Shojo Beat

OTOMEN

Story & Art by
Aya Kanno

Volume
FOURTEEN

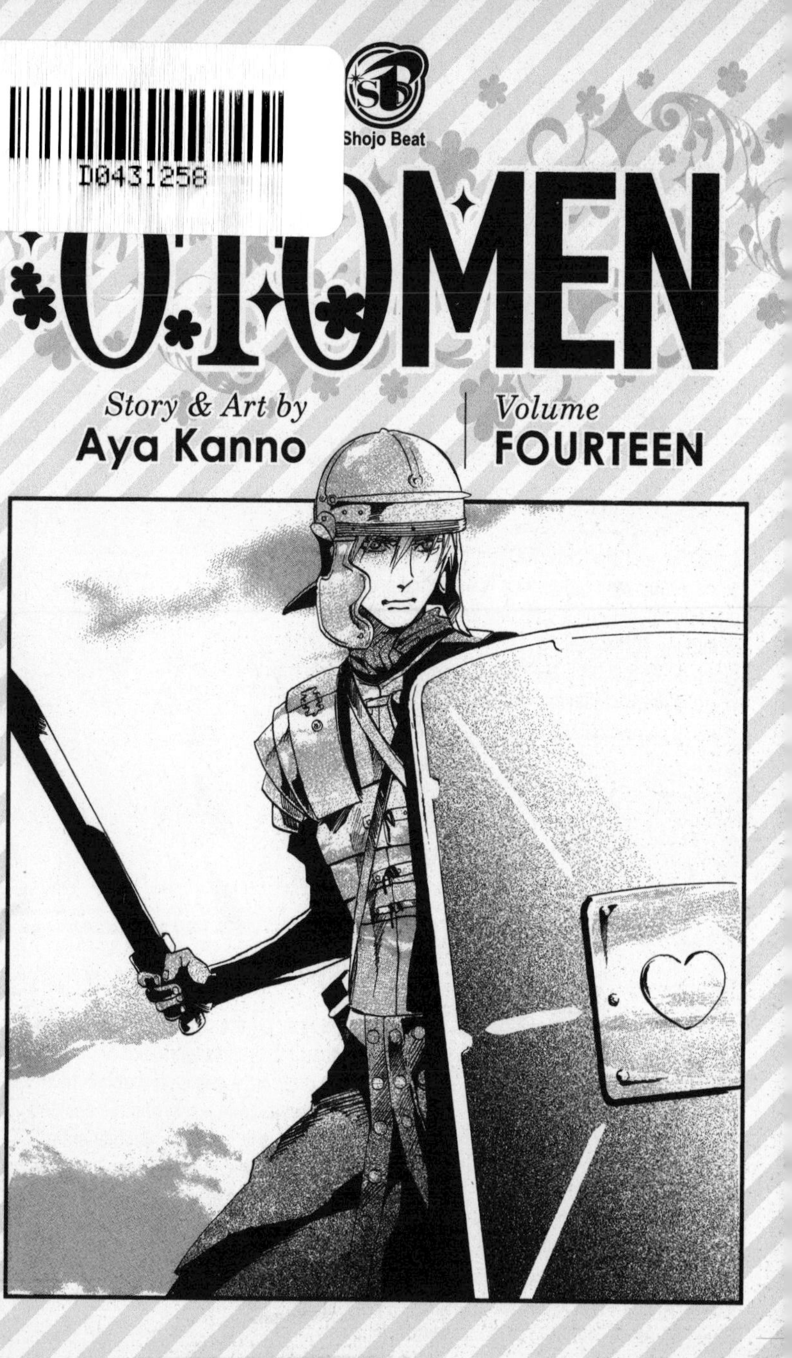

OTOMEN Characters & Story

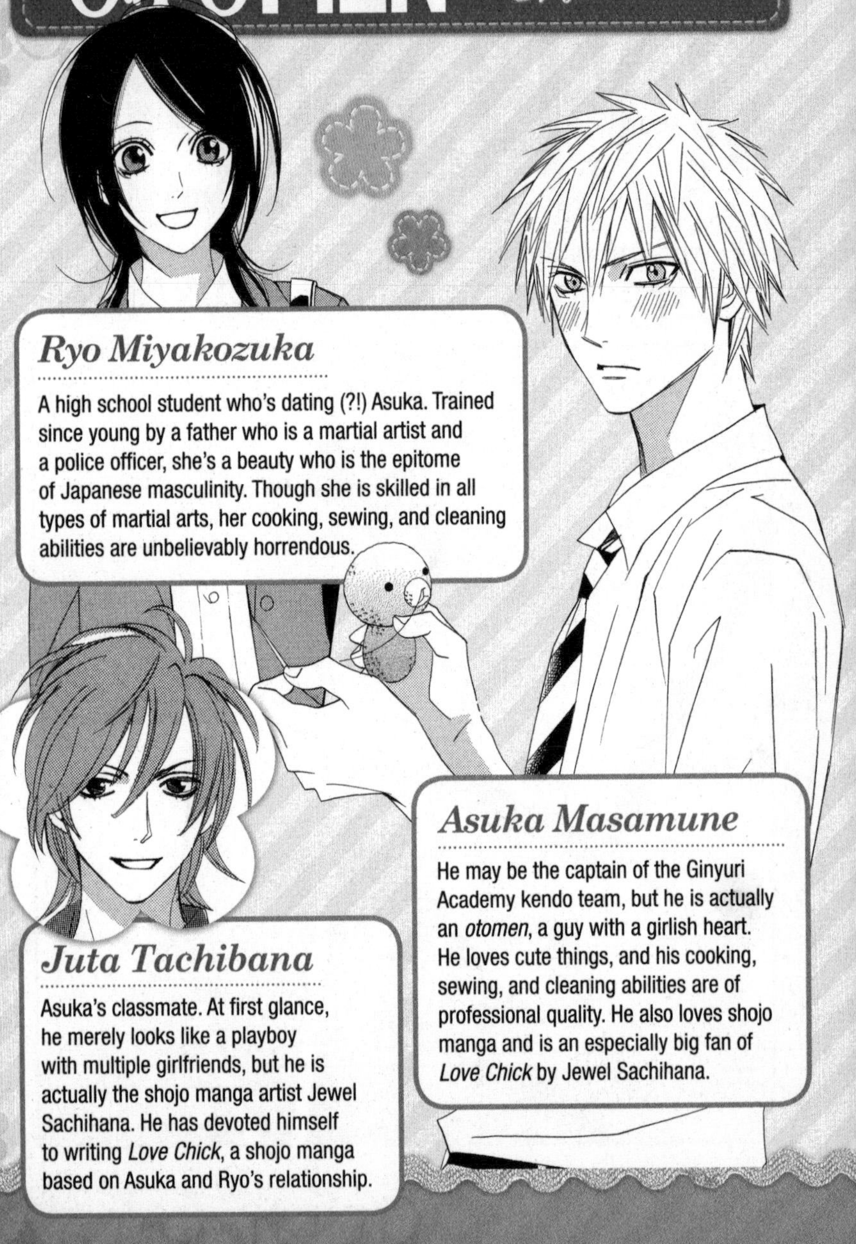

Ryo Miyakozuka

A high school student who's dating (?!) Asuka. Trained since young by a father who is a martial artist and a police officer, she's a beauty who is the epitome of Japanese masculinity. Though she is skilled in all types of martial arts, her cooking, sewing, and cleaning abilities are unbelievably horrendous.

Asuka Masamune

He may be the captain of the Ginyuri Academy kendo team, but he is actually an *otomen*, a guy with a girlish heart. He loves cute things, and his cooking, sewing, and cleaning abilities are of professional quality. He also loves shojo manga and is an especially big fan of *Love Chick* by Jewel Sachihana.

Juta Tachibana

Asuka's classmate. At first glance, he merely looks like a playboy with multiple girlfriends, but he is actually the shojo manga artist Jewel Sachihana. He has devoted himself to writing *Love Chick*, a shojo manga based on Asuka and Ryo's relationship.

STORY

Asuka works hard at making a Valentine's Day cake at a baking class for men at Patisserie Violet. He's happy to hear that people think he's good enough to become a pastry chef, but he becomes worried when he sees how seriously Ryo and his friends are thinking about their futures. In the end, he realizes he wants Ryo to be with him always, so he tells her his feelings.

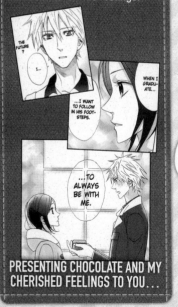

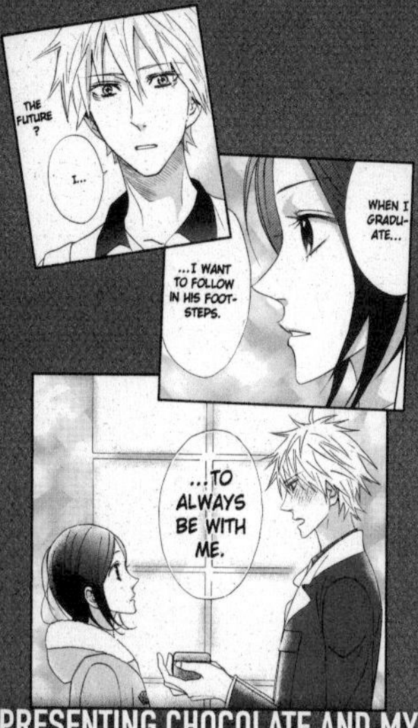
THE FUTURE?
I...
WHEN I GRADUATE...
...I WANT TO FOLLOW IN HIS FOOTSTEPS.
...TO ALWAYS BE WITH ME.

PRESENTING CHOCOLATE AND MY CHERISHED FEELINGS TO YOU...

OTHER OTOMEN

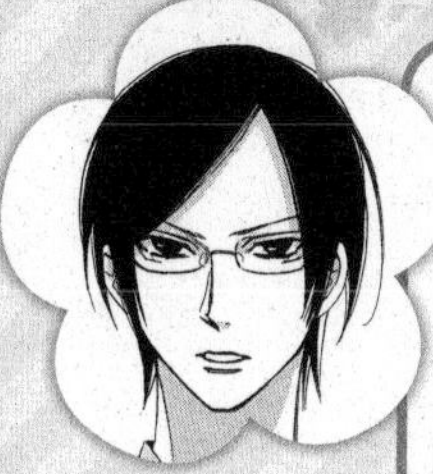

Hajime Tonomine

The captain of the Kinbara High School kendo team, he considers Asuka his sworn rival. He is actually an *otomen* who is good with cosmetics.

Yamato Ariake

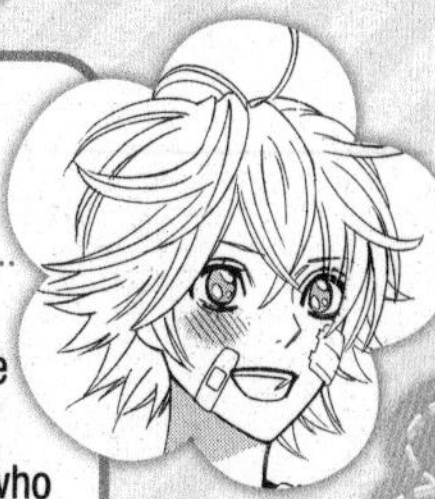

He is younger than Asuka and looks like a cute girl. He is a delusional *otomen* who admires manliness.

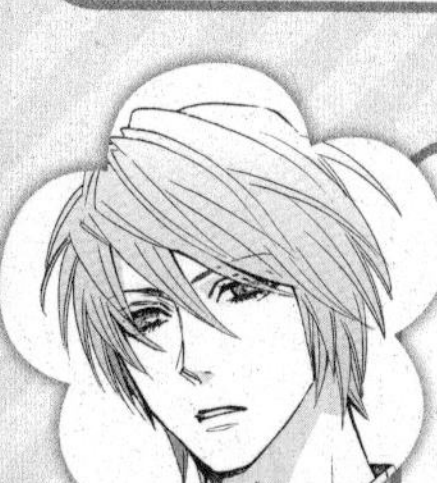

Kitora Kurokawa

Asuka's classmate. A man who is captivated by the beauty of flowers. He is an obsessed *otomen* who wants to cover the world in flowers.

OTOMEN

volume 14

CONTENTS

OTOMEN 05

NOTES 190

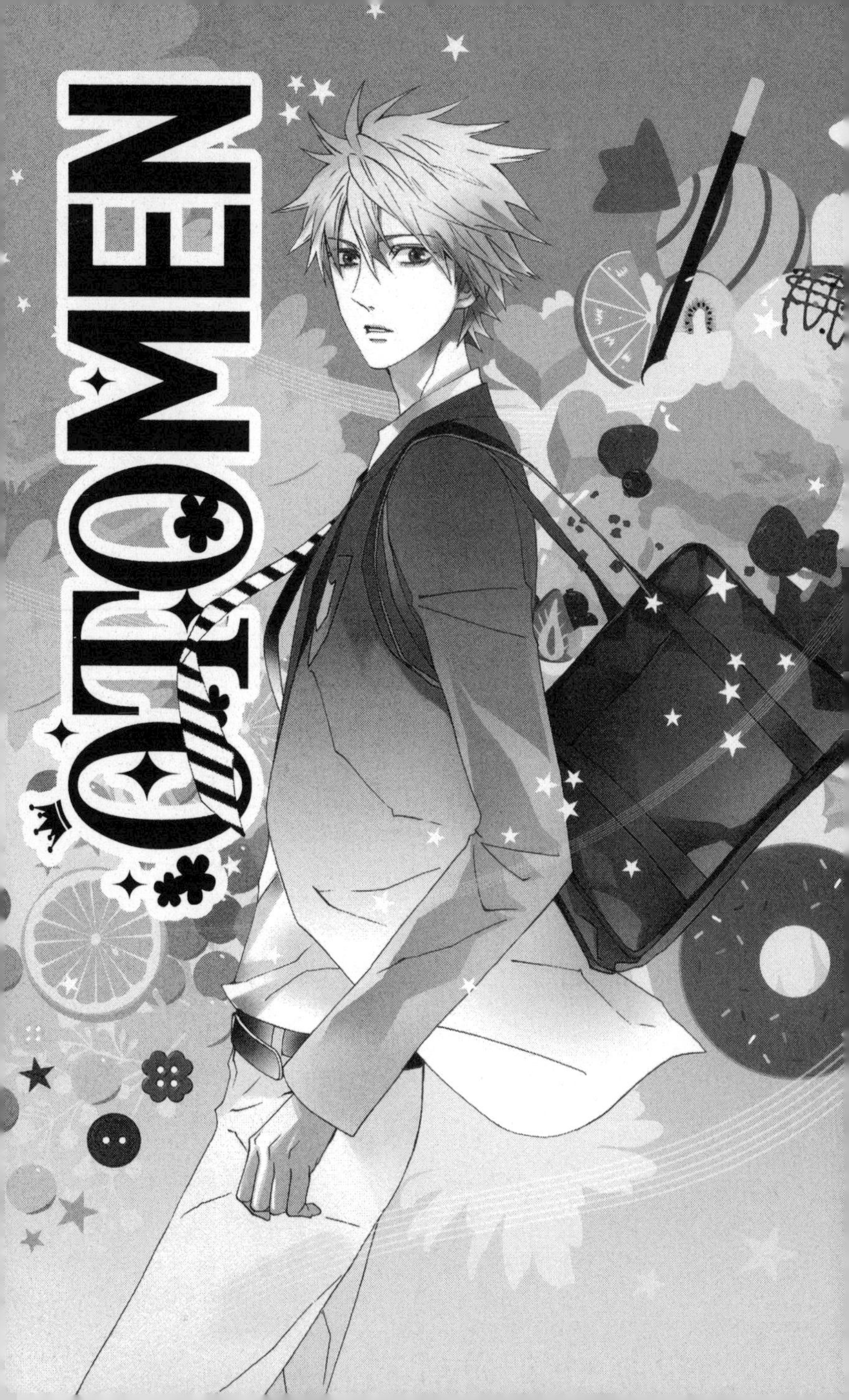
OTOMEN

OTOMEN

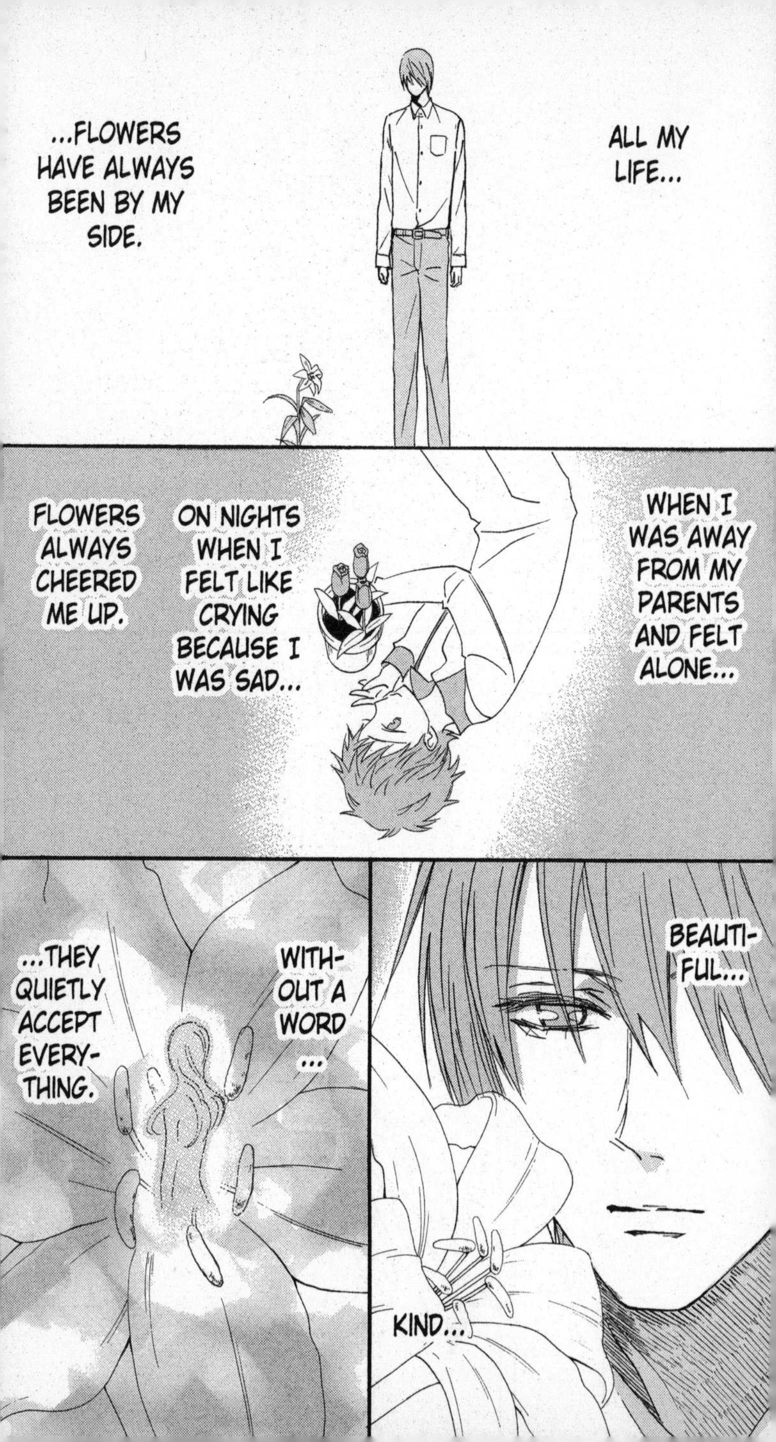
ALL MY LIFE...
...FLOWERS HAVE ALWAYS BEEN BY MY SIDE.
WHEN I WAS AWAY FROM MY PARENTS AND FELT ALONE...
ON NIGHTS WHEN I FELT LIKE CRYING BECAUSE I WAS SAD...
FLOWERS ALWAYS CHEERED ME UP.
BEAUTIFUL...
KIND...
WITHOUT A WORD...
...THEY QUIETLY ACCEPT EVERYTHING.

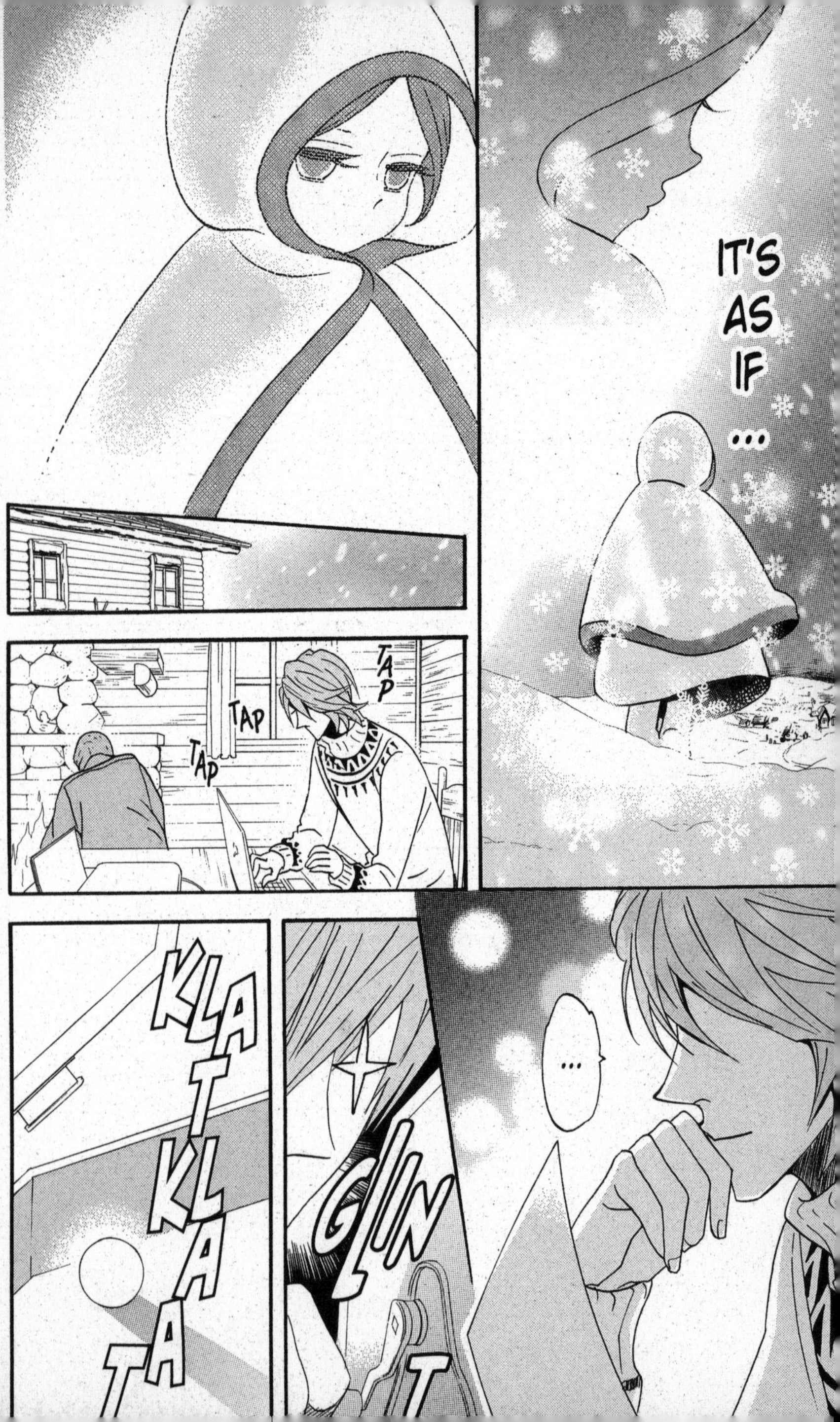
IT'S AS IF...
TAP TAP TAP
...
GLINT
KLATKLATAT

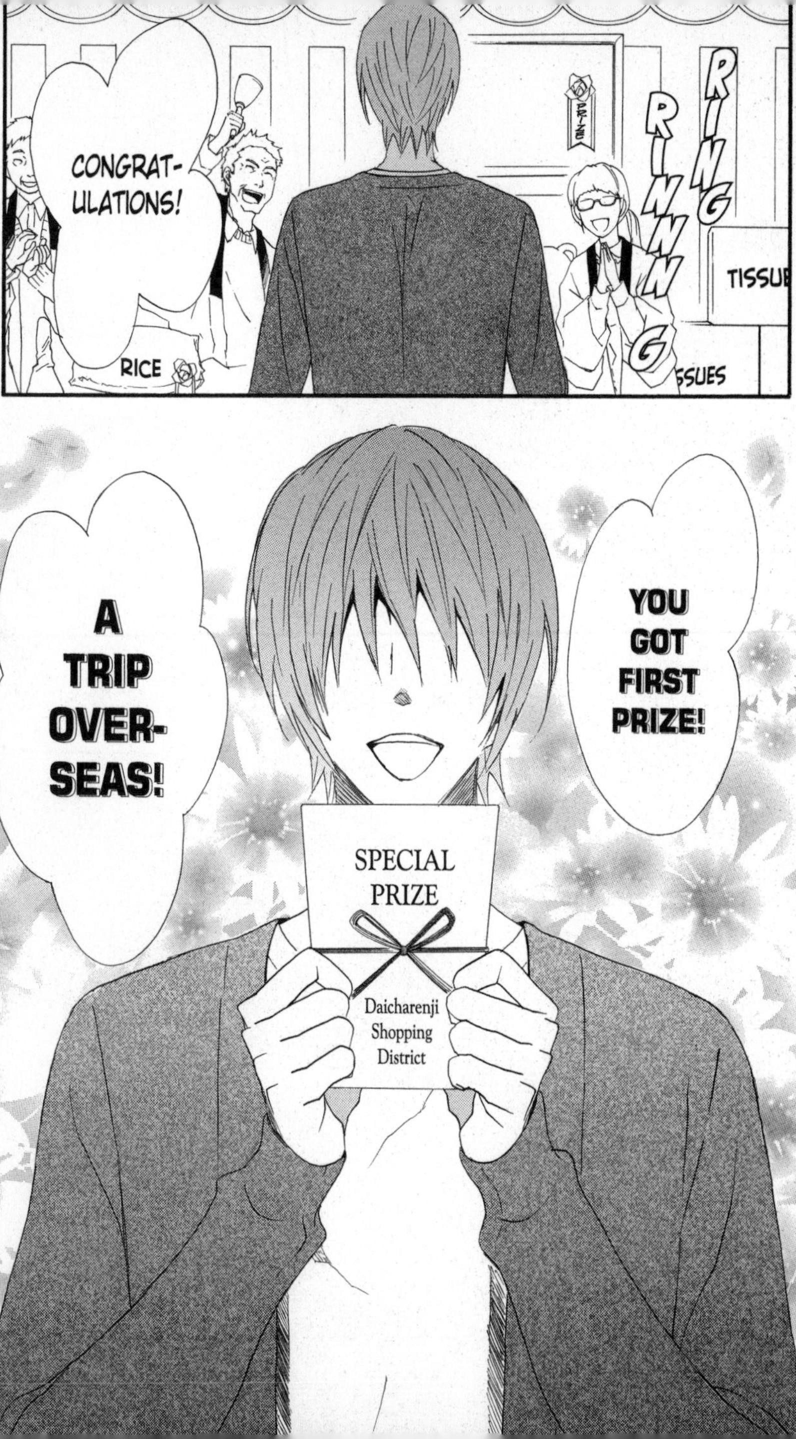
RING
RINNNG
PRIZE
TISSUE
CONGRAT-ULATIONS!
RICE
SSUES
YOU GOT FIRST PRIZE!
A TRIP OVER-SEAS!
SPECIAL PRIZE
Daicharenji Shopping District

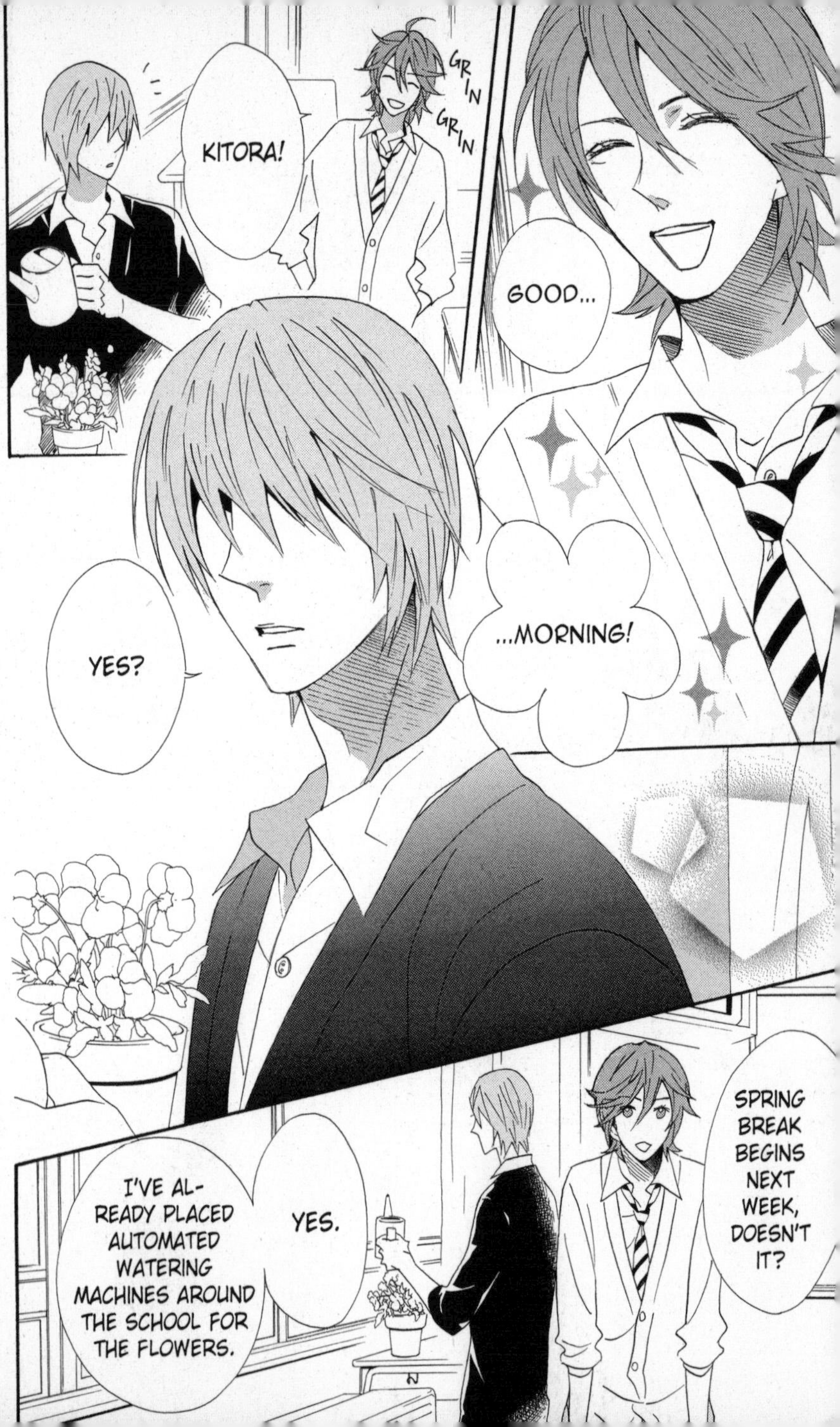
GOOD...
...MORNING!
KITORA!
GRIN GRIN
YES?
SPRING BREAK BEGINS NEXT WEEK, DOESN'T IT?
YES.
I'VE AL-READY PLACED AUTOMATED WATERING MACHINES AROUND THE SCHOOL FOR THE FLOWERS.

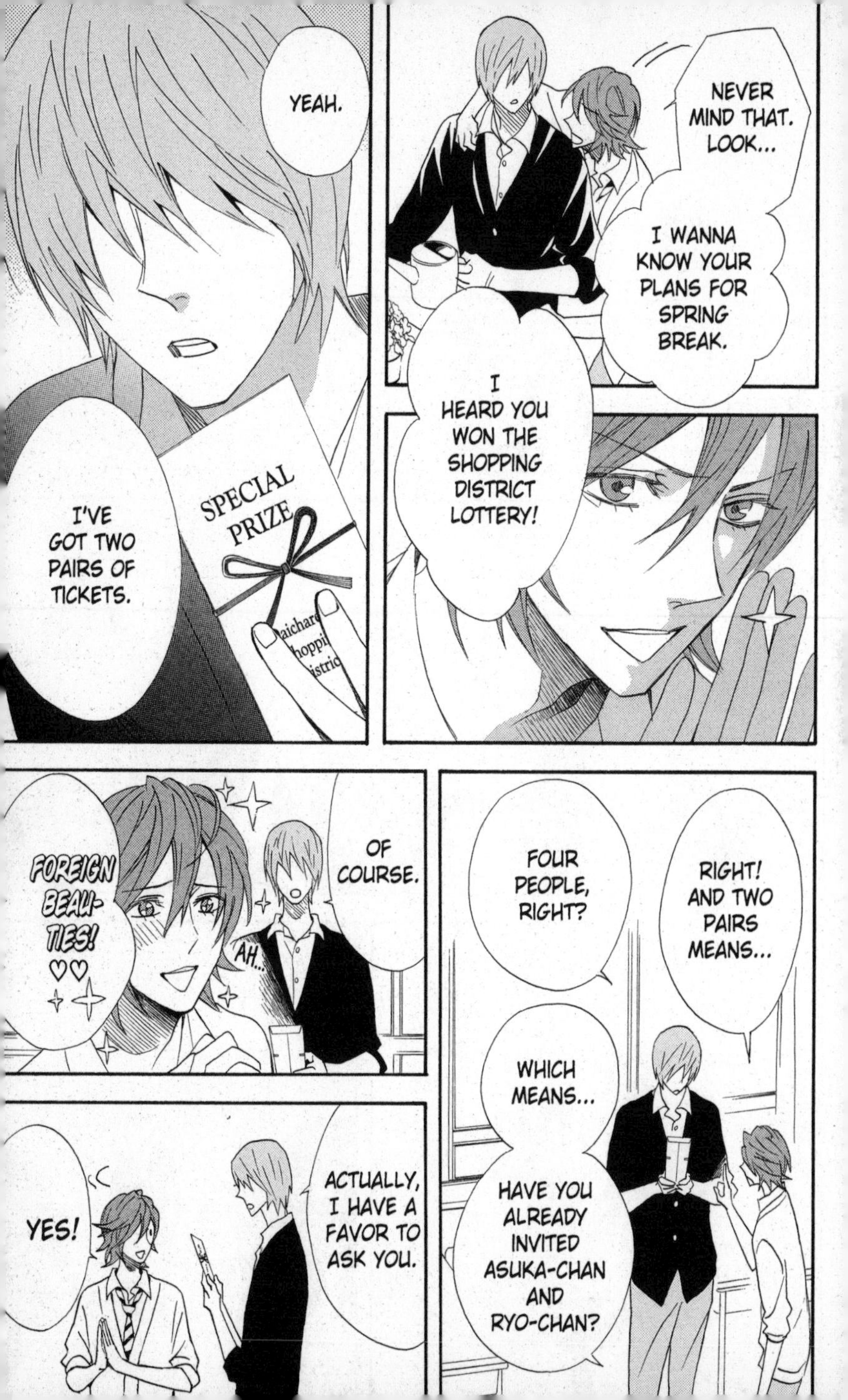
NEVER MIND THAT. LOOK...
I WANNA KNOW YOUR PLANS FOR SPRING BREAK.
I HEARD YOU WON THE SHOPPING DISTRICT LOTTERY!
YEAH.
SPECIAL PRIZE
I'VE GOT TWO PAIRS OF TICKETS.
RIGHT! AND TWO PAIRS MEANS...
FOUR PEOPLE, RIGHT?
WHICH MEANS...
HAVE YOU ALREADY INVITED ASUKA-CHAN AND RYO-CHAN?
OF COURSE.
AH...
FOREIGN BEAUTIES! ♡♡
ACTUALLY, I HAVE A FAVOR TO ASK YOU.
YES!

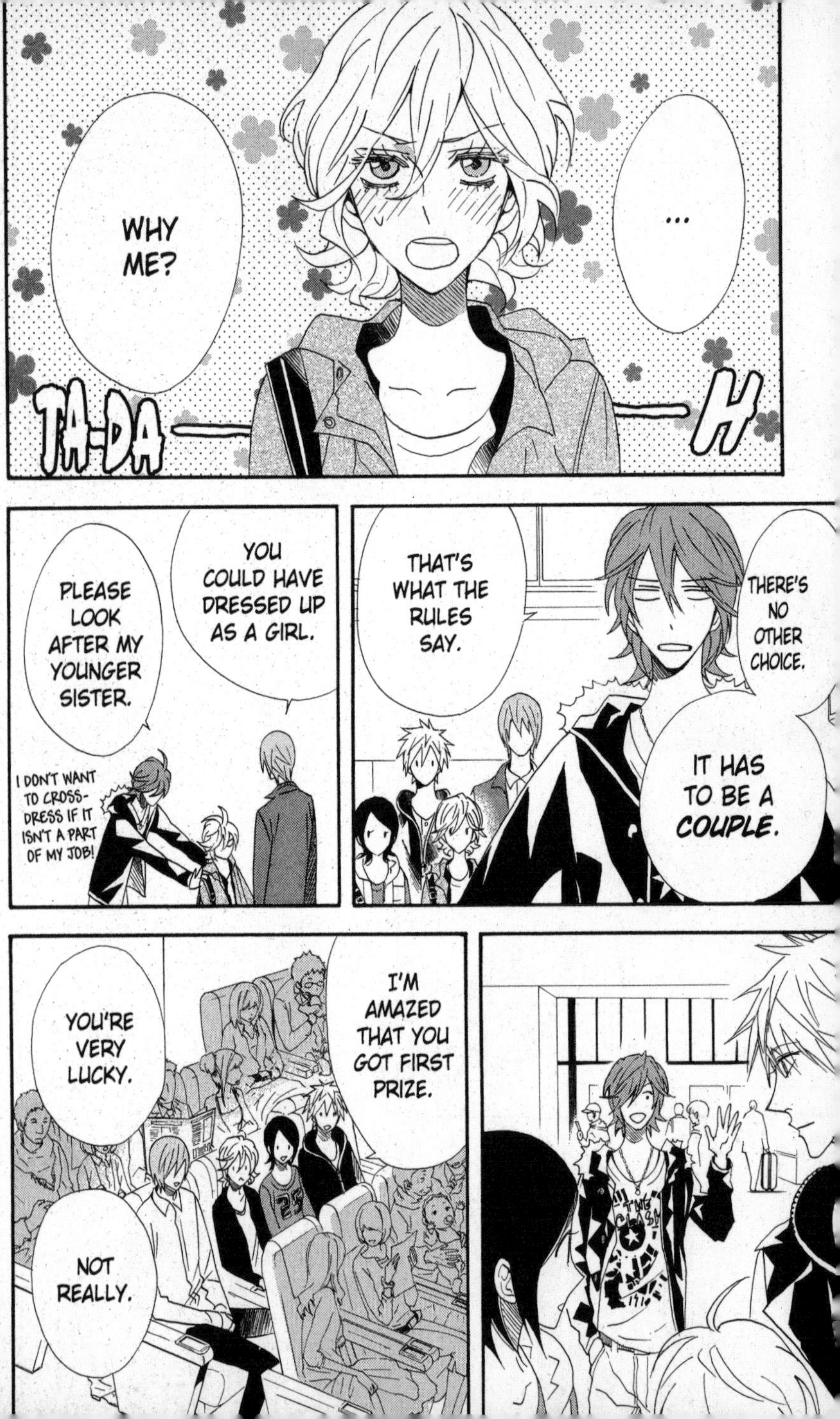
...
WHY ME?
TA-DA—H
THERE'S NO OTHER CHOICE.
IT HAS TO BE A COUPLE.
THAT'S WHAT THE RULES SAY.
YOU COULD HAVE DRESSED UP AS A GIRL.
PLEASE LOOK AFTER MY YOUNGER SISTER.
I DON'T WANT TO CROSS-DRESS IF IT ISN'T A PART OF MY JOB!
I'M AMAZED THAT YOU GOT FIRST PRIZE.
YOU'RE VERY LUCKY.
NOT REALLY.

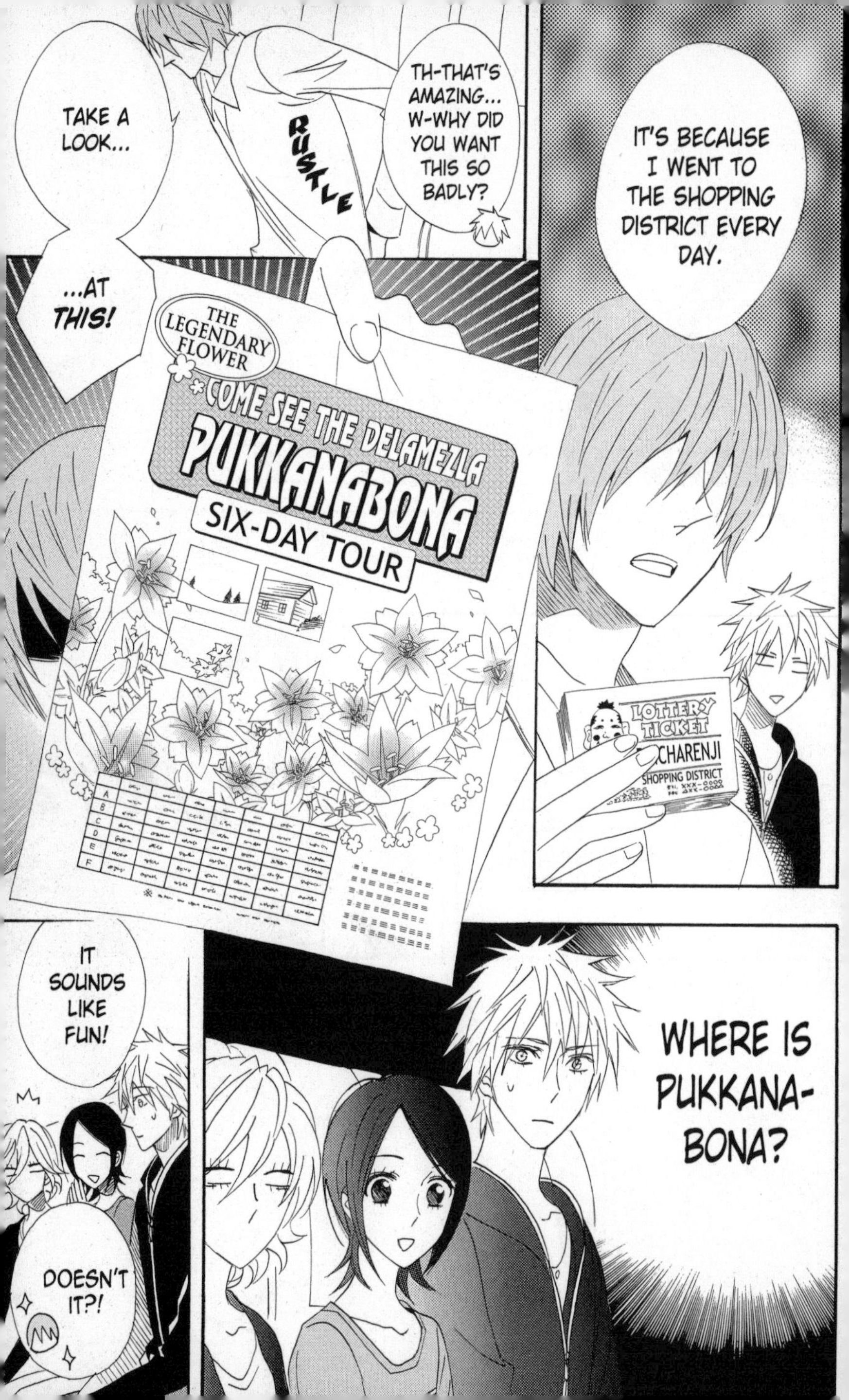
IT'S BECAUSE I WENT TO THE SHOPPING DISTRICT EVERY DAY.
LOTTERY TICKET
CHARENJI
SHOPPING DISTRICT
TH-THAT'S AMAZING... W-WHY DID YOU WANT THIS SO BADLY?
RUSTLE
TAKE A LOOK...
...AT THIS!
THE LEGENDARY FLOWER
COME SEE THE DELAMEZLA
PUKKANABONA
SIX-DAY TOUR
WHERE IS PUKKANA-BONA?
IT SOUNDS LIKE FUN!
DOESN'T IT?!

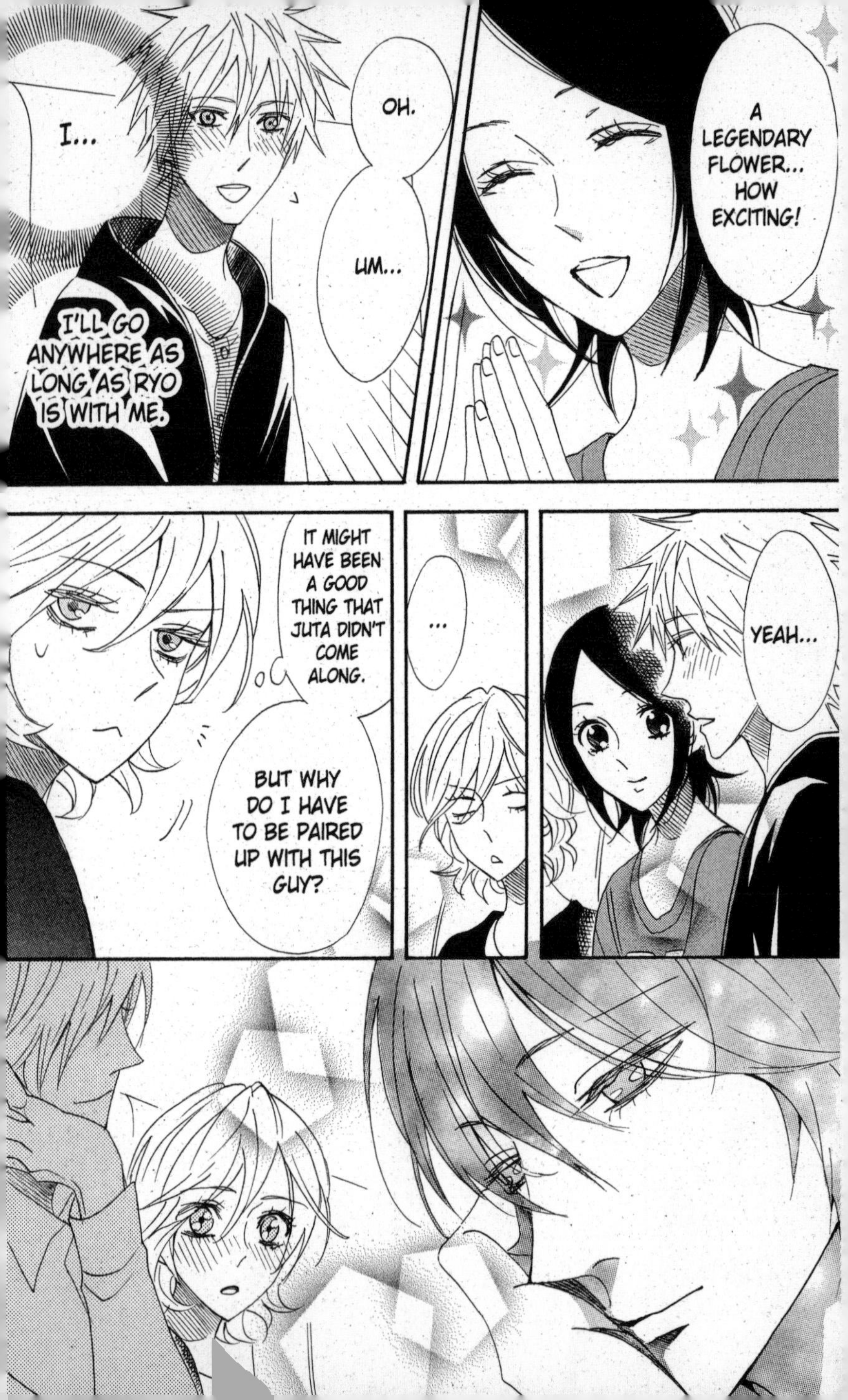
A LEGENDARY FLOWER... HOW EXCITING!
OH.
UM...
I...
I'LL GO ANYWHERE AS LONG AS RYO IS WITH ME.
YEAH...
...
IT MIGHT HAVE BEEN A GOOD THING THAT JUTA DIDN'T COME ALONG.
BUT WHY DO I HAVE TO BE PAIRED UP WITH THIS GUY?

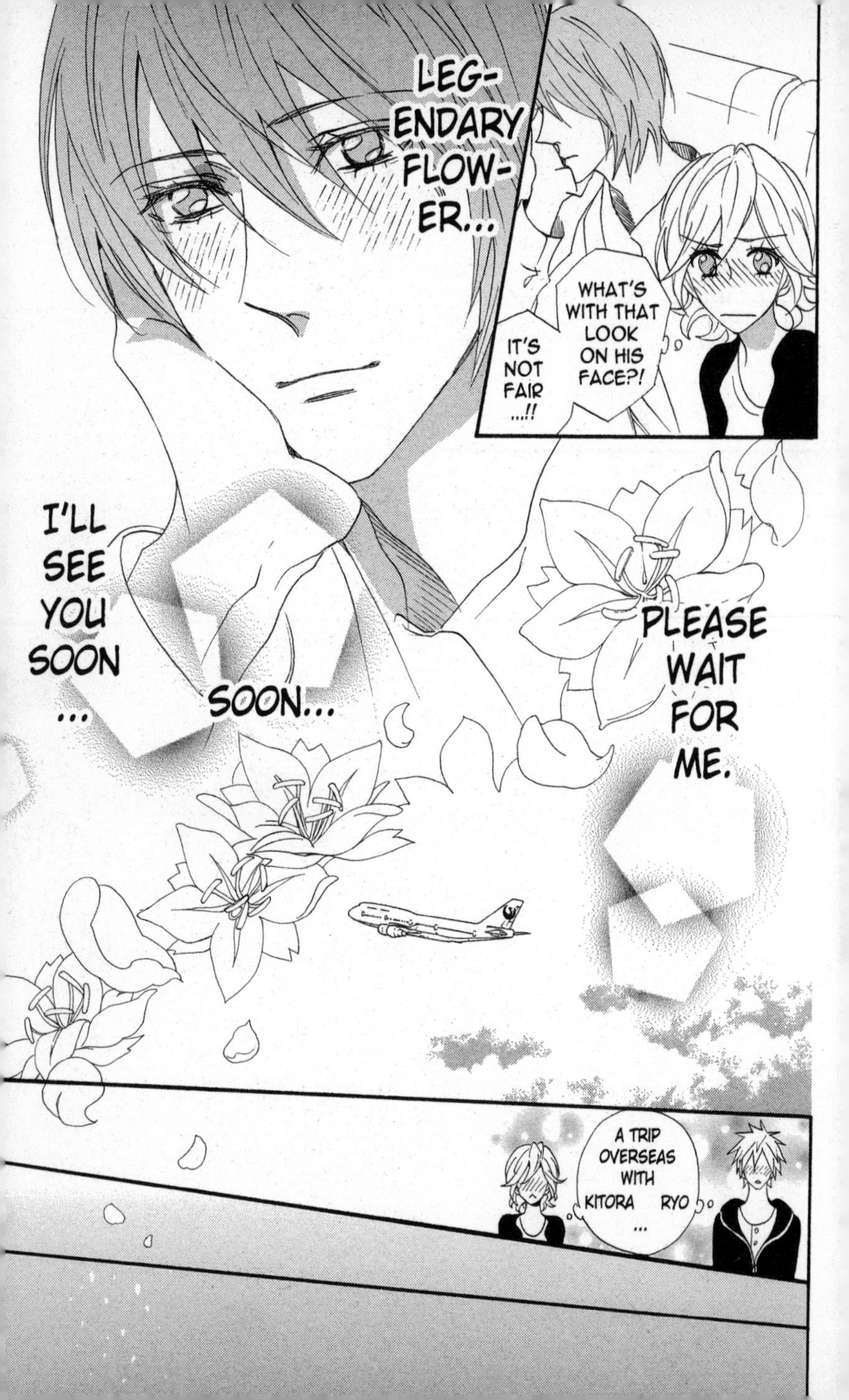
WHAT'S WITH THAT LOOK ON HIS FACE?!
IT'S NOT FAIR ...!!
LEG-ENDARY FLOW-ER...
PLEASE WAIT FOR ME.
SOON...
I'LL SEE YOU SOON ...
A TRIP OVERSEAS WITH KITORA RYO ...

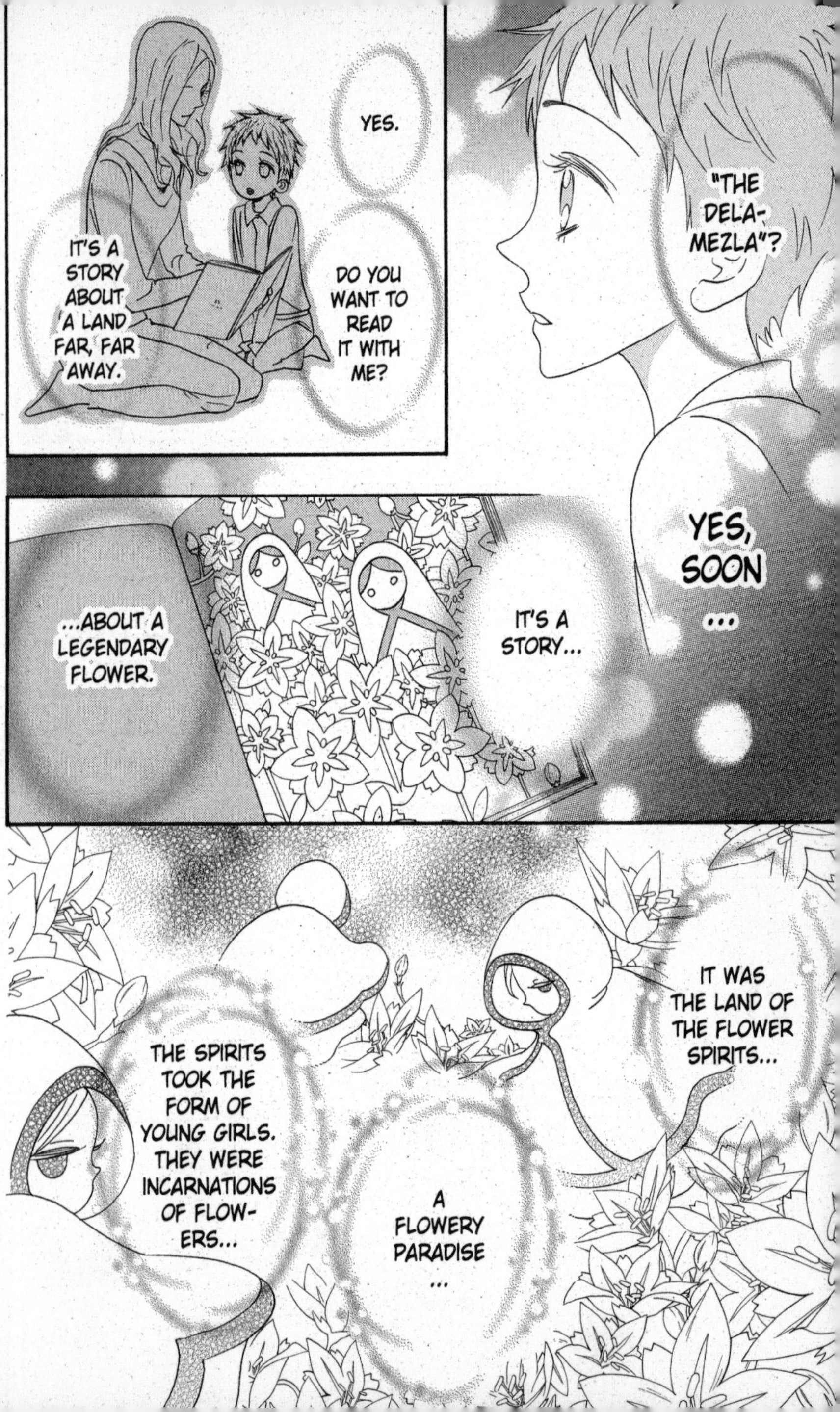
"THE DELA-MEZLA"?
YES, SOON ...
YES.
DO YOU WANT TO READ IT WITH ME?
IT'S A STORY ABOUT A LAND FAR, FAR AWAY.
IT'S A STORY...
...ABOUT A LEGENDARY FLOWER.
IT WAS THE LAND OF THE FLOWER SPIRITS...
A FLOWERY PARADISE ...
THE SPIRITS TOOK THE FORM OF YOUNG GIRLS. THEY WERE INCARNATIONS OF FLOW-ERS...

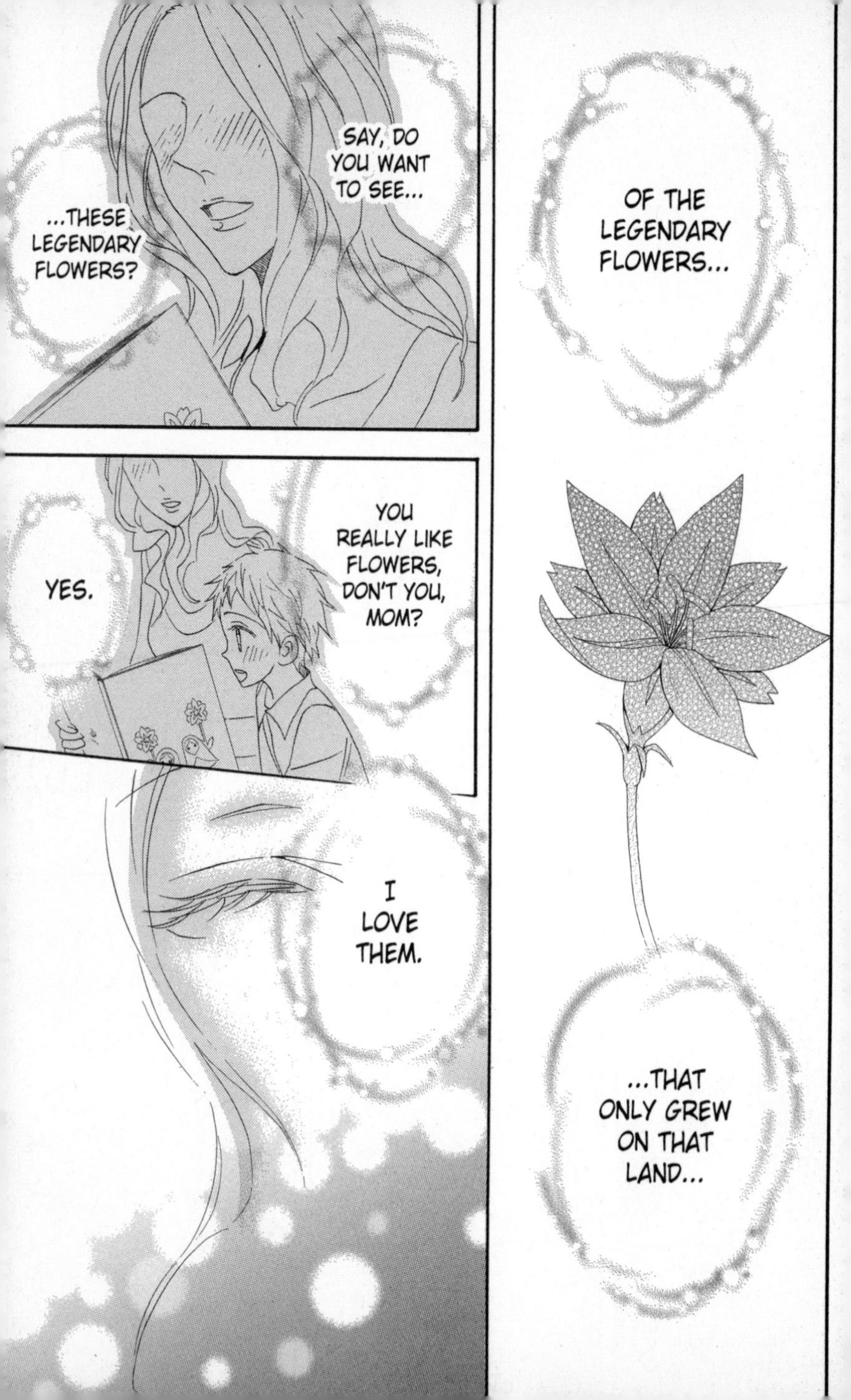
OF THE LEGENDARY FLOWERS...
...THAT ONLY GREW ON THAT LAND...
SAY, DO YOU WANT TO SEE...
...THESE LEGENDARY FLOWERS?
YOU REALLY LIKE FLOWERS, DON'T YOU, MOM?
YES.
I LOVE THEM.

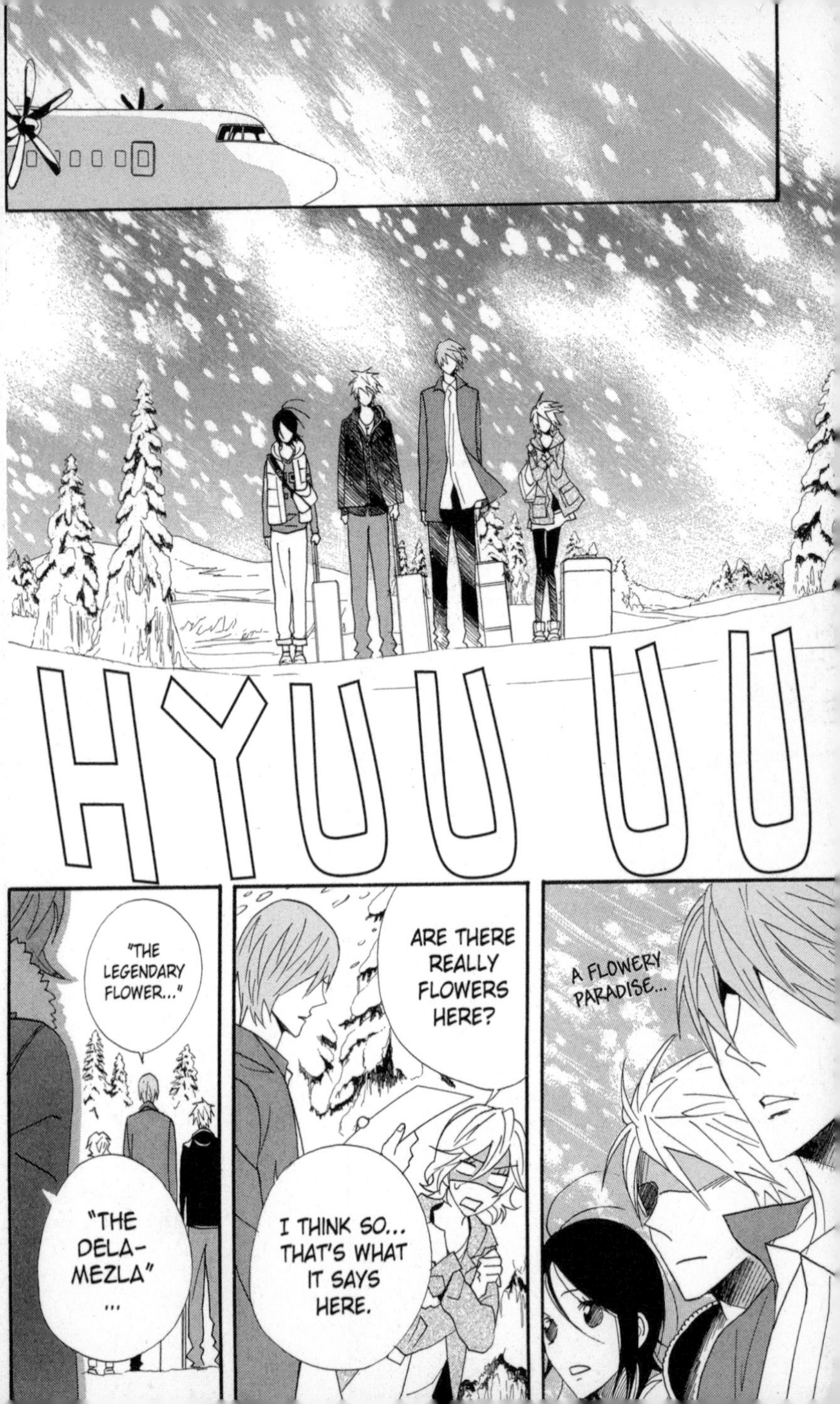
HYUU UU
A FLOWERY PARADISE...
ARE THERE REALLY FLOWERS HERE?
I THINK SO... THAT'S WHAT IT SAYS HERE.
"THE LEGENDARY FLOWER..."
"THE DELA-MEZLA" ...

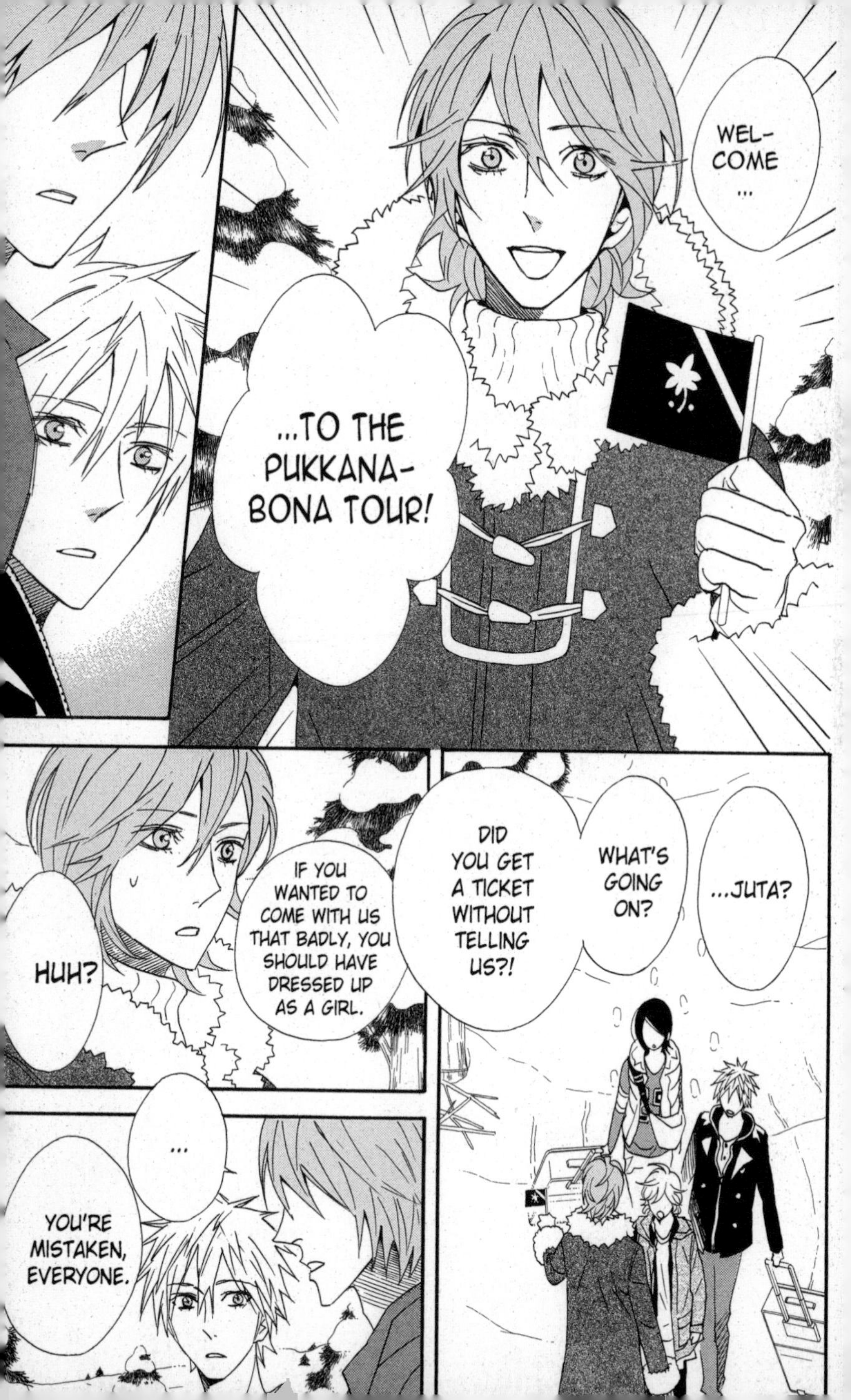
WEL-COME ...
...TO THE PUKKANA-BONA TOUR!
...JUTA?
WHAT'S GOING ON?
DID YOU GET A TICKET WITHOUT TELLING US?!
IF YOU WANTED TO COME WITH US THAT BADLY, YOU SHOULD HAVE DRESSED UP AS A GIRL.
HUH?
...
YOU'RE MISTAKEN, EVERYONE.

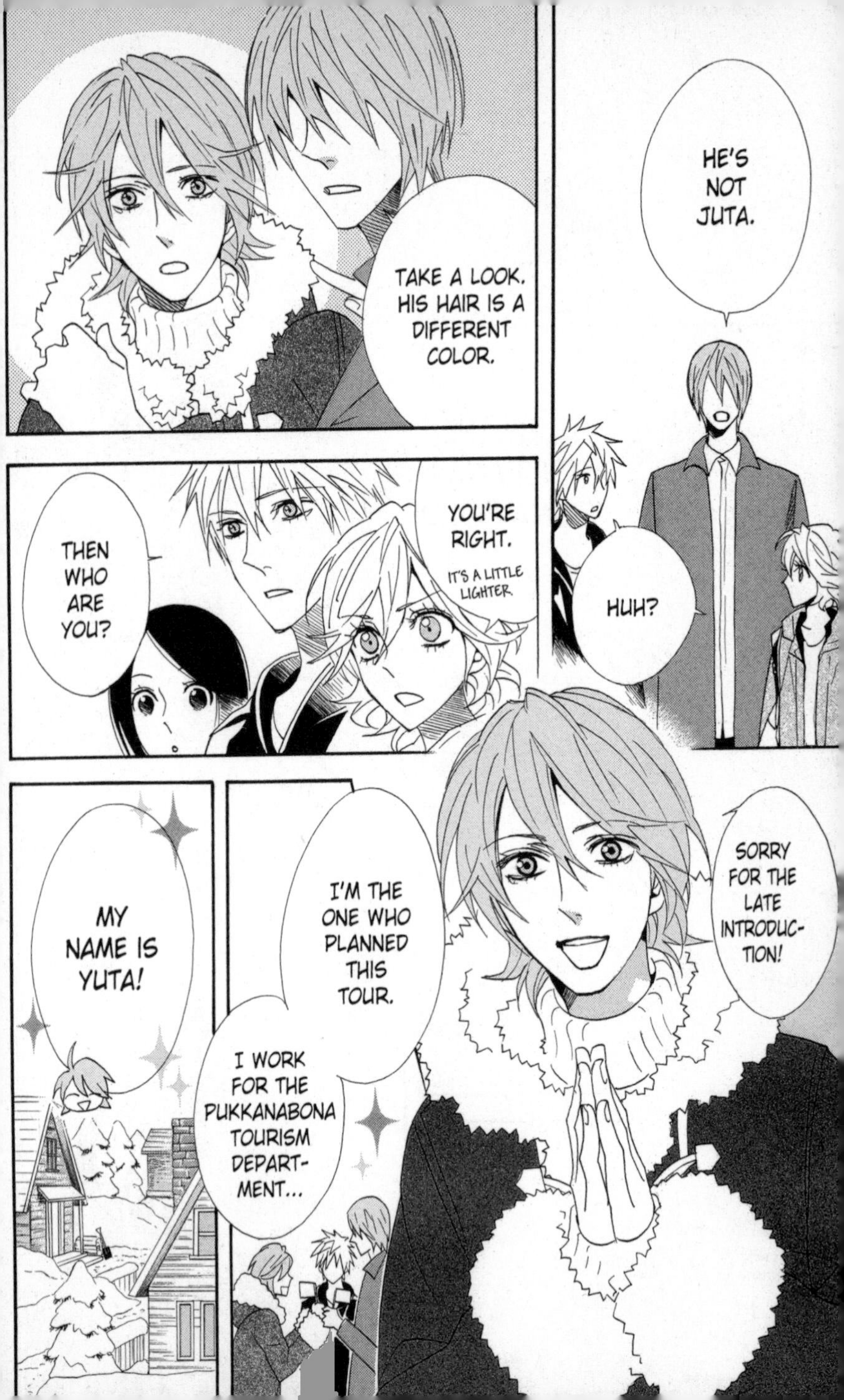
HE'S NOT JUTA.
HUH?
TAKE A LOOK. HIS HAIR IS A DIFFERENT COLOR.
YOU'RE RIGHT.
IT'S A LITTLE LIGHTER.
THEN WHO ARE YOU?
SORRY FOR THE LATE INTRODUC-TION!
I'M THE ONE WHO PLANNED THIS TOUR.
I WORK FOR THE PUKKANABONA TOURISM DEPART-MENT...
MY NAME IS YUTA!

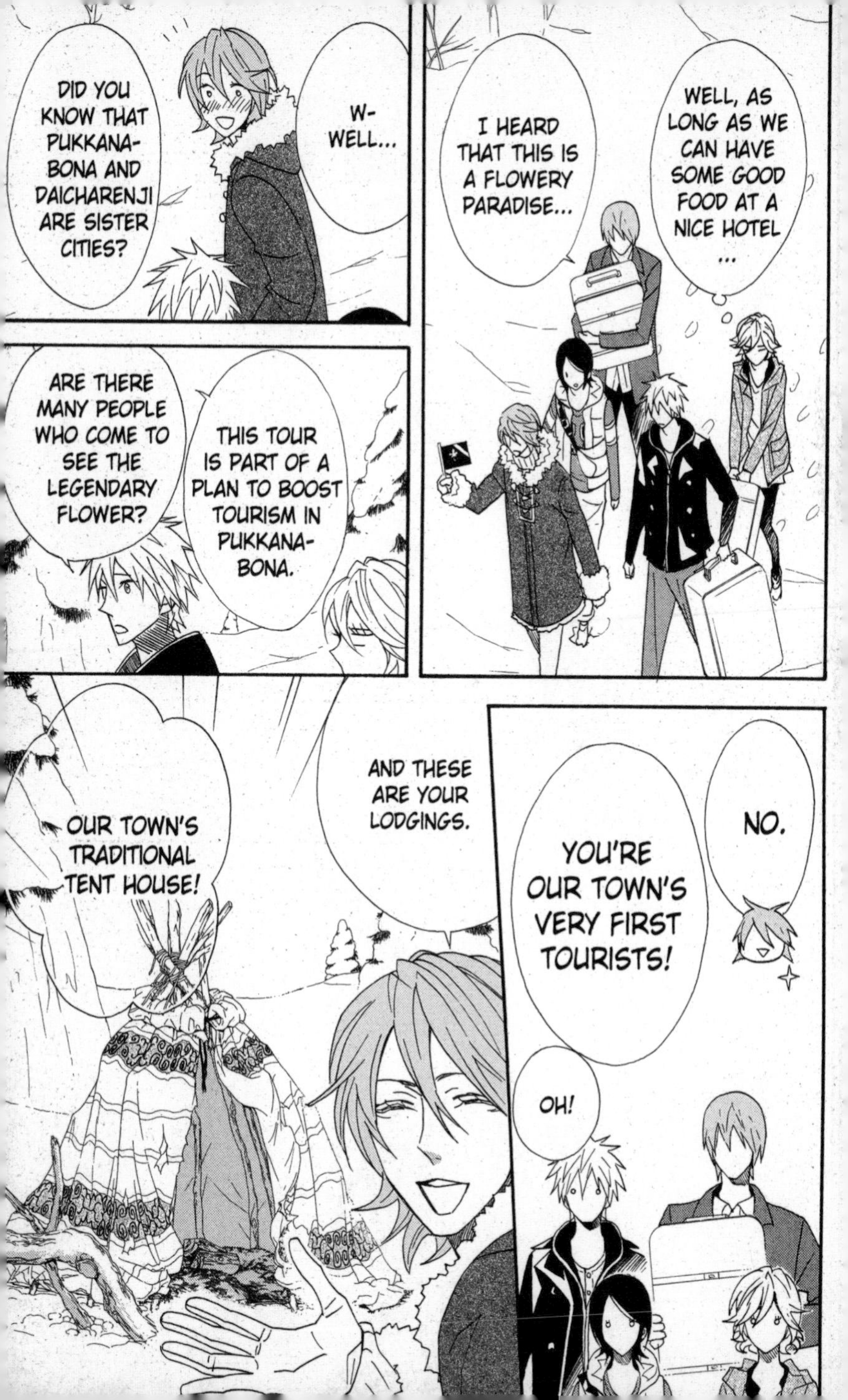
WELL, AS LONG AS WE CAN HAVE SOME GOOD FOOD AT A NICE HOTEL ...
I HEARD THAT THIS IS A FLOWERY PARADISE...
W-WELL...
DID YOU KNOW THAT PUKKANA-BONA AND DAICHARENJI ARE SISTER CITIES?
THIS TOUR IS PART OF A PLAN TO BOOST TOURISM IN PUKKANA-BONA.
ARE THERE MANY PEOPLE WHO COME TO SEE THE LEGENDARY FLOWER?
NO.
YOU'RE OUR TOWN'S VERY FIRST TOURISTS!
OH!
AND THESE ARE YOUR LODGINGS.
OUR TOWN'S TRADITIONAL TENT HOUSE!

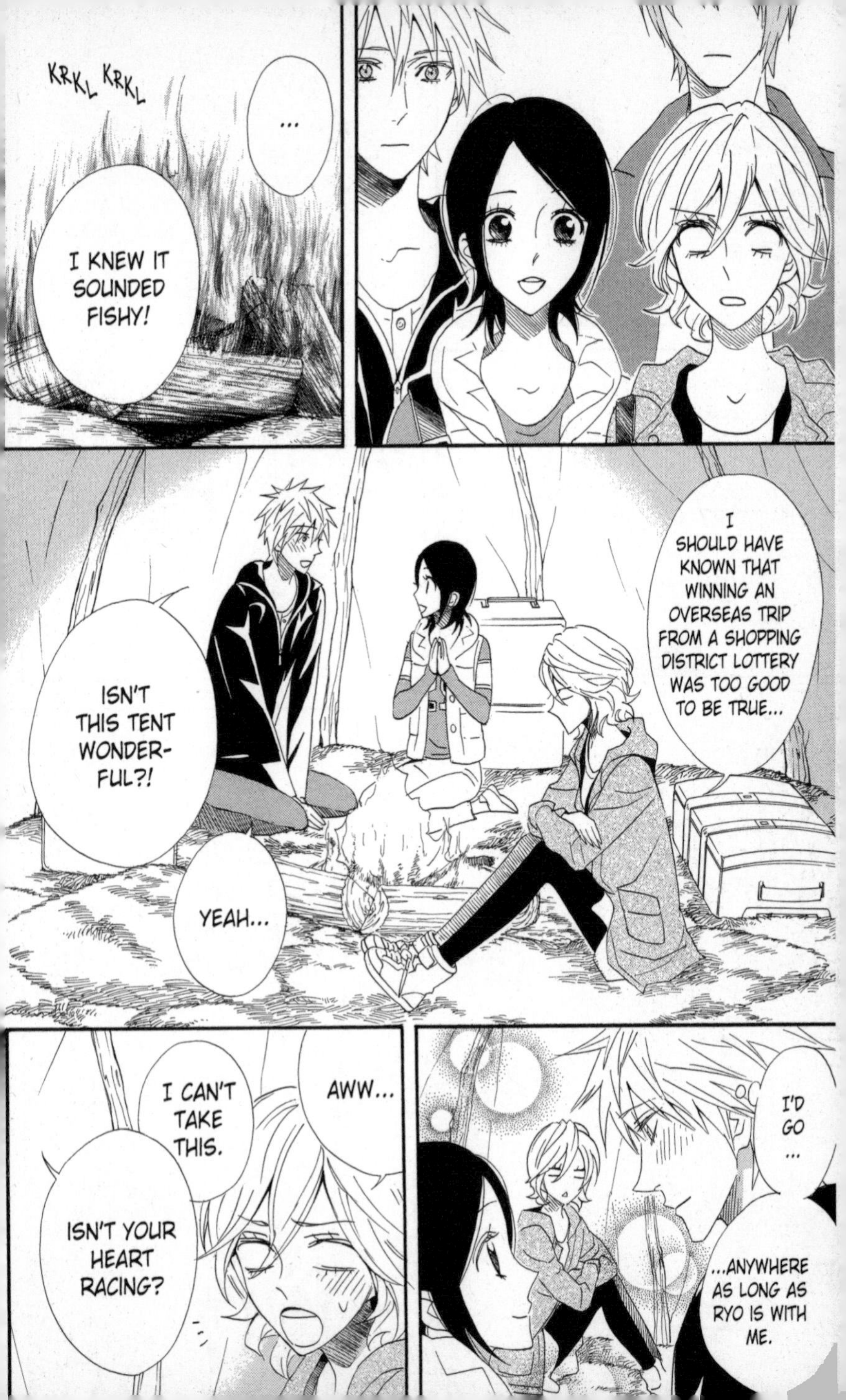
...
KRKL KRKL
I KNEW IT SOUNDED FISHY!
I SHOULD HAVE KNOWN THAT WINNING AN OVERSEAS TRIP FROM A SHOPPING DISTRICT LOTTERY WAS TOO GOOD TO BE TRUE...
ISN'T THIS TENT WONDER-FUL?!
YEAH...
I'D GO...
...ANYWHERE AS LONG AS RYO IS WITH ME.
AWW...
I CAN'T TAKE THIS.
ISN'T YOUR HEART RACING?

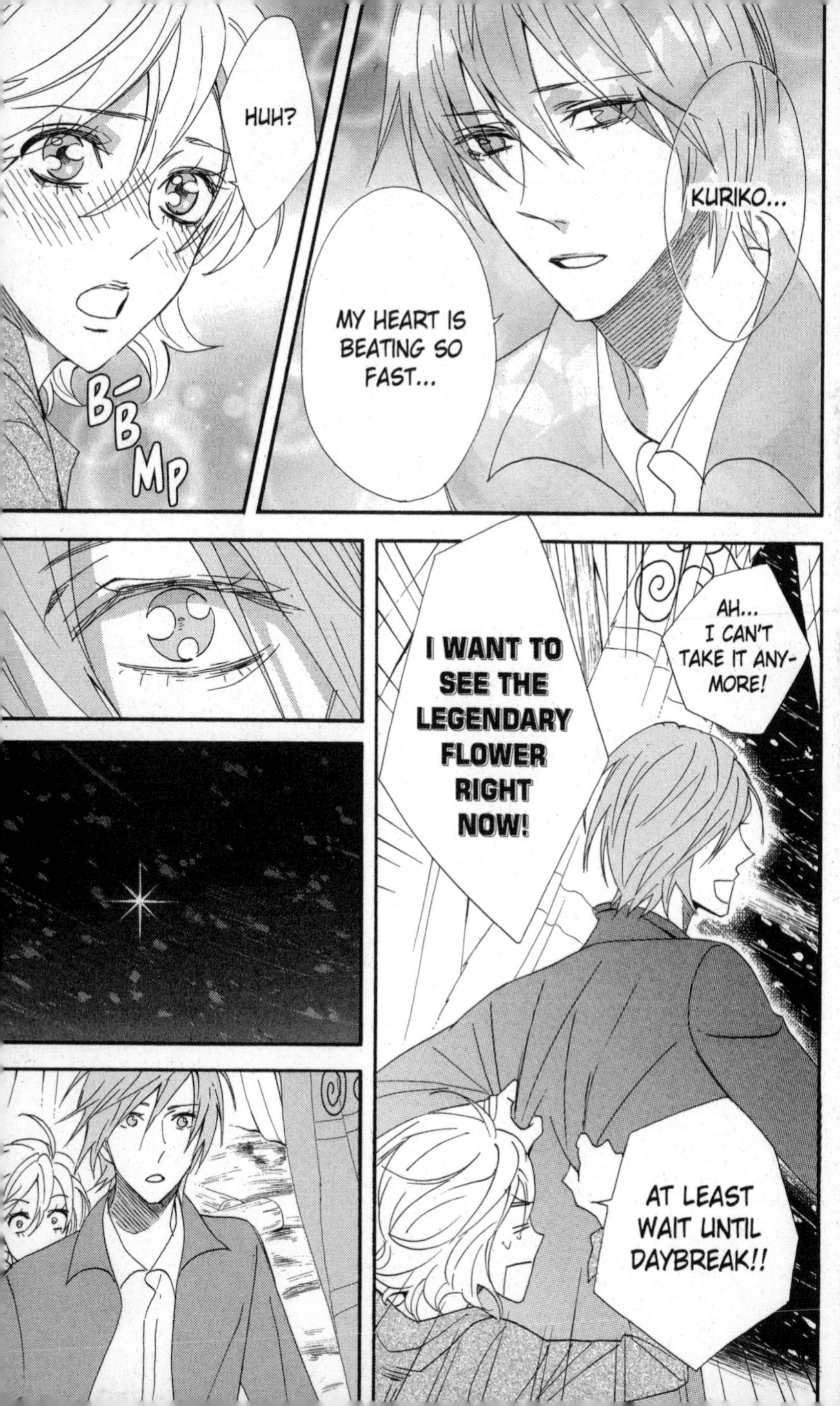
KURIKO...
MY HEART IS BEATING SO FAST...
HUH?
B-BMP
AH... I CAN'T TAKE IT ANY-MORE!
I WANT TO SEE THE LEGENDARY FLOWER RIGHT NOW!
AT LEAST WAIT UNTIL DAYBREAK!!

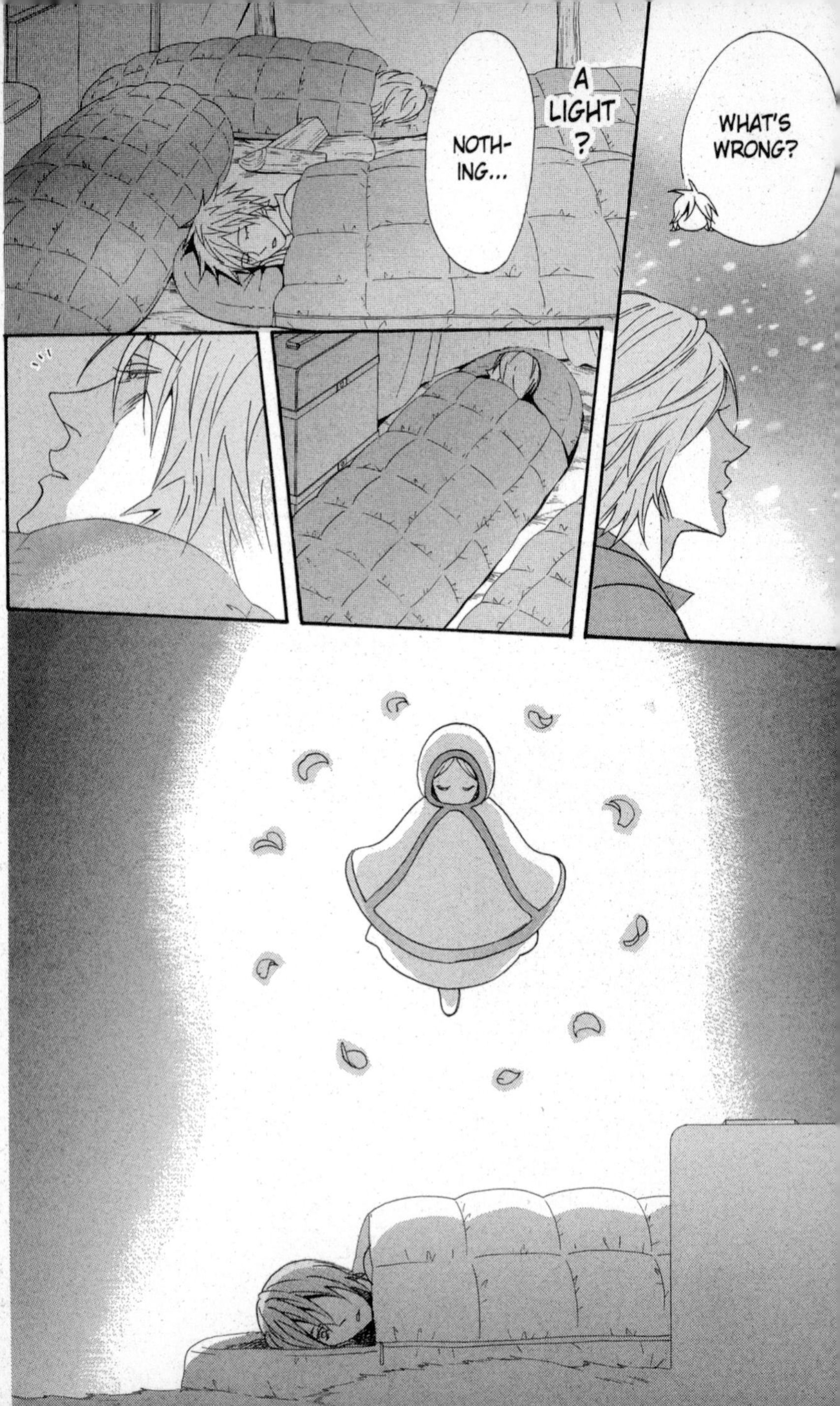
WHAT'S WRONG?
A LIGHT?
NOTH-ING...

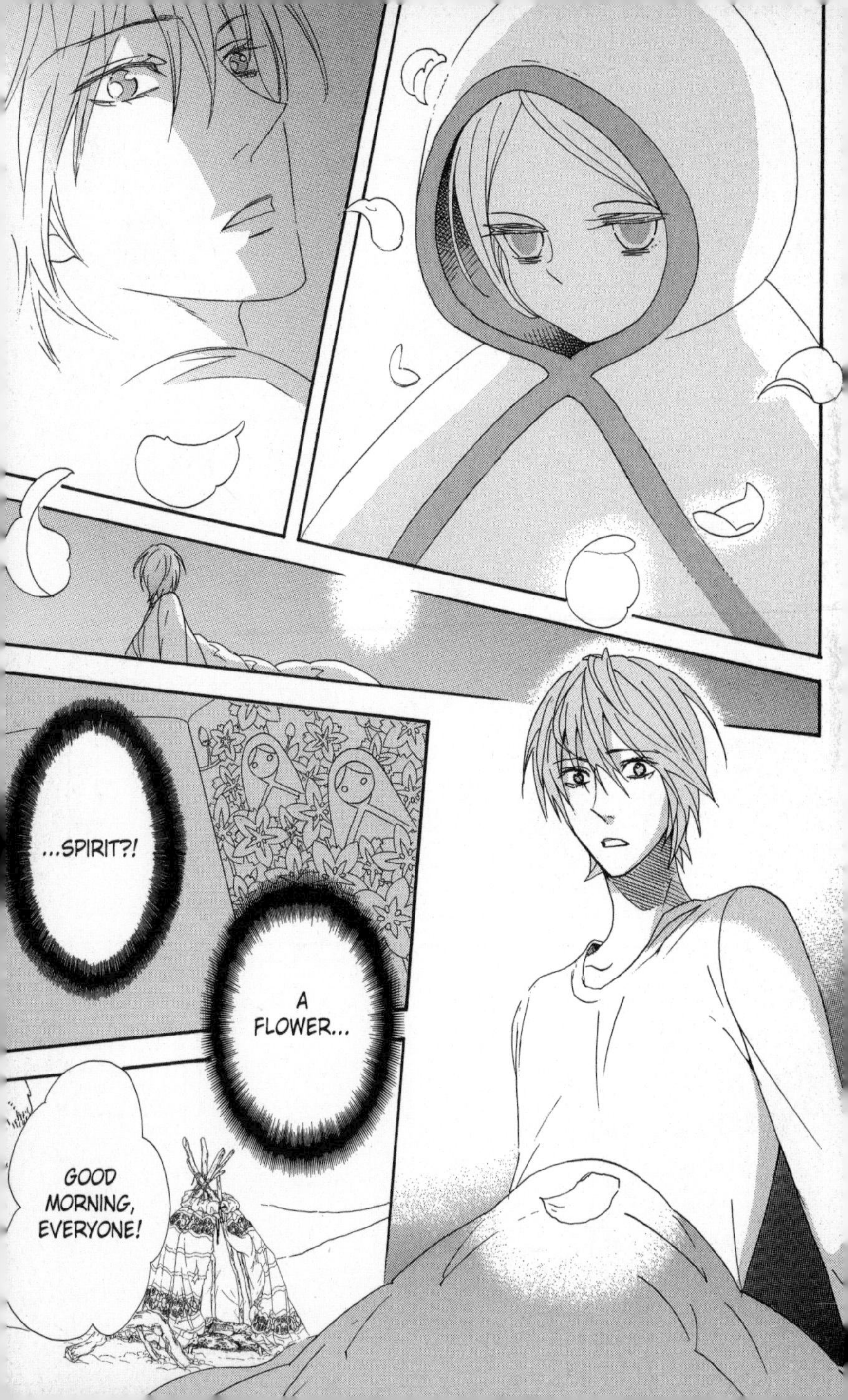
A FLOWER...
...SPIRIT?!
GOOD MORNING, EVERYONE!

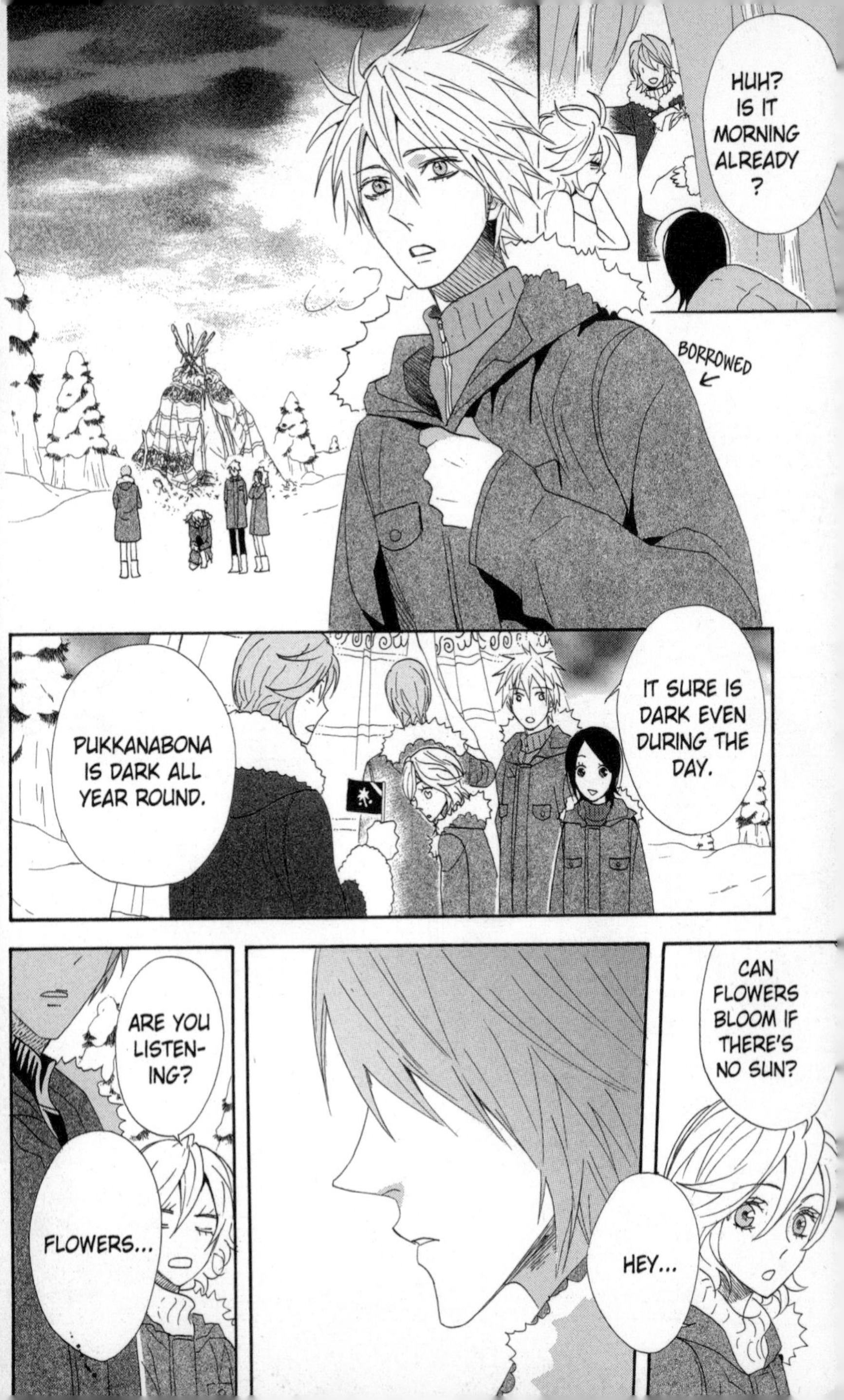
HUH? IS IT MORNING ALREADY?
BORROWED
IT SURE IS DARK EVEN DURING THE DAY.
PUKKANABONA IS DARK ALL YEAR ROUND.
CAN FLOWERS BLOOM IF THERE'S NO SUN?
HEY...
ARE YOU LISTEN-ING?
FLOWERS...

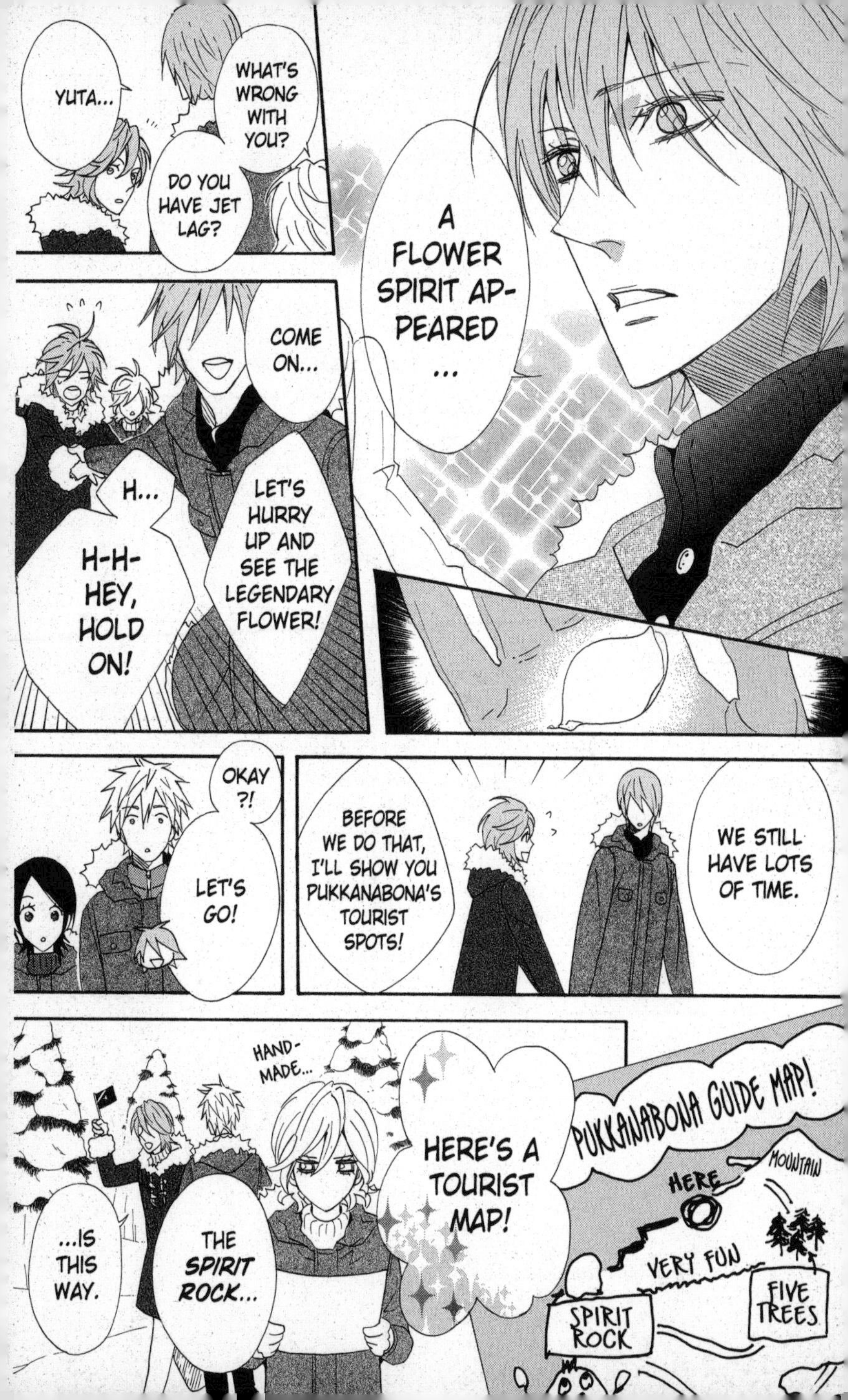
A FLOWER SPIRIT APPEARED...
WHAT'S WRONG WITH YOU?
YUTA...
DO YOU HAVE JET LAG?
COME ON...
LET'S HURRY UP AND SEE THE LEGENDARY FLOWER!
H...
H-H-HEY, HOLD ON!
WE STILL HAVE LOTS OF TIME.
BEFORE WE DO THAT, I'LL SHOW YOU PUKKANABONA'S TOURIST SPOTS!
OKAY?!
LET'S GO!
PUKKANABONA GUIDE MAP!
MOUNTAIN
HERE
VERY FUN
FIVE TREES
SPIRIT ROCK
HERE'S A TOURIST MAP!
HAND-MADE...
THE SPIRIT ROCK...
...IS THIS WAY.

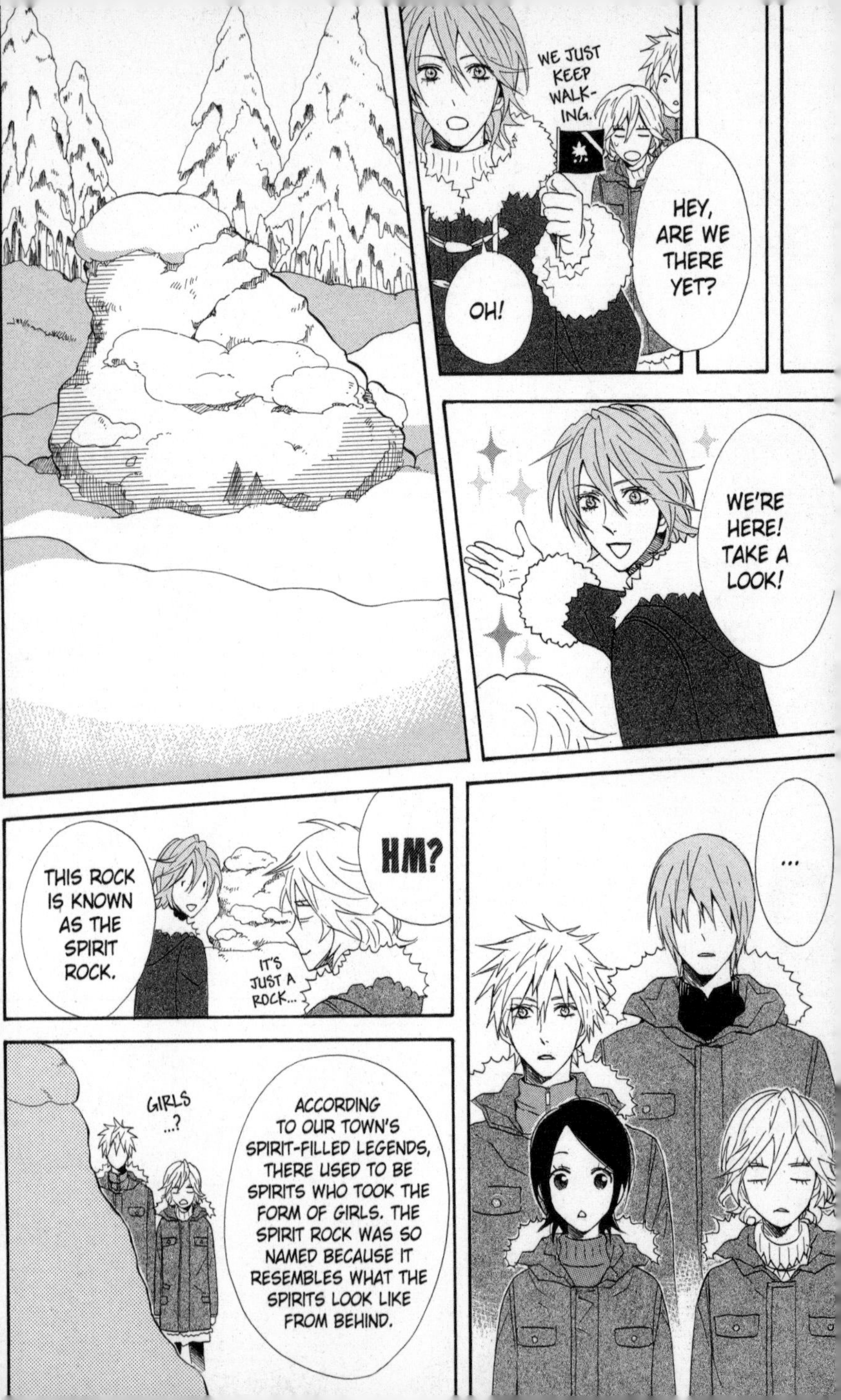
HEY, ARE WE THERE YET?
WE JUST KEEP WALK-ING.
OH!
WE'RE HERE! TAKE A LOOK!
...
HM?
THIS ROCK IS KNOWN AS THE SPIRIT ROCK.
IT'S JUST A ROCK...
ACCORDING TO OUR TOWN'S SPIRIT-FILLED LEGENDS, THERE USED TO BE SPIRITS WHO TOOK THE FORM OF GIRLS. THE SPIRIT ROCK WAS SO NAMED BECAUSE IT RESEMBLES WHAT THE SPIRITS LOOK LIKE FROM BEHIND.
GIRLS ...?

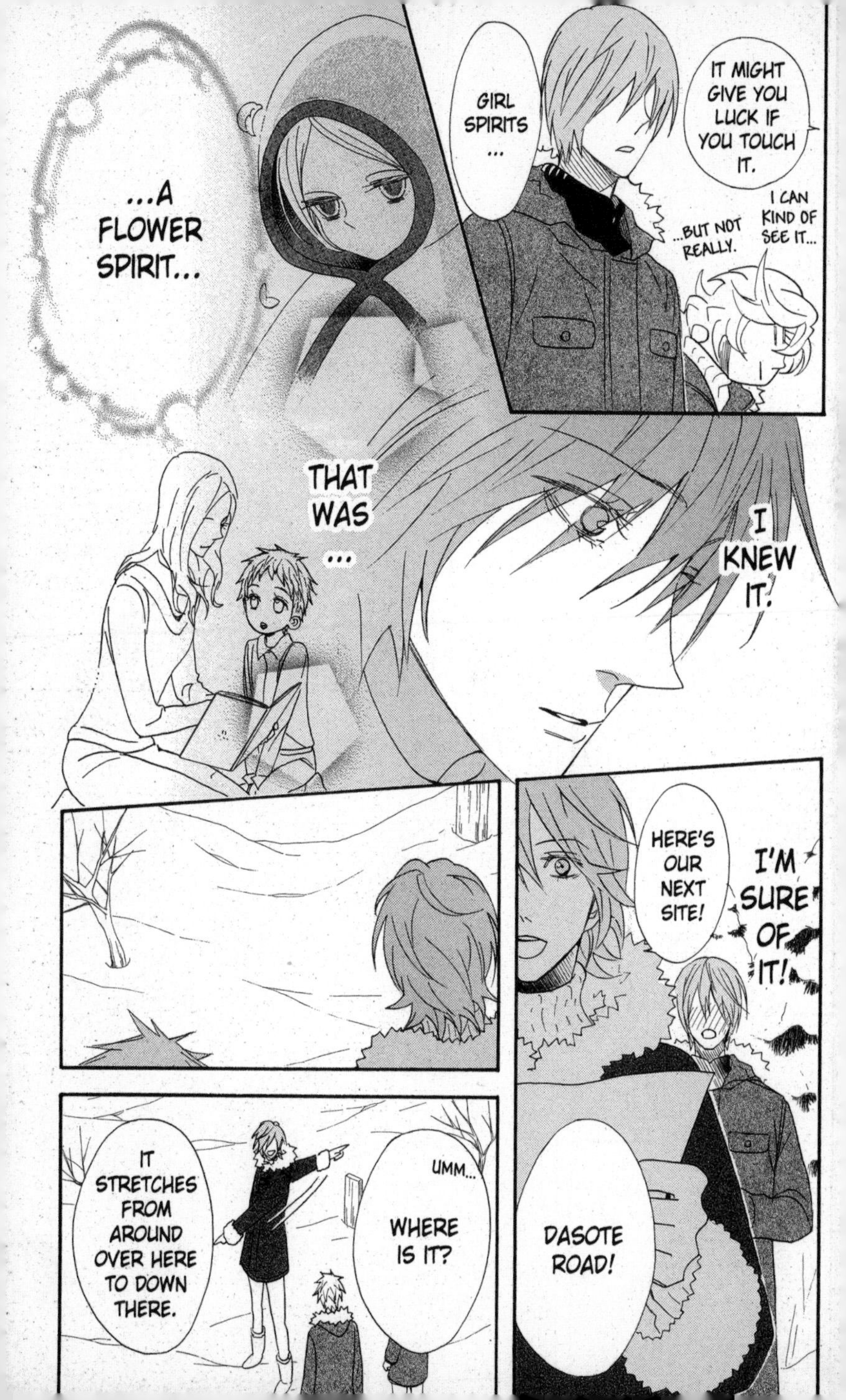

IT MIGHT GIVE YOU LUCK IF YOU TOUCH IT.
I CAN KIND OF SEE IT...
...BUT NOT REALLY.
GIRL SPIRITS...
...A FLOWER SPIRIT...
THAT WAS...
I KNEW IT.
I'M SURE OF IT!
HERE'S OUR NEXT SITE!
DASOTE ROAD!
UMM...
WHERE IS IT?
IT STRETCHES FROM AROUND OVER HERE TO DOWN THERE.

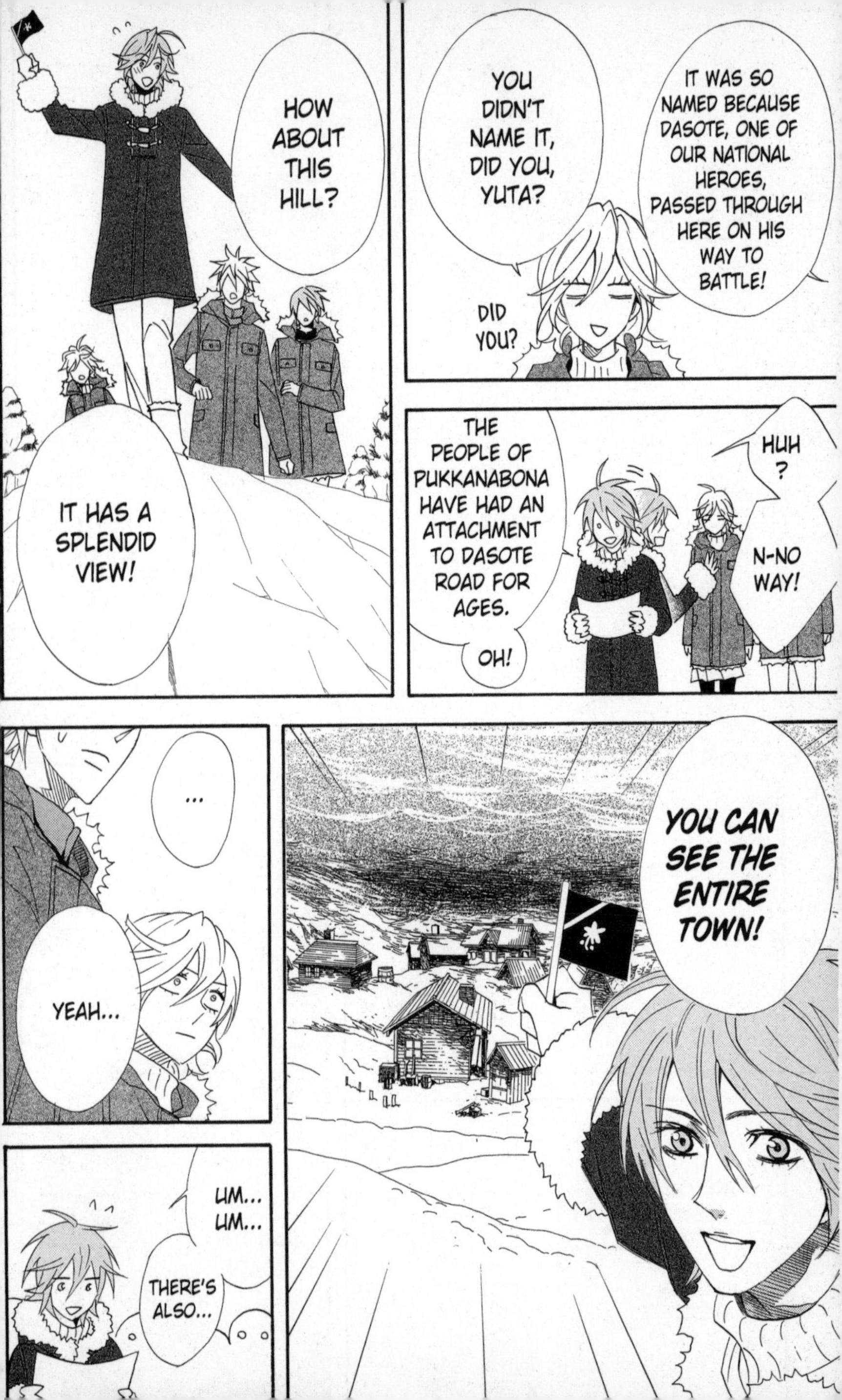
IT WAS SO NAMED BECAUSE DASOTE, ONE OF OUR NATIONAL HEROES, PASSED THROUGH HERE ON HIS WAY TO BATTLE!
YOU DIDN'T NAME IT, DID YOU, YUTA?
DID YOU?
HUH?
N-NO WAY!
THE PEOPLE OF PUKKANABONA HAVE HAD AN ATTACHMENT TO DASOTE ROAD FOR AGES.
OH!
HOW ABOUT THIS HILL?
IT HAS A SPLENDID VIEW!
YOU CAN SEE THE ENTIRE TOWN!
...
YEAH...
UM... UM...
THERE'S ALSO...

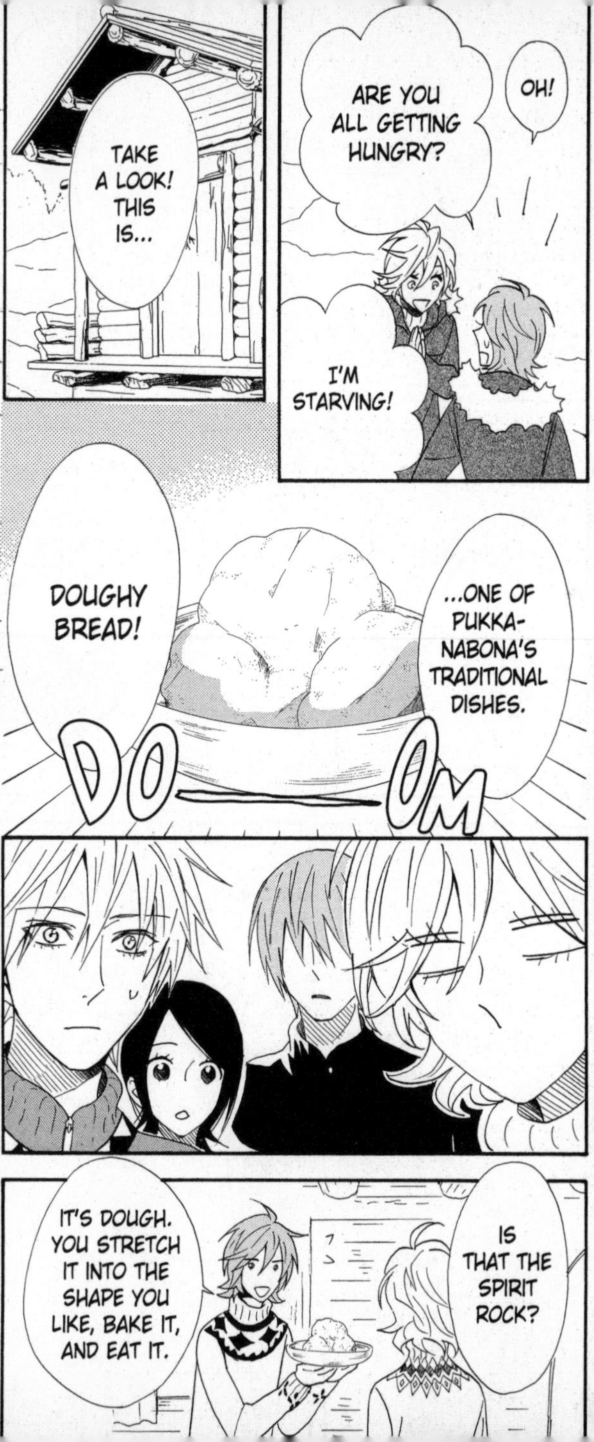
OH!
ARE YOU ALL GETTING HUNGRY?
I'M STARVING!
TAKE A LOOK! THIS IS...
...ONE OF PUKKA-NABONA'S TRADITIONAL DISHES.
DOUGHY BREAD!
DO—OM
IS THAT THE SPIRIT ROCK?
IT'S DOUGH. YOU STRETCH IT INTO THE SHAPE YOU LIKE, BAKE IT, AND EAT IT.

Hello there!
This is volume 14.

Finally... I finally got him on the cover this time.

I thought it would be kind of funny to not have him on any of the covers, but I ran out of ideas for covers. Heh.

That was one of my reasons, but he was the main focus in the serialized comic at the time, so I finally decided to put him on a cover.

I make fun of him all the time, but I love him a lot.

He'll play an active role in a later volume.

He hardly appears at all in this one. Hee.

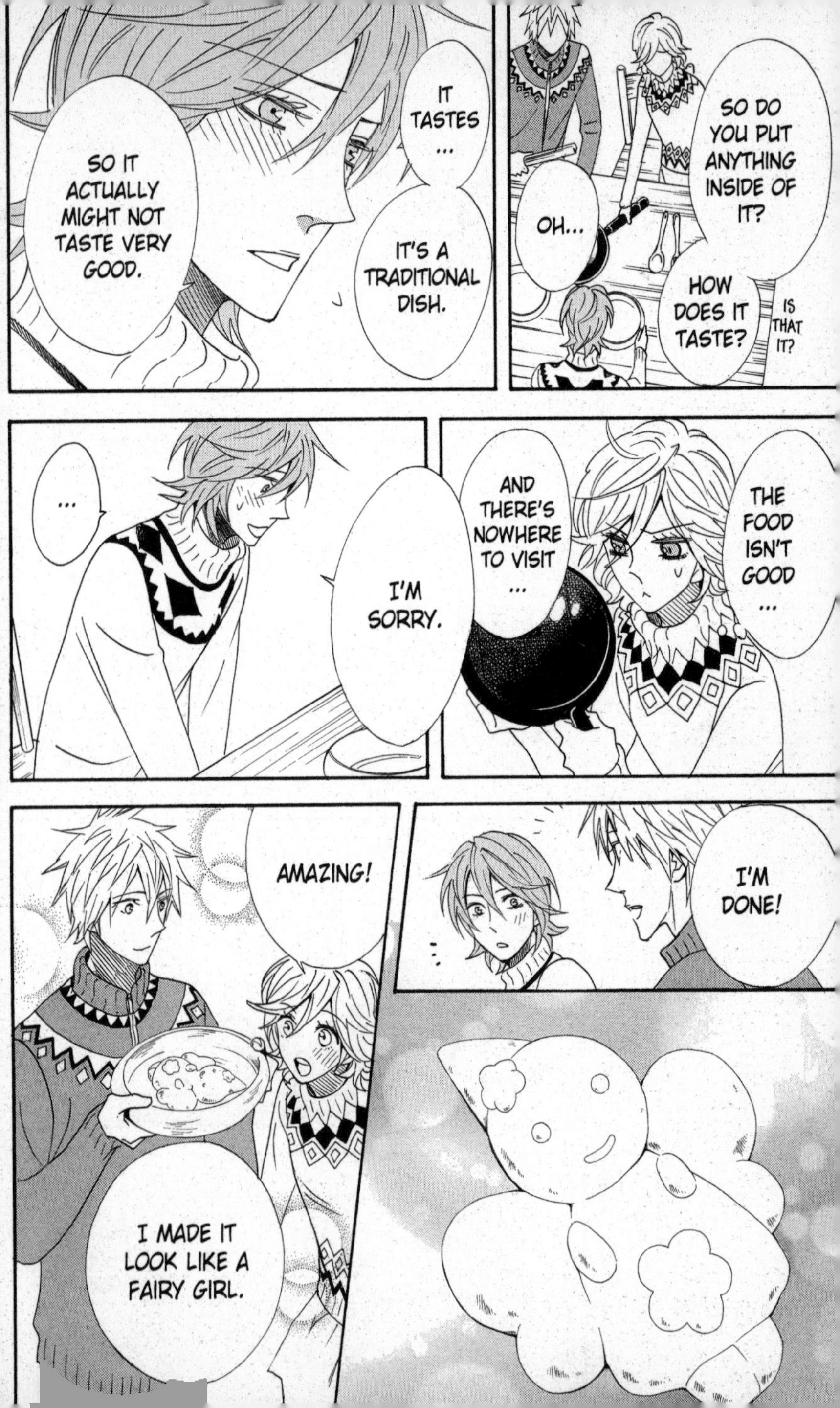
SO DO YOU PUT ANYTHING INSIDE OF IT?
IS THAT IT?
HOW DOES IT TASTE?
OH...
IT TASTES ...
IT'S A TRADITIONAL DISH.
SO IT ACTUALLY MIGHT NOT TASTE VERY GOOD.
THE FOOD ISN'T GOOD ...
AND THERE'S NOWHERE TO VISIT ...
I'M SORRY.
...
I'M DONE!
AMAZING!
I MADE IT LOOK LIKE A FAIRY GIRL.

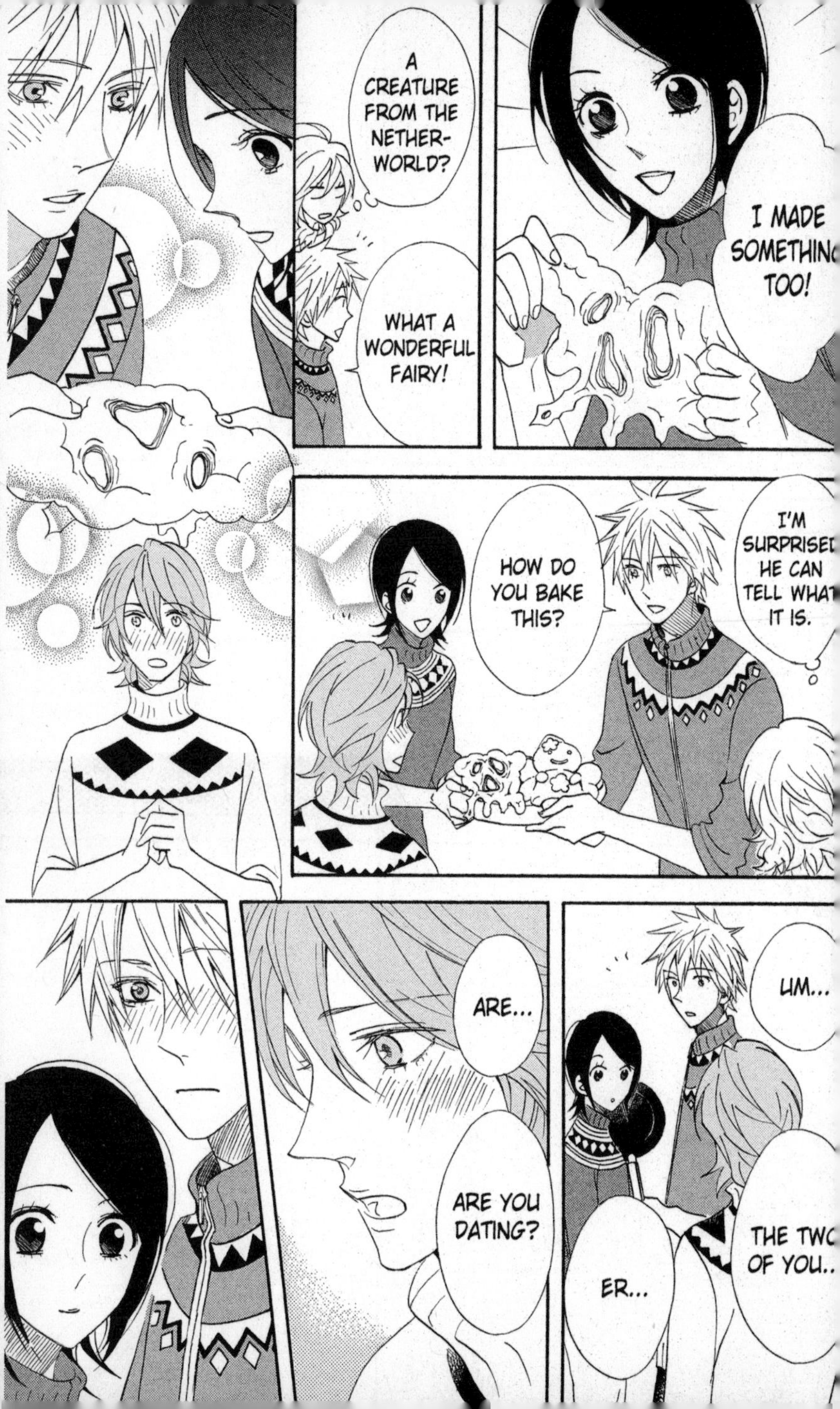
I MADE SOMETHING TOO!
A CREATURE FROM THE NETHER-WORLD?
WHAT A WONDERFUL FAIRY!
I'M SURPRISED HE CAN TELL WHAT IT IS.
HOW DO YOU BAKE THIS?
UM...
THE TWO OF YOU...
ER...
ARE...
ARE YOU DATING?

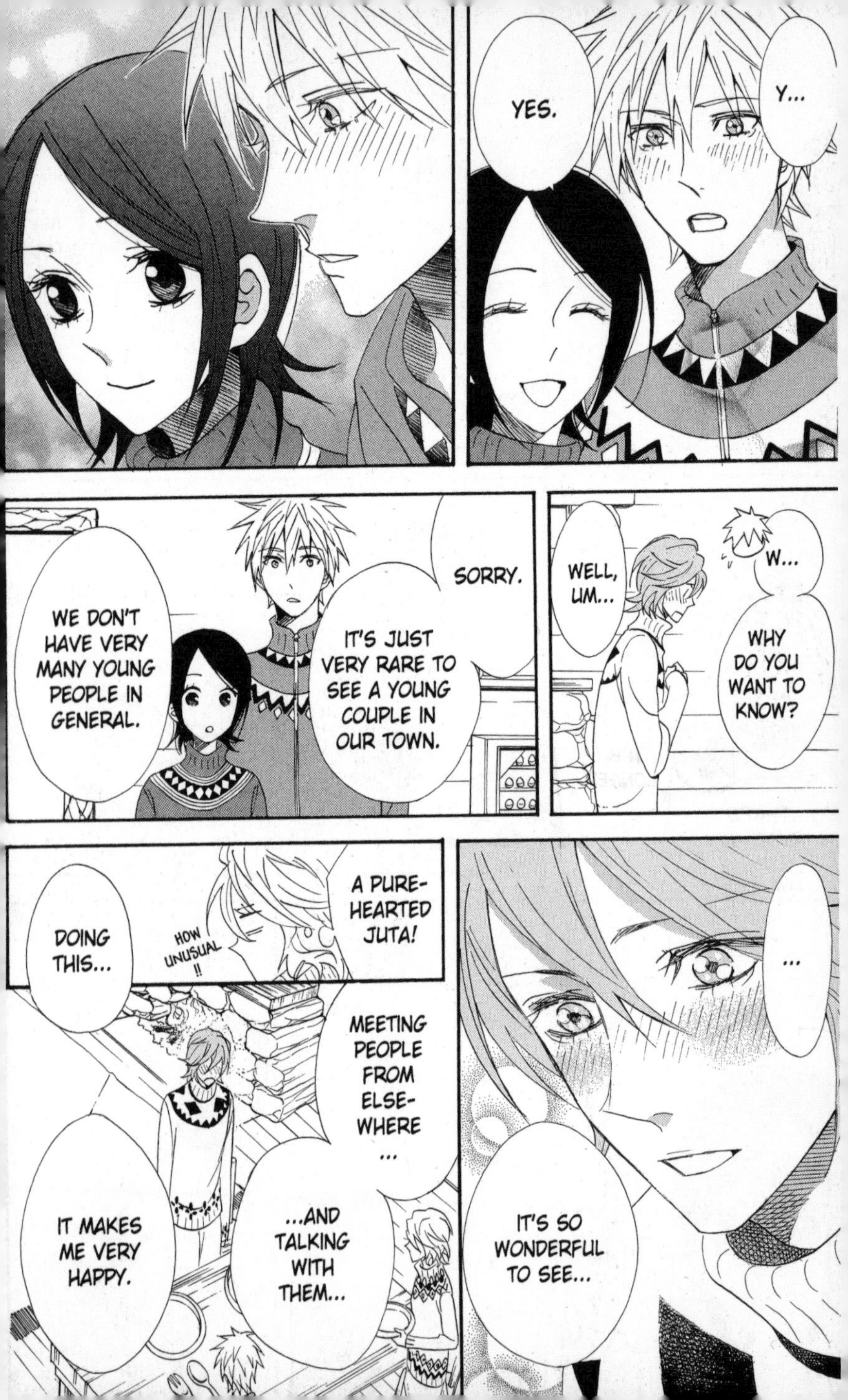
Y...
YES.
W...
WHY DO YOU WANT TO KNOW?
WELL, UM...
SORRY.
IT'S JUST VERY RARE TO SEE A YOUNG COUPLE IN OUR TOWN.
WE DON'T HAVE VERY MANY YOUNG PEOPLE IN GENERAL.
...
IT'S SO WONDERFUL TO SEE...
A PURE-HEARTED JUTA!
HOW UNUSUAL!!
DOING THIS...
MEETING PEOPLE FROM ELSEWHERE...
...AND TALKING WITH THEM...
IT MAKES ME VERY HAPPY.

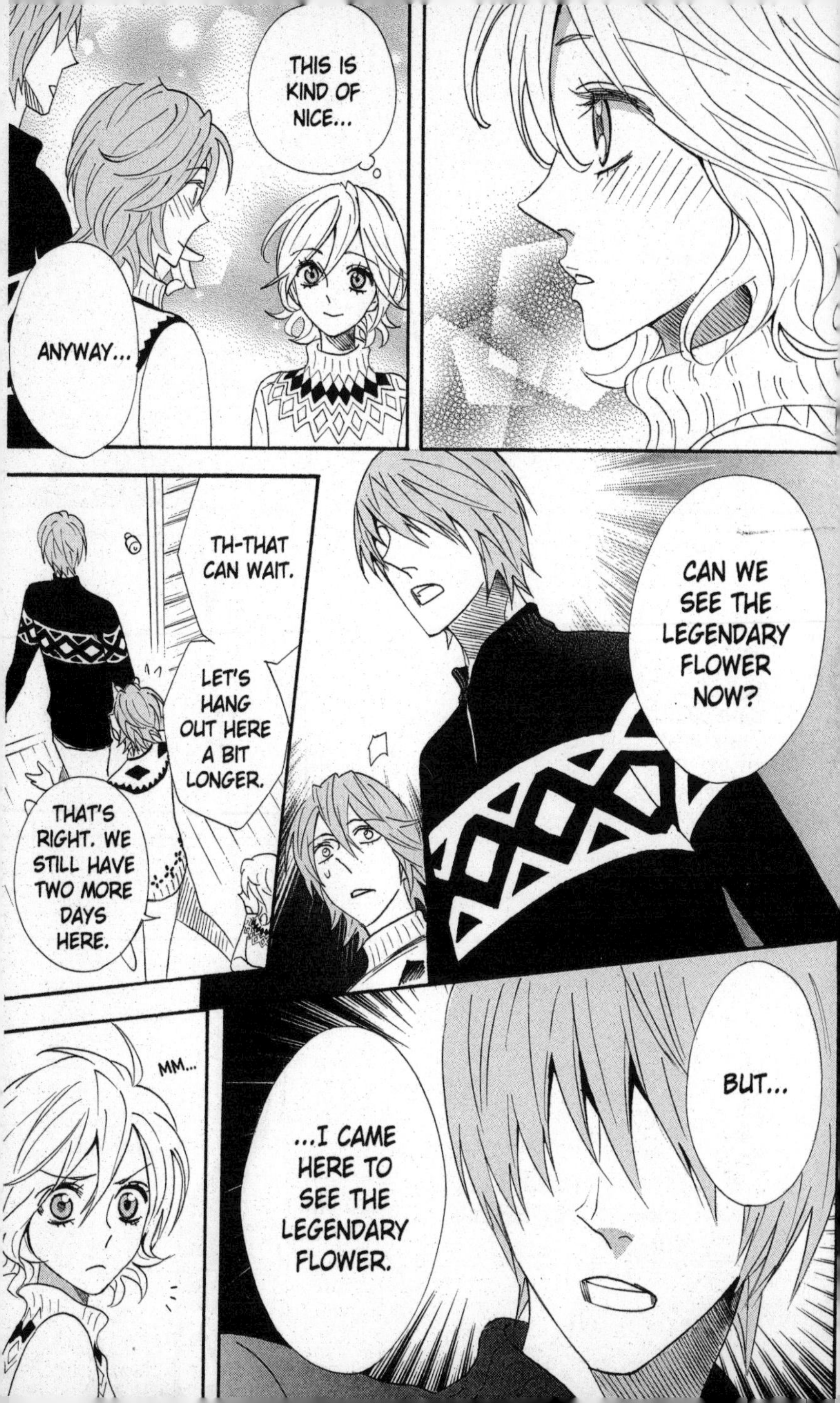
THIS IS KIND OF NICE...
ANYWAY...
CAN WE SEE THE LEGENDARY FLOWER NOW?
TH-THAT CAN WAIT.
LET'S HANG OUT HERE A BIT LONGER.
THAT'S RIGHT. WE STILL HAVE TWO MORE DAYS HERE.
BUT...
...I CAME HERE TO SEE THE LEGENDARY FLOWER.
MM...

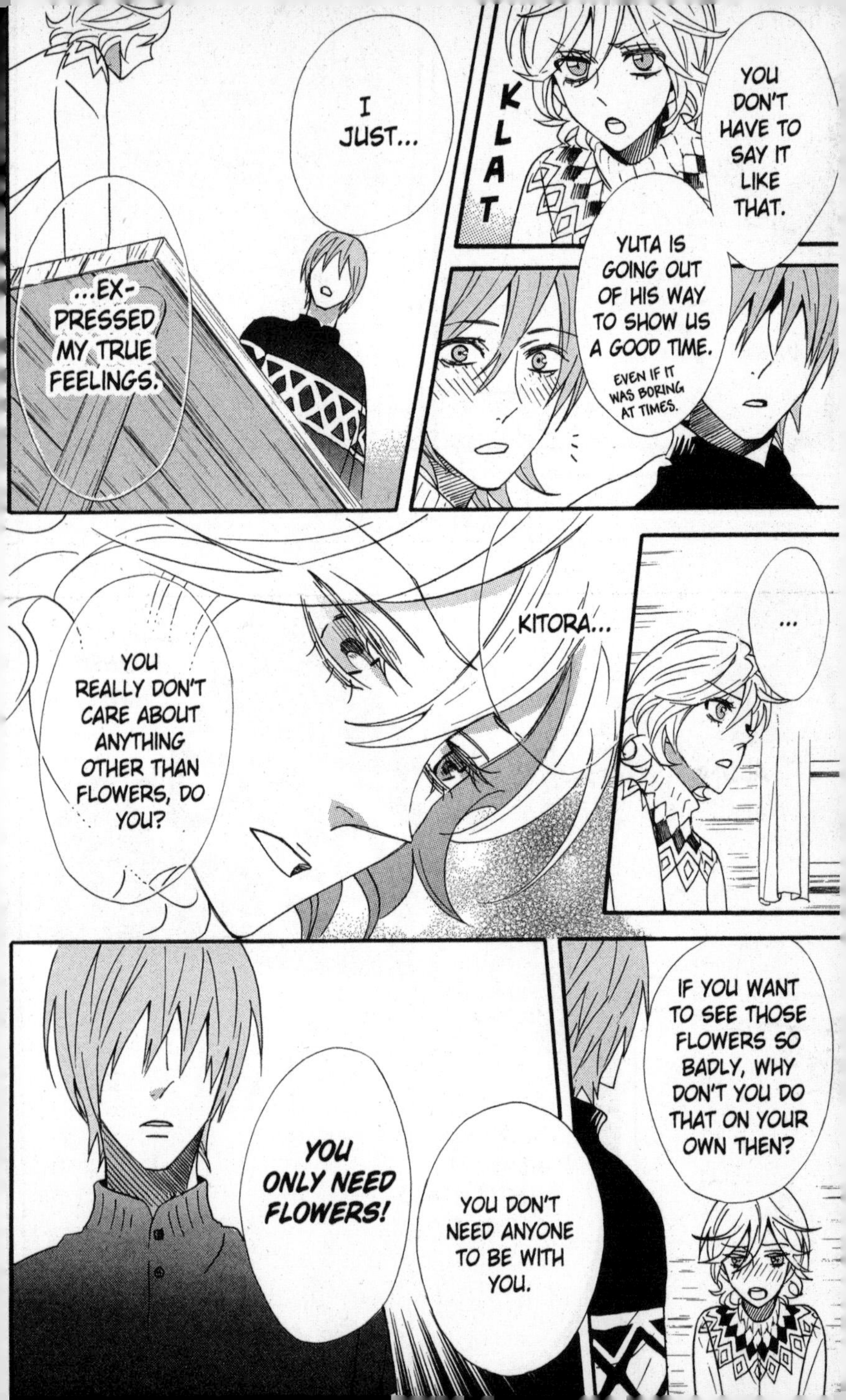
KLAT
YOU DON'T HAVE TO SAY IT LIKE THAT.
YUTA IS GOING OUT OF HIS WAY TO SHOW US A GOOD TIME.
EVEN IF IT WAS BORING AT TIMES.
I JUST...
...EX-PRESSED MY TRUE FEELINGS.
...
KITORA...
YOU REALLY DON'T CARE ABOUT ANYTHING OTHER THAN FLOWERS, DO YOU?
IF YOU WANT TO SEE THOSE FLOWERS SO BADLY, WHY DON'T YOU DO THAT ON YOUR OWN THEN?
YOU DON'T NEED ANYONE TO BE WITH YOU.
YOU ONLY NEED FLOWERS!

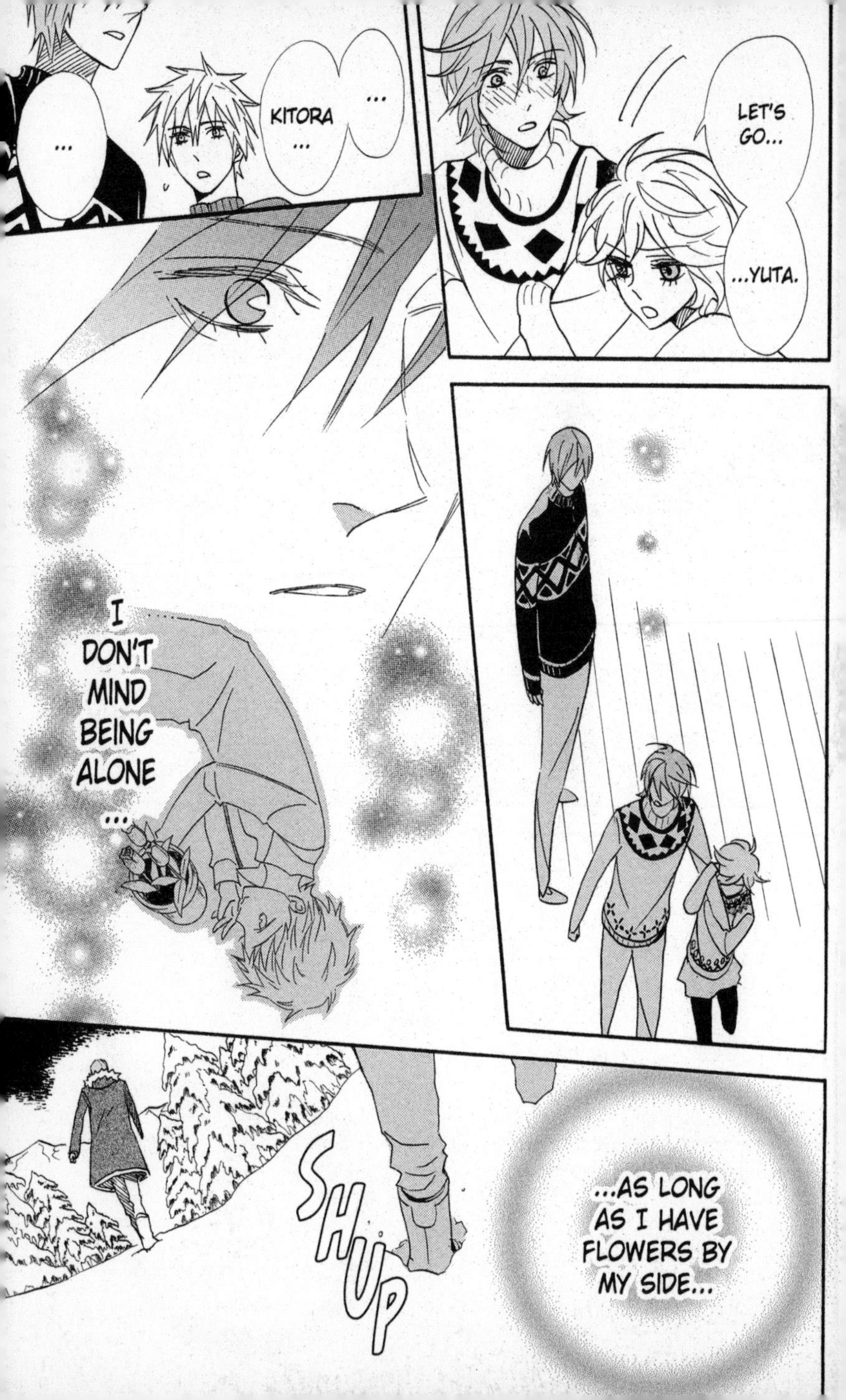
LET'S GO...
...YUTA.
... KITORA ...
...
I DON'T MIND BEING ALONE ...
...AS LONG AS I HAVE FLOWERS BY MY SIDE...
SHUP

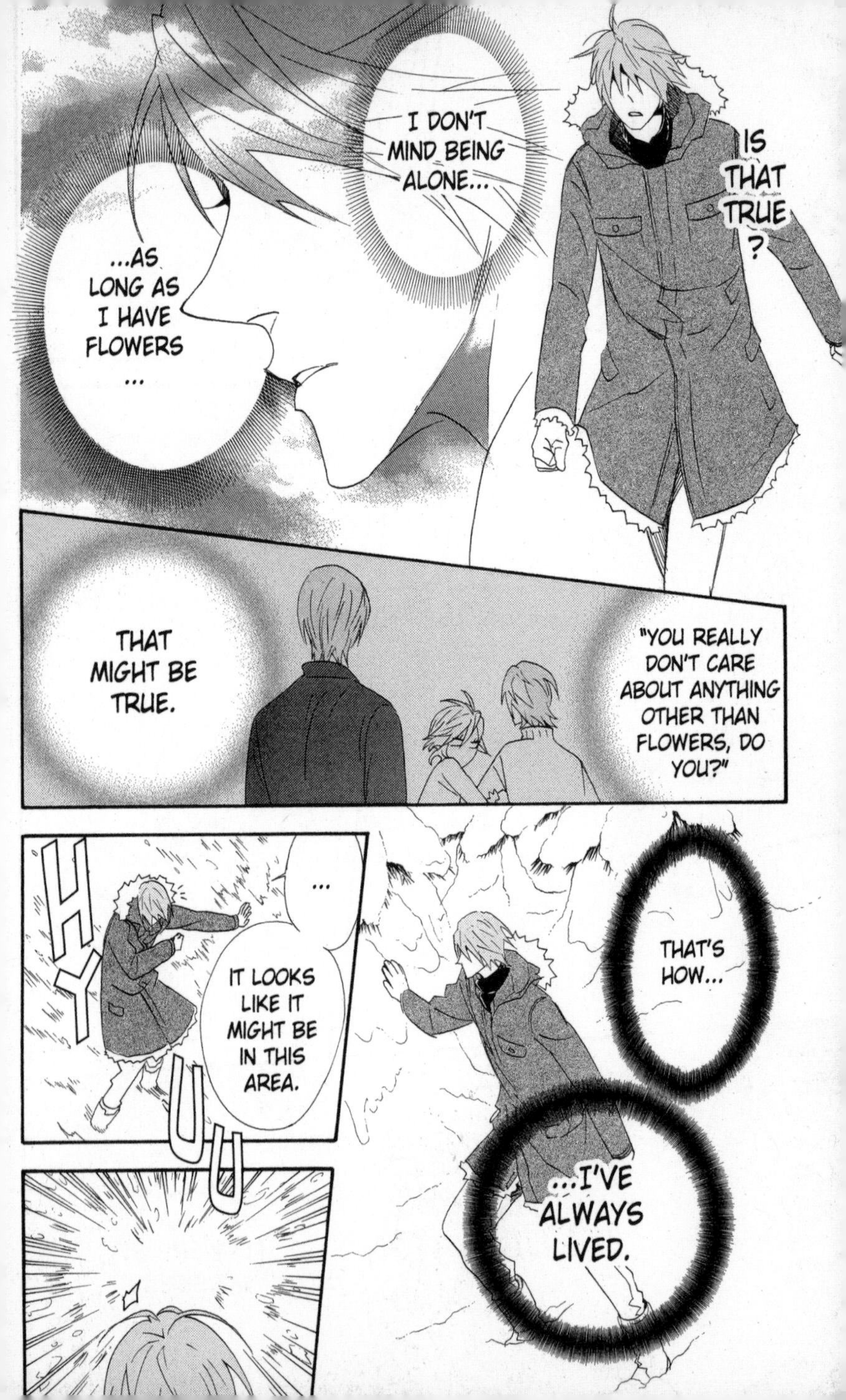
IS THAT TRUE?
I DON'T MIND BEING ALONE...
...AS LONG AS I HAVE FLOWERS...
"YOU REALLY DON'T CARE ABOUT ANYTHING OTHER THAN FLOWERS, DO YOU?"
THAT MIGHT BE TRUE.
THAT'S HOW...
...I'VE ALWAYS LIVED.
HYUU
...
IT LOOKS LIKE IT MIGHT BE IN THIS AREA.

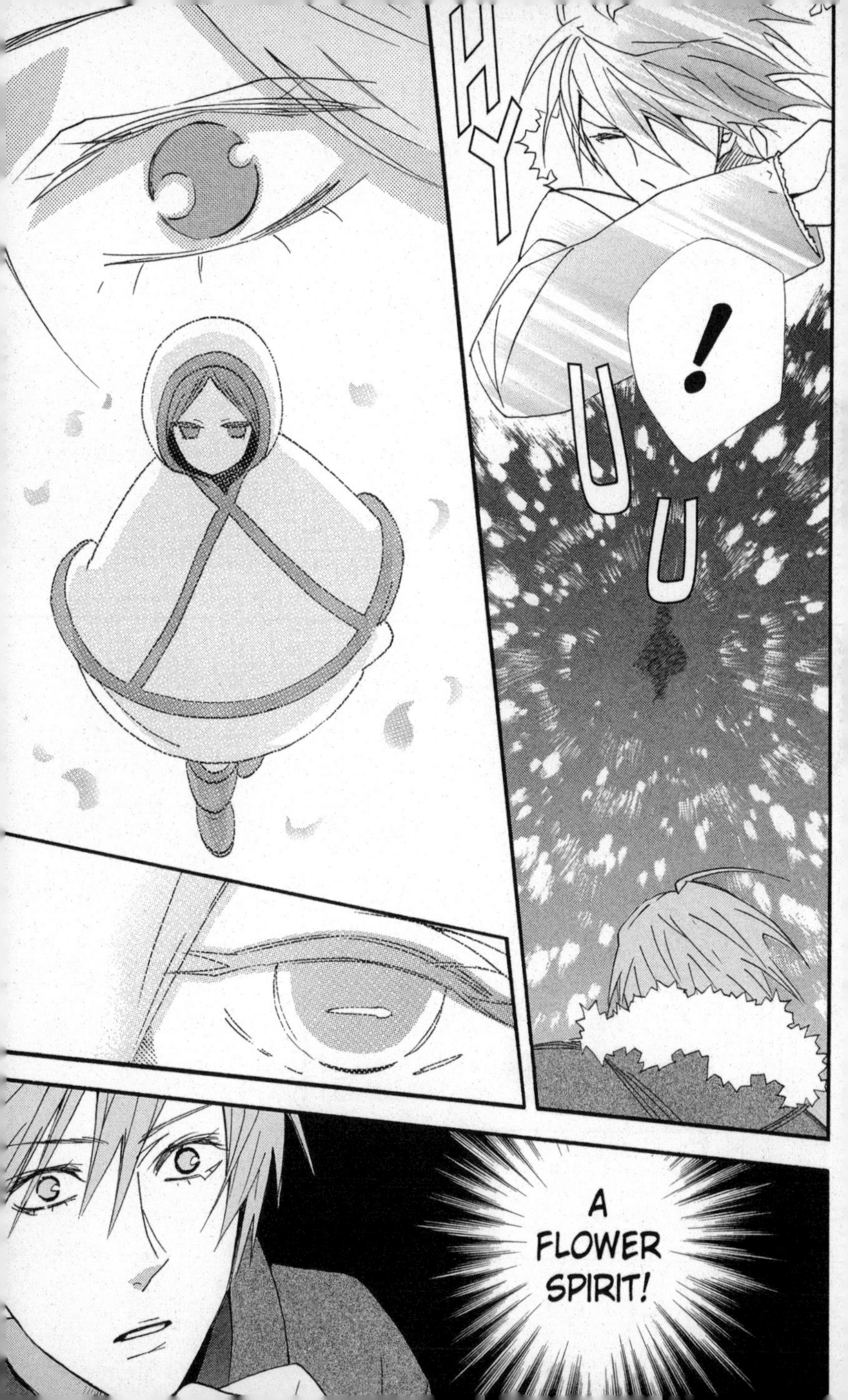
!
UUU
A FLOWER SPIRIT!

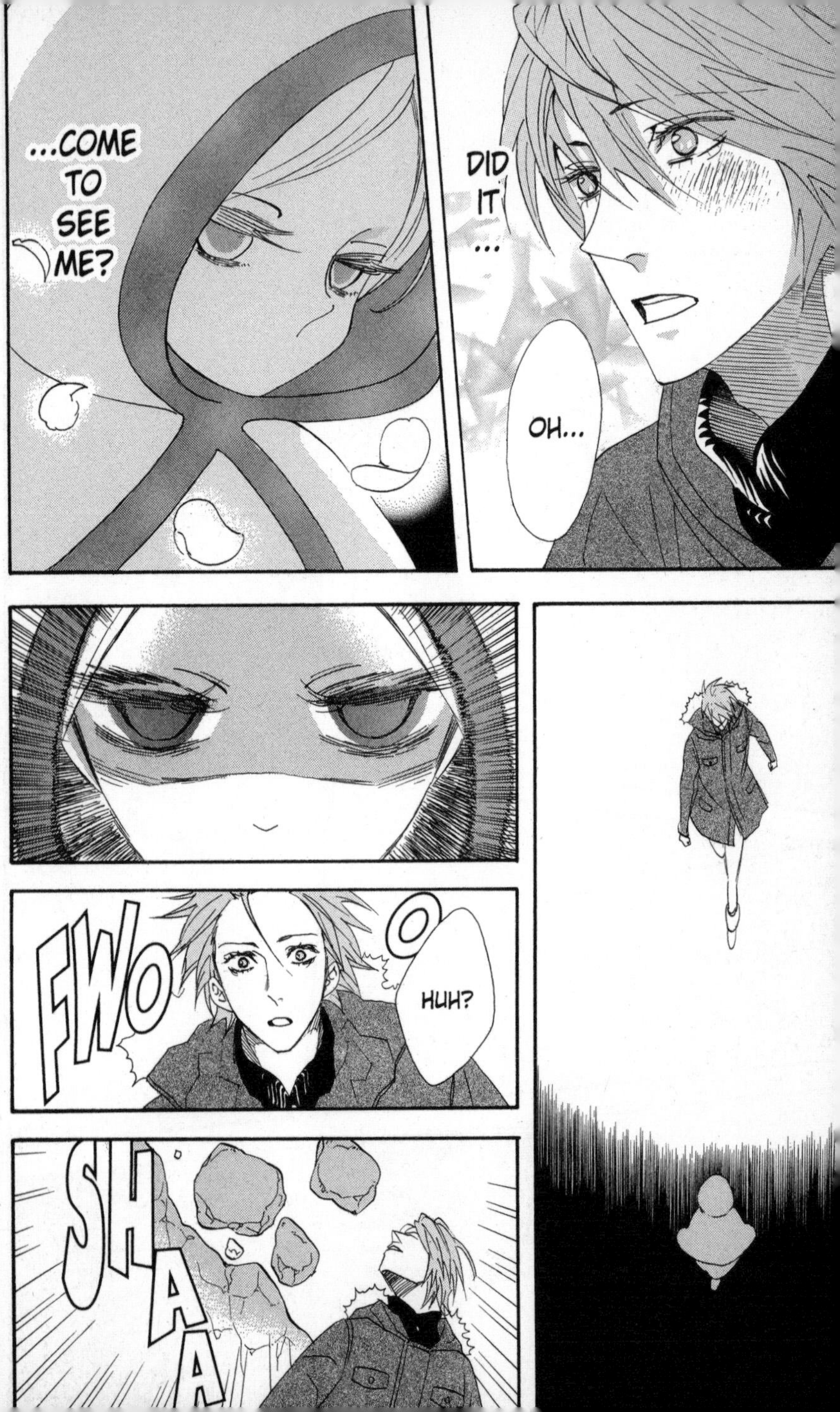

DID IT ...
OH...
...COME TO SEE ME?
FWOO
HUH?
SHAA

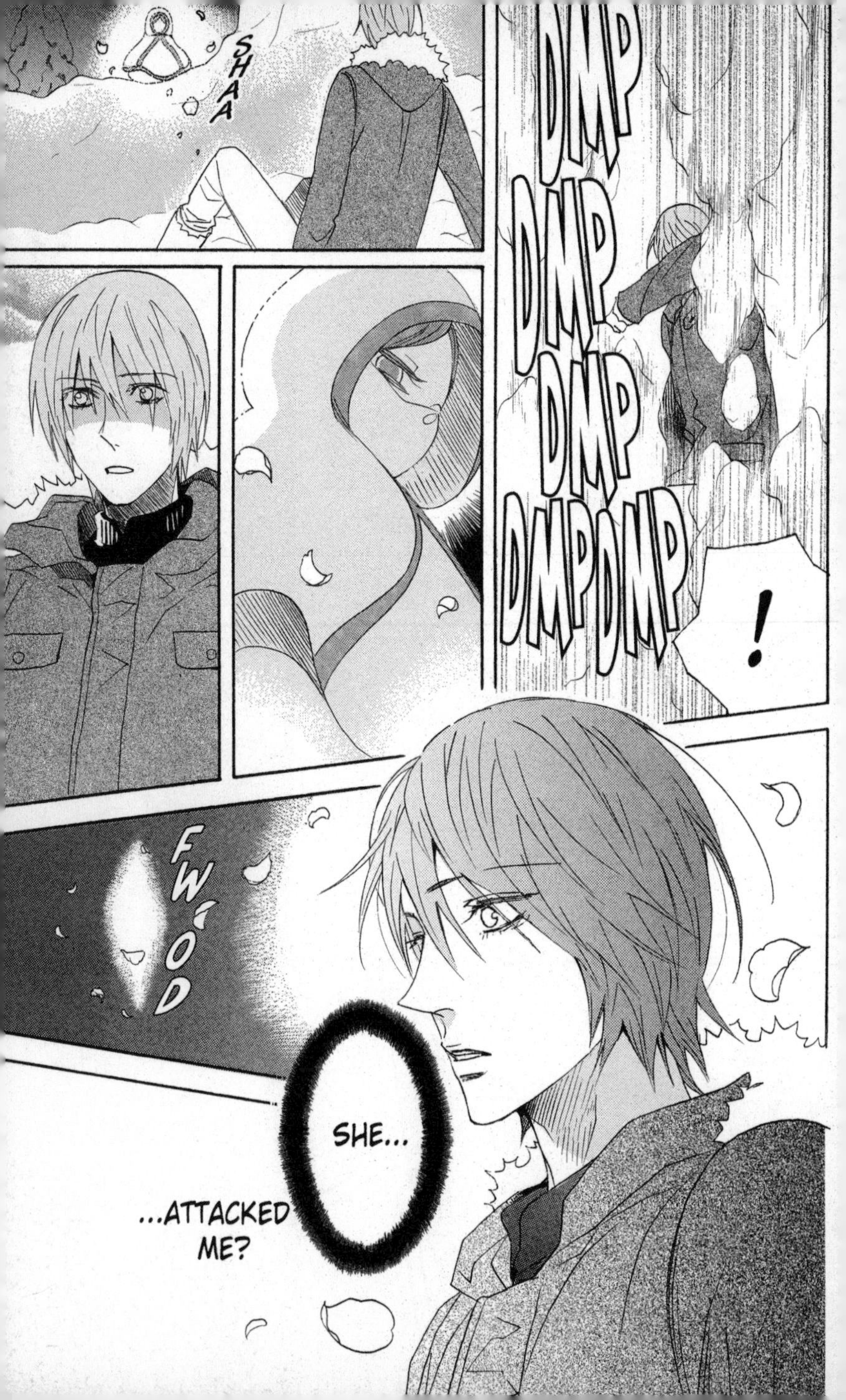
DMP DMP DMP DMP DMPDMP
!
SHAA
FWOOD
SHE...
...ATTACKED ME?

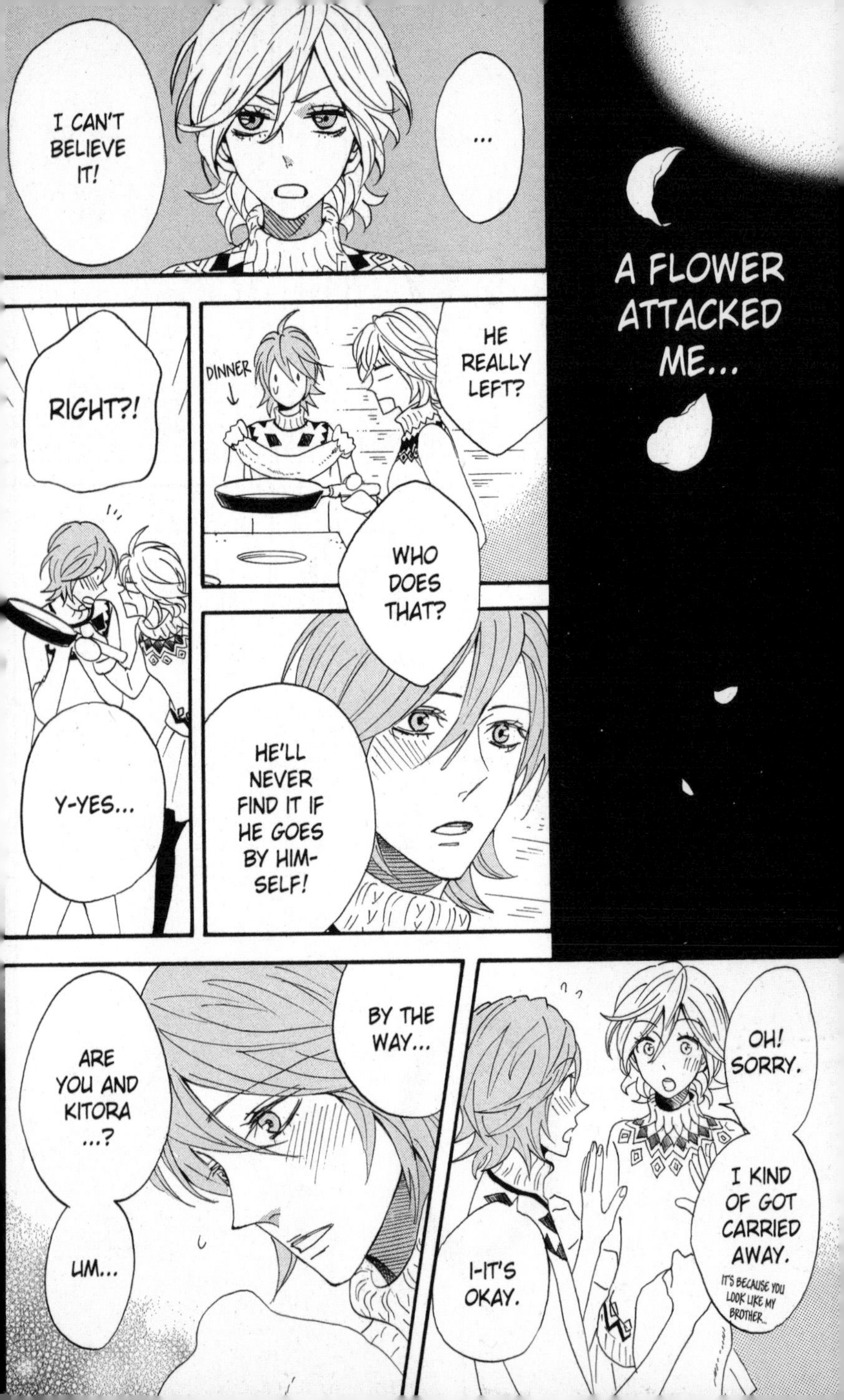
A FLOWER ATTACKED ME...
...
I CAN'T BELIEVE IT!
HE REALLY LEFT?
DINNER
RIGHT?!
WHO DOES THAT?
HE'LL NEVER FIND IT IF HE GOES BY HIM-SELF!
Y-YES...
OH! SORRY.
I KIND OF GOT CARRIED AWAY.
IT'S BECAUSE YOU LOOK LIKE MY BROTHER...
I-IT'S OKAY.
BY THE WAY...
ARE YOU AND KITORA ...?
UM...

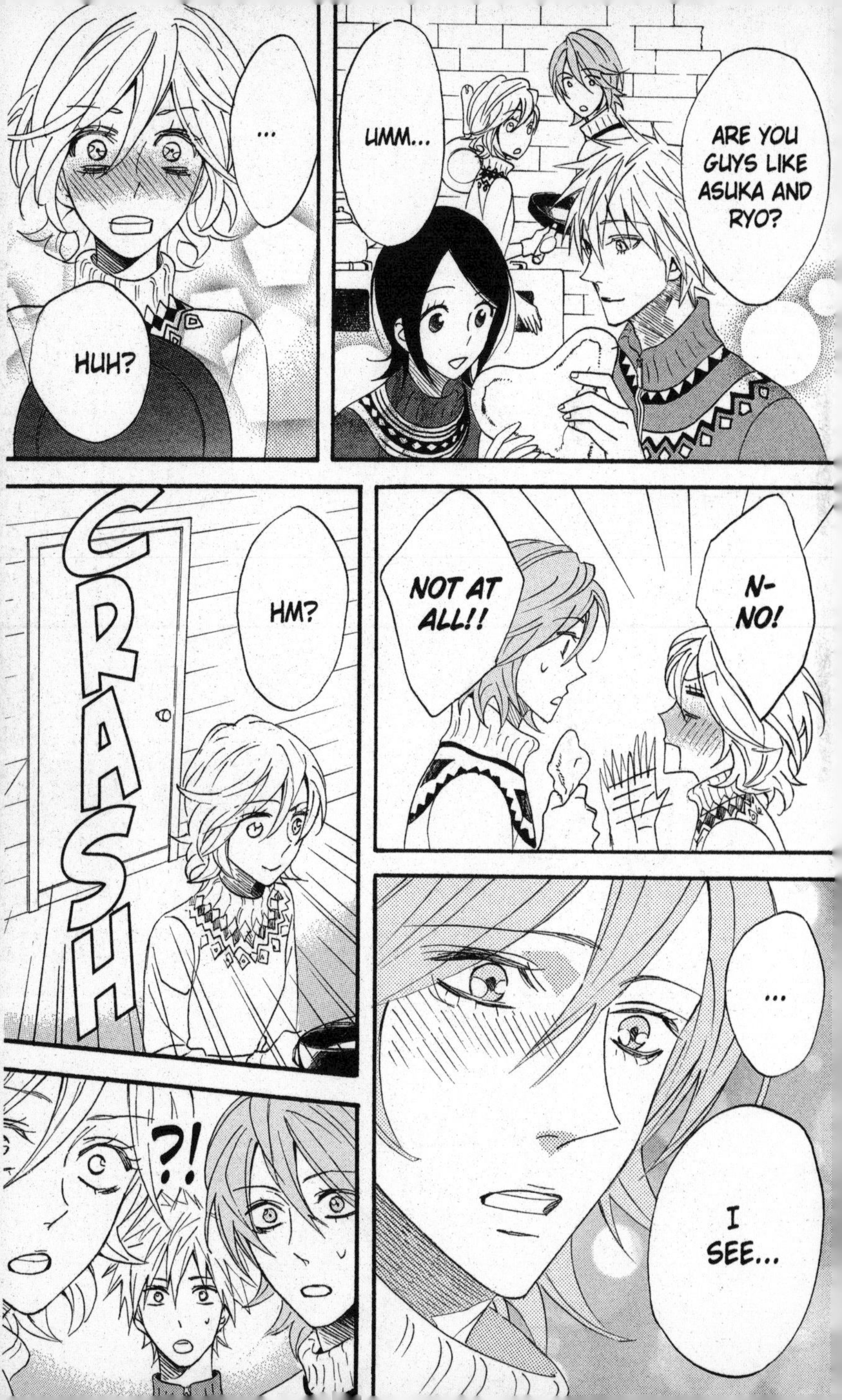
ARE YOU GUYS LIKE ASUKA AND RYO?
UMM...
...
HUH?
N-NO!
NOT AT ALL!!
...
I SEE...
HM?
CRASH
?!

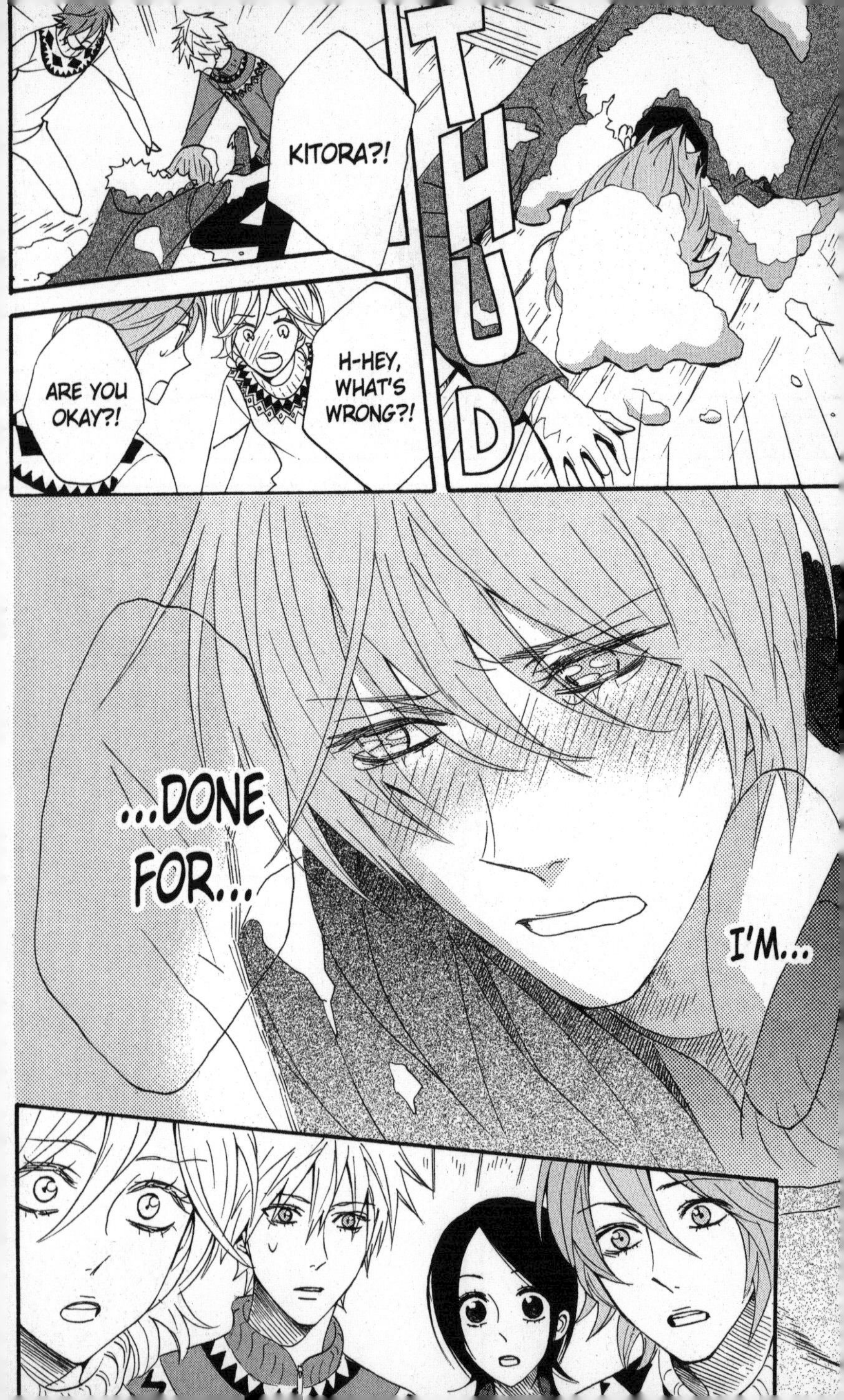
THUD
KITORA?!
H-HEY, WHAT'S WRONG?!
ARE YOU OKAY?!
I'M...
...DONE FOR...

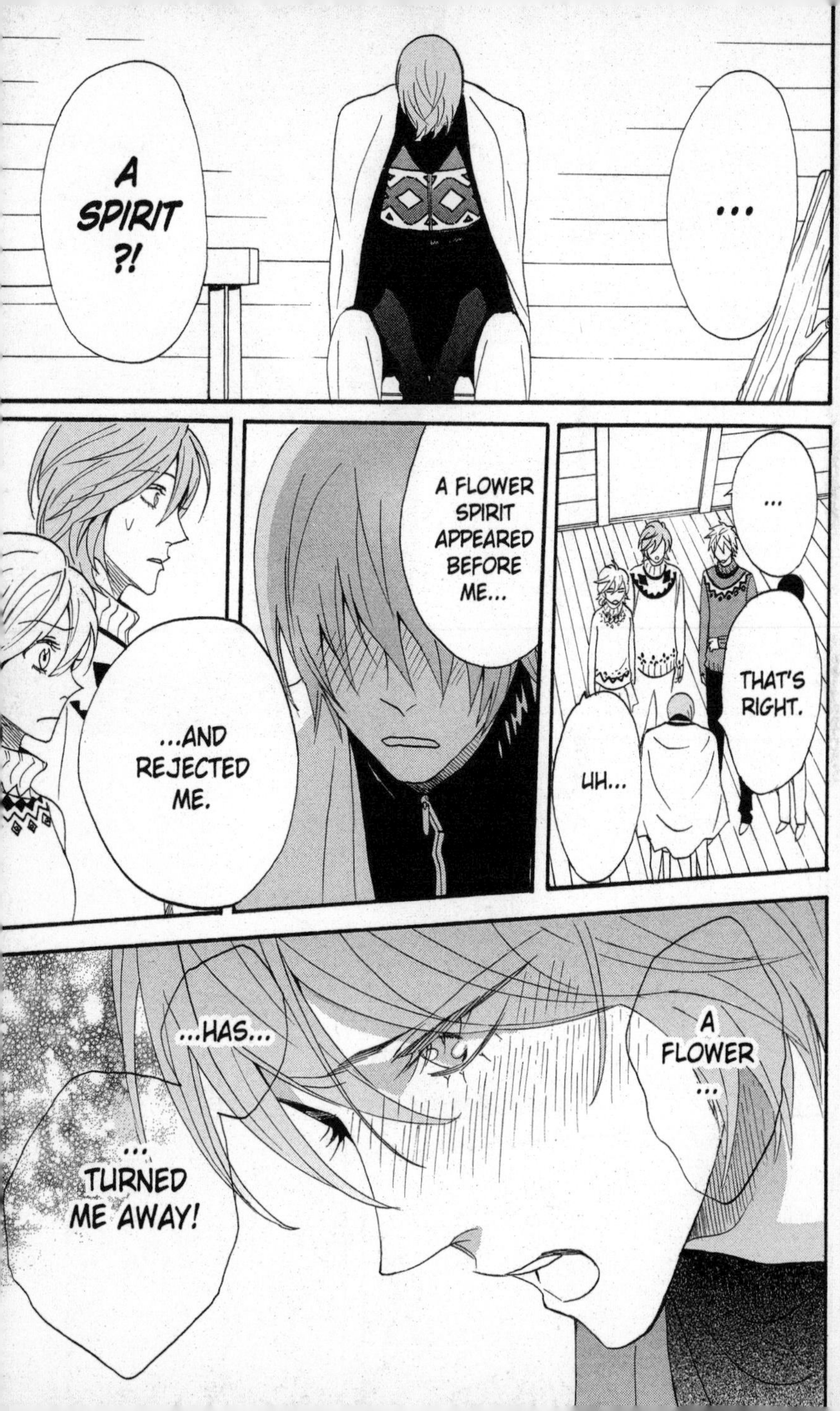
...
A SPIRIT ?!
...
THAT'S RIGHT.
UH...
A FLOWER SPIRIT APPEARED BEFORE ME...
...AND REJECTED ME.
A FLOWER...
...HAS...
...TURNED ME AWAY!

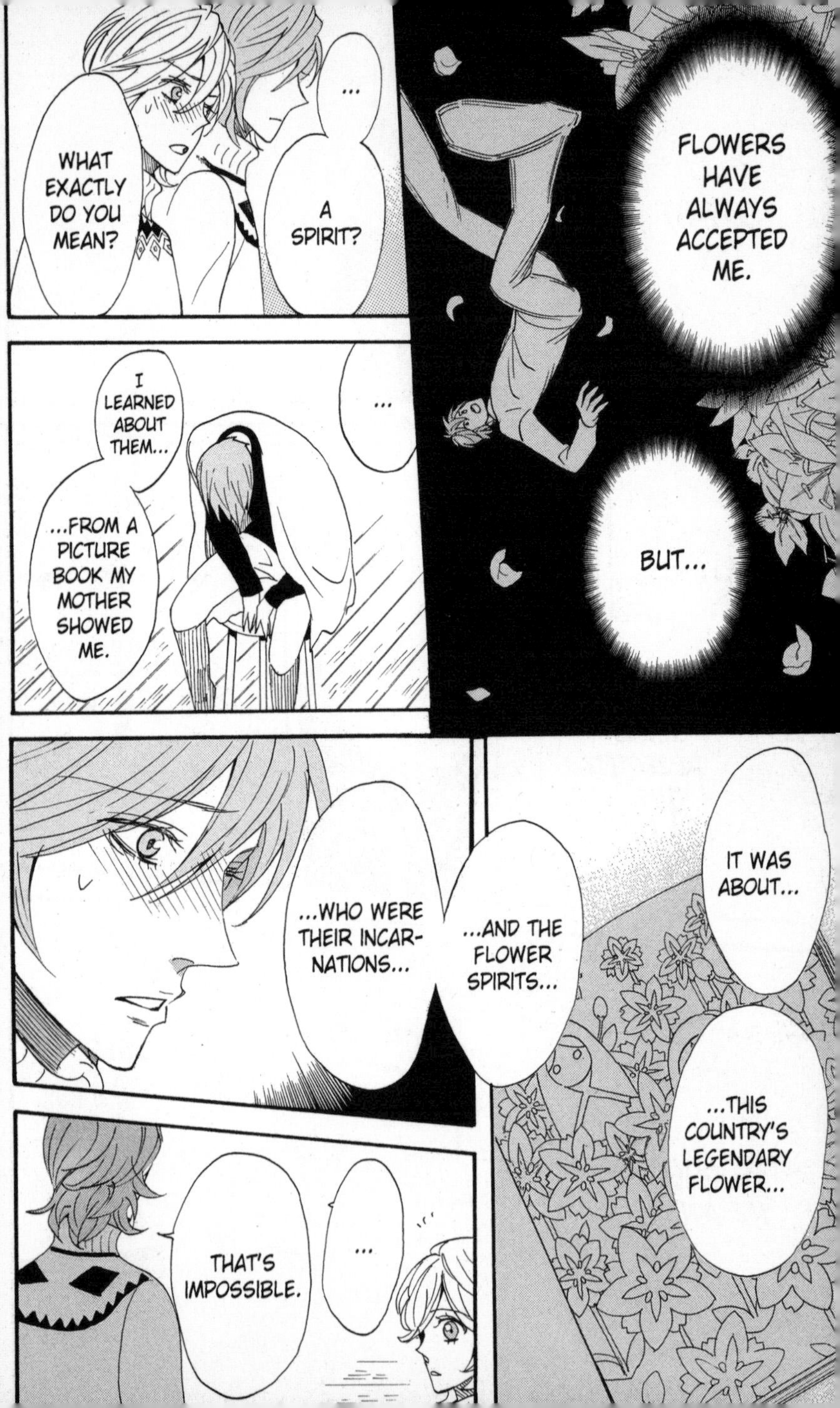
FLOWERS HAVE ALWAYS ACCEPTED ME.
BUT...
...
A SPIRIT?
WHAT EXACTLY DO YOU MEAN?
...
I LEARNED ABOUT THEM...
...FROM A PICTURE BOOK MY MOTHER SHOWED ME.
IT WAS ABOUT...
...THIS COUNTRY'S LEGENDARY FLOWER...
...AND THE FLOWER SPIRITS...
...WHO WERE THEIR INCAR-NATIONS...
...
THAT'S IMPOSSIBLE.

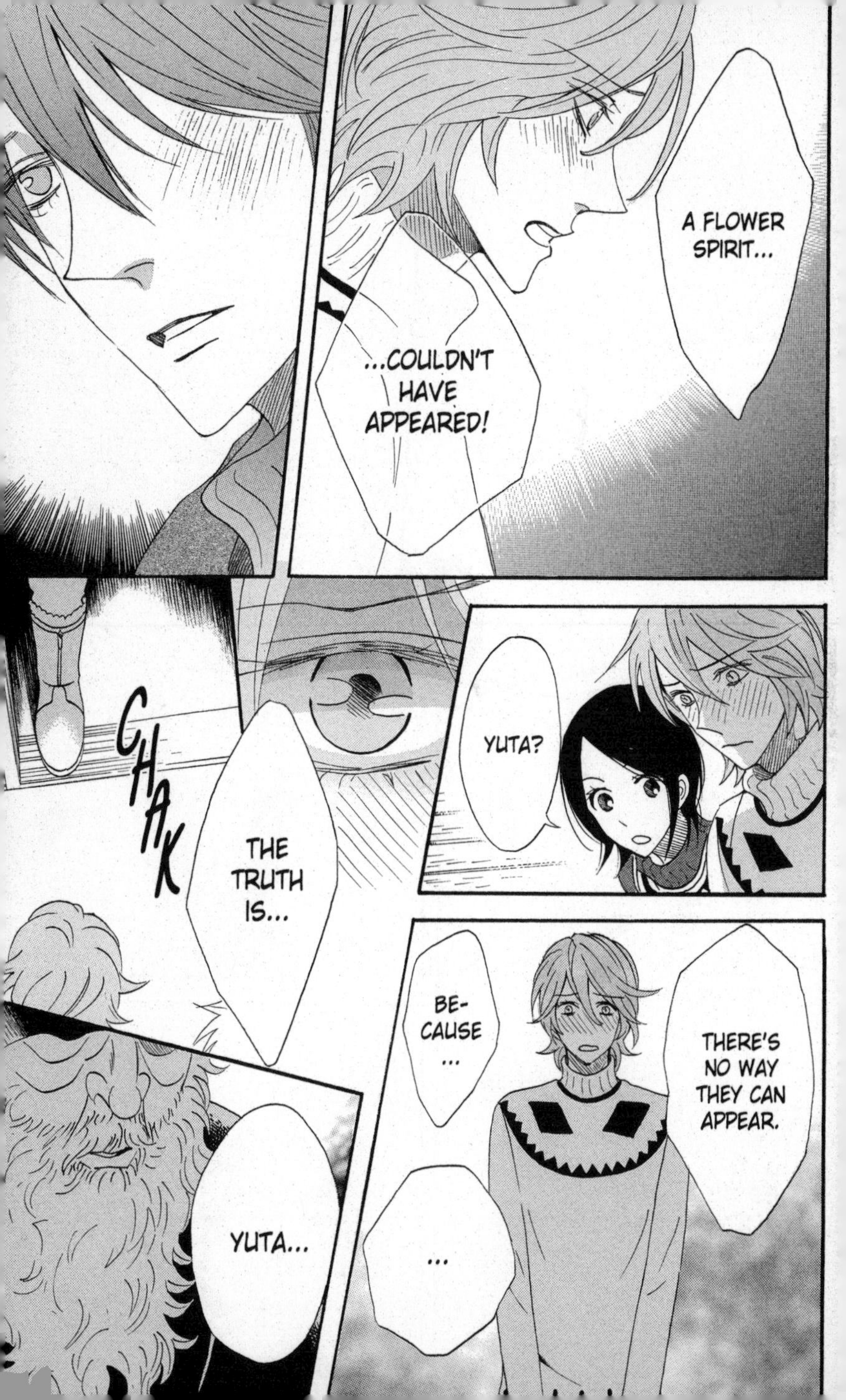
A FLOWER SPIRIT...
...COULDN'T HAVE APPEARED!
YUTA?
THE TRUTH IS...
CHAK
THERE'S NO WAY THEY CAN APPEAR.
BE-CAUSE ...
...
YUTA...

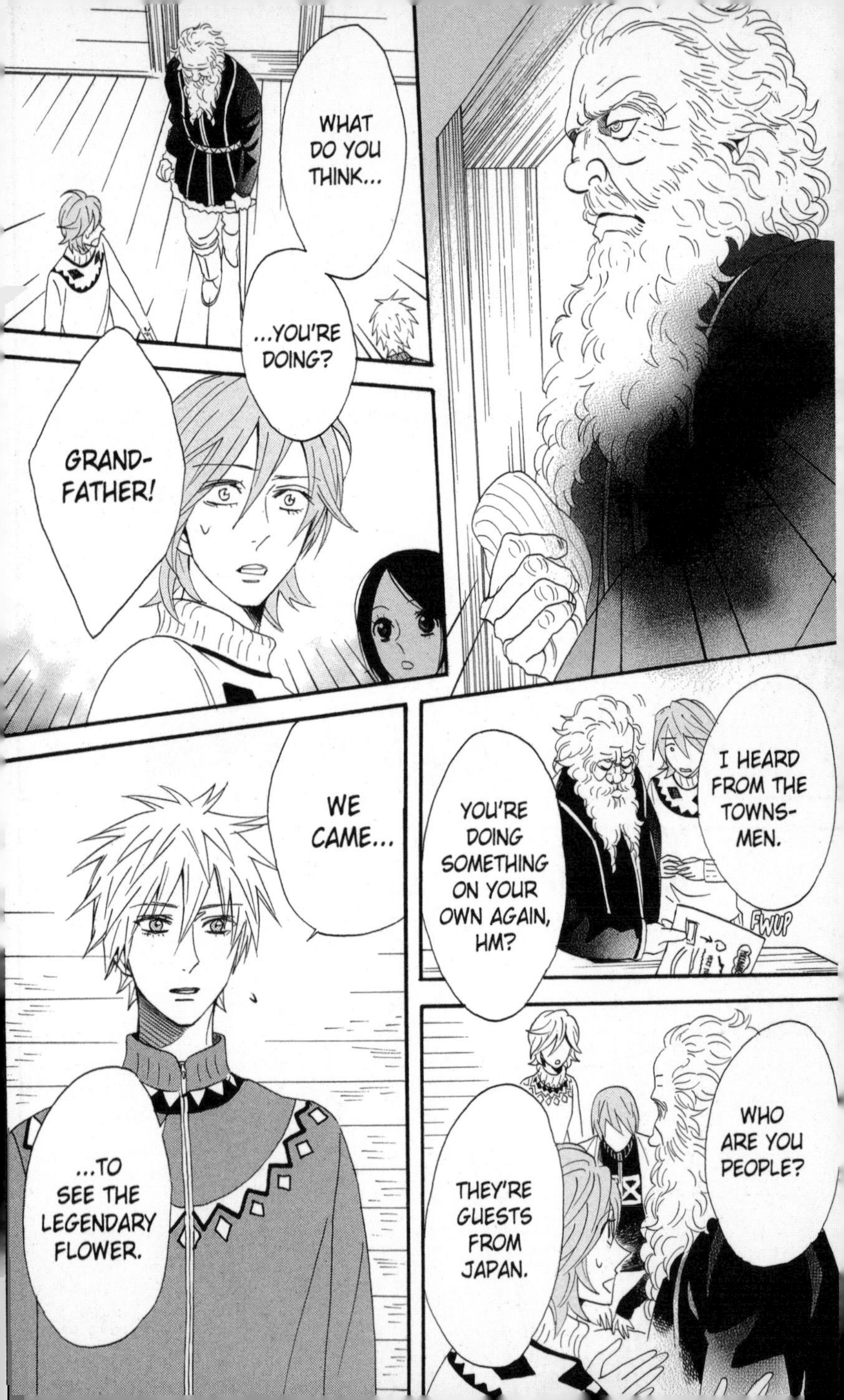
WHAT DO YOU THINK...
...YOU'RE DOING?
GRAND-FATHER!
I HEARD FROM THE TOWNS-MEN.
YOU'RE DOING SOMETHING ON YOUR OWN AGAIN, HM?
FWUP
WHO ARE YOU PEOPLE?
THEY'RE GUESTS FROM JAPAN.
WE CAME...
...TO SEE THE LEGENDARY FLOWER.

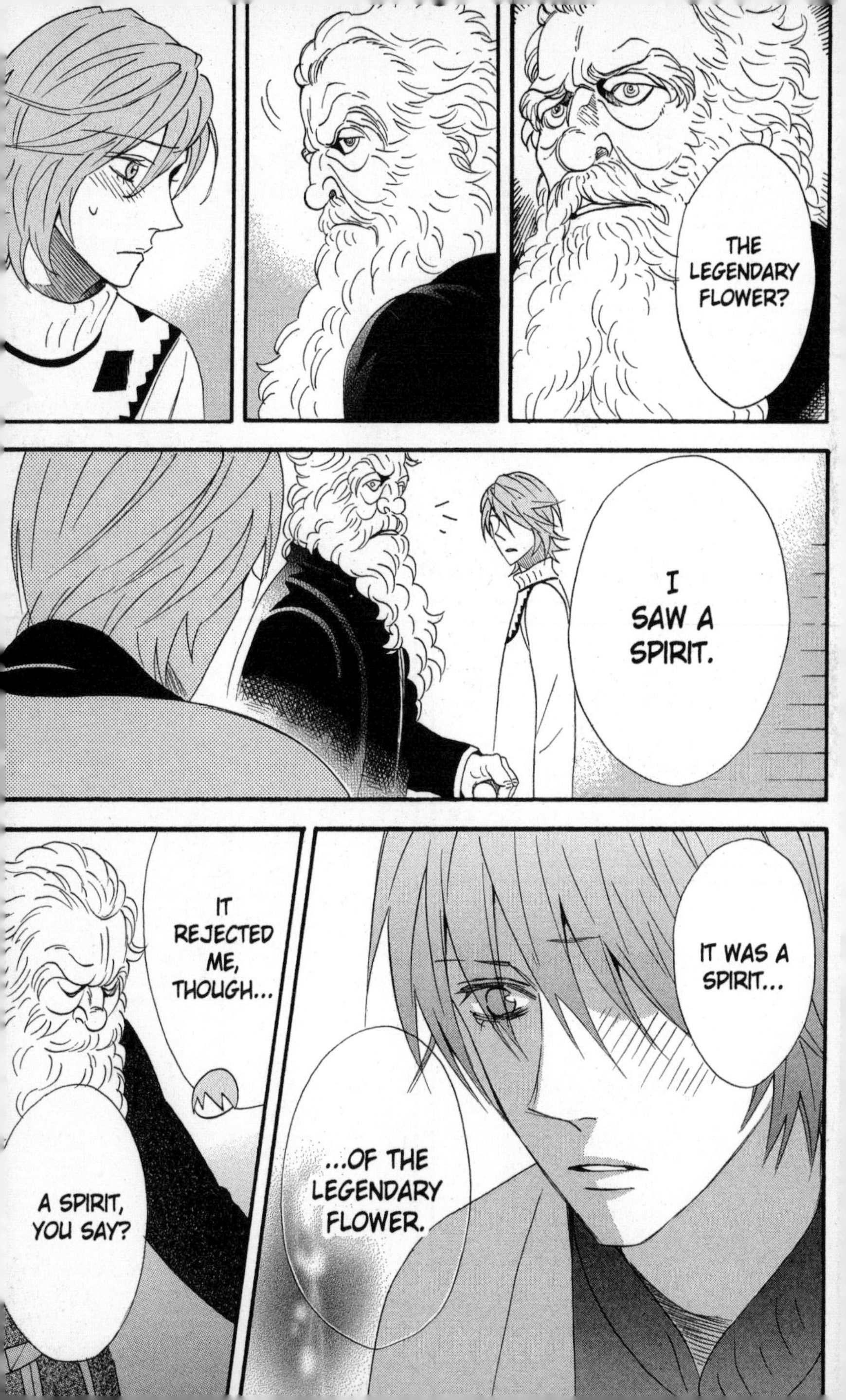
THE LEGENDARY FLOWER?
I SAW A SPIRIT.
IT WAS A SPIRIT...
...OF THE LEGENDARY FLOWER.
IT REJECTED ME, THOUGH...
A SPIRIT, YOU SAY?

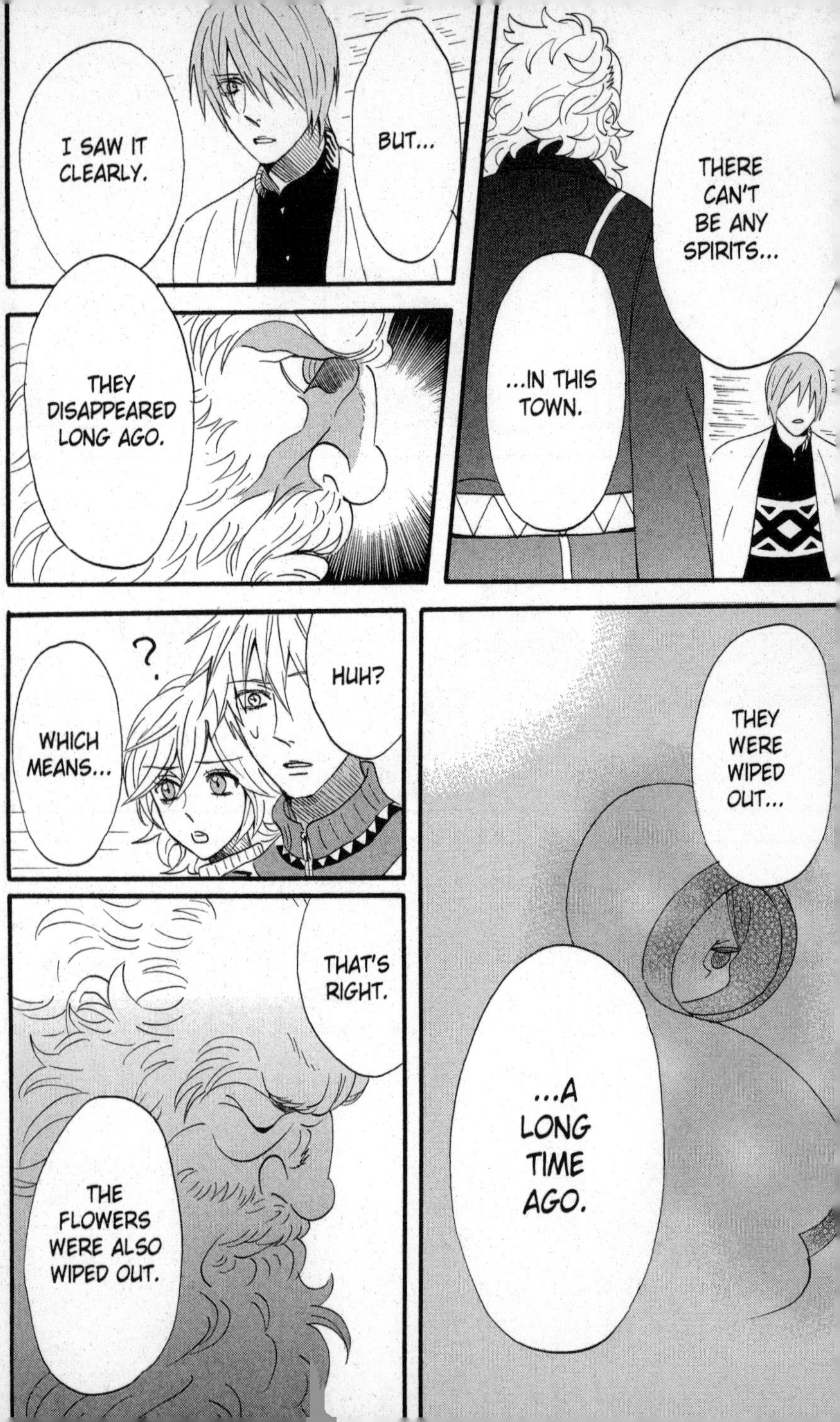
THERE CAN'T BE ANY SPIRITS...
...IN THIS TOWN.
BUT...
I SAW IT CLEARLY.
THEY DISAPPEARED LONG AGO.
THEY WERE WIPED OUT...
...A LONG TIME AGO.
HUH?
?
WHICH MEANS...
THAT'S RIGHT.
THE FLOWERS WERE ALSO WIPED OUT.

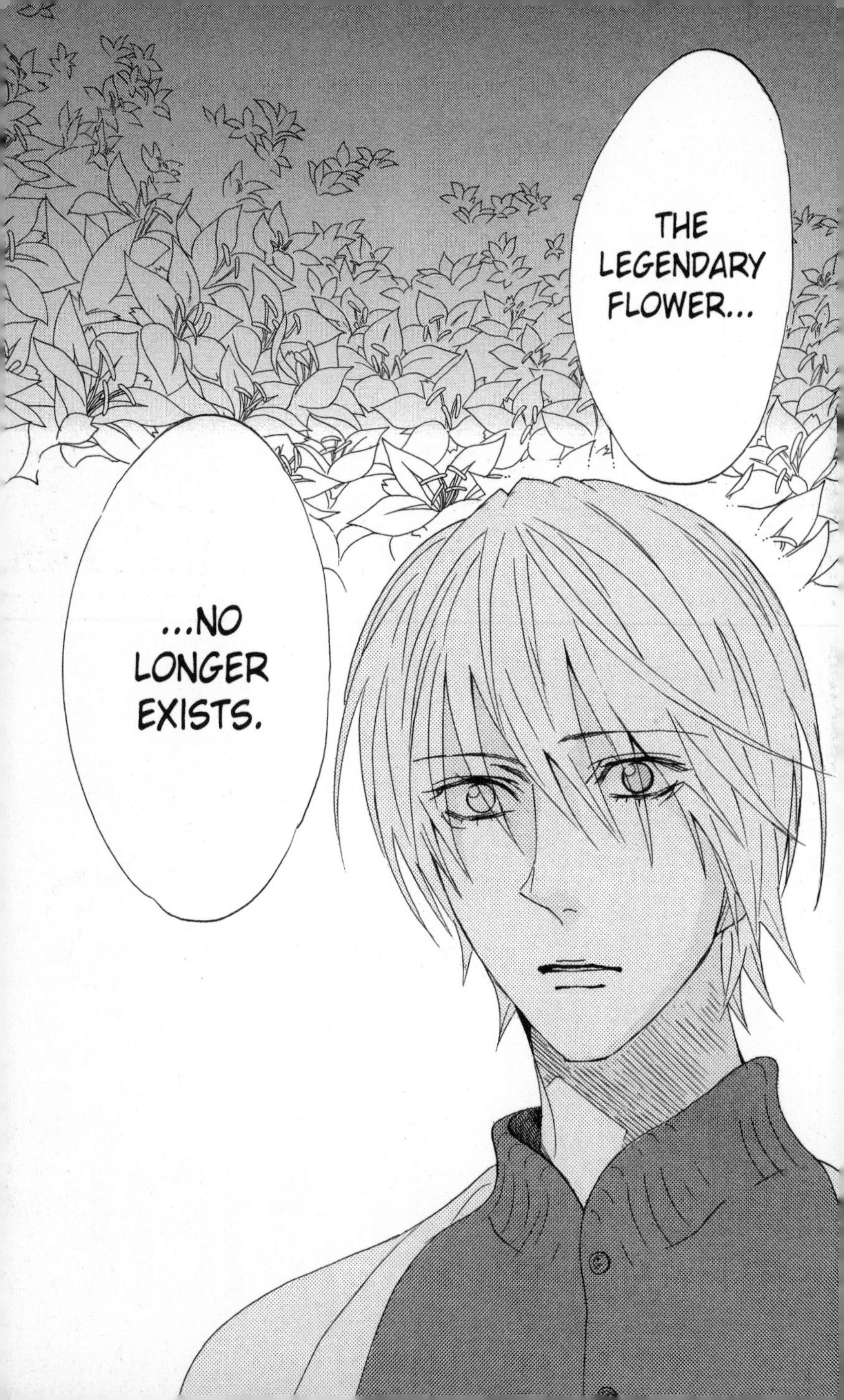
THE LEGENDARY FLOWER...
...NO LONGER EXISTS.

OTOMEN

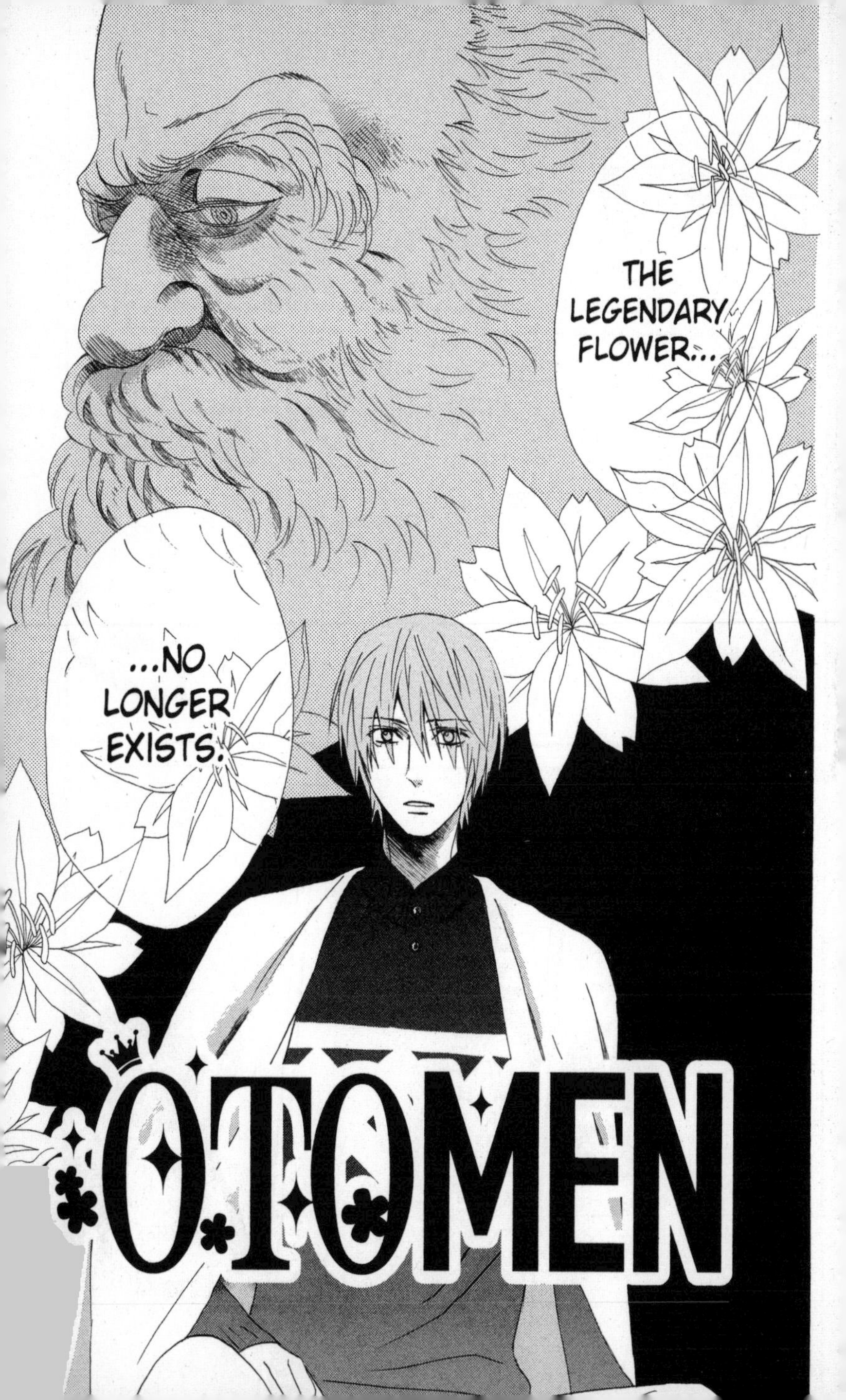
THE LEGENDARY FLOWER...
...NO LONGER EXISTS.
OTOMEN

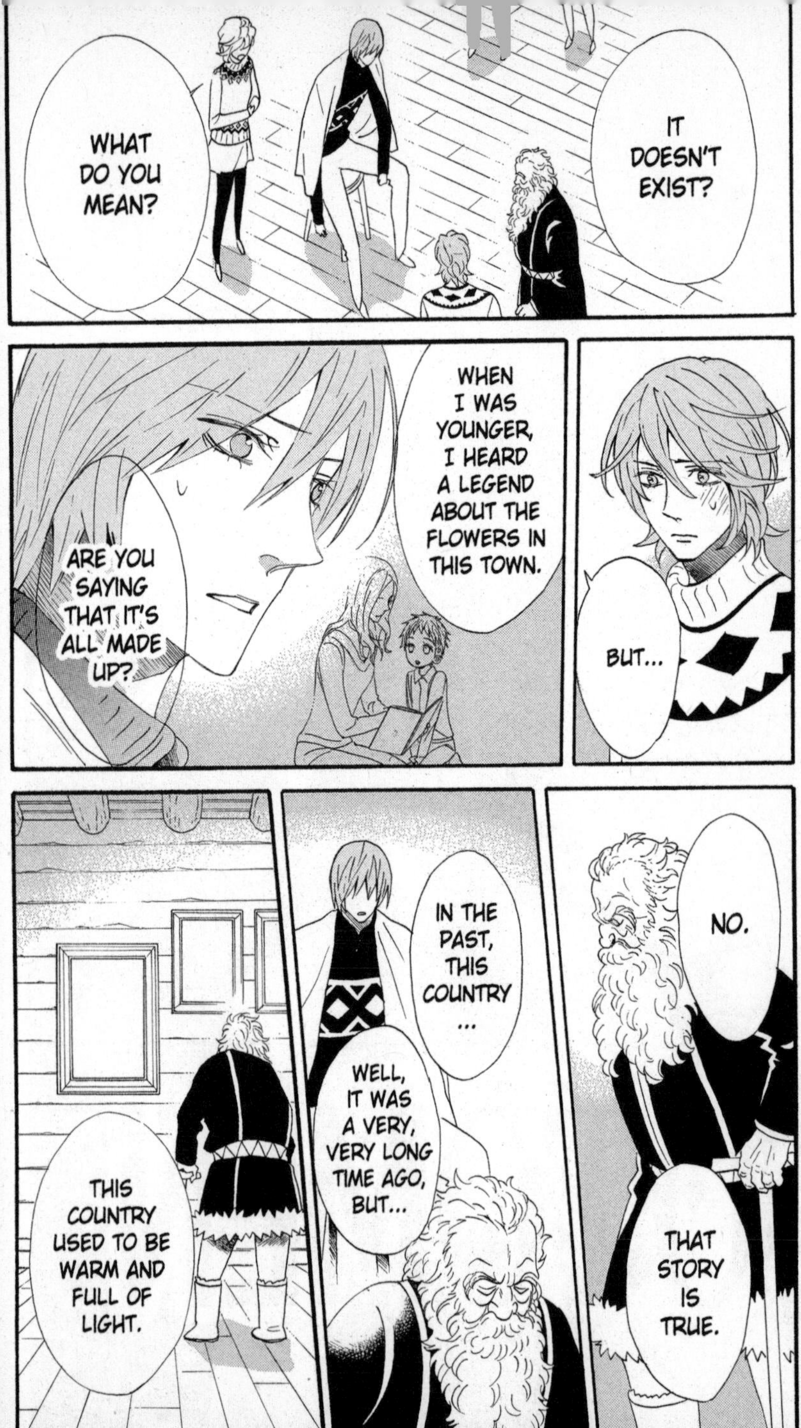
IT DOESN'T EXIST?
WHAT DO YOU MEAN?
BUT...
WHEN I WAS YOUNGER, I HEARD A LEGEND ABOUT THE FLOWERS IN THIS TOWN.
ARE YOU SAYING THAT IT'S ALL MADE UP?
NO.
THAT STORY IS TRUE.
IN THE PAST, THIS COUNTRY ...
WELL, IT WAS A VERY, VERY LONG TIME AGO, BUT...
THIS COUNTRY USED TO BE WARM AND FULL OF LIGHT.

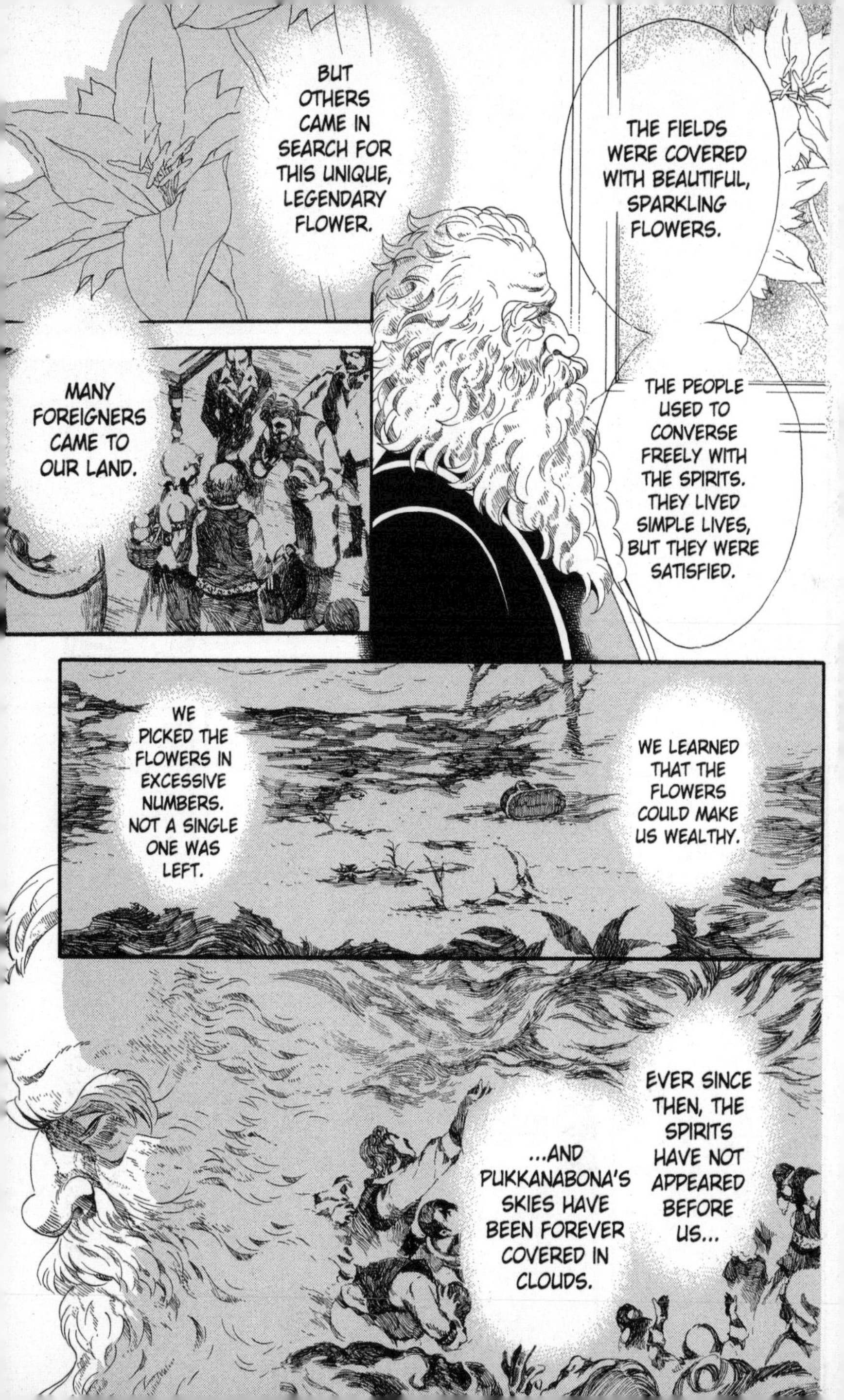
THE FIELDS WERE COVERED WITH BEAUTIFUL, SPARKLING FLOWERS.
THE PEOPLE USED TO CONVERSE FREELY WITH THE SPIRITS. THEY LIVED SIMPLE LIVES, BUT THEY WERE SATISFIED.
BUT OTHERS CAME IN SEARCH FOR THIS UNIQUE, LEGENDARY FLOWER.
MANY FOREIGNERS CAME TO OUR LAND.
WE LEARNED THAT THE FLOWERS COULD MAKE US WEALTHY.
WE PICKED THE FLOWERS IN EXCESSIVE NUMBERS. NOT A SINGLE ONE WAS LEFT.
EVER SINCE THEN, THE SPIRITS HAVE NOT APPEARED BEFORE US...
...AND PUKKANABONA'S SKIES HAVE BEEN FOREVER COVERED IN CLOUDS.

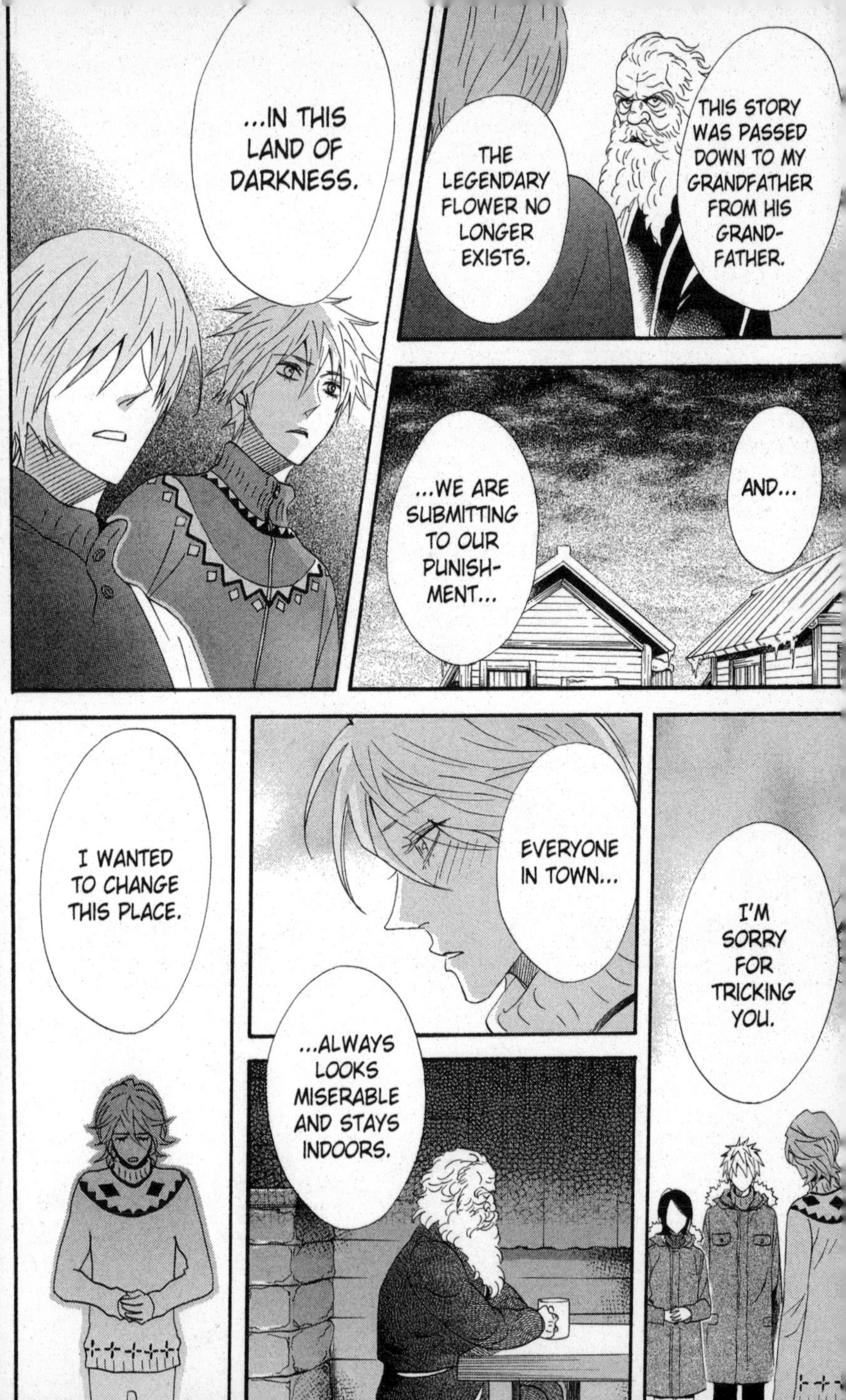
THIS STORY WAS PASSED DOWN TO MY GRANDFATHER FROM HIS GRAND-FATHER.
THE LEGENDARY FLOWER NO LONGER EXISTS.
...IN THIS LAND OF DARKNESS.
AND...
...WE ARE SUBMITTING TO OUR PUNISH-MENT...
I'M SORRY FOR TRICKING YOU.
EVERYONE IN TOWN...
...ALWAYS LOOKS MISERABLE AND STAYS INDOORS.
I WANTED TO CHANGE THIS PLACE.

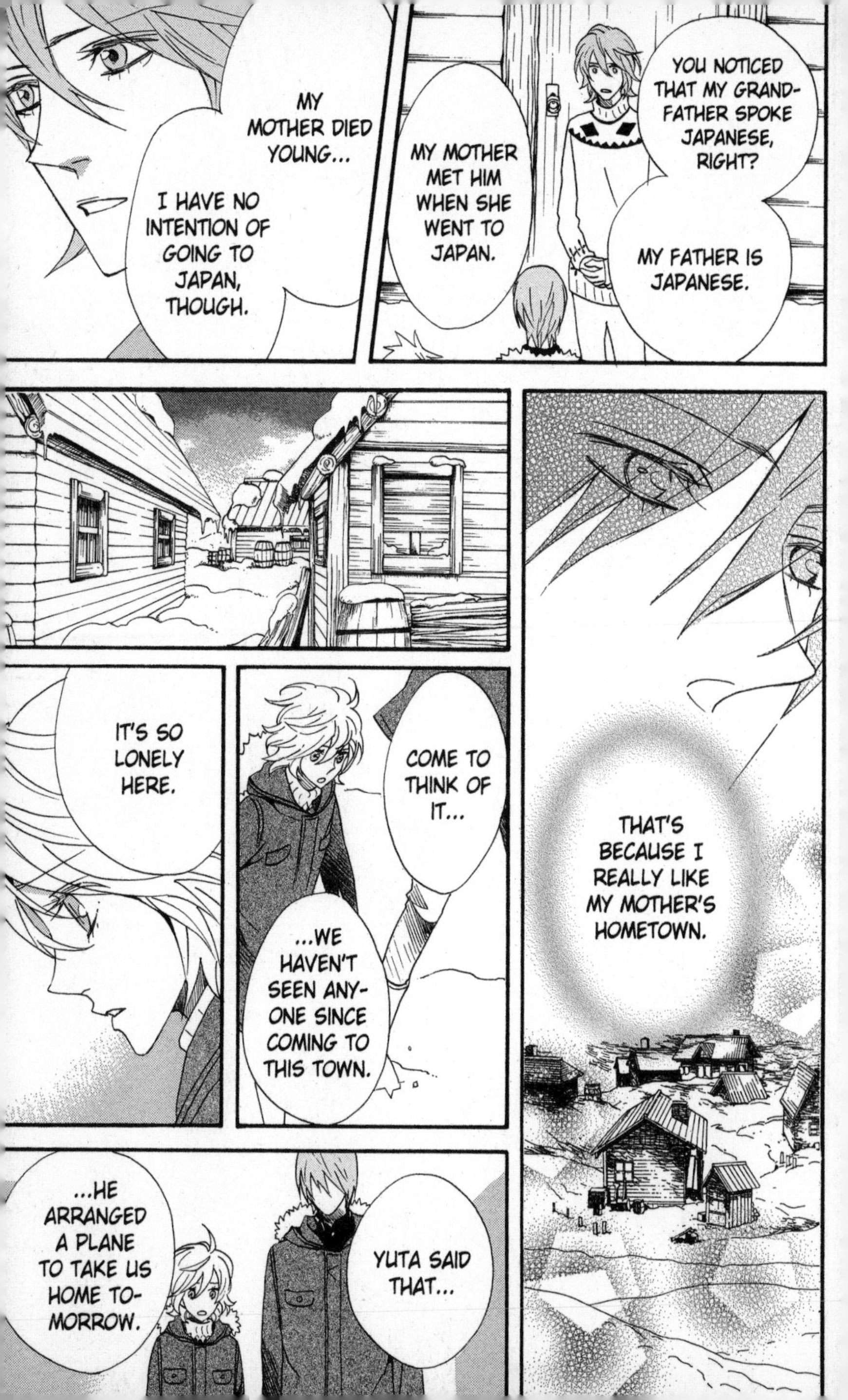
YOU NOTICED THAT MY GRAND-FATHER SPOKE JAPANESE, RIGHT?
MY FATHER IS JAPANESE.
MY MOTHER MET HIM WHEN SHE WENT TO JAPAN.
MY MOTHER DIED YOUNG...
I HAVE NO INTENTION OF GOING TO JAPAN, THOUGH.
THAT'S BECAUSE I REALLY LIKE MY MOTHER'S HOMETOWN.
COME TO THINK OF IT...
...WE HAVEN'T SEEN ANY-ONE SINCE COMING TO THIS TOWN.
IT'S SO LONELY HERE.
YUTA SAID THAT...
...HE ARRANGED A PLANE TO TAKE US HOME TO-MORROW.

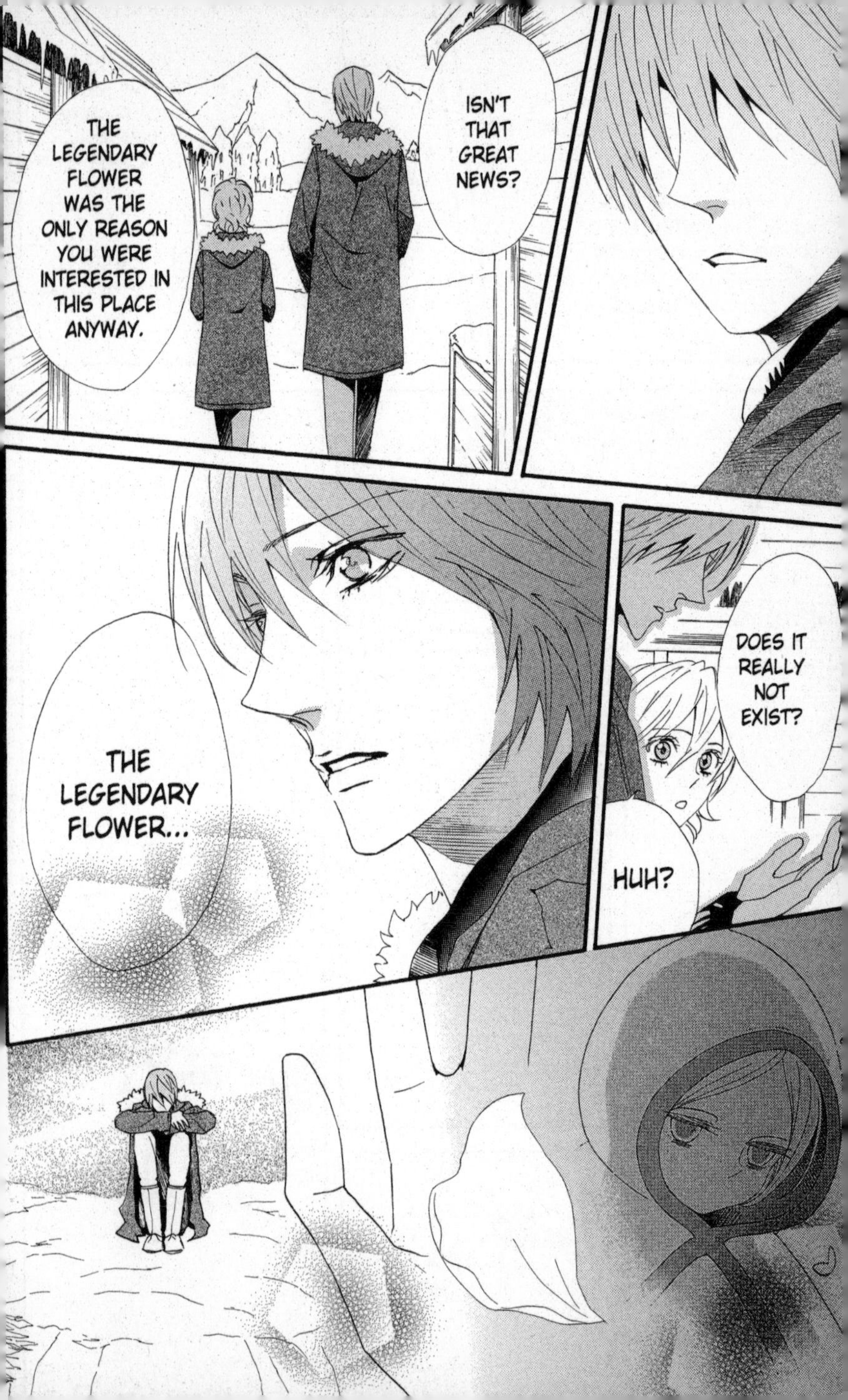
ISN'T THAT GREAT NEWS?
THE LEGENDARY FLOWER WAS THE ONLY REASON YOU WERE INTERESTED IN THIS PLACE ANYWAY.
DOES IT REALLY NOT EXIST?
HUH?
THE LEGENDARY FLOWER...

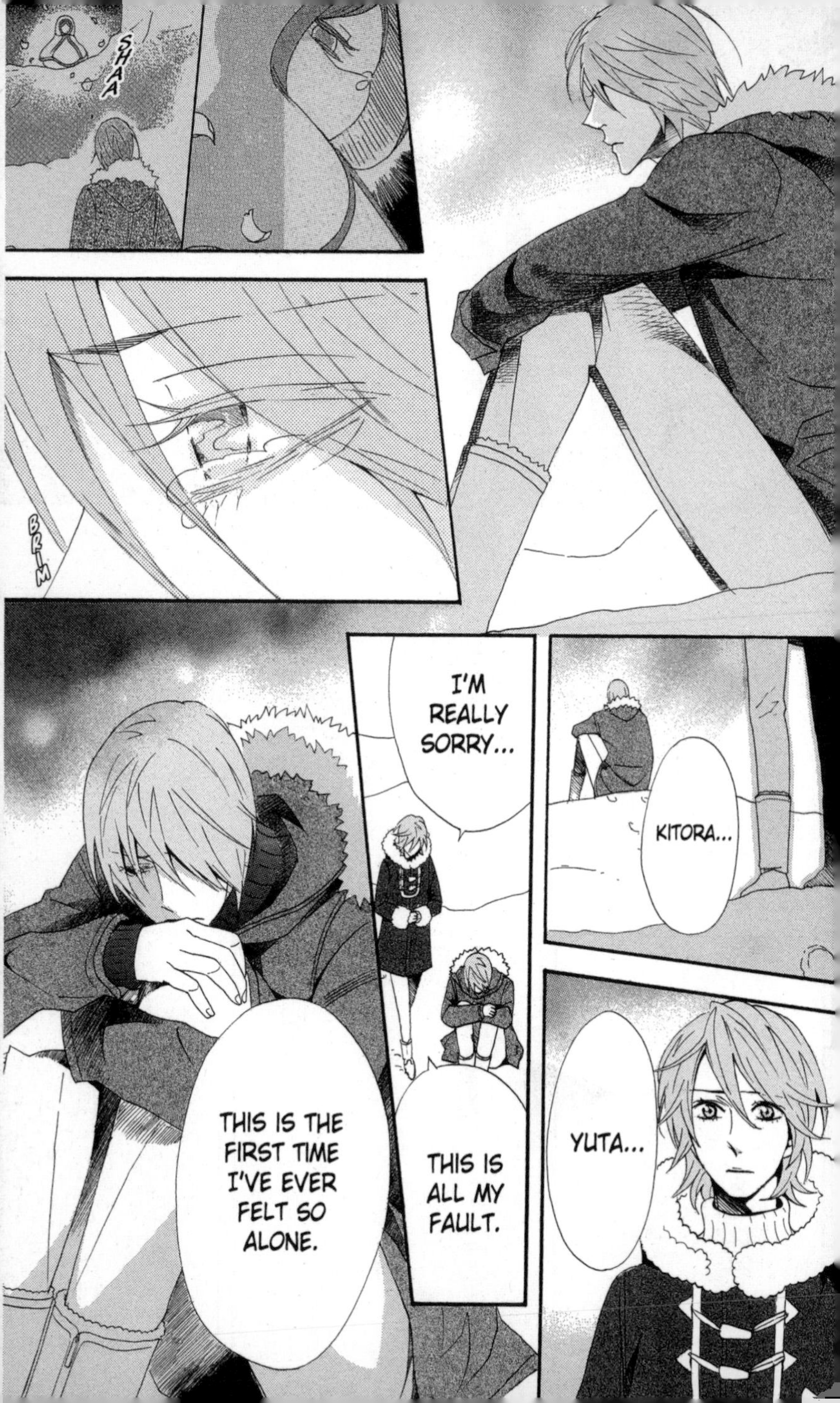
SHAA
BRIM
KITORA...
YUTA...
I'M REALLY SORRY...
THIS IS ALL MY FAULT.
THIS IS THE FIRST TIME I'VE EVER FELT SO ALONE.

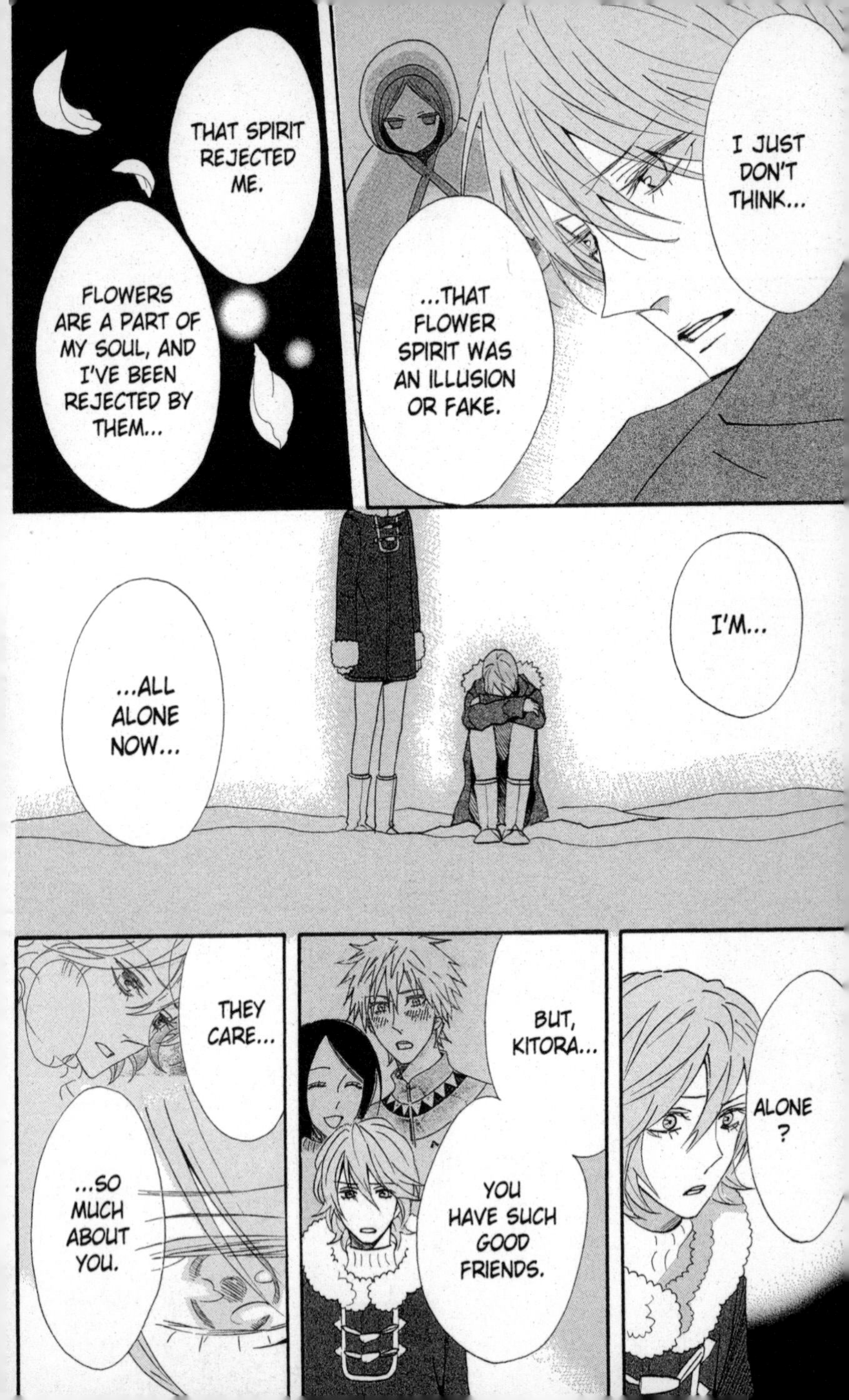
I JUST DON'T THINK...
...THAT FLOWER SPIRIT WAS AN ILLUSION OR FAKE.
THAT SPIRIT REJECTED ME.
FLOWERS ARE A PART OF MY SOUL, AND I'VE BEEN REJECTED BY THEM...
I'M...
...ALL ALONE NOW...
ALONE?
BUT, KITORA...
YOU HAVE SUCH GOOD FRIENDS.
THEY CARE...
...SO MUCH ABOUT YOU.

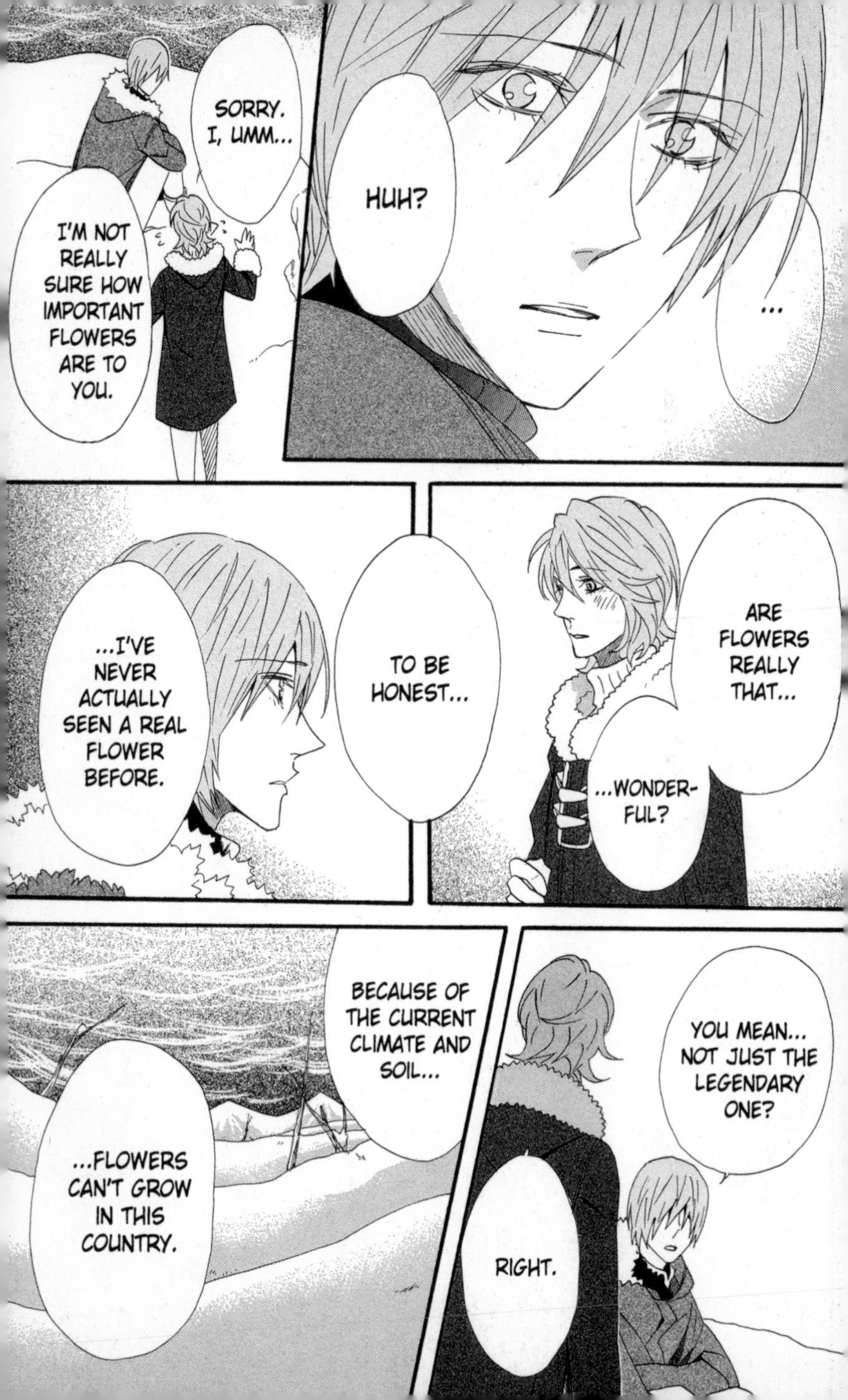
...
HUH?
SORRY. I, UMM...
I'M NOT REALLY SURE HOW IMPORTANT FLOWERS ARE TO YOU.
ARE FLOWERS REALLY THAT...
...WONDER-FUL?
TO BE HONEST...
...I'VE NEVER ACTUALLY SEEN A REAL FLOWER BEFORE.
YOU MEAN... NOT JUST THE LEGENDARY ONE?
RIGHT.
BECAUSE OF THE CURRENT CLIMATE AND SOIL...
...FLOWERS CAN'T GROW IN THIS COUNTRY.

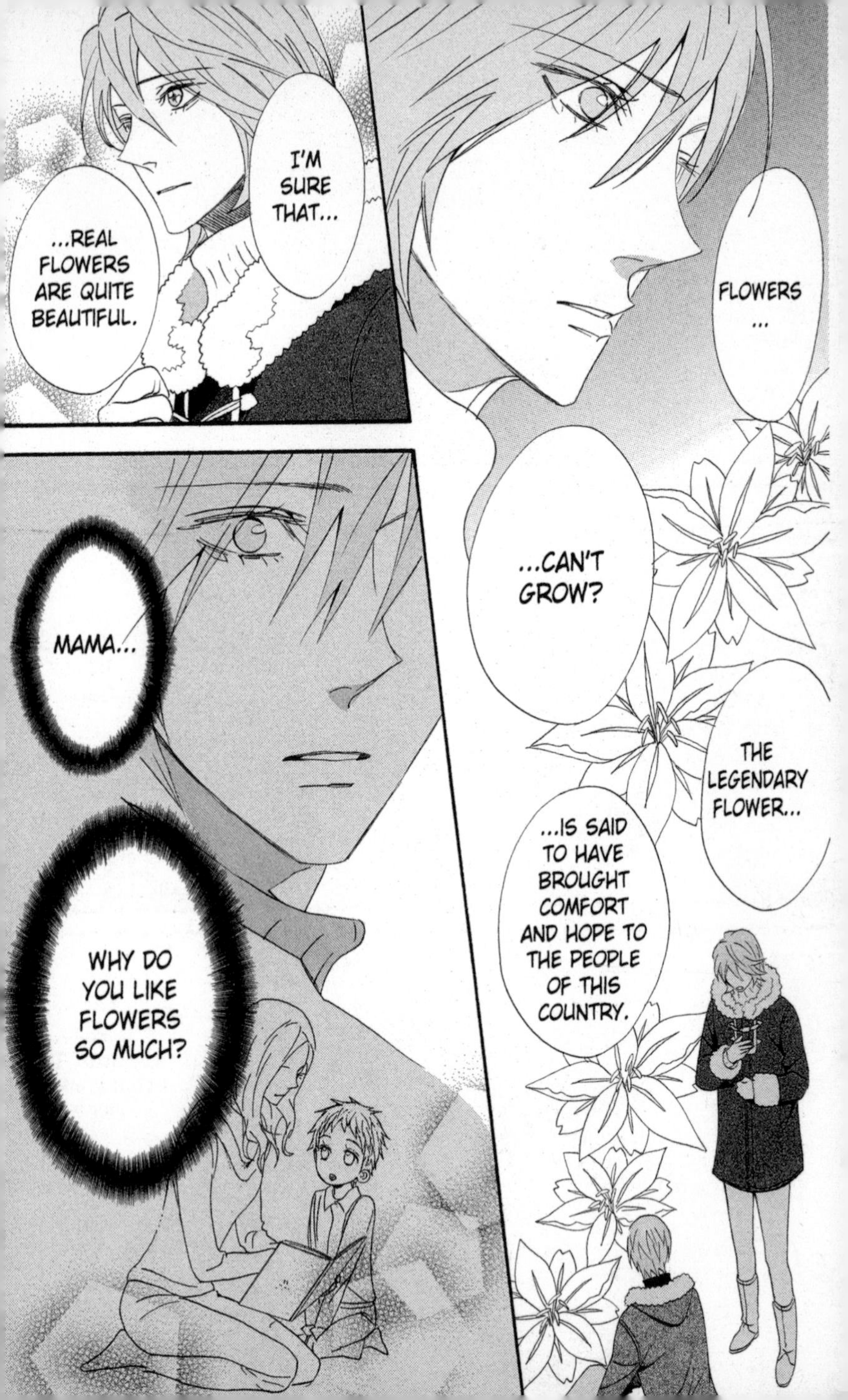
FLOWERS ...
...CAN'T GROW?
THE LEGENDARY FLOWER...
...IS SAID TO HAVE BROUGHT COMFORT AND HOPE TO THE PEOPLE OF THIS COUNTRY.
I'M SURE THAT...
...REAL FLOWERS ARE QUITE BEAUTIFUL.
MAMA...
WHY DO YOU LIKE FLOWERS SO MUCH?

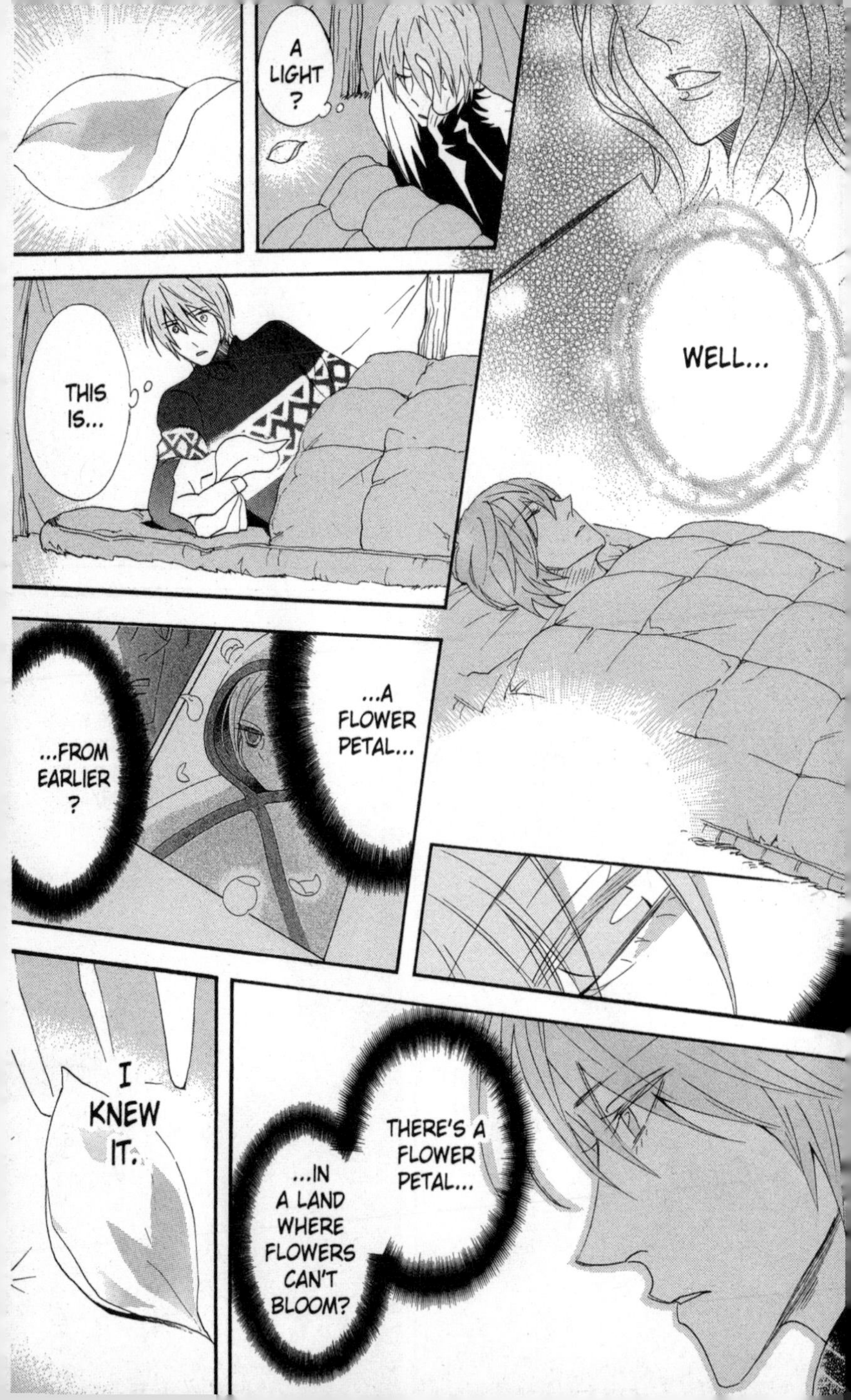
WELL...
A LIGHT?
THIS IS...
...A FLOWER PETAL...
...FROM EARLIER?
THERE'S A FLOWER PETAL...
...IN A LAND WHERE FLOWERS CAN'T BLOOM?
I KNEW IT.

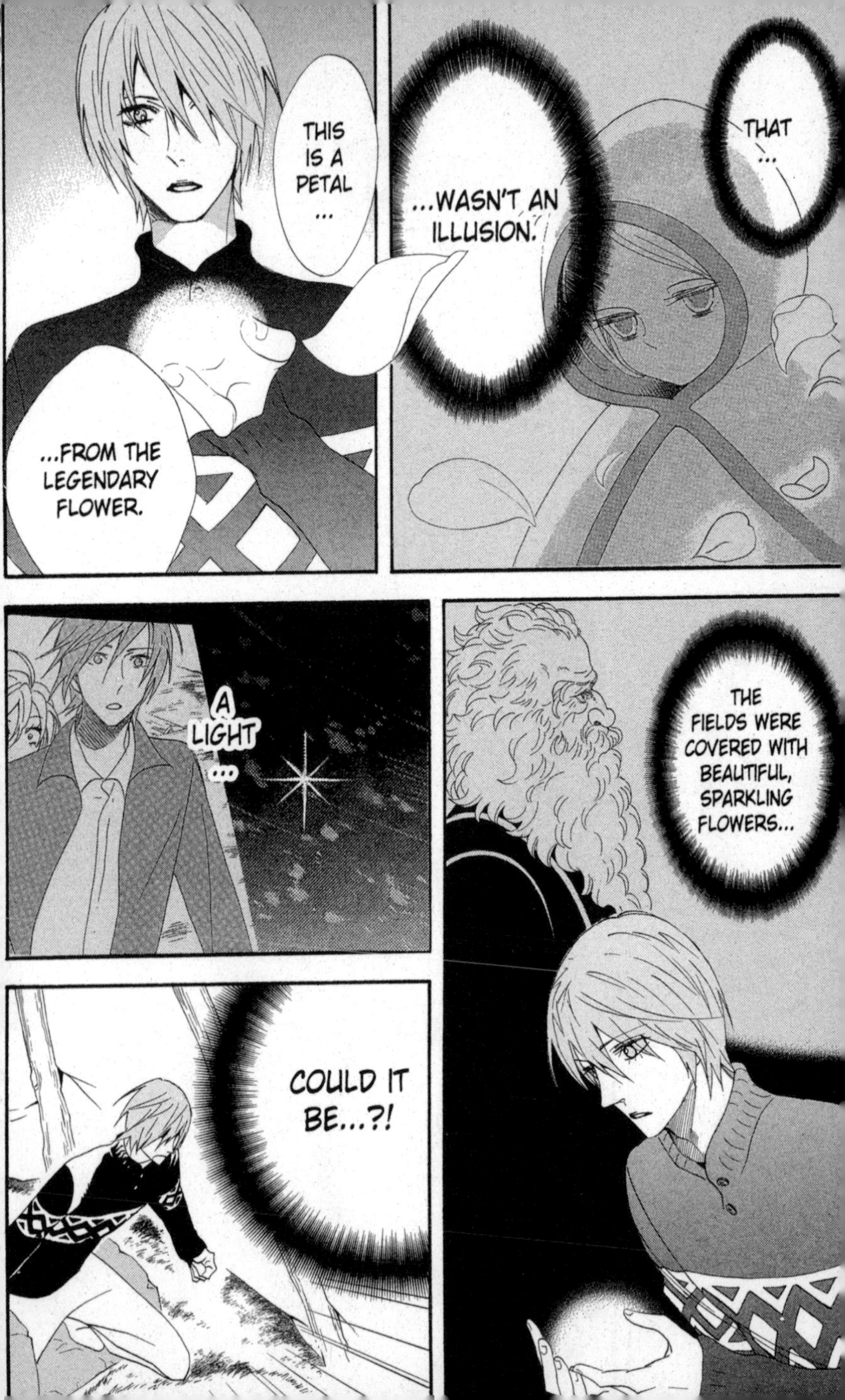
THAT...
...WASN'T AN ILLUSION.
THIS IS A PETAL...
...FROM THE LEGENDARY FLOWER.
THE FIELDS WERE COVERED WITH BEAUTIFUL, SPARKLING FLOWERS...
A LIGHT...
COULD IT BE...?!

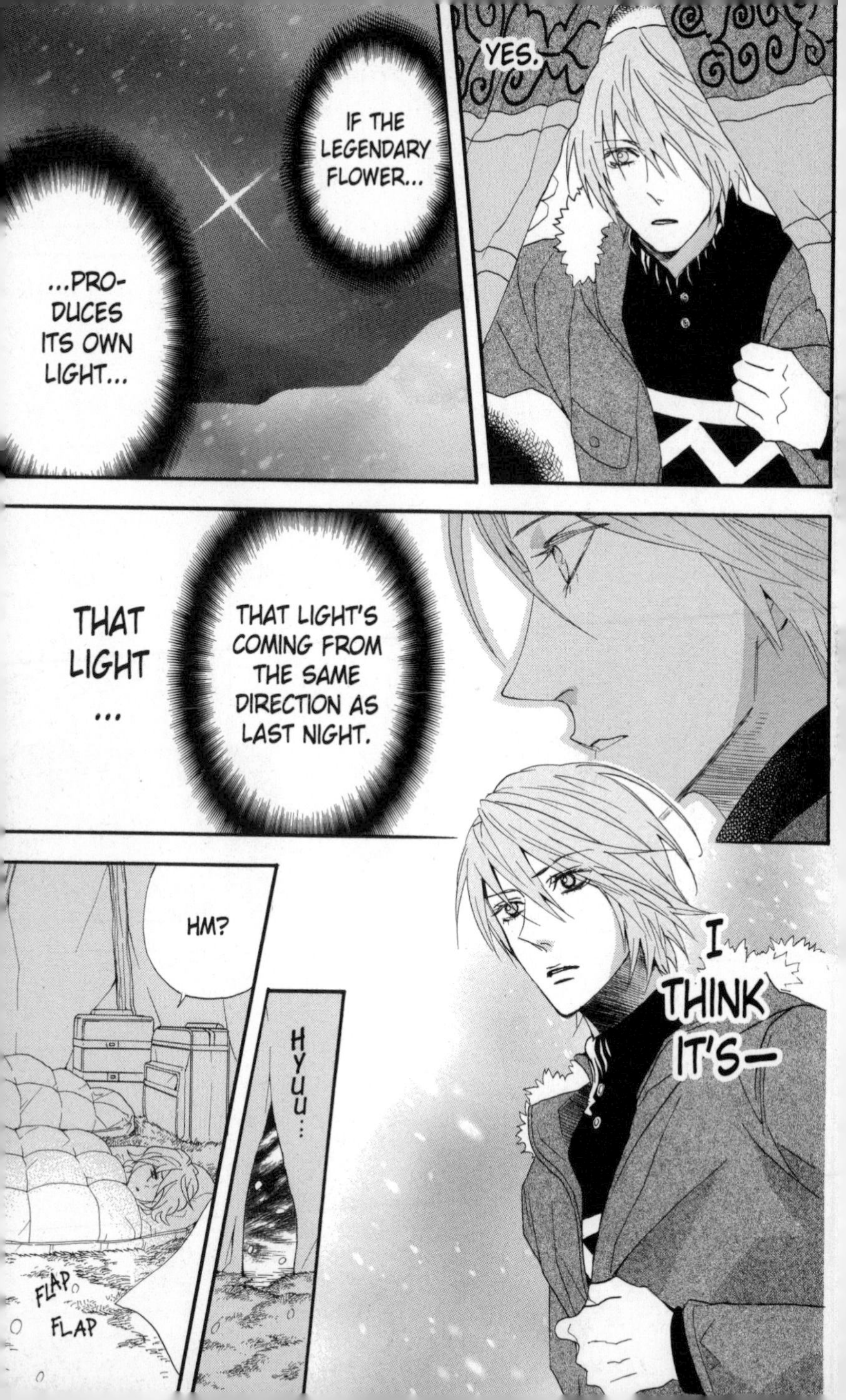
YES.
IF THE LEGENDARY FLOWER...
...PRO-DUCES ITS OWN LIGHT...
THAT LIGHT'S COMING FROM THE SAME DIRECTION AS LAST NIGHT.
THAT LIGHT ...
I THINK IT'S—
HYUU...
HM?
FLAP FLAP

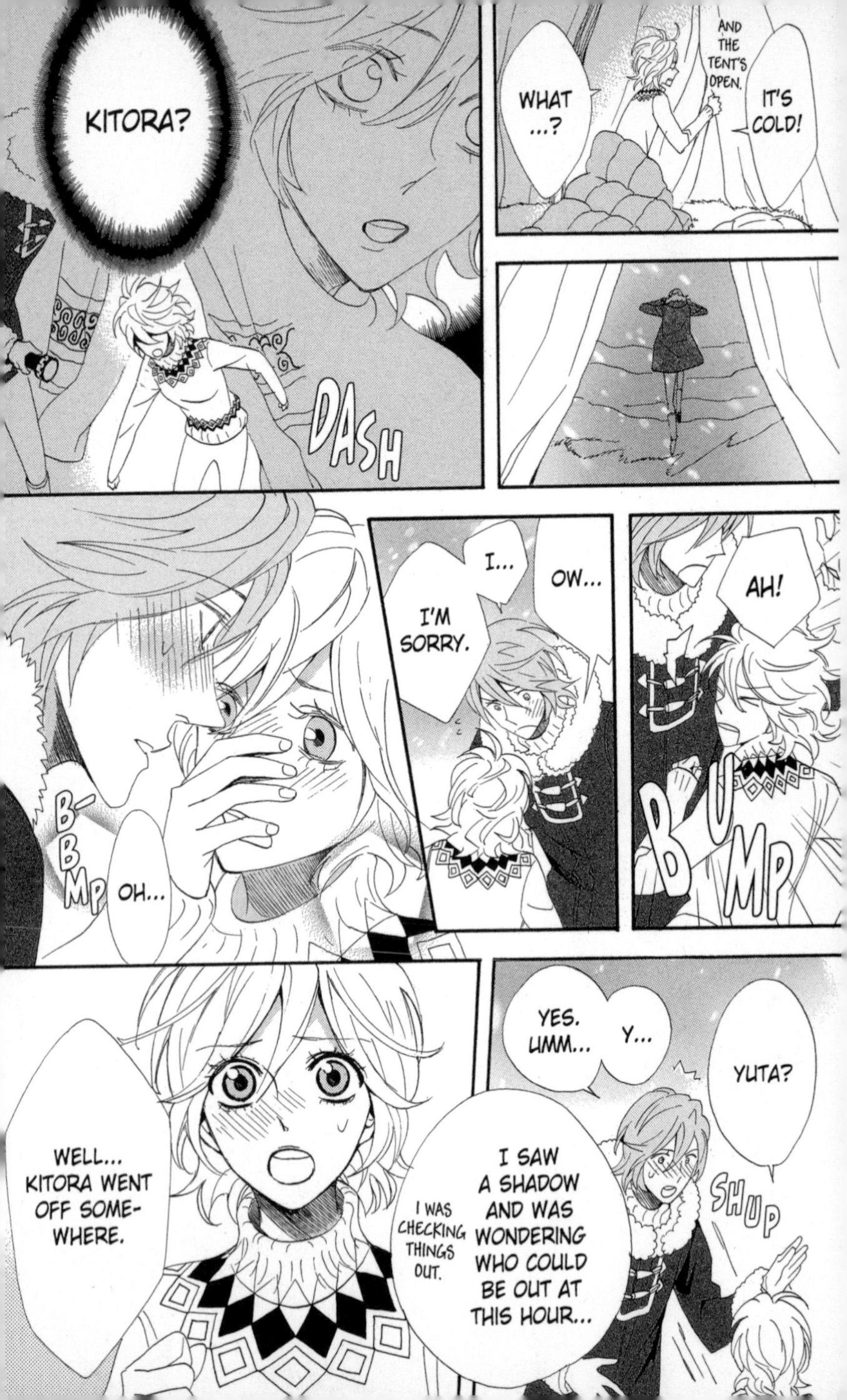
IT'S COLD!
AND THE TENT'S OPEN.
WHAT ...?
KITORA?
DASH
AH!
BUMP
OW...
I...
I'M SORRY.
B-BMP
OH...
YUTA?
Y...
YES. UMM...
SHUP
I SAW A SHADOW AND WAS WONDERING WHO COULD BE OUT AT THIS HOUR...
I WAS CHECKING THINGS OUT.
WELL... KITORA WENT OFF SOME-WHERE.

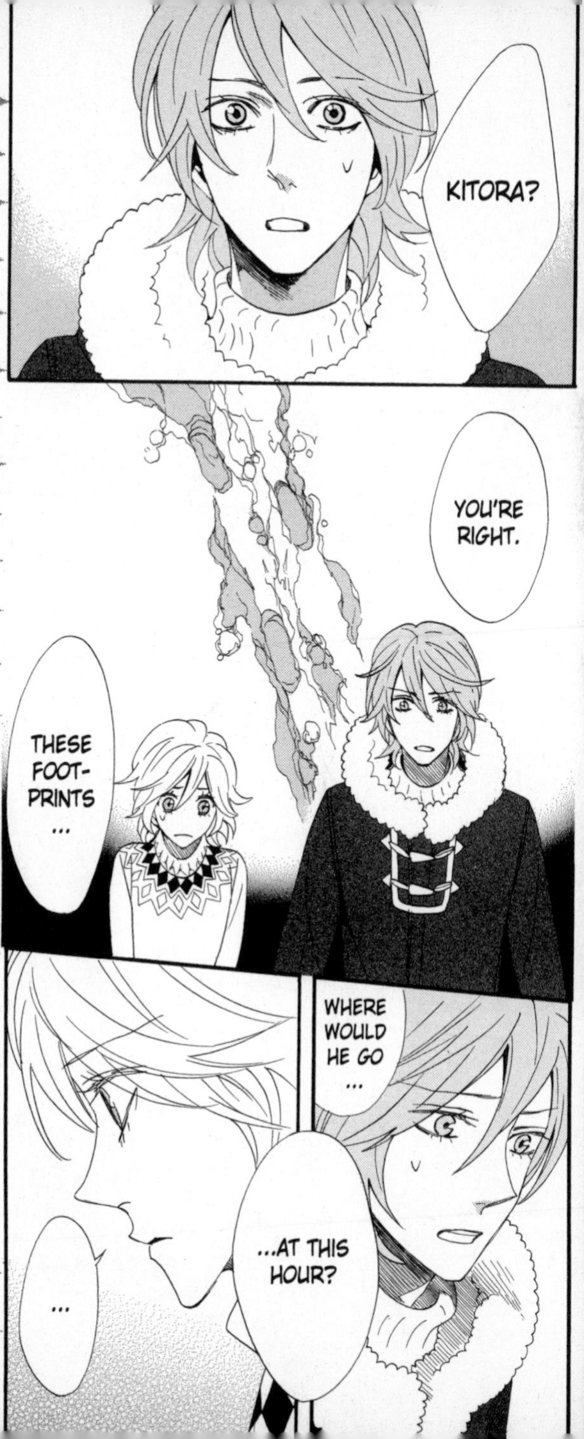
KITORA?
YOU'RE RIGHT.
THESE FOOT-PRINTS ...
WHERE WOULD HE GO ...
...AT THIS HOUR?
...

Sorry about suddenly doing a fantasy story.

Kitora is a mysterious character, so I figured that I could do anything with him.

Honestly, I had planned on making an entirely different story, but the Tohoku Earthquake happened around the time I was writing this.

I would be lying if I said I wasn't affected by it.

I hope from the bottom of my heart that the affected area will make a full recovery.

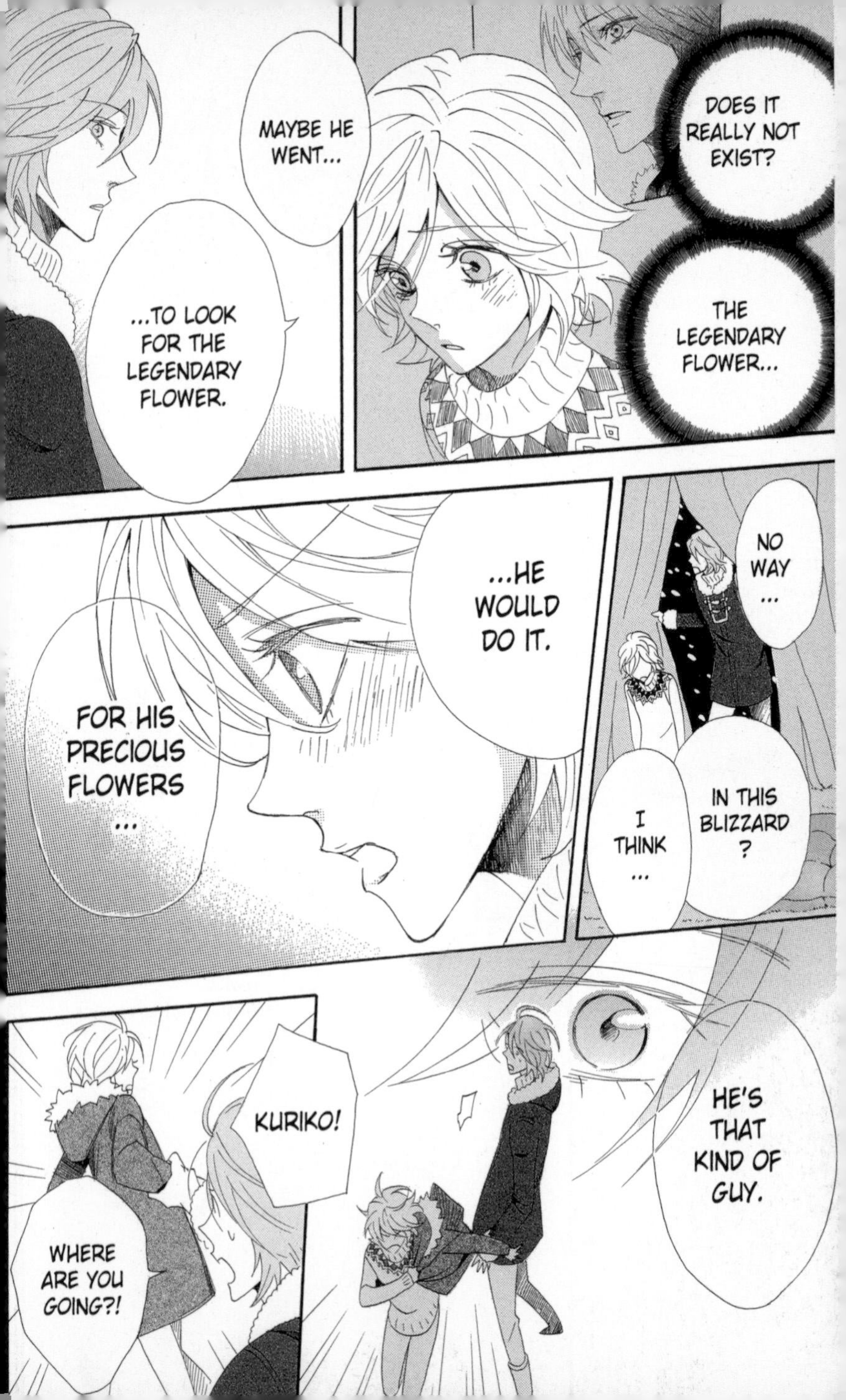
DOES IT REALLY NOT EXIST?
THE LEGENDARY FLOWER...
MAYBE HE WENT...
...TO LOOK FOR THE LEGENDARY FLOWER.
NO WAY...
IN THIS BLIZZARD?
I THINK...
...HE WOULD DO IT.
FOR HIS PRECIOUS FLOWERS...
HE'S THAT KIND OF GUY.
KURIKO!
WHERE ARE YOU GOING?!

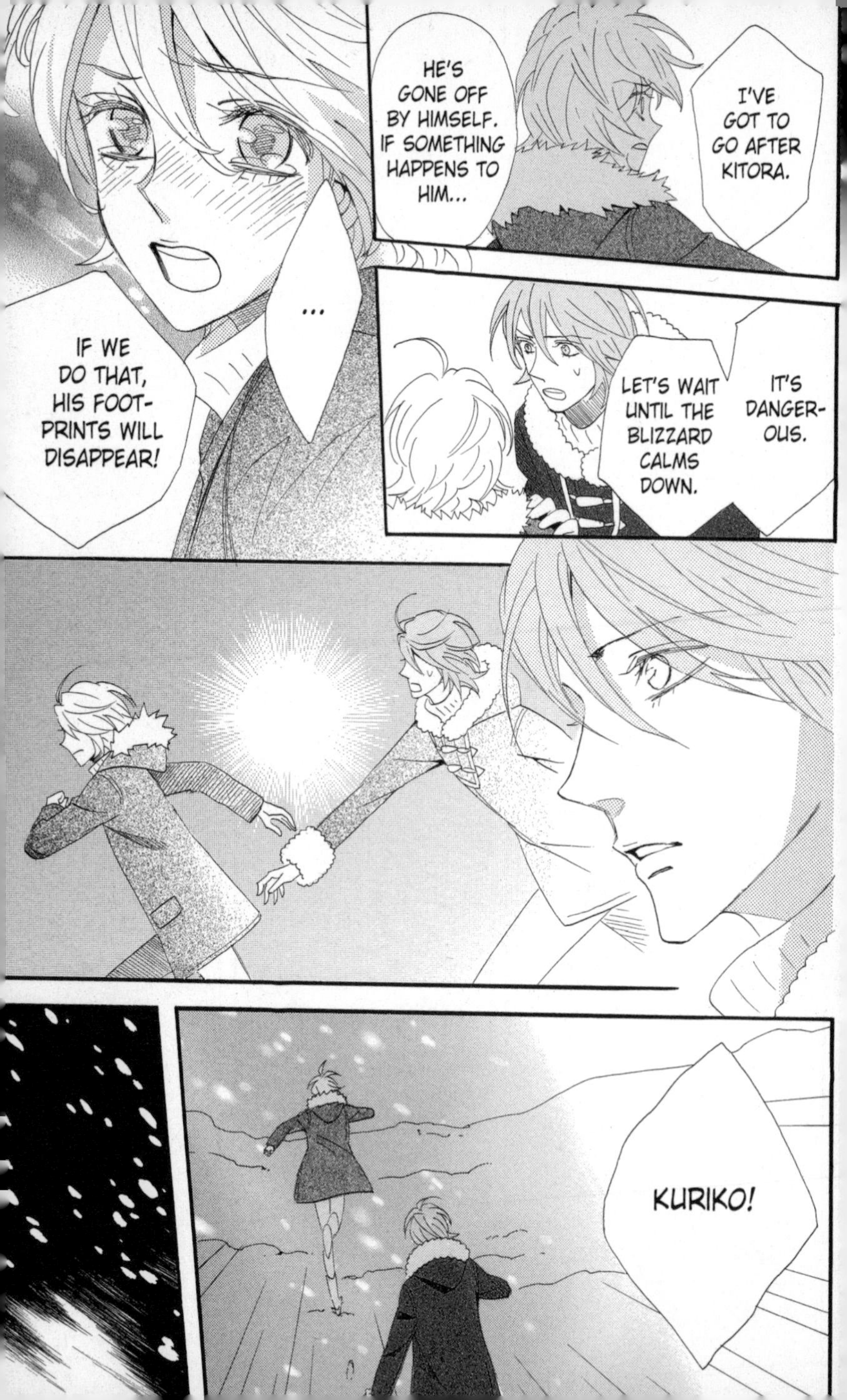
I'VE GOT TO GO AFTER KITORA.
HE'S GONE OFF BY HIMSELF. IF SOMETHING HAPPENS TO HIM...
IT'S DANGER-OUS.
LET'S WAIT UNTIL THE BLIZZARD CALMS DOWN.
...
IF WE DO THAT, HIS FOOT-PRINTS WILL DISAPPEAR!
KURIKO!

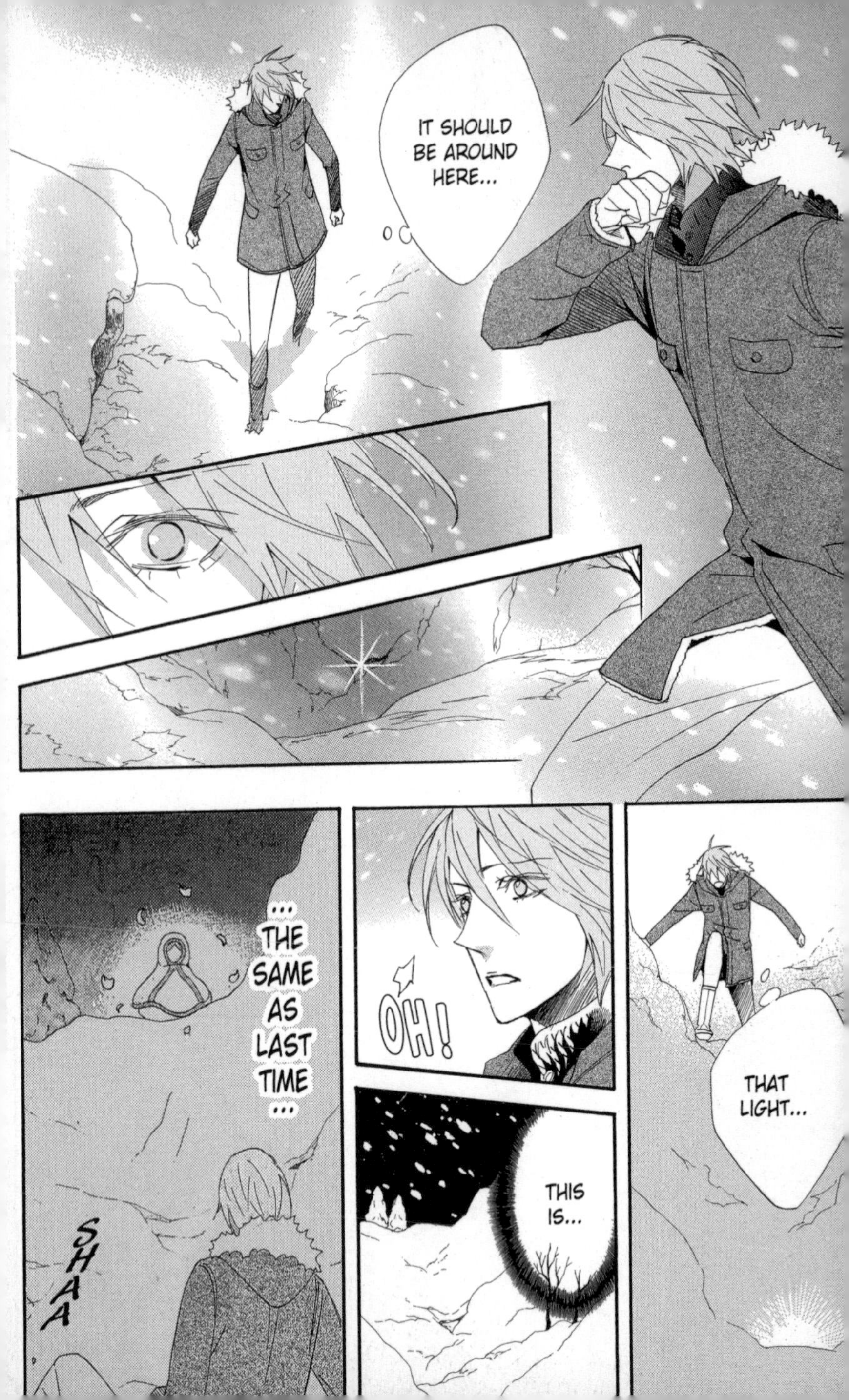
IT SHOULD BE AROUND HERE...
THAT LIGHT...
OH!
...THE SAME AS LAST TIME...
THIS IS...
SHAA

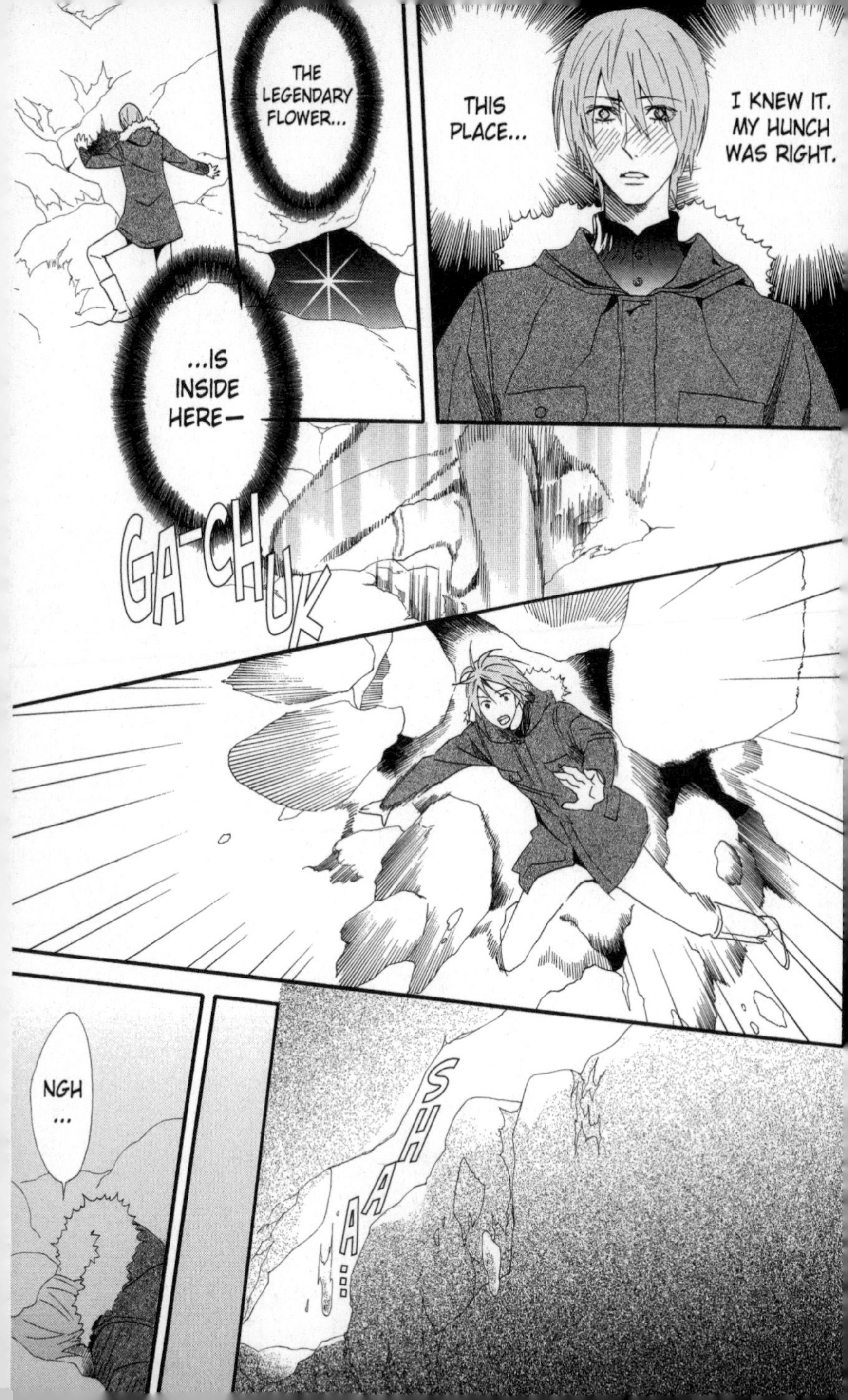
I KNEW IT. MY HUNCH WAS RIGHT.
THIS PLACE...
THE LEGENDARY FLOWER...
...IS INSIDE HERE—
GA-CHUK
SHHAAA...
NGH...

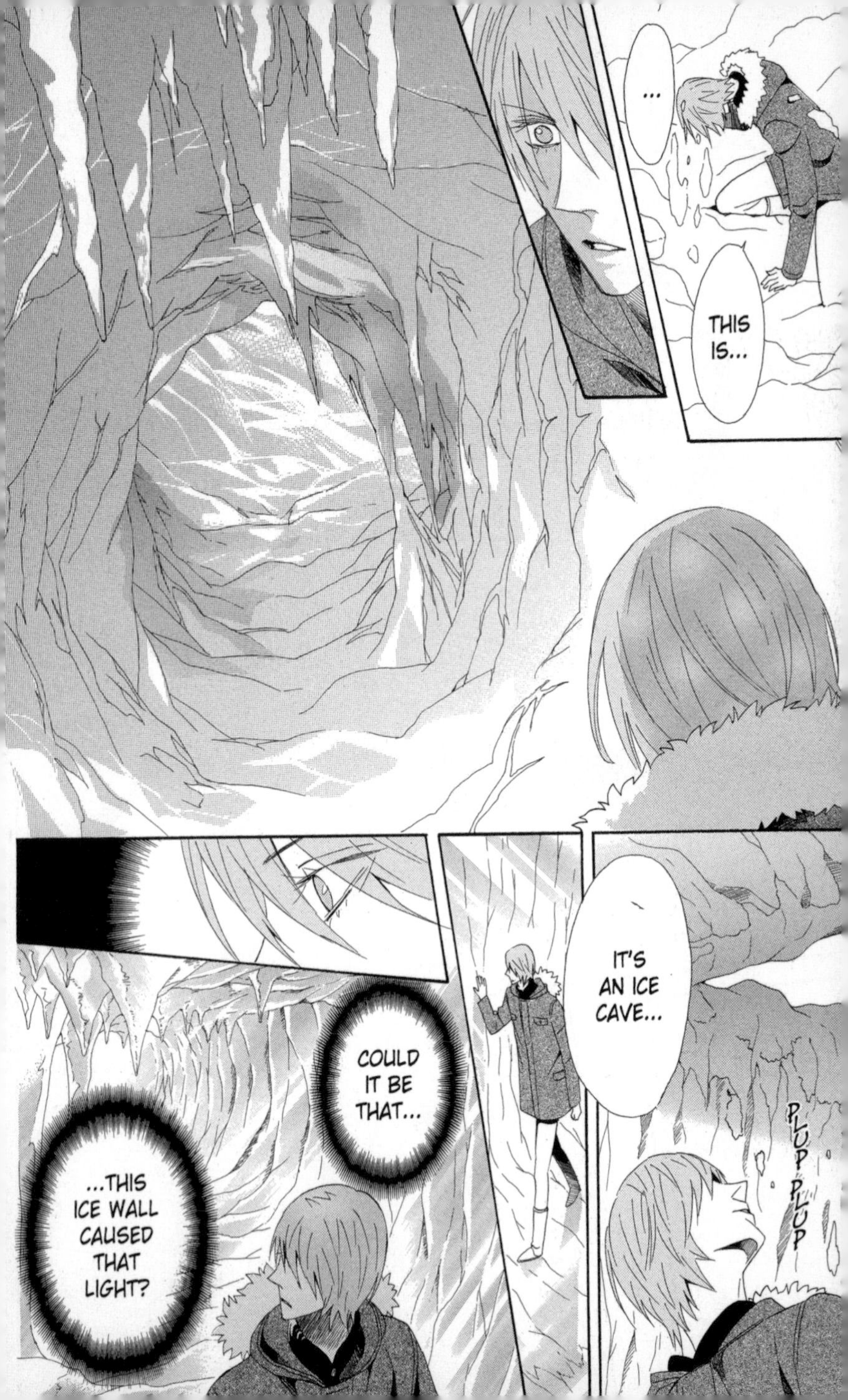
...
THIS IS...
IT'S AN ICE CAVE...
PLUP PLUP PLUP
COULD IT BE THAT...
...THIS ICE WALL CAUSED THAT LIGHT?

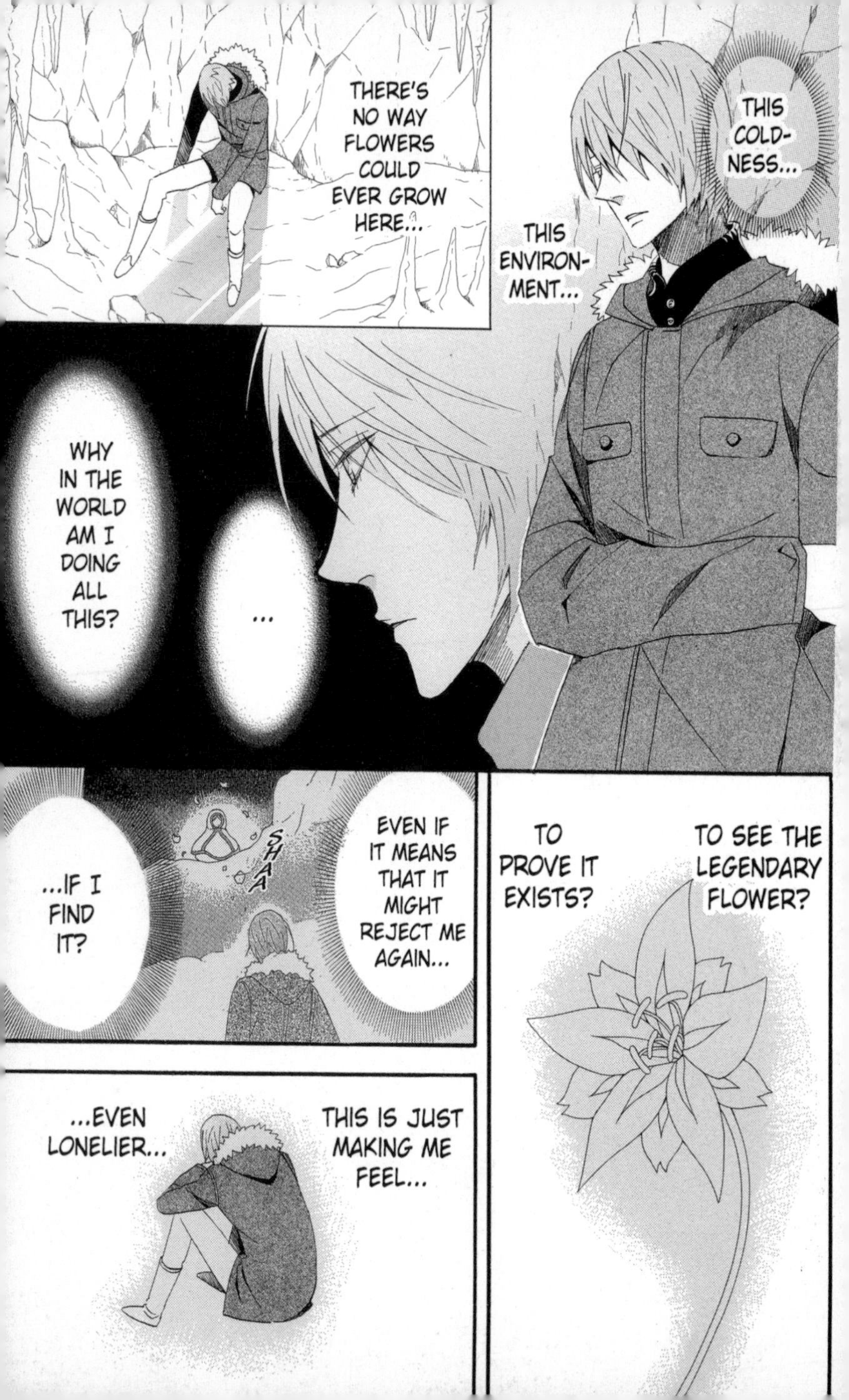
THIS COLDNESS...
THIS ENVIRONMENT...
THERE'S NO WAY FLOWERS COULD EVER GROW HERE...
...
WHY IN THE WORLD AM I DOING ALL THIS?
TO SEE THE LEGENDARY FLOWER?
TO PROVE IT EXISTS?
EVEN IF IT MEANS THAT IT MIGHT REJECT ME AGAIN...
SHAA
...IF I FIND IT?
THIS IS JUST MAKING ME FEEL...
...EVEN LONELIER...

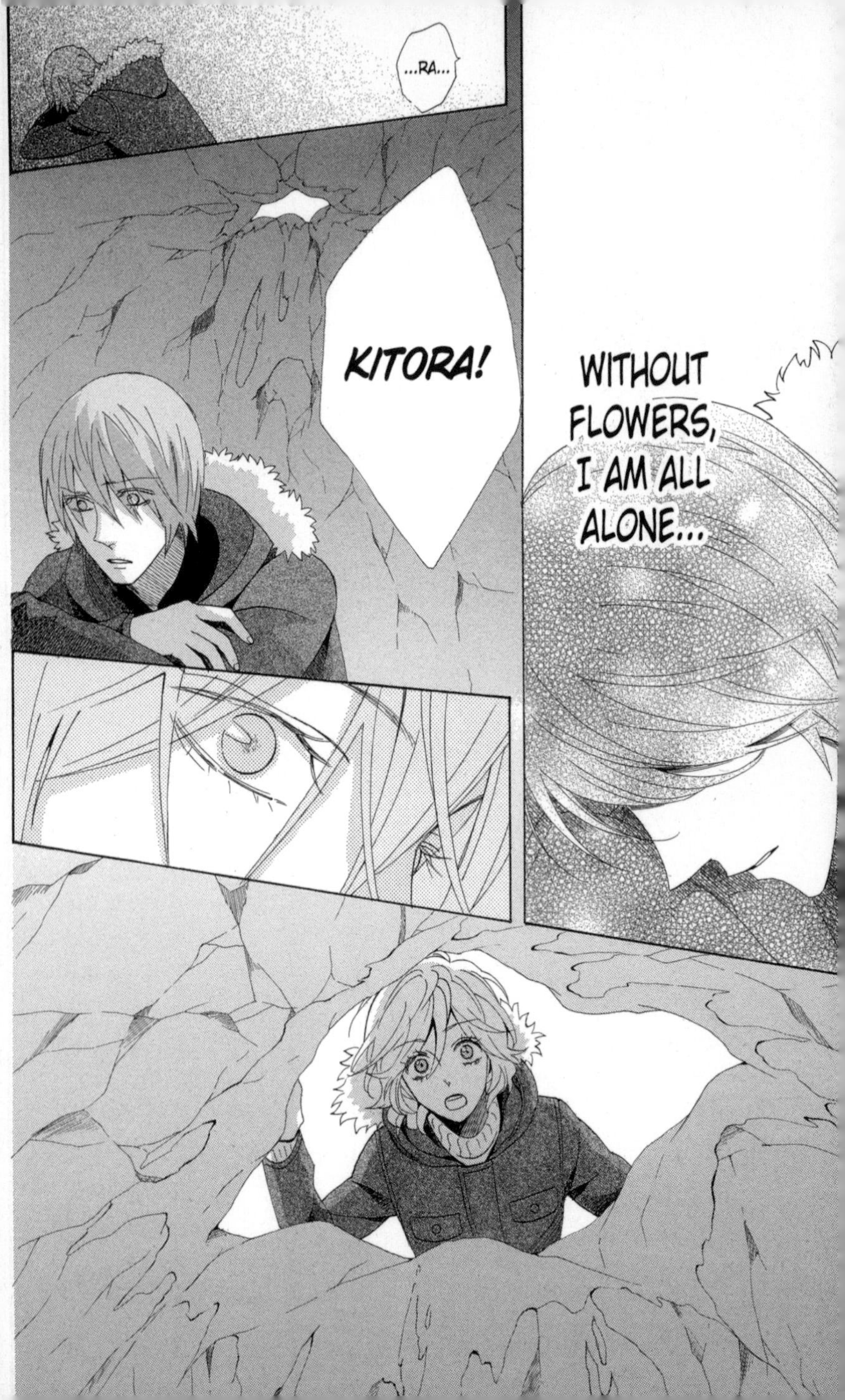

WITHOUT FLOWERS, I AM ALL ALONE...
...RA...
KITORA!

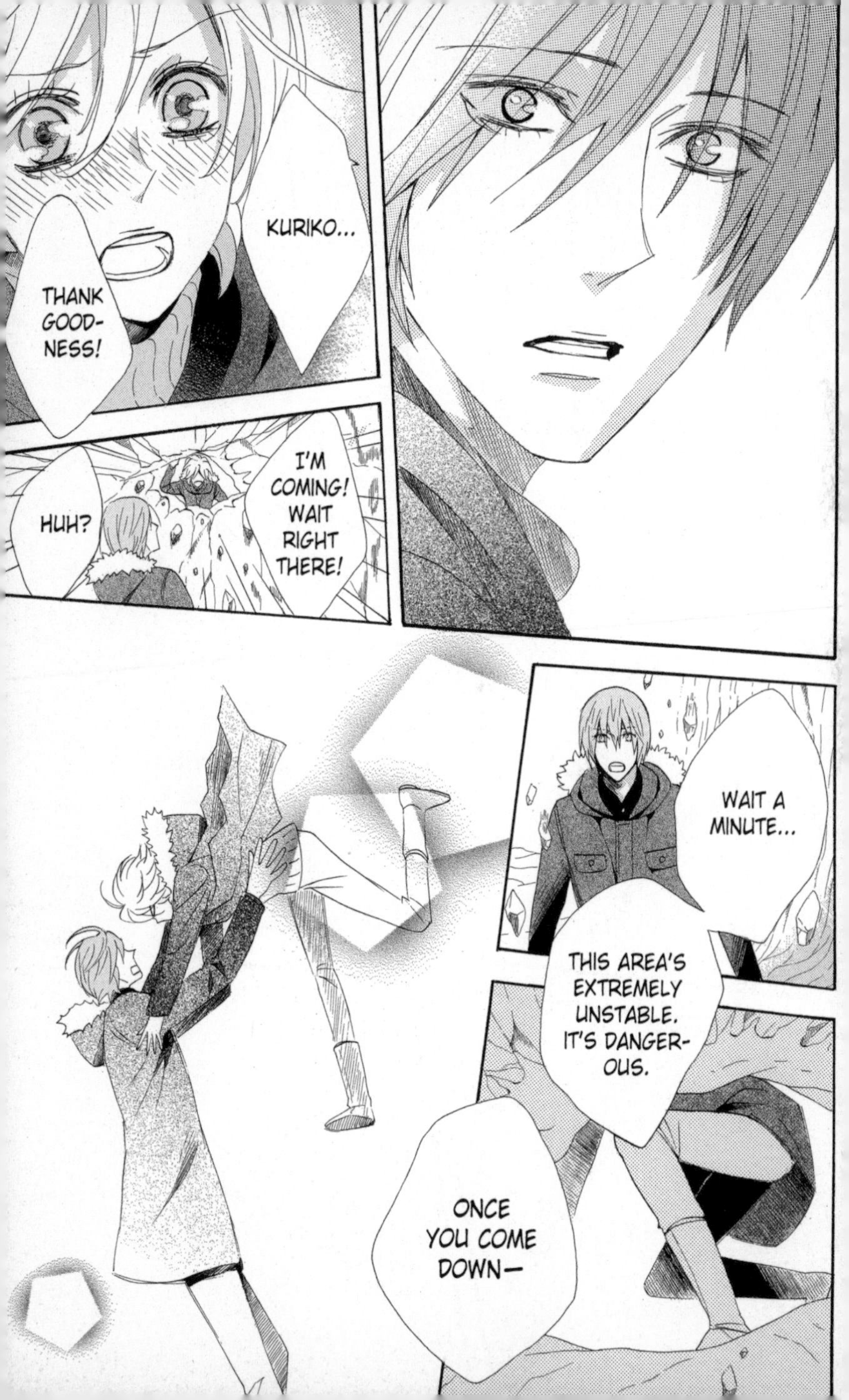
KURIKO...
THANK GOOD-NESS!
I'M COMING! WAIT RIGHT THERE!
HUH?
WAIT A MINUTE...
THIS AREA'S EXTREMELY UNSTABLE. IT'S DANGER-OUS.
ONCE YOU COME DOWN—

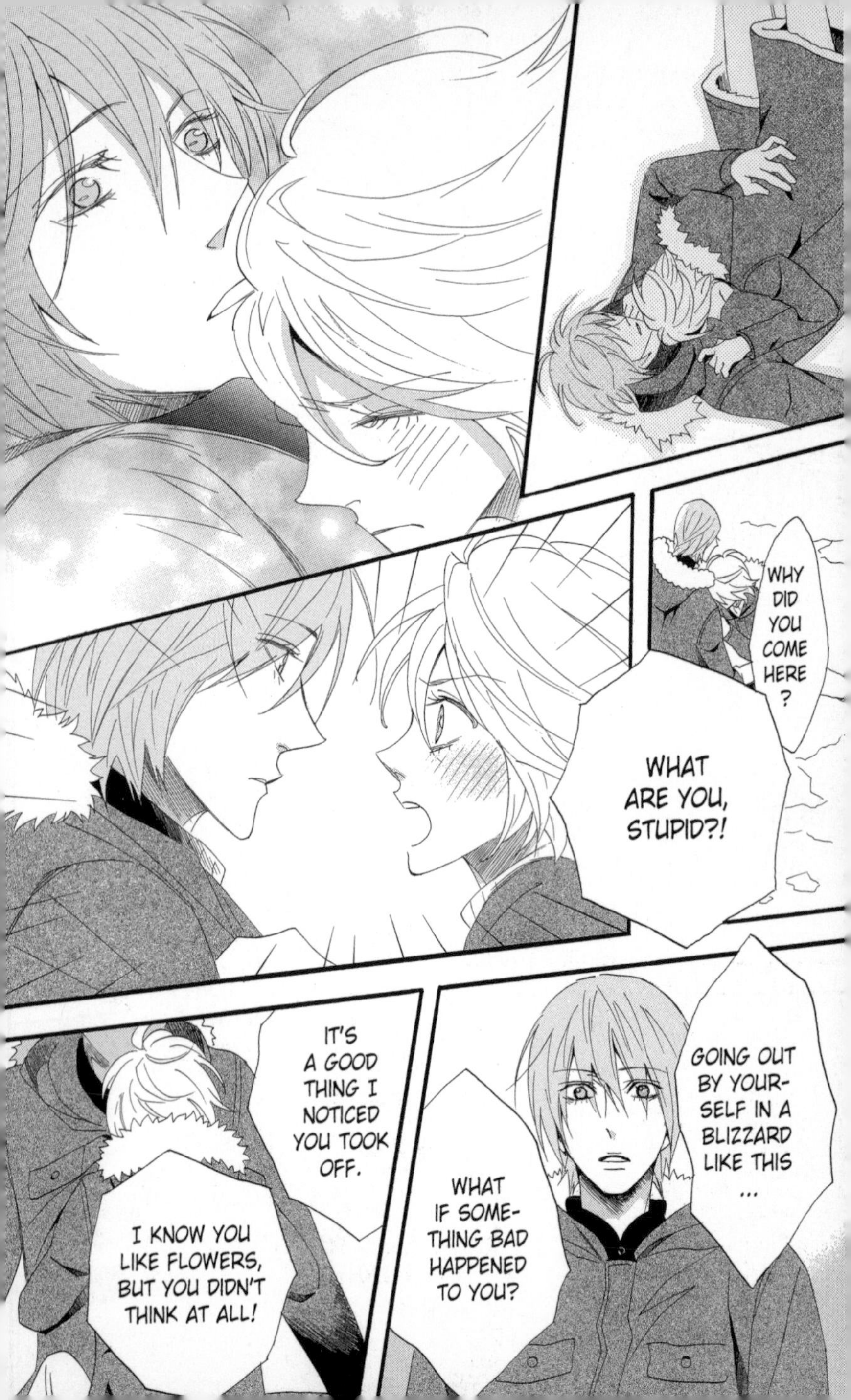
WHY DID YOU COME HERE?
WHAT ARE YOU, STUPID?!
GOING OUT BY YOURSELF IN A BLIZZARD LIKE THIS...
WHAT IF SOMETHING BAD HAPPENED TO YOU?
IT'S A GOOD THING I NOTICED YOU TOOK OFF.
I KNOW YOU LIKE FLOWERS, BUT YOU DIDN'T THINK AT ALL!

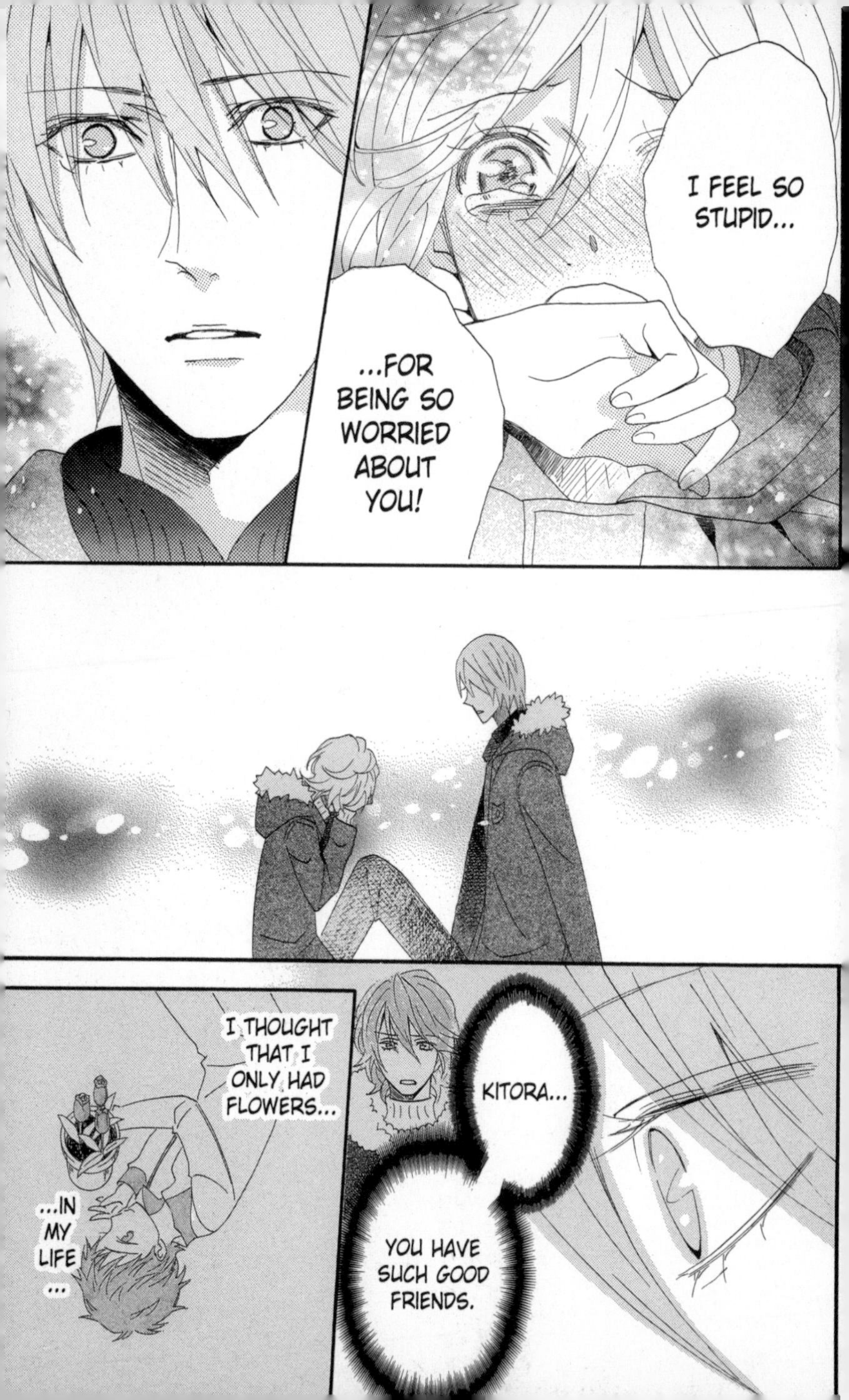
I FEEL SO STUPID...
...FOR BEING SO WORRIED ABOUT YOU!
KITORA...
YOU HAVE SUCH GOOD FRIENDS.
I THOUGHT THAT I ONLY HAD FLOWERS...
...IN MY LIFE ...

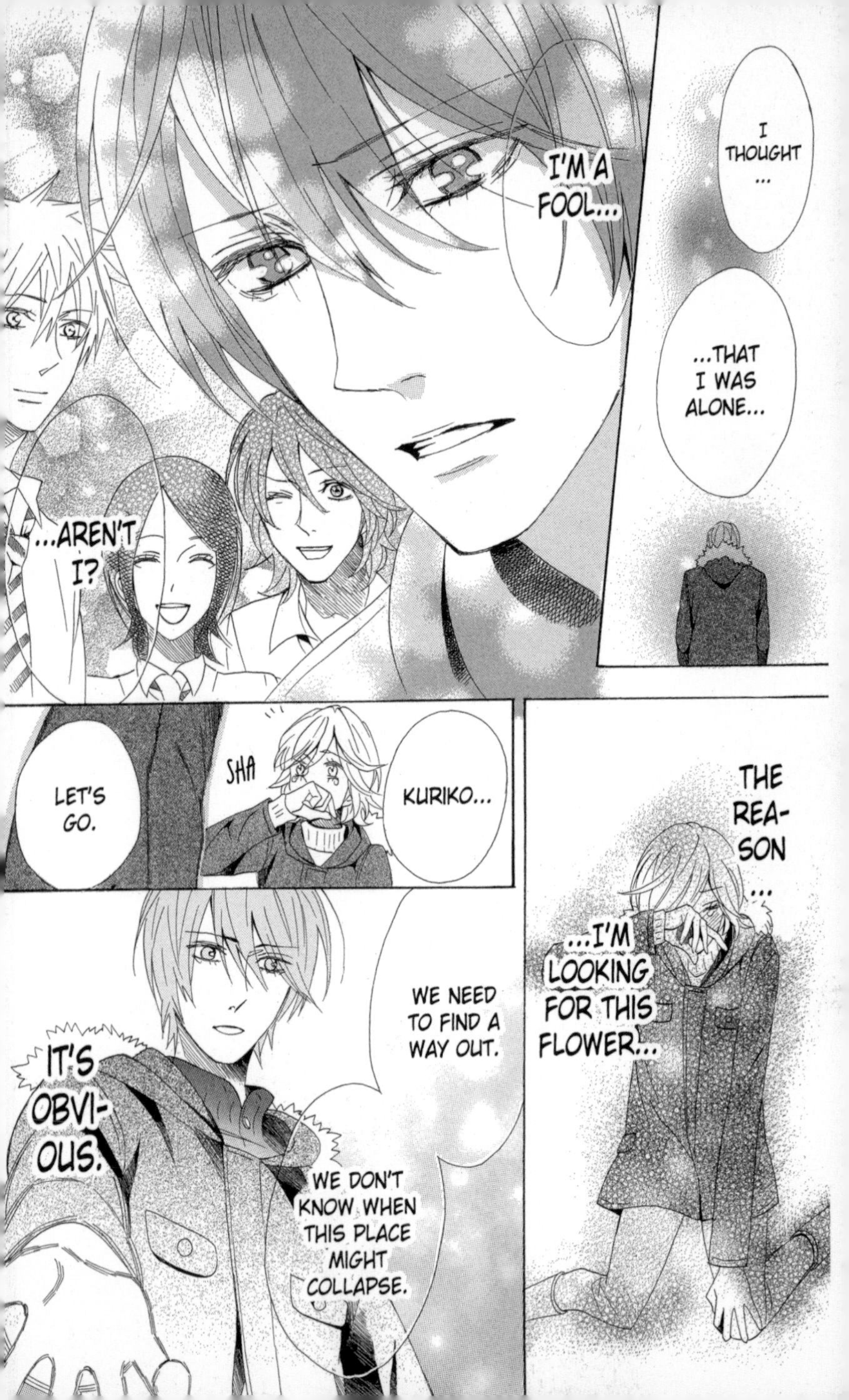
I THOUGHT ...
...THAT I WAS ALONE...
I'M A FOOL...
...AREN'T I?
THE REA-SON ...
...I'M LOOKING FOR THIS FLOWER...
KURIKO...
SHA
LET'S GO.
WE NEED TO FIND A WAY OUT.
IT'S OBVI-OUS.
WE DON'T KNOW WHEN THIS PLACE MIGHT COLLAPSE.

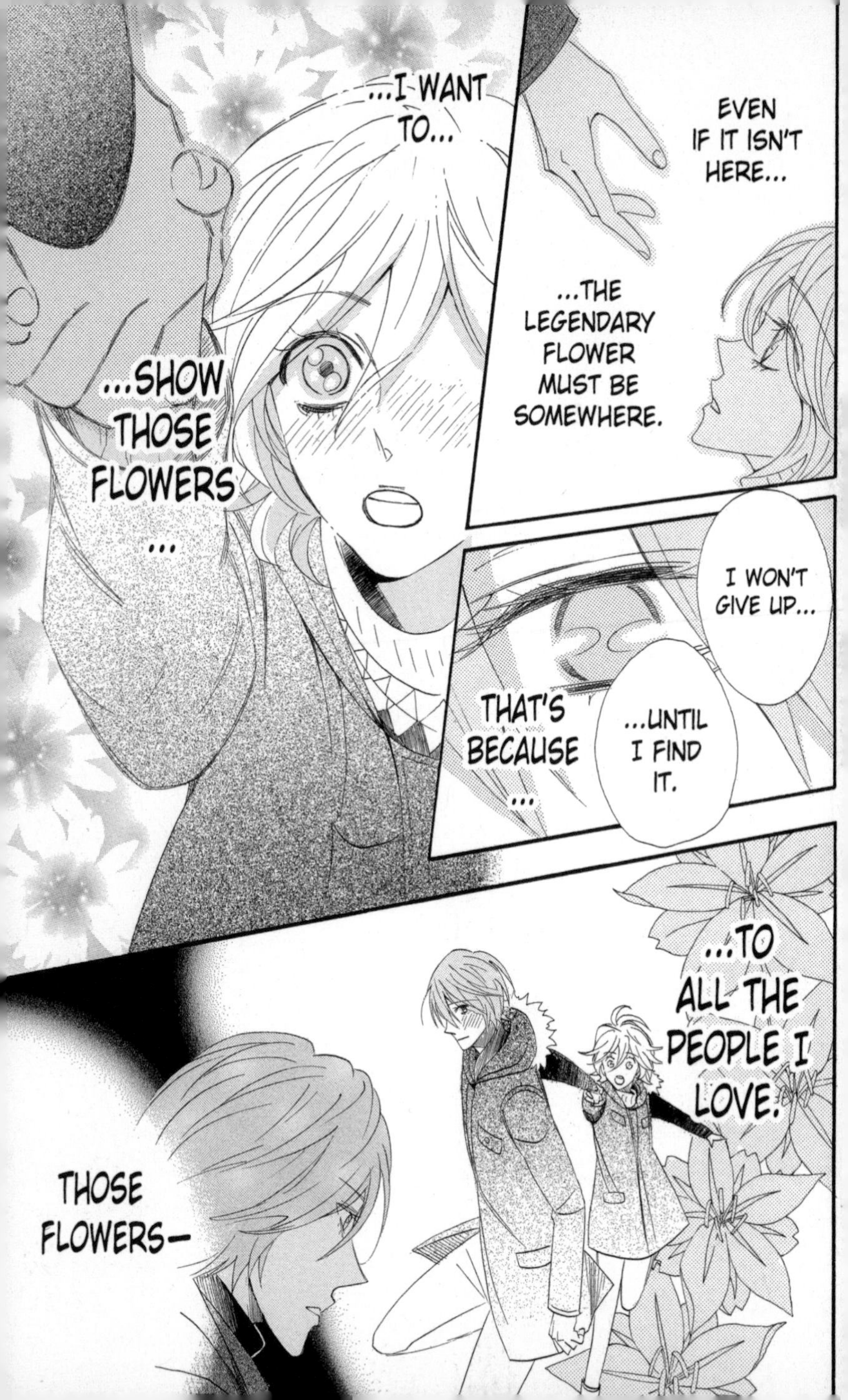
EVEN IF IT ISN'T HERE...
...THE LEGENDARY FLOWER MUST BE SOMEWHERE.
I WON'T GIVE UP...
...UNTIL I FIND IT.
THAT'S BECAUSE ...
...I WANT TO...
...SHOW THOSE FLOWERS ...
...TO ALL THE PEOPLE I LOVE.
THOSE FLOWERS—

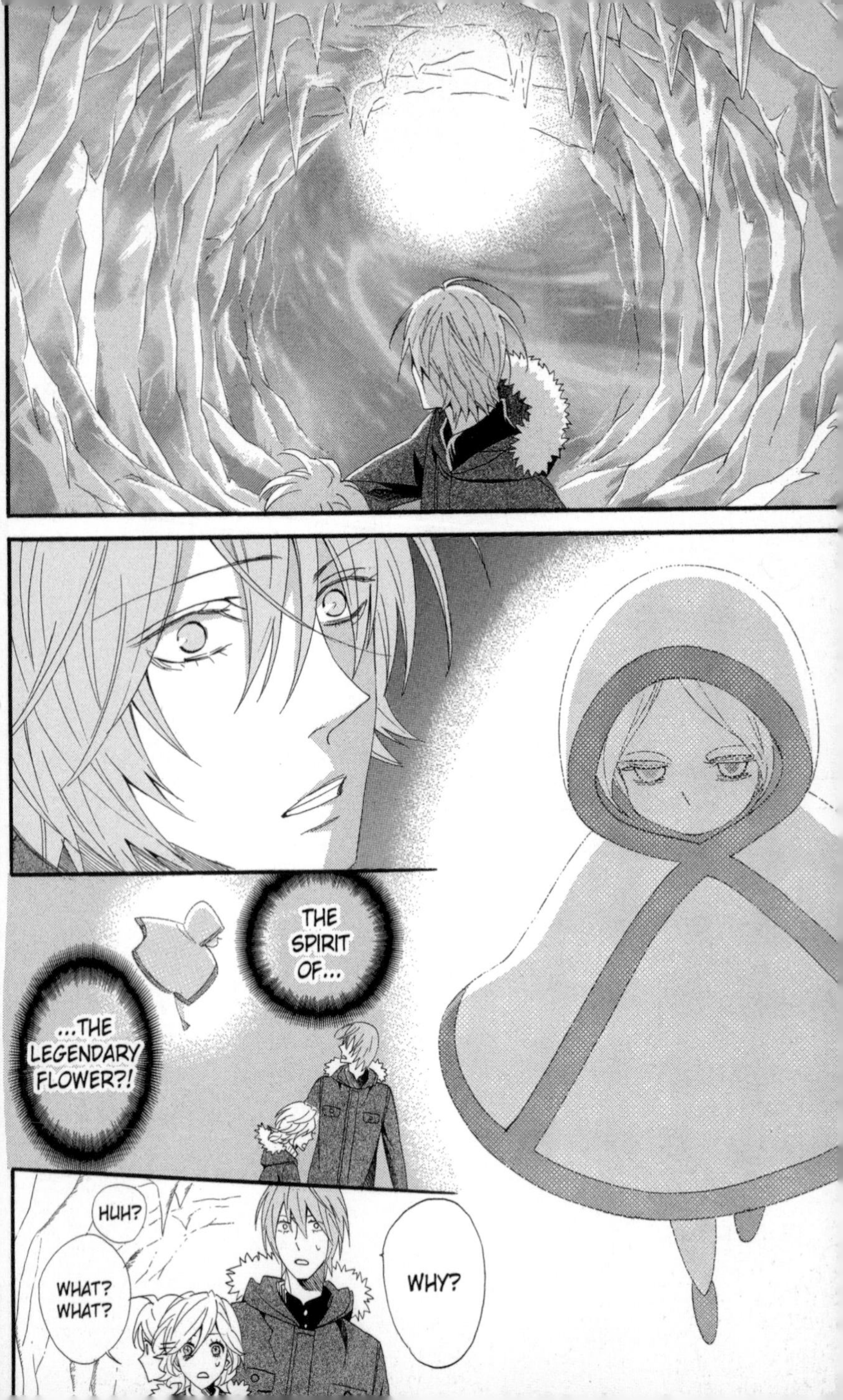
THE SPIRIT OF...
...THE LEGENDARY FLOWER?!
WHY?
HUH?
WHAT? WHAT?

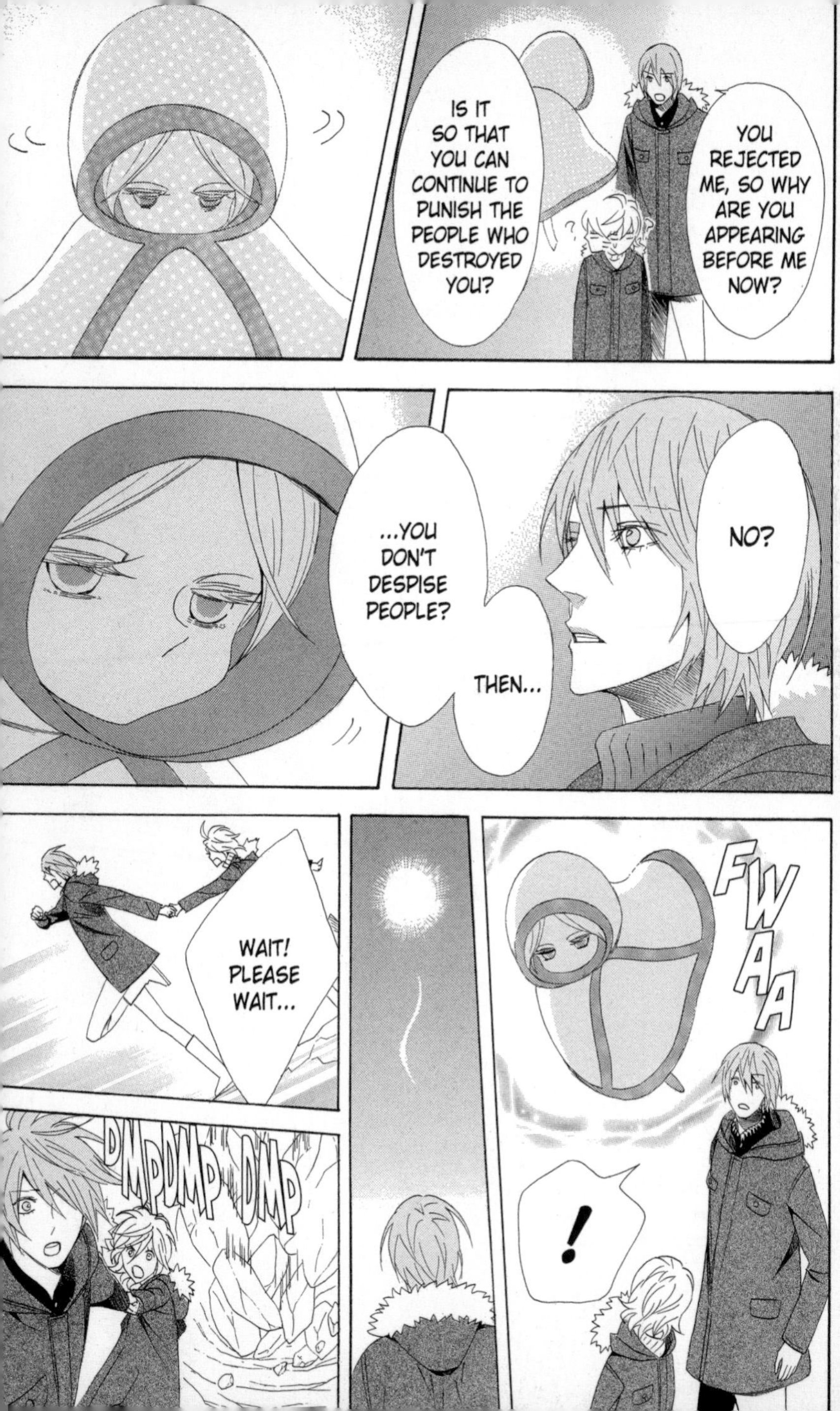
YOU REJECTED ME, SO WHY ARE YOU APPEARING BEFORE ME NOW?
IS IT SO THAT YOU CAN CONTINUE TO PUNISH THE PEOPLE WHO DESTROYED YOU?
NO?
...YOU DON'T DESPISE PEOPLE?
THEN...
FWAAA
!
WAIT! PLEASE WAIT...
DMP DMP DMP DMP

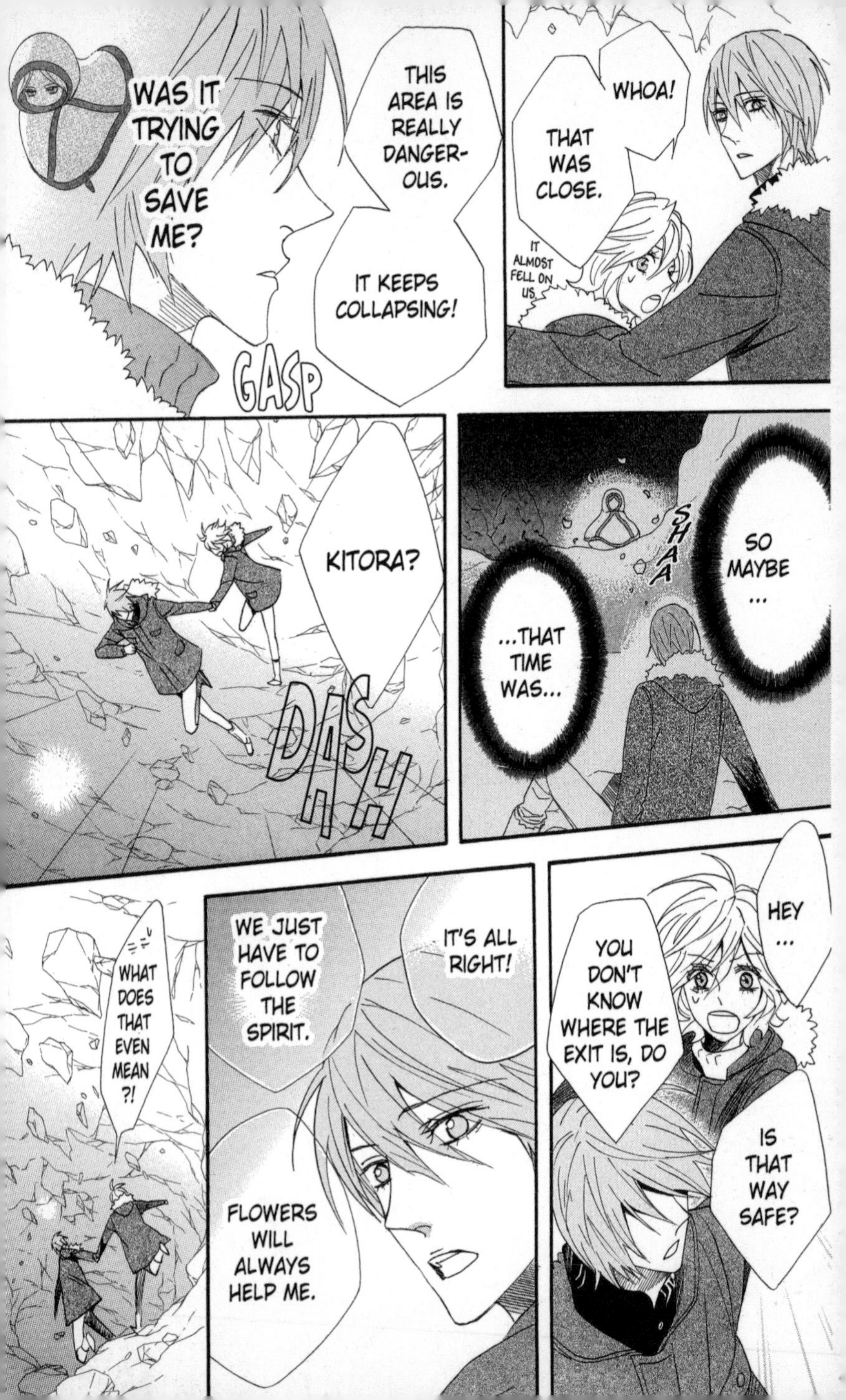
WHOA!
THAT WAS CLOSE.
IT ALMOST FELL ON US.
THIS AREA IS REALLY DANGER-OUS.
IT KEEPS COLLAPSING!
WAS IT TRYING TO SAVE ME?
GASP
SHAA
SO MAYBE...
...THAT TIME WAS...
KITORA?
DASH
HEY...
YOU DON'T KNOW WHERE THE EXIT IS, DO YOU?
IS THAT WAY SAFE?
IT'S ALL RIGHT!
WE JUST HAVE TO FOLLOW THE SPIRIT.
FLOWERS WILL ALWAYS HELP ME.
WHAT DOES THAT EVEN MEAN?!

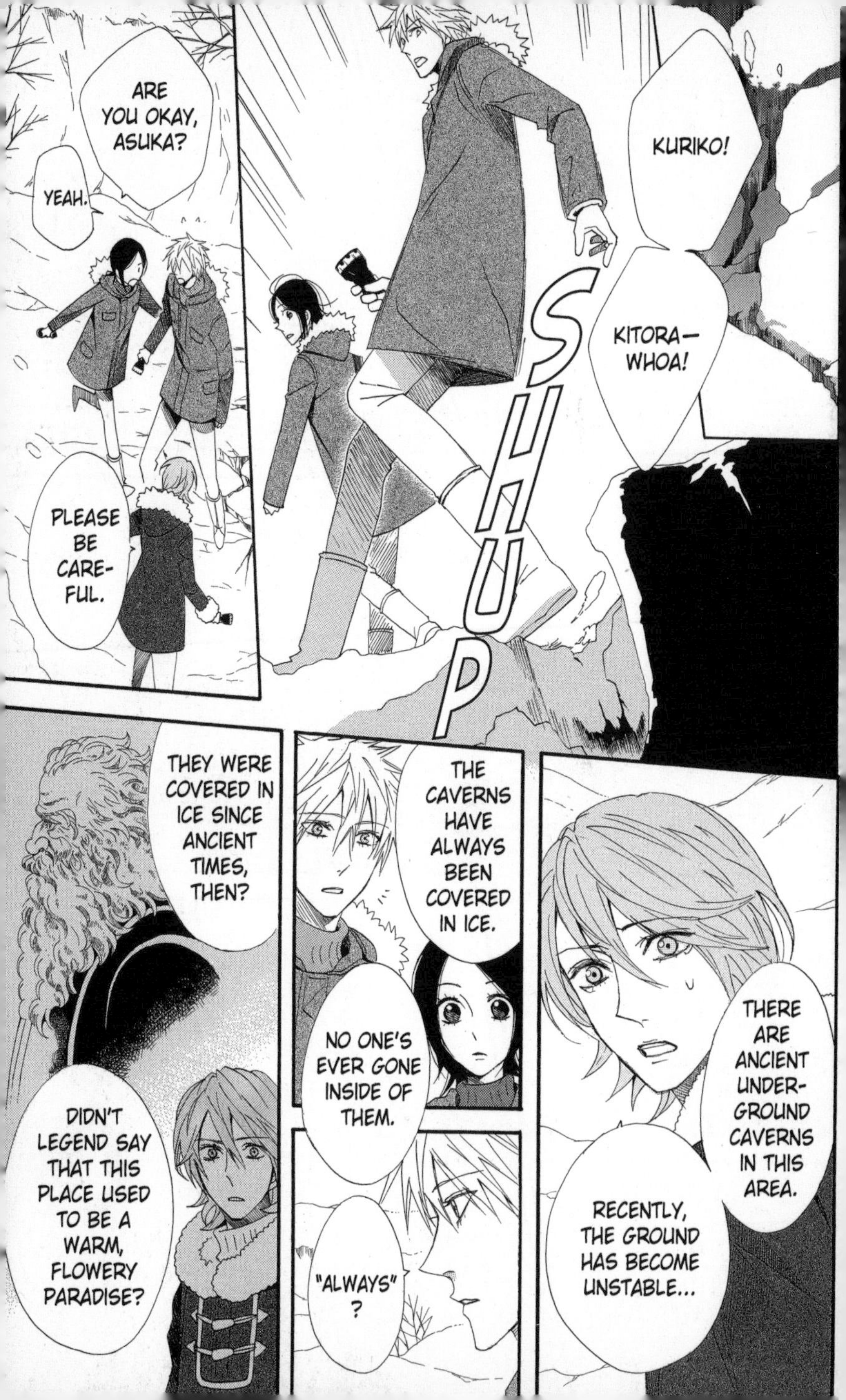

KURIKO!
KITORA—WHOA!
SHUP
ARE YOU OKAY, ASUKA?
YEAH.
PLEASE BE CARE-FUL.
THERE ARE ANCIENT UNDER-GROUND CAVERNS IN THIS AREA.
RECENTLY, THE GROUND HAS BECOME UNSTABLE...
THE CAVERNS HAVE ALWAYS BEEN COVERED IN ICE.
NO ONE'S EVER GONE INSIDE OF THEM.
"ALWAYS"?
THEY WERE COVERED IN ICE SINCE ANCIENT TIMES, THEN?
DIDN'T LEGEND SAY THAT THIS PLACE USED TO BE A WARM, FLOWERY PARADISE?

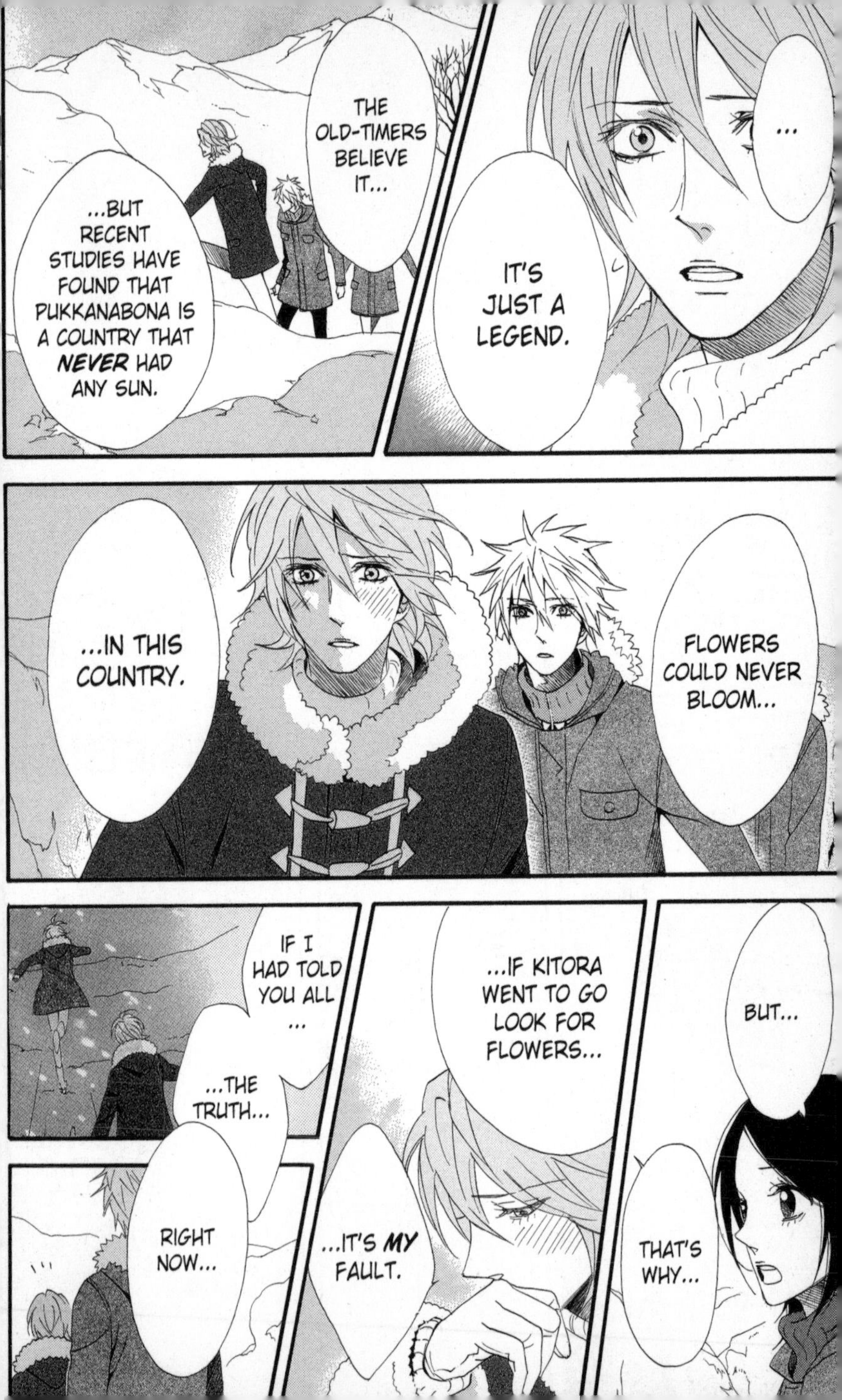
...
IT'S JUST A LEGEND.
THE OLD-TIMERS BELIEVE IT...
...BUT RECENT STUDIES HAVE FOUND THAT PUKKANABONA IS A COUNTRY THAT ***NEVER*** HAD ANY SUN.
FLOWERS COULD NEVER BLOOM...
...IN THIS COUNTRY.
BUT...
THAT'S WHY...
...IF KITORA WENT TO GO LOOK FOR FLOWERS...
...IT'S ***MY*** FAULT.
IF I HAD TOLD YOU ALL ...
...THE TRUTH...
RIGHT NOW...

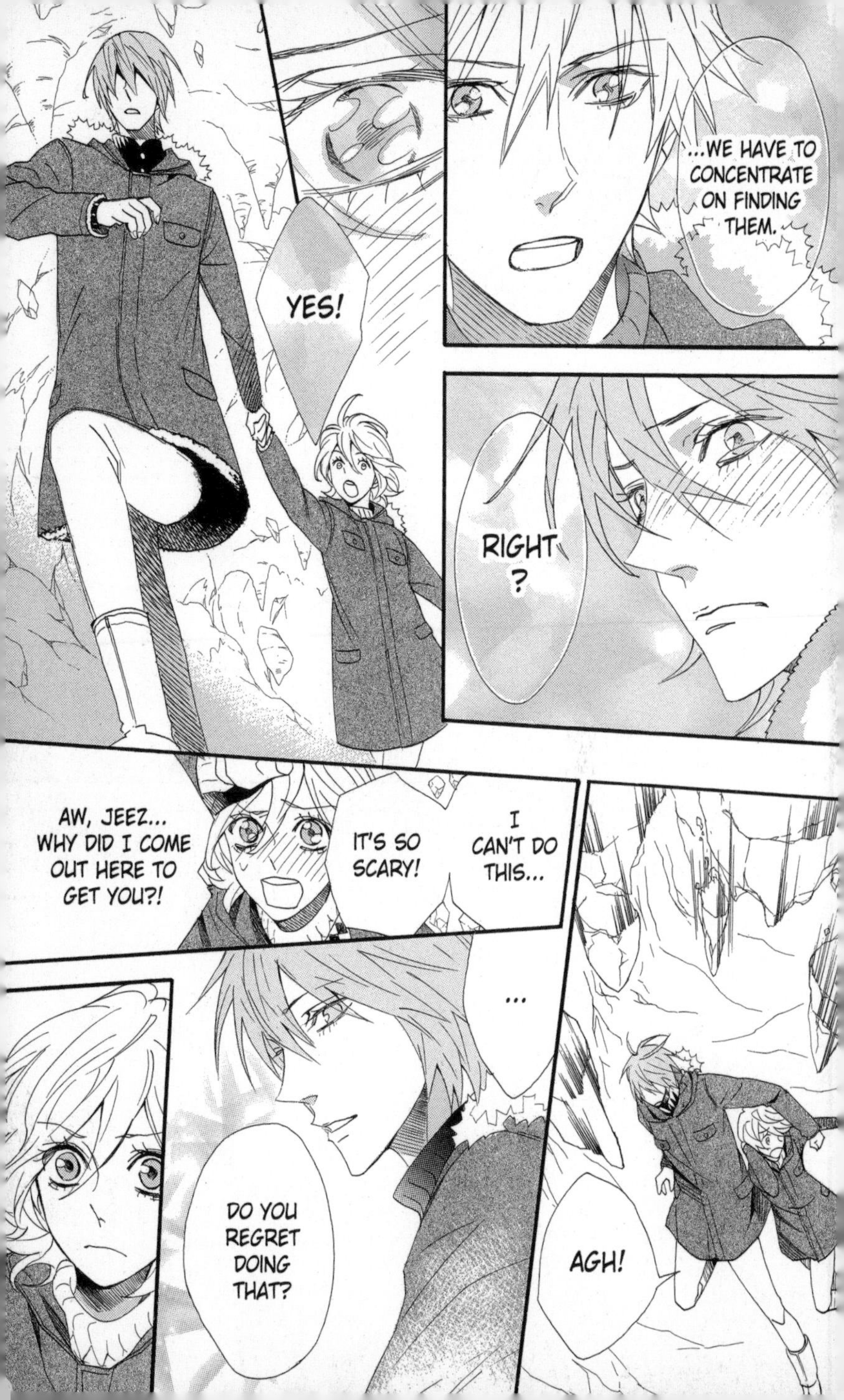
...WE HAVE TO CONCENTRATE ON FINDING THEM.
RIGHT ?
YES!
AGH!
I CAN'T DO THIS...
IT'S SO SCARY!
AW, JEEZ... WHY DID I COME OUT HERE TO GET YOU?!
...
DO YOU REGRET DOING THAT?

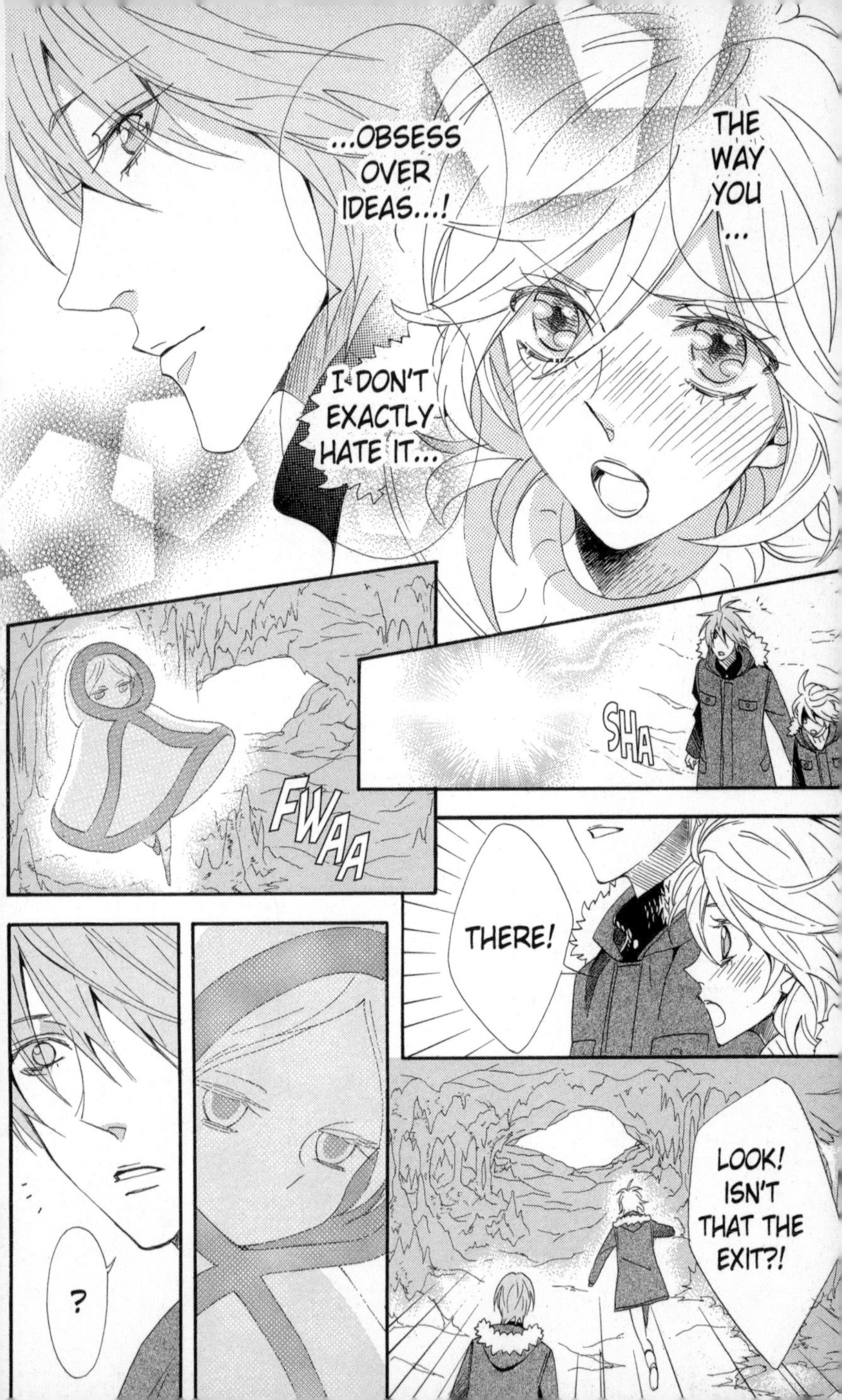
THE WAY YOU...
...OBSESS OVER IDEAS...!
I DON'T EXACTLY HATE IT...
SHA
FWAA
THERE!
LOOK! ISN'T THAT THE EXIT?!
?

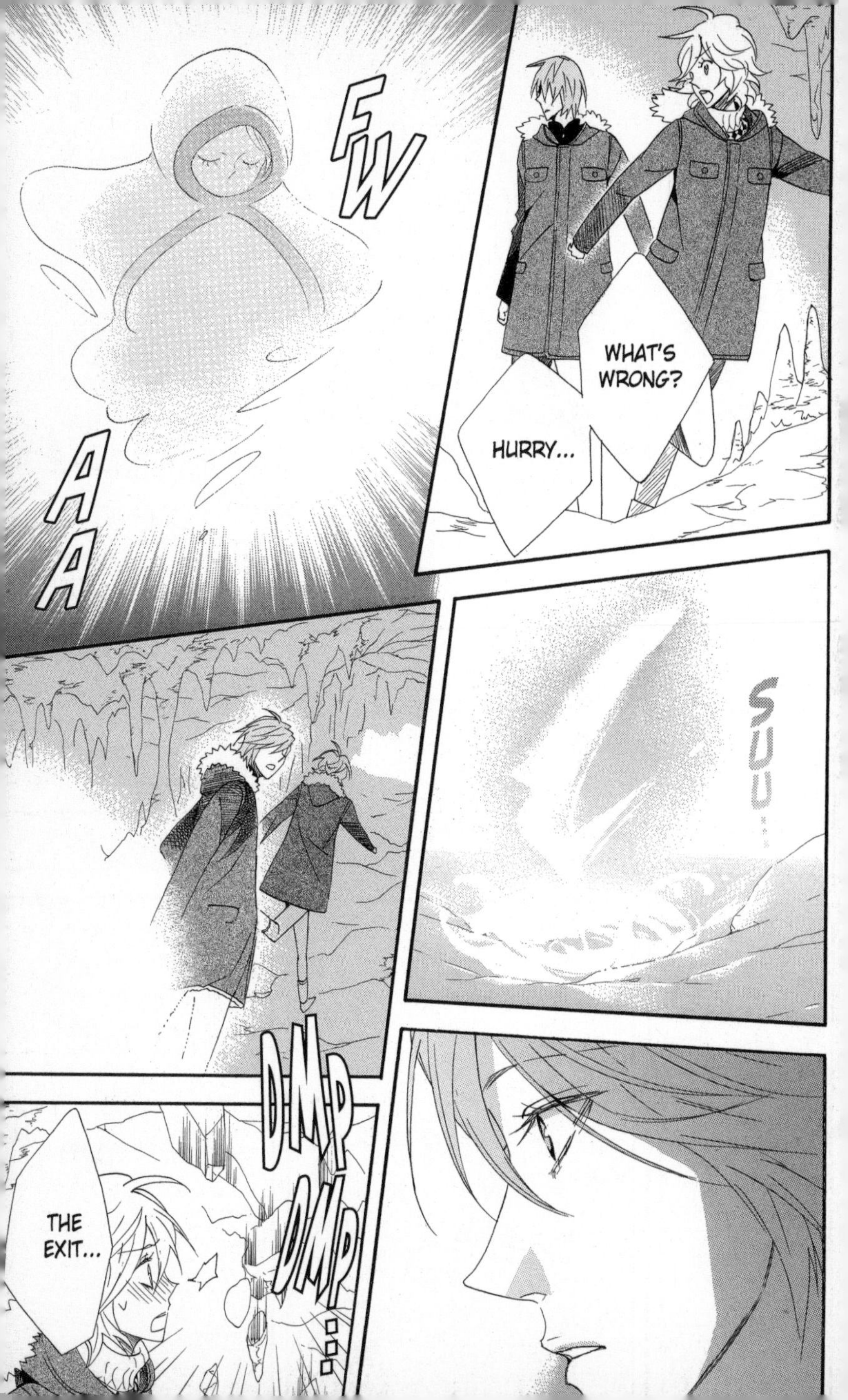
WHAT'S WRONG?
HURRY...
FW
AA
SUU...
DMP
DMP...
THE EXIT...

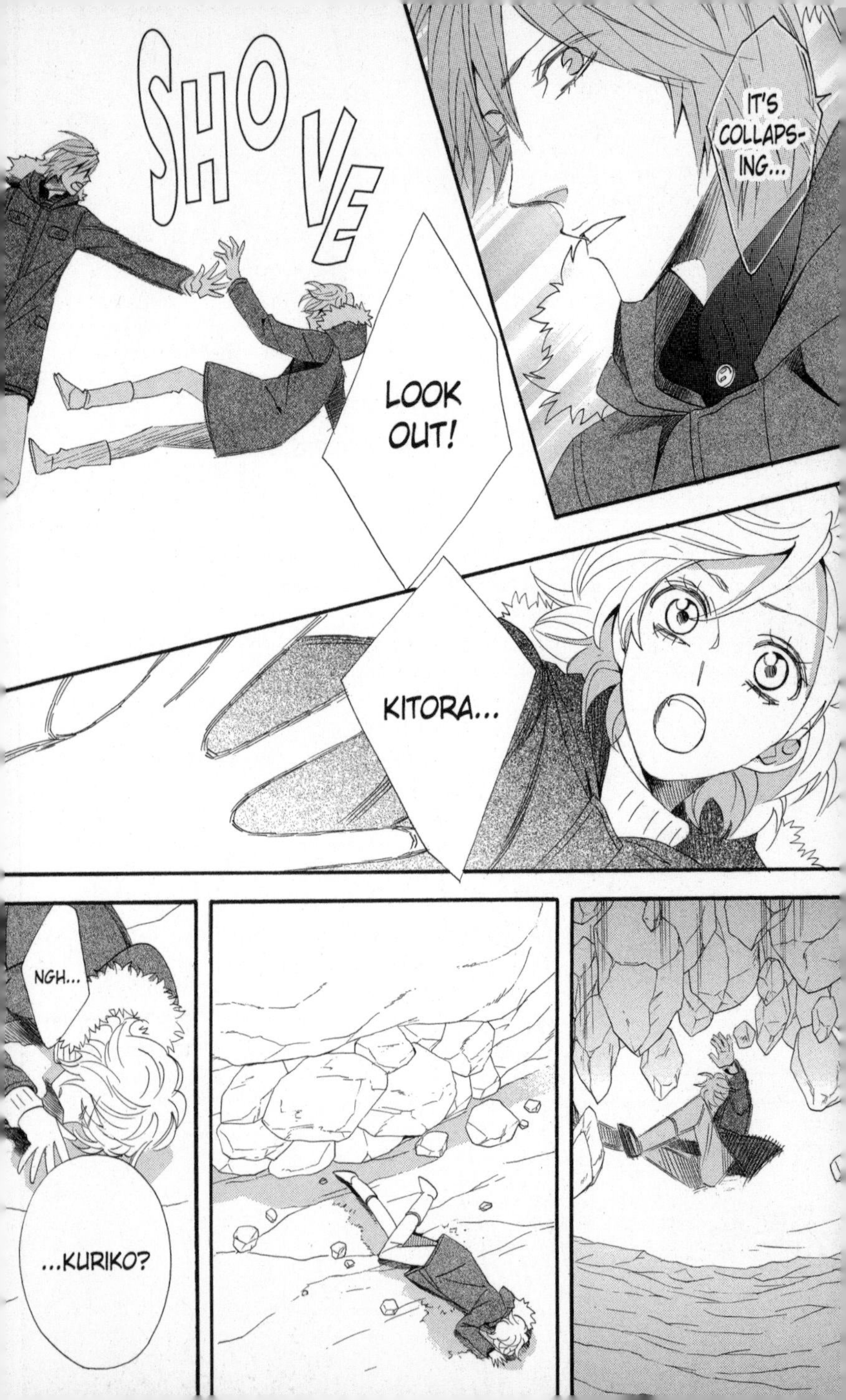
IT'S COLLAPSING...
SHOVE
LOOK OUT!
KITORA...
NGH...
...KURIKO?

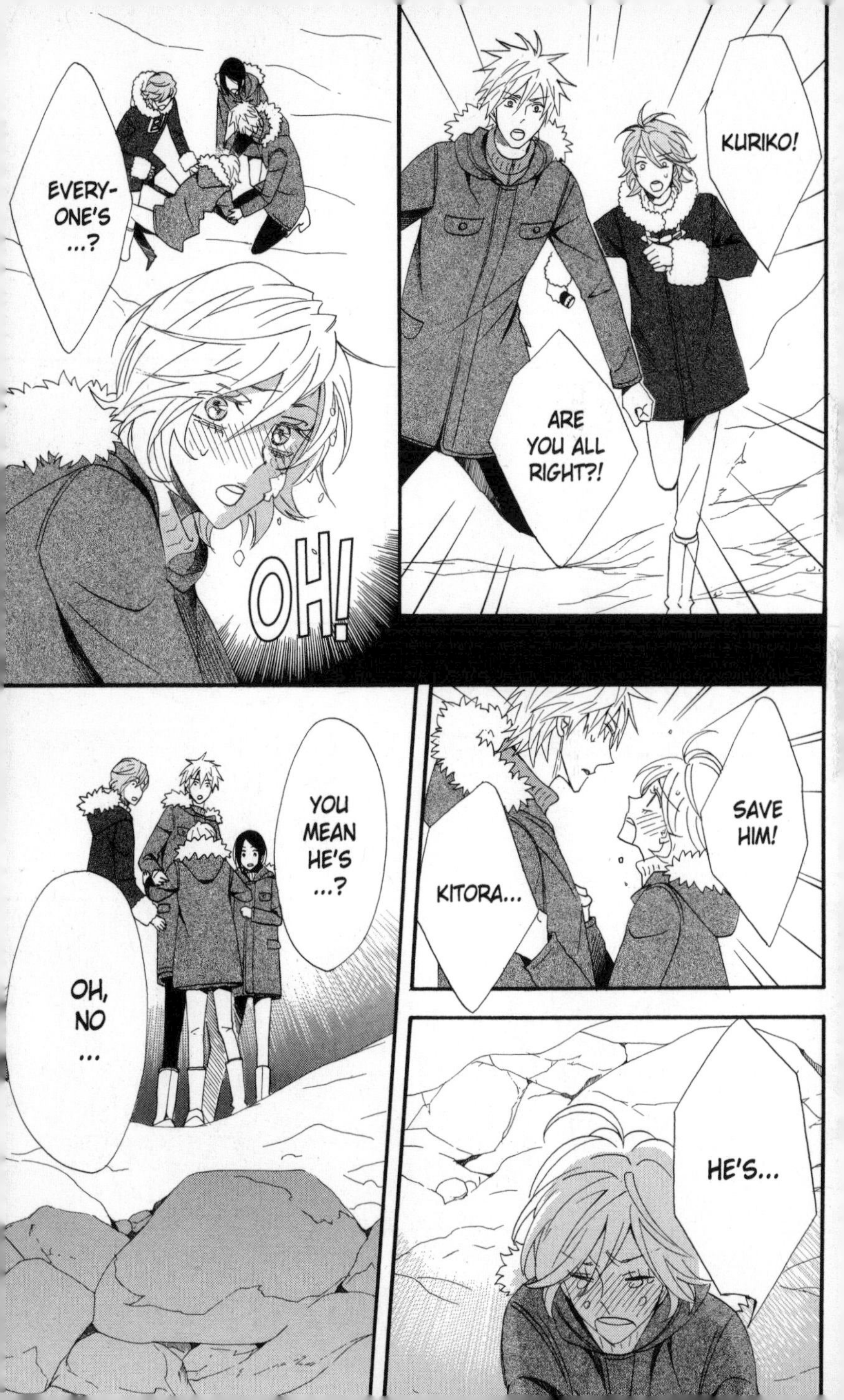
KURIKO!
ARE YOU ALL RIGHT?!
EVERY-ONE'S ...?
OH!
SAVE HIM!
KITORA...
HE'S...
YOU MEAN HE'S ...?
OH, NO ...

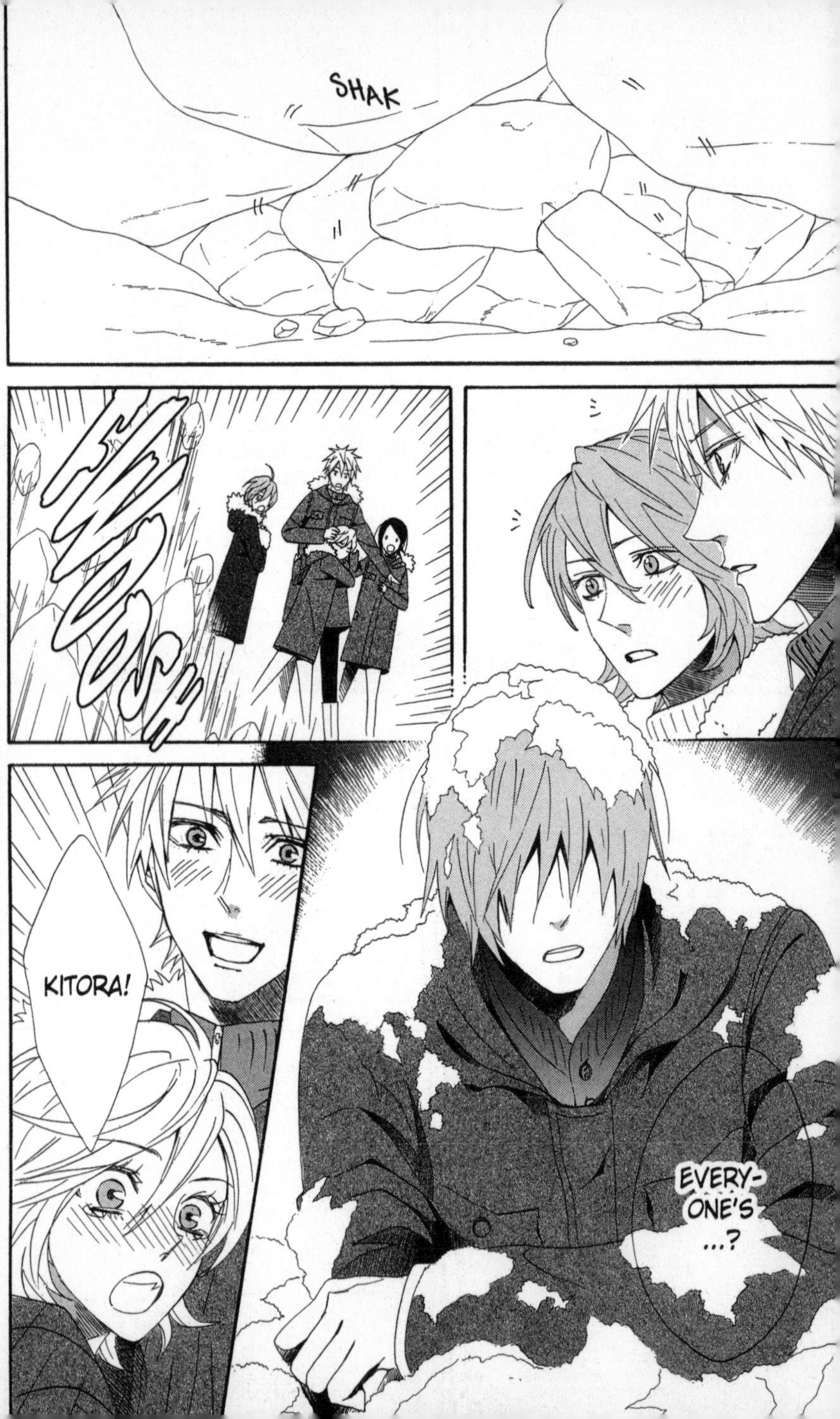
SHAK
WHOOSH
EVERY-ONE'S ...?
KITORA!

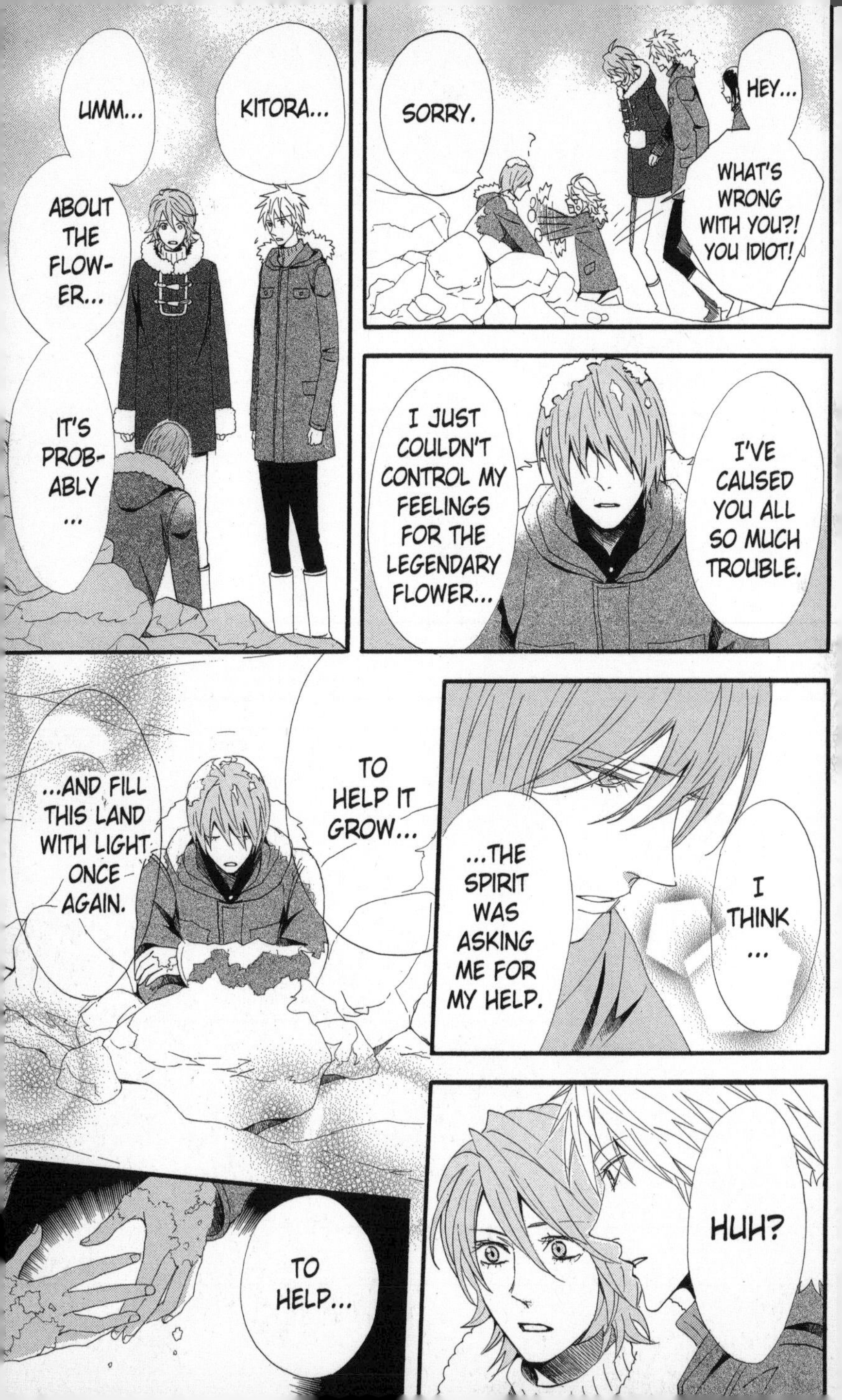
HEY...
WHAT'S WRONG WITH YOU?! YOU IDIOT!
SORRY.
I'VE CAUSED YOU ALL SO MUCH TROUBLE.
I JUST COULDN'T CONTROL MY FEELINGS FOR THE LEGENDARY FLOWER...
KITORA...
UMM...
ABOUT THE FLOWER...
IT'S PROBABLY...
I THINK...
...THE SPIRIT WAS ASKING ME FOR MY HELP.
HUH?
TO HELP IT GROW...
...AND FILL THIS LAND WITH LIGHT ONCE AGAIN.
TO HELP...

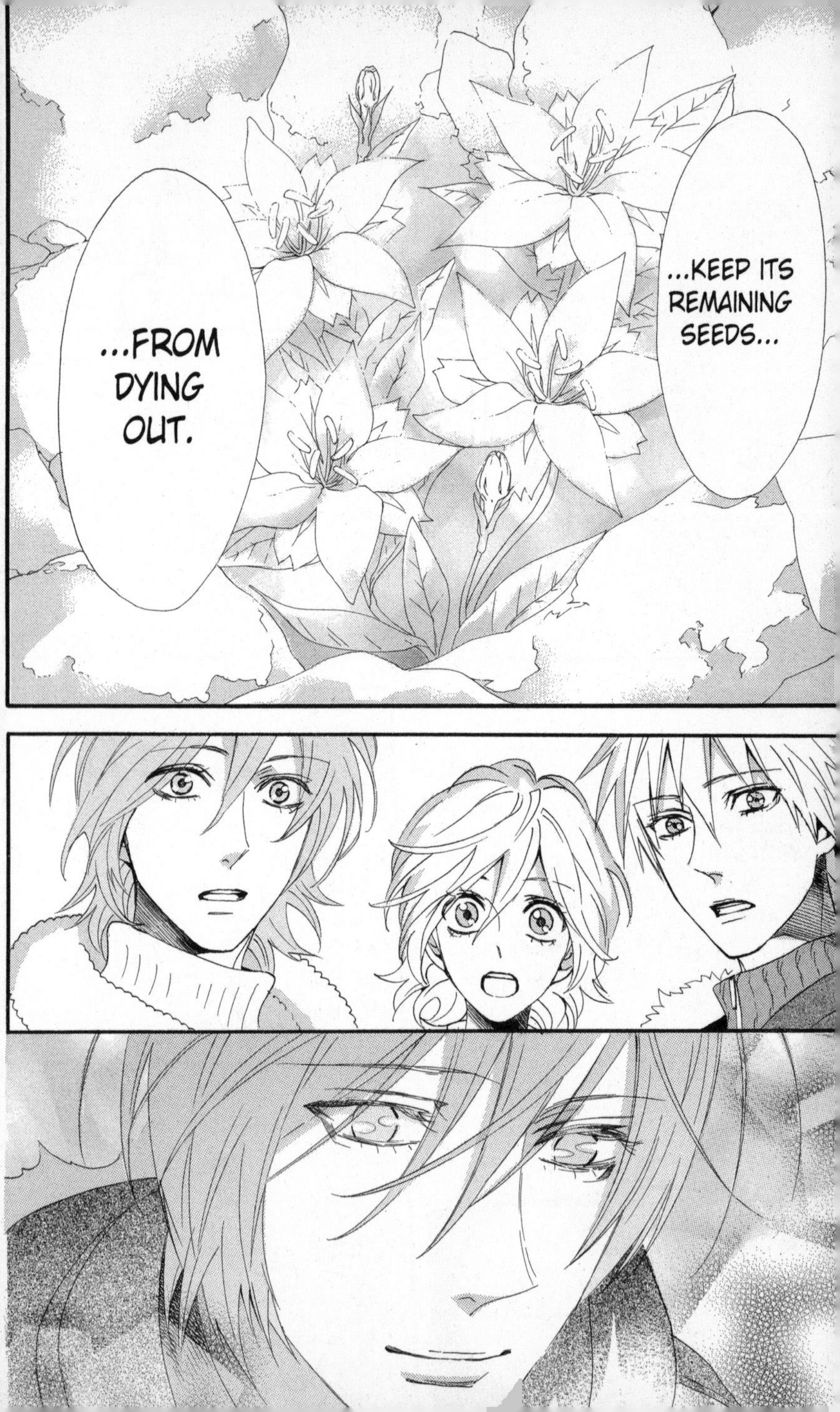
...KEEP ITS REMAINING SEEDS...
...FROM DYING OUT.

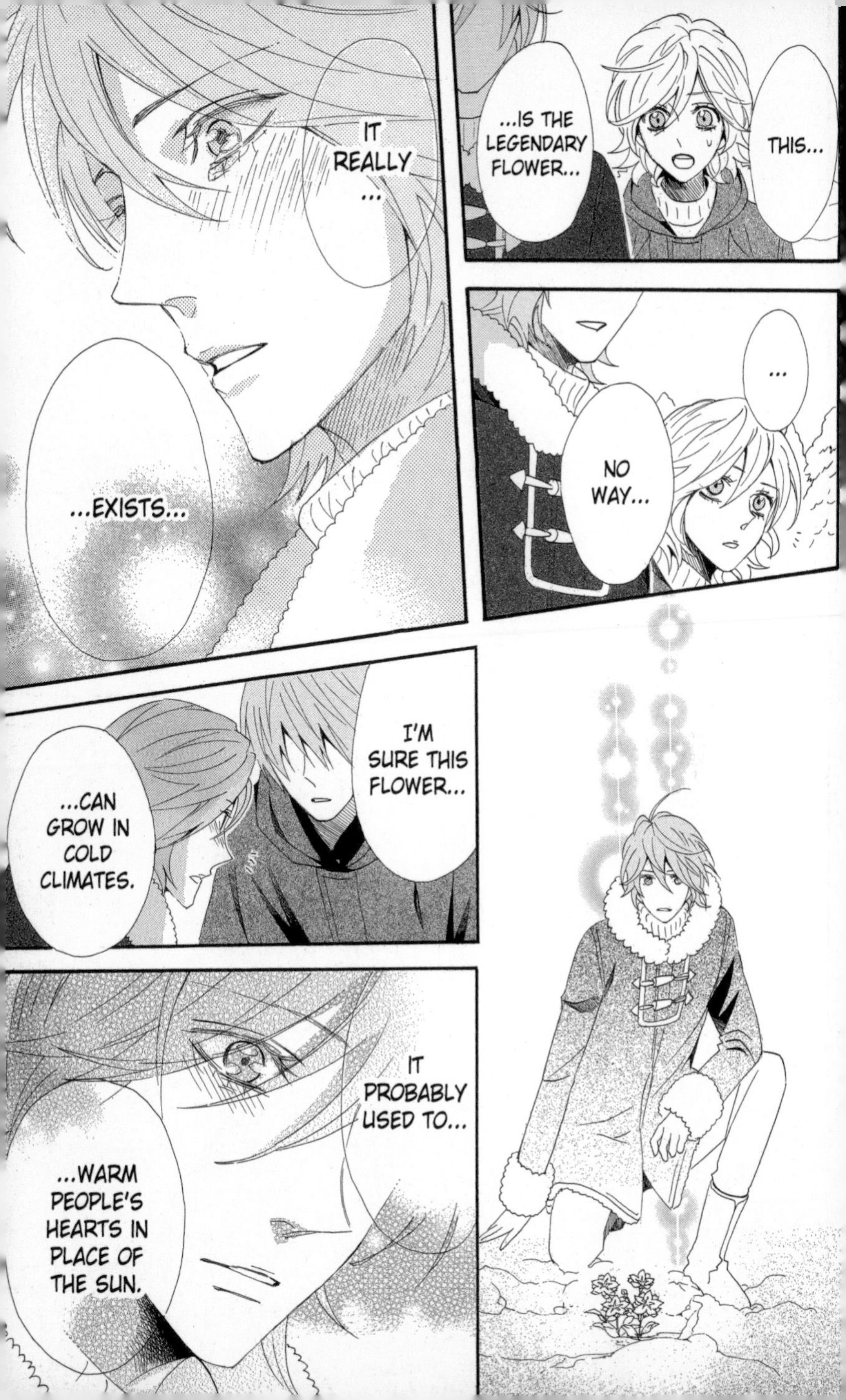
THIS...
...IS THE LEGENDARY FLOWER...
...
NO WAY...
IT REALLY...
...EXISTS...
I'M SURE THIS FLOWER...
...CAN GROW IN COLD CLIMATES.
IT PROBABLY USED TO...
...WARM PEOPLE'S HEARTS IN PLACE OF THE SUN.

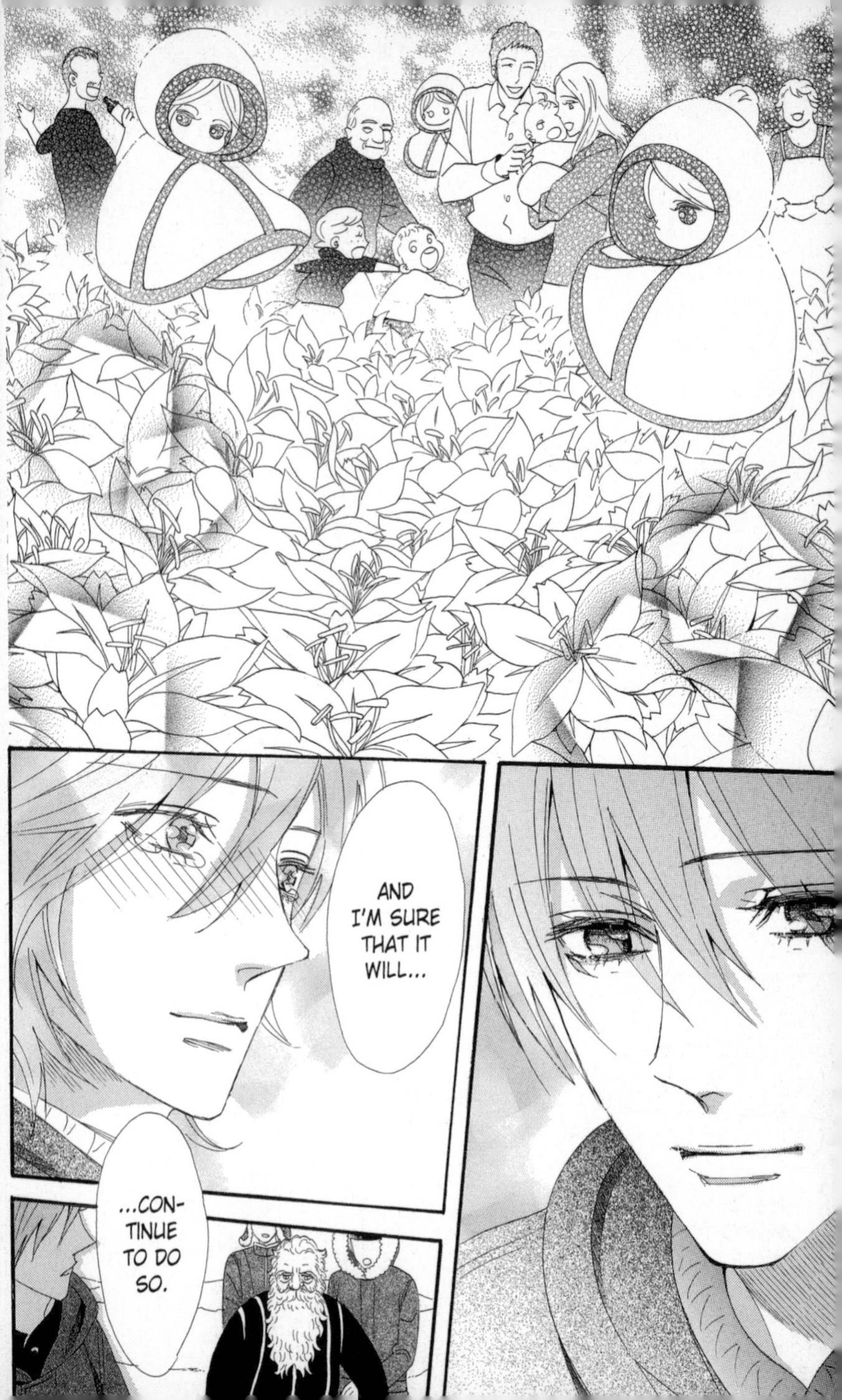
AND I'M SURE THAT IT WILL...
...CON-TINUE TO DO SO.

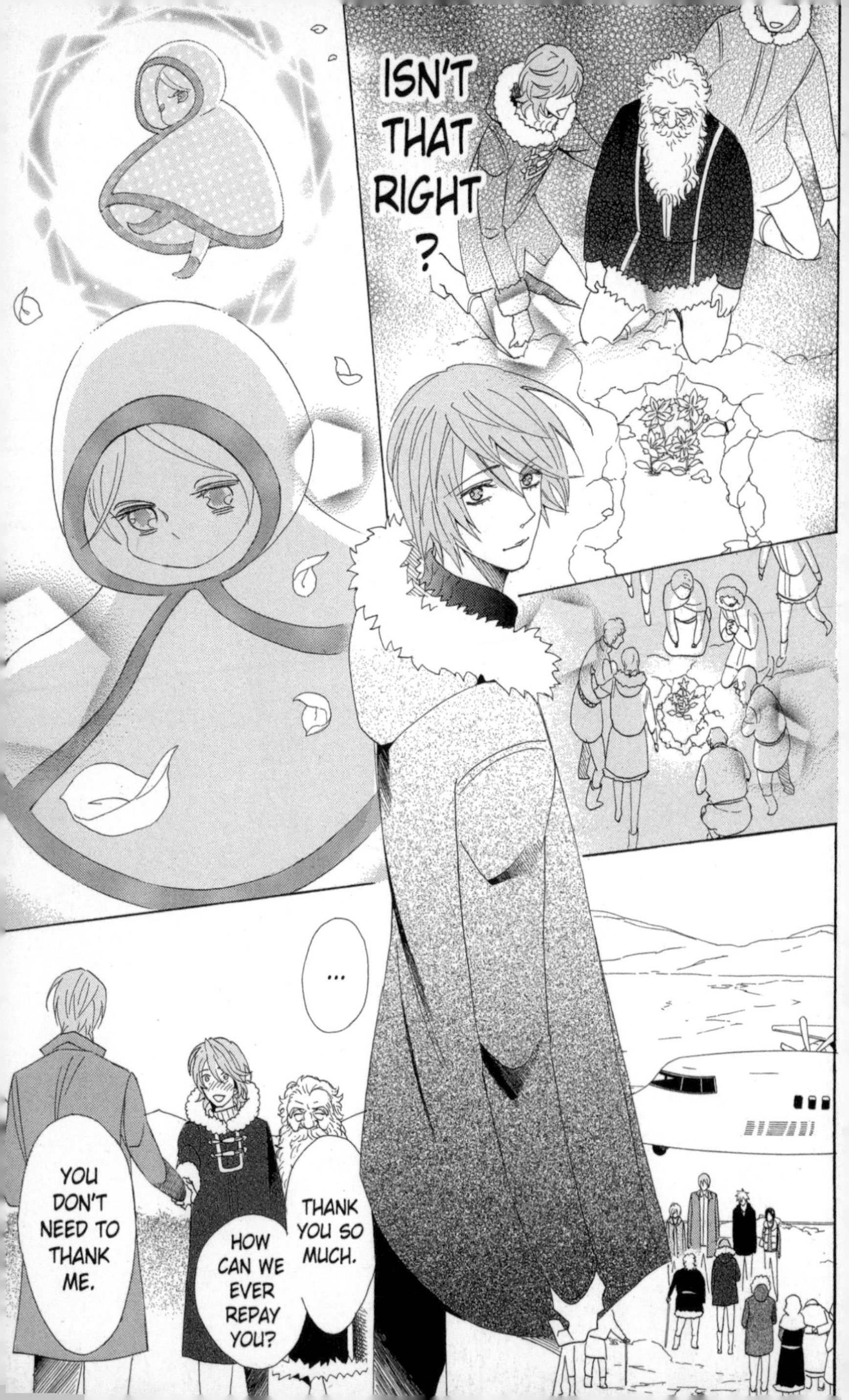
ISN'T THAT RIGHT?
...
THANK YOU SO MUCH.
HOW CAN WE EVER REPAY YOU?
YOU DON'T NEED TO THANK ME.

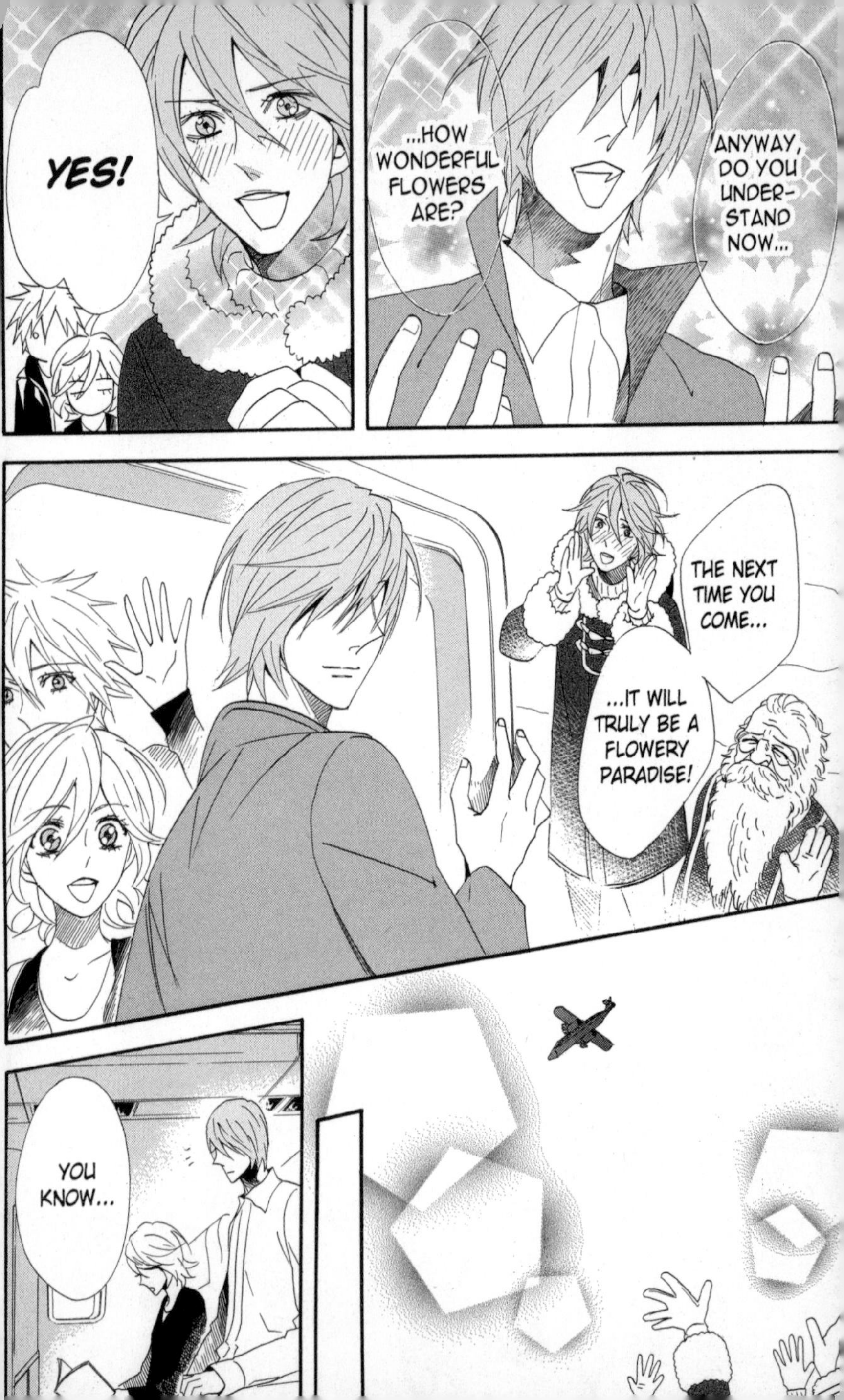
ANYWAY, DO YOU UNDER-STAND NOW...
...HOW WONDERFUL FLOWERS ARE?
YES!
THE NEXT TIME YOU COME...
...IT WILL TRULY BE A FLOWERY PARADISE!
YOU KNOW...

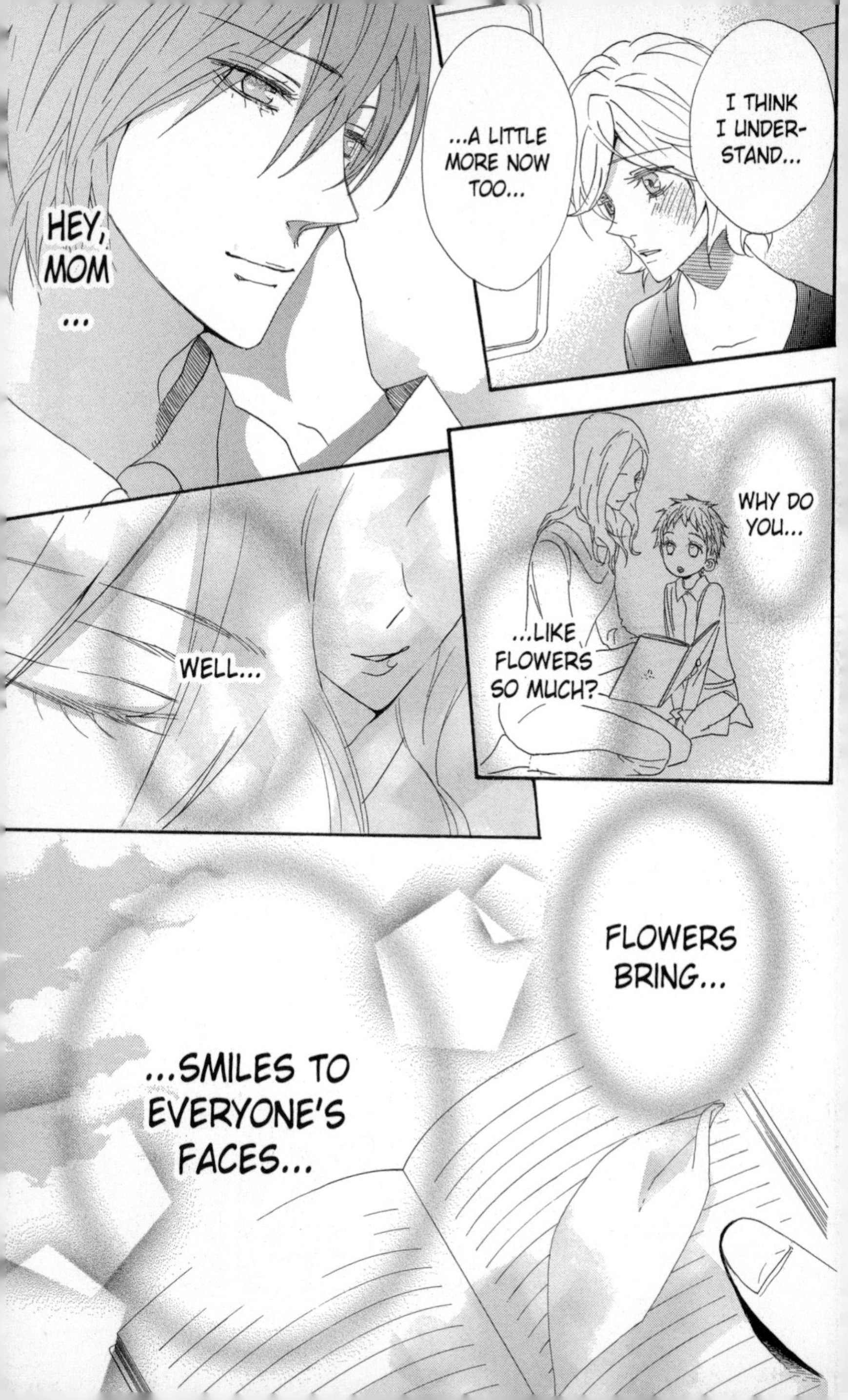
I THINK I UNDER-STAND...
...A LITTLE MORE NOW TOO...
HEY, MOM ...
WHY DO YOU...
...LIKE FLOWERS SO MUCH?
WELL...
FLOWERS BRING...
...SMILES TO EVERYONE'S FACES...

OTOMEN

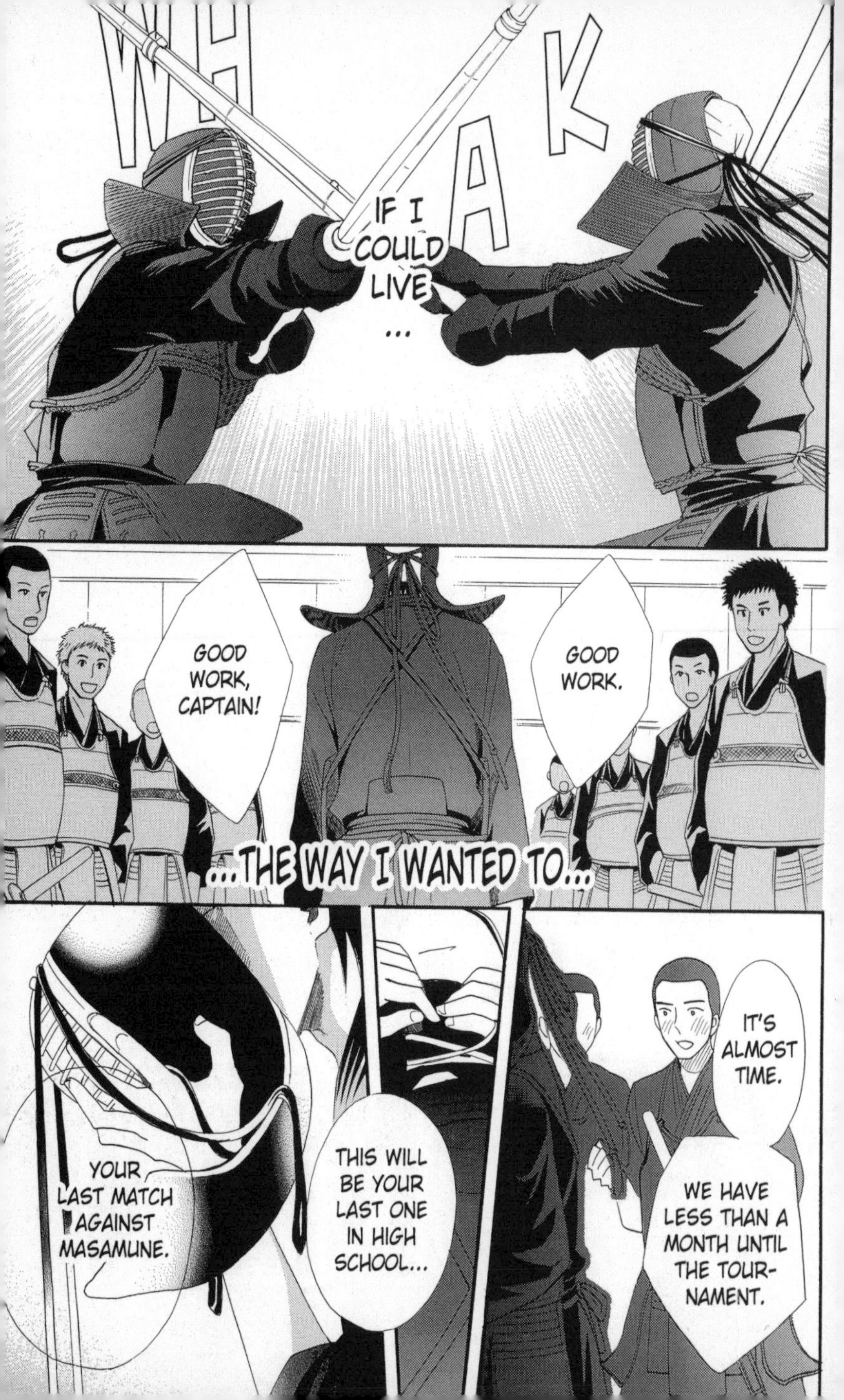
WHAK
IF I COULD LIVE...
GOOD WORK.
GOOD WORK, CAPTAIN!
...THE WAY I WANTED TO...
IT'S ALMOST TIME.
WE HAVE LESS THAN A MONTH UNTIL THE TOUR-NAMENT.
THIS WILL BE YOUR LAST ONE IN HIGH SCHOOL...
YOUR LAST MATCH AGAINST MASAMUNE.

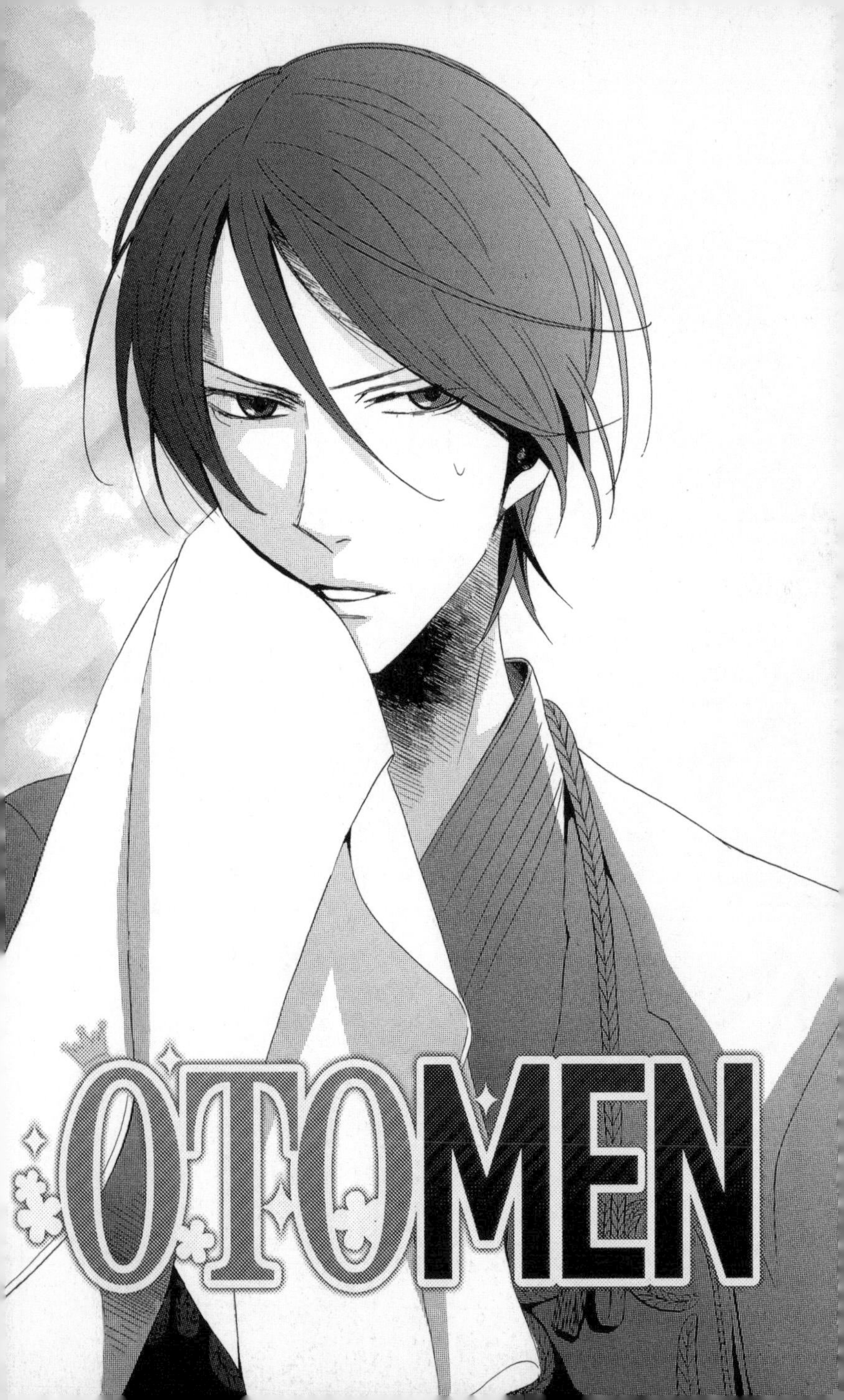
OTOMEN

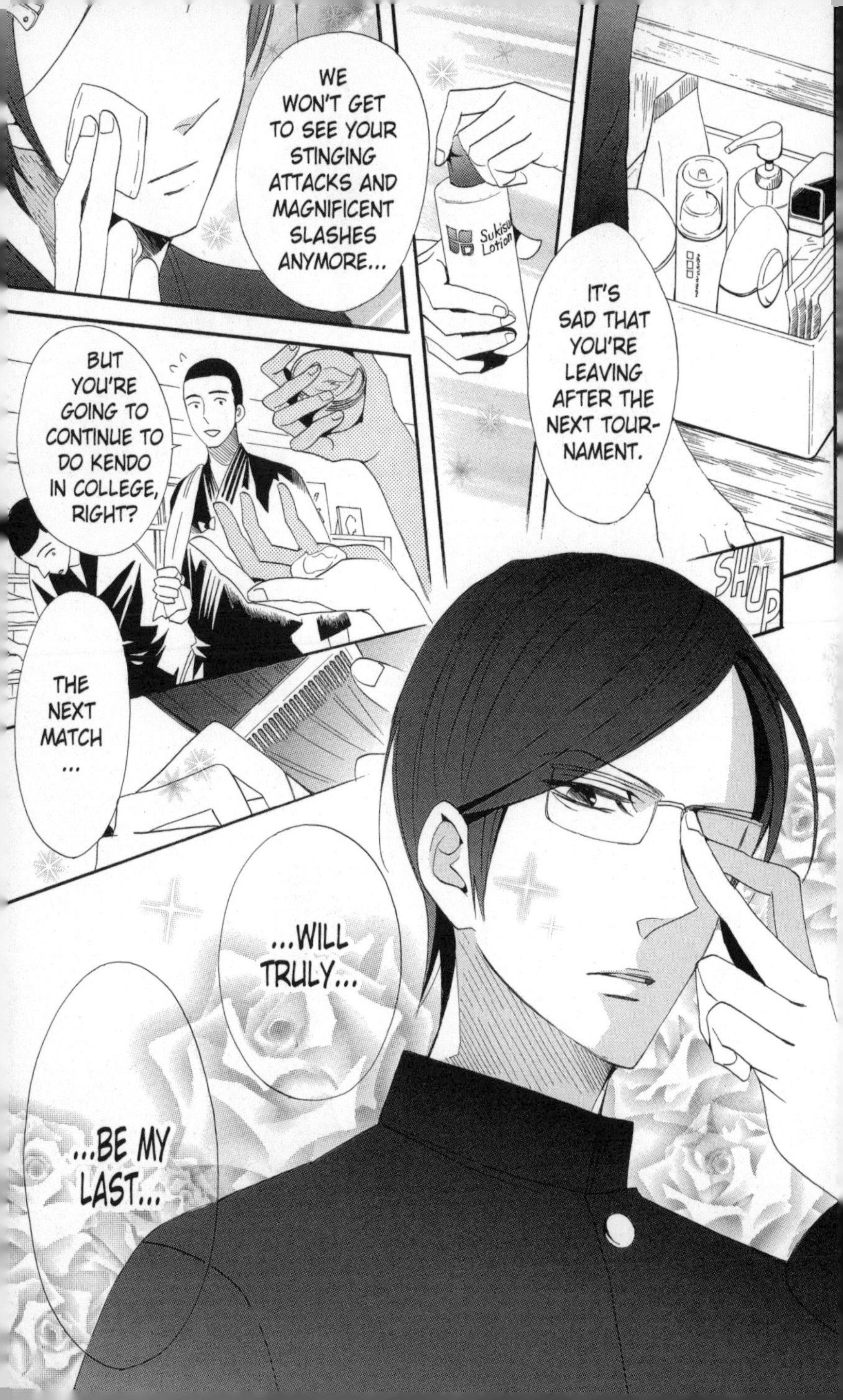
IT'S SAD THAT YOU'RE LEAVING AFTER THE NEXT TOUR-NAMENT.
WE WON'T GET TO SEE YOUR STINGING ATTACKS AND MAGNIFICENT SLASHES ANYMORE...
BUT YOU'RE GOING TO CONTINUE TO DO KENDO IN COLLEGE, RIGHT?
SHUP
THE NEXT MATCH ...
...WILL TRULY...
...BE MY LAST...

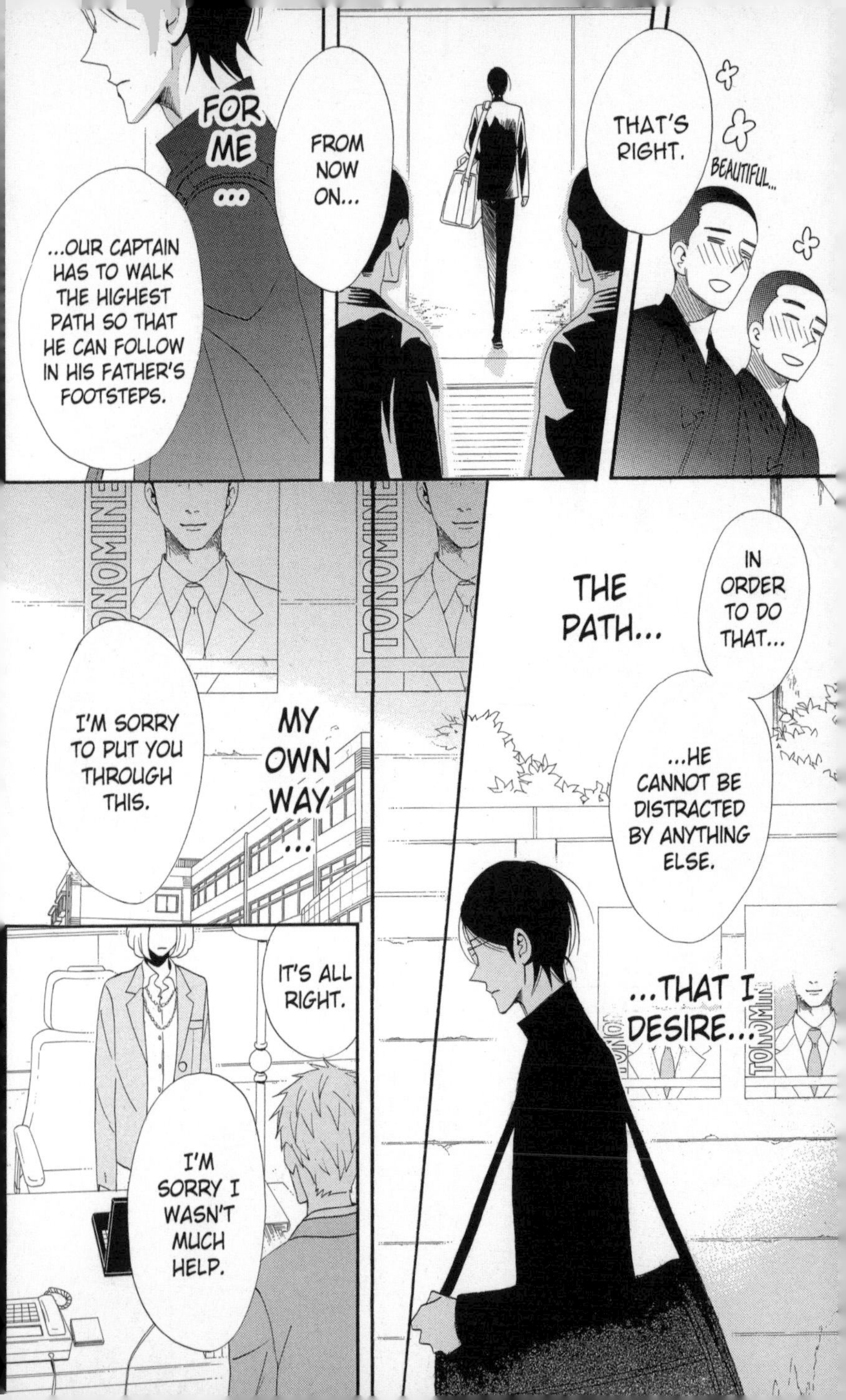
THAT'S RIGHT.
BEAUTIFUL...
FROM NOW ON...
FOR ME ...
...OUR CAPTAIN HAS TO WALK THE HIGHEST PATH SO THAT HE CAN FOLLOW IN HIS FATHER'S FOOTSTEPS.
IN ORDER TO DO THAT...
THE PATH...
...HE CANNOT BE DISTRACTED BY ANYTHING ELSE.
...THAT I DESIRE...
MY OWN WAY...!
I'M SORRY TO PUT YOU THROUGH THIS.
IT'S ALL RIGHT.
I'M SORRY I WASN'T MUCH HELP.

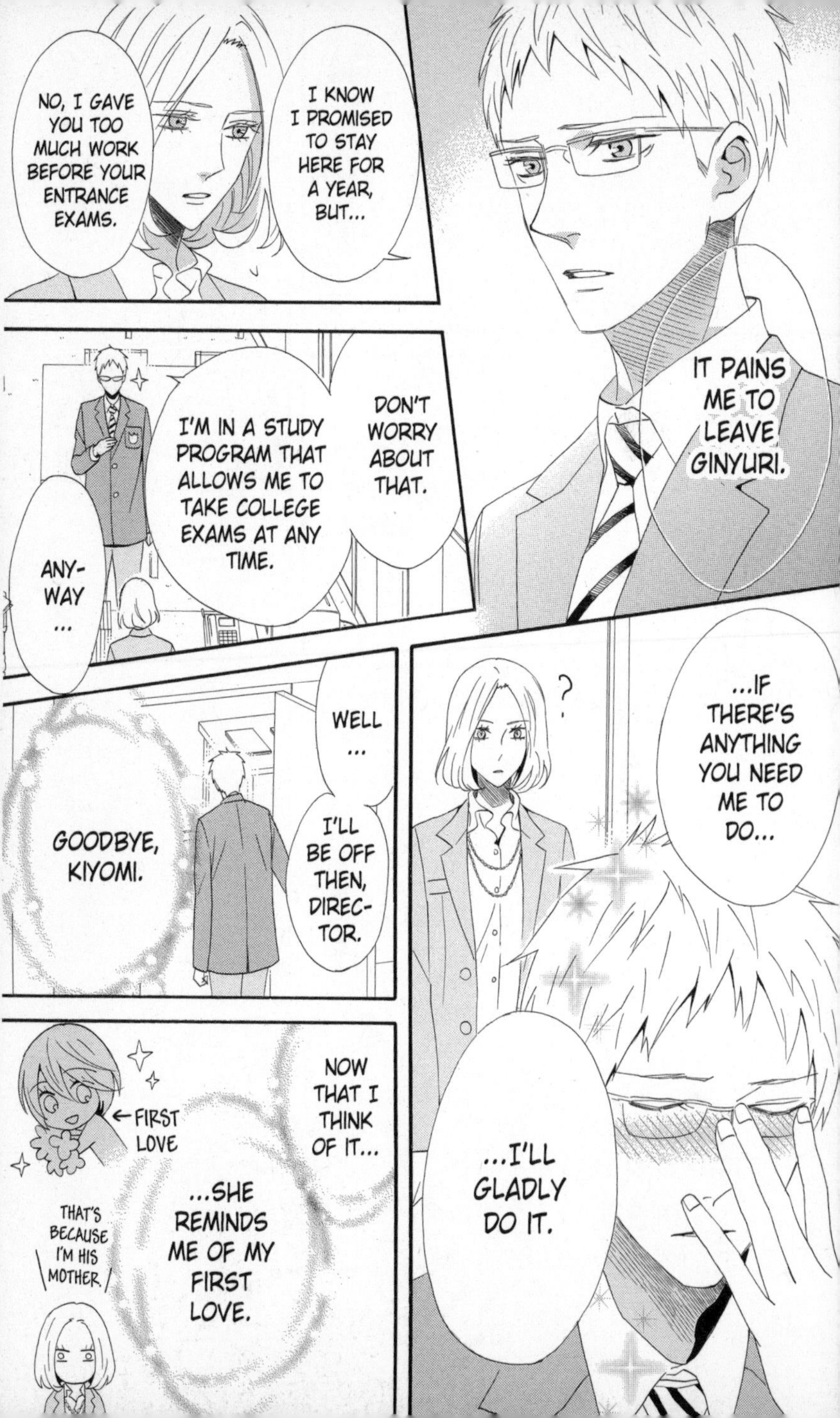
IT PAINS ME TO LEAVE GINYURI.
I KNOW I PROMISED TO STAY HERE FOR A YEAR, BUT...
NO, I GAVE YOU TOO MUCH WORK BEFORE YOUR ENTRANCE EXAMS.
DON'T WORRY ABOUT THAT.
I'M IN A STUDY PROGRAM THAT ALLOWS ME TO TAKE COLLEGE EXAMS AT ANY TIME.
ANY-WAY...
...IF THERE'S ANYTHING YOU NEED ME TO DO...
...I'LL GLADLY DO IT.
WELL...
I'LL BE OFF THEN, DIRECTOR.
GOODBYE, KIYOMI.
NOW THAT I THINK OF IT...
...SHE REMINDS ME OF MY FIRST LOVE.
FIRST LOVE
THAT'S BECAUSE I'M HIS MOTHER.

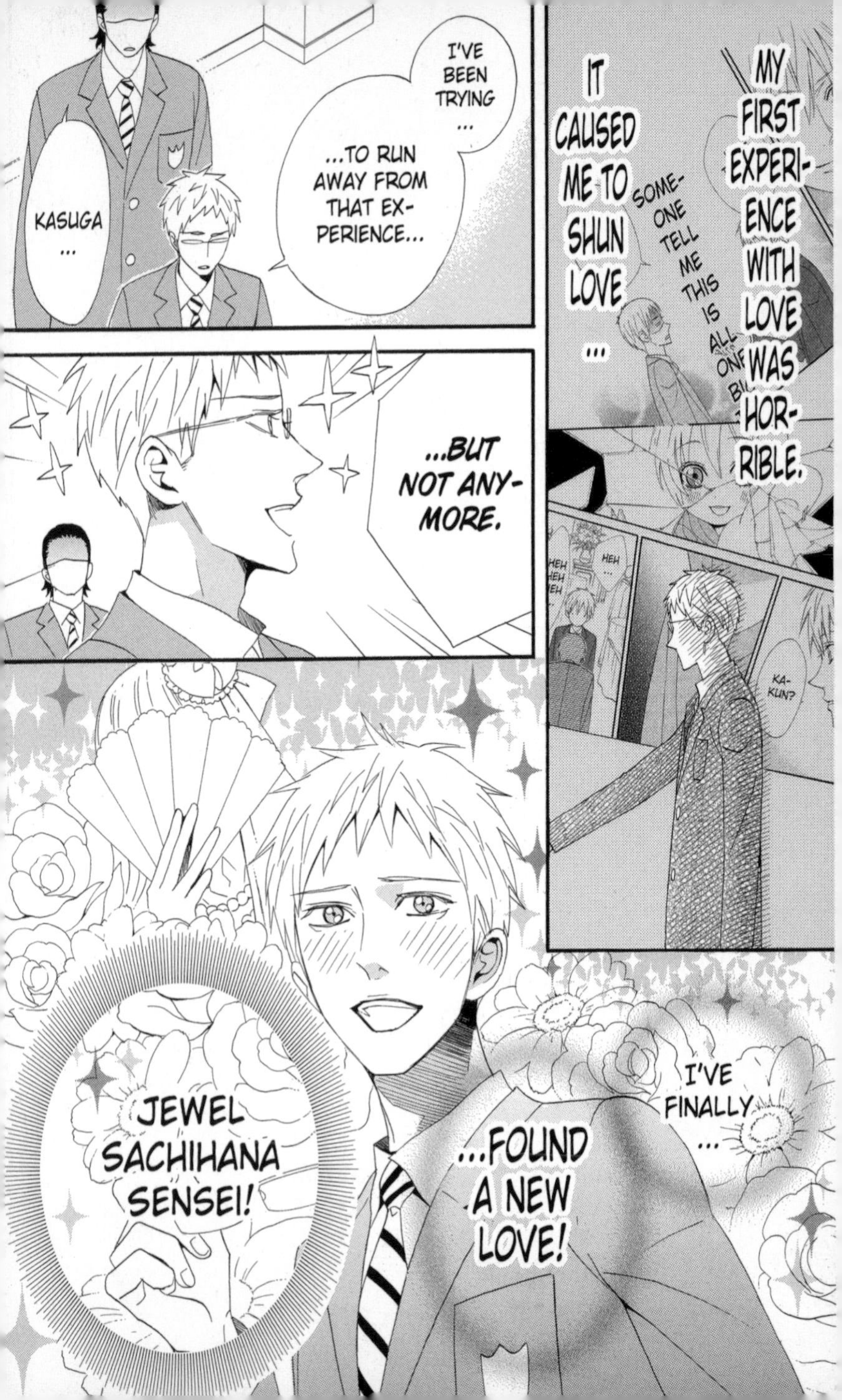

MY FIRST EXPERI-ENCE WITH LOVE WAS HOR-RIBLE.
SOME-ONE TELL ME THIS IS ALL
IT CAUSED ME TO SHUN LOVE...
HEH HEH HEH
HEH...
KA-KUN?
I'VE BEEN TRYING...
...TO RUN AWAY FROM THAT EX-PERIENCE...
KASUGA...
...BUT NOT ANY-MORE.
I'VE FINALLY...
...FOUND A NEW LOVE!
JEWEL SACHIHANA SENSEI!

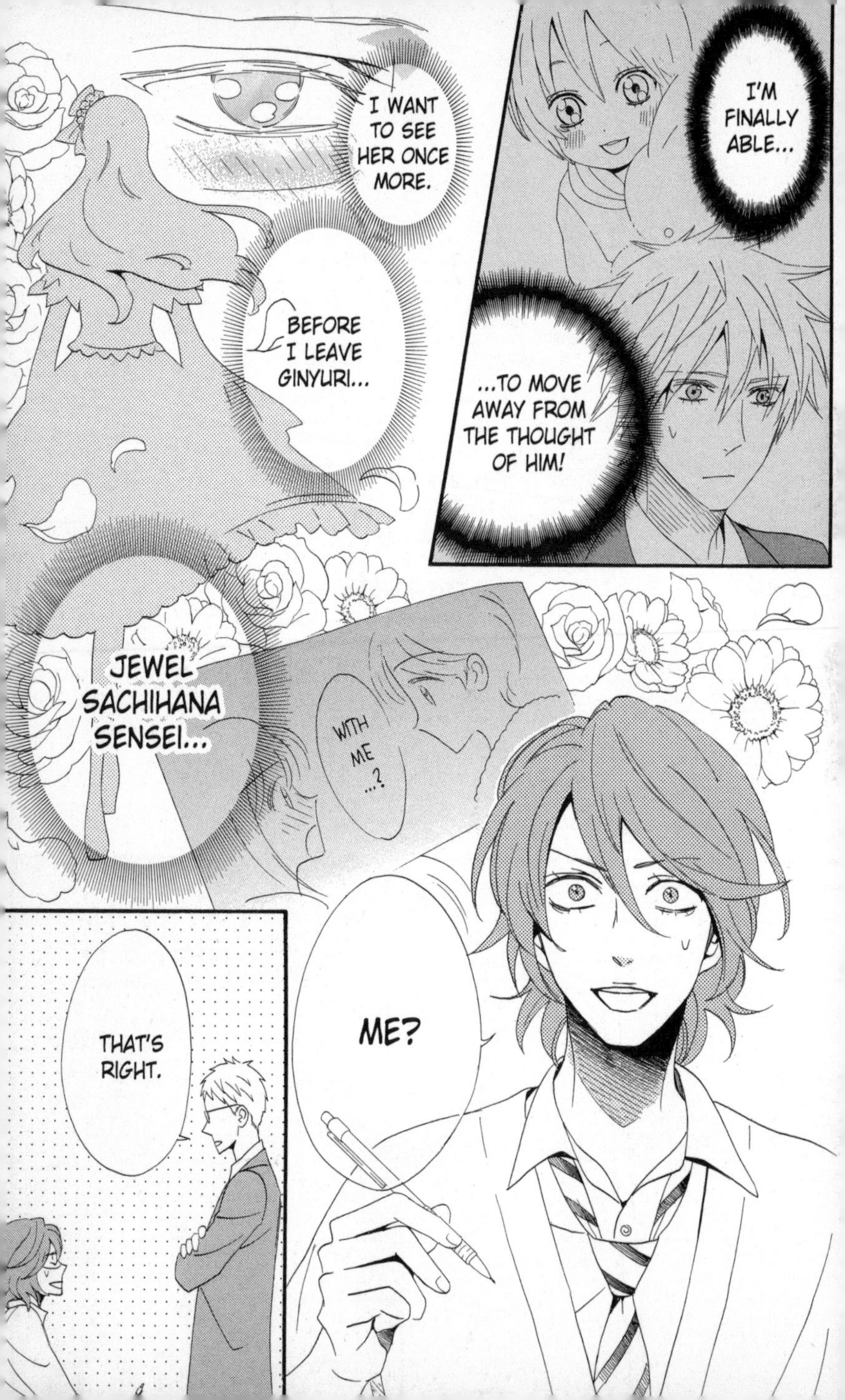
I'M FINALLY ABLE...
...TO MOVE AWAY FROM THE THOUGHT OF HIM!
I WANT TO SEE HER ONCE MORE.
BEFORE I LEAVE GINYURI...
JEWEL SACHIHANA SENSEI...
WITH ME ...?
ME?
THAT'S RIGHT.

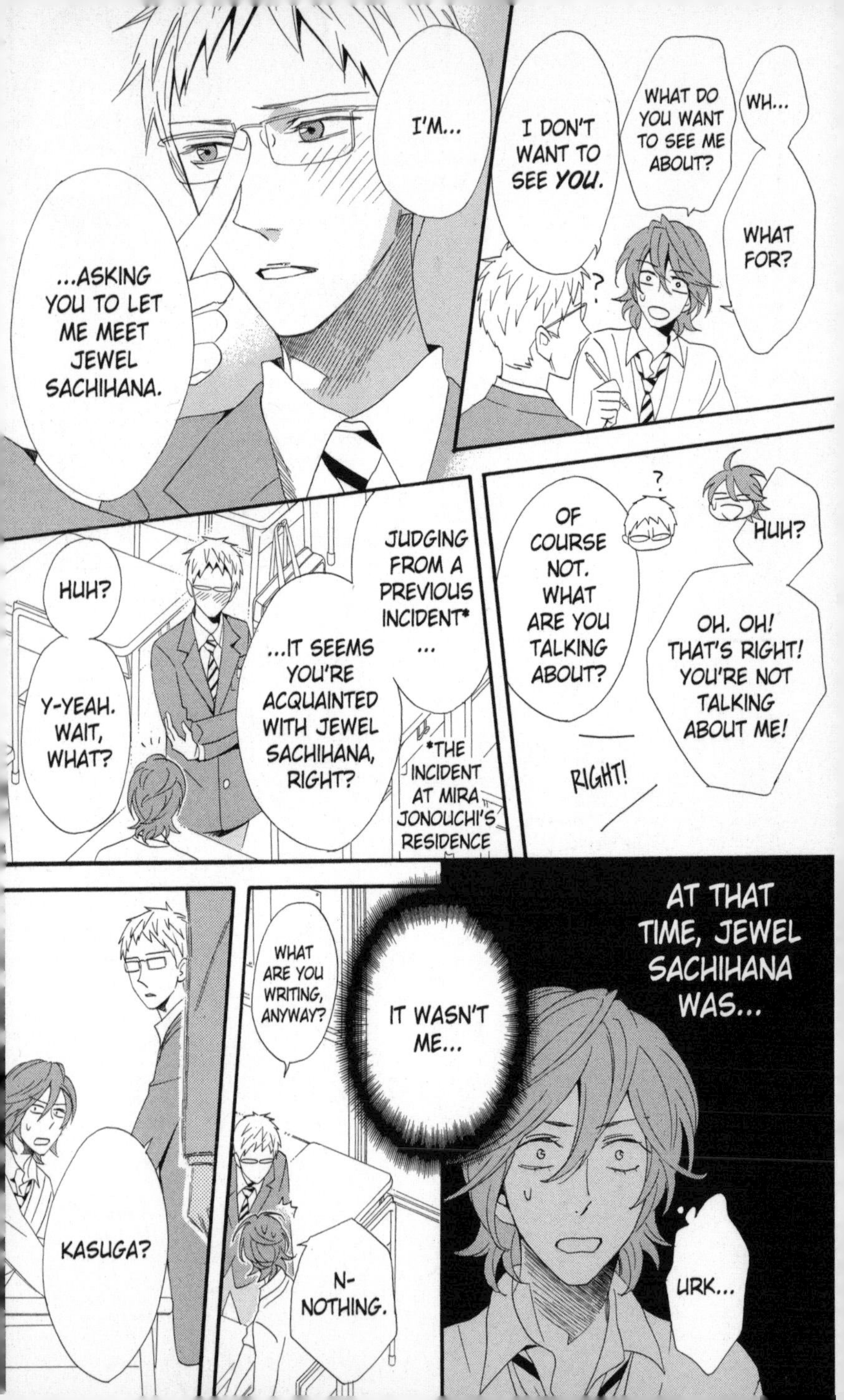
WH...
WHAT FOR?
WHAT DO YOU WANT TO SEE ME ABOUT?
I DON'T WANT TO SEE *YOU*.
I'M...
...ASKING YOU TO LET ME MEET JEWEL SACHIHANA.
HUH?
OF COURSE NOT. WHAT ARE YOU TALKING ABOUT?
OH. OH! THAT'S RIGHT! YOU'RE NOT TALKING ABOUT ME!
RIGHT!
JUDGING FROM A PREVIOUS INCIDENT* ...
...IT SEEMS YOU'RE ACQUAINTED WITH JEWEL SACHIHANA, RIGHT?
*THE INCIDENT AT MIRA JONOUCHI'S RESIDENCE
HUH?
Y-YEAH. WAIT, WHAT?
AT THAT TIME, JEWEL SACHIHANA WAS...
IT WASN'T ME...
URK...
WHAT ARE YOU WRITING, ANYWAY?
N-NOTHING.
KASUGA?

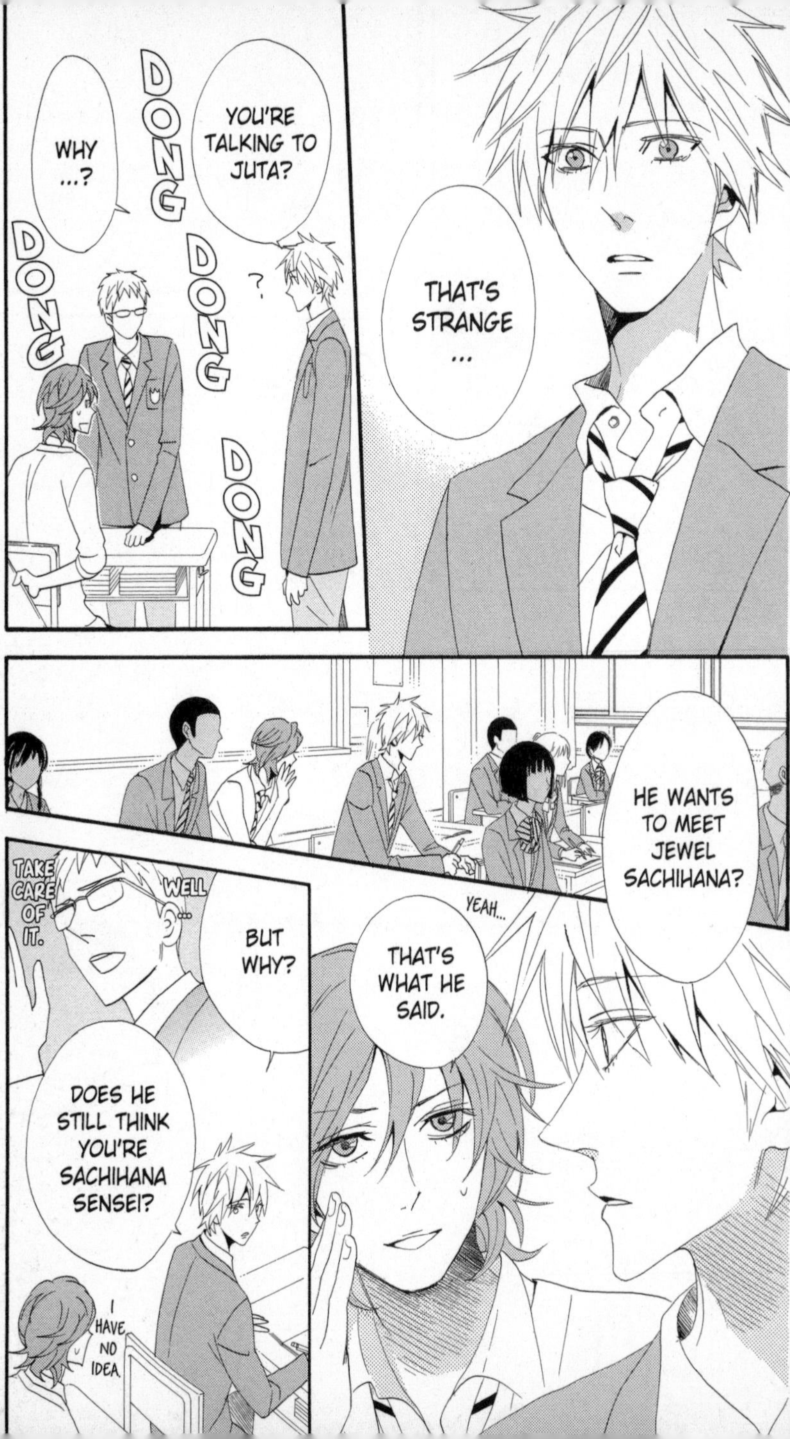
THAT'S STRANGE ...
YOU'RE TALKING TO JUTA?
DONG DONG
?
WHY ...?
DONG DONG
DONG DONG
HE WANTS TO MEET JEWEL SACHIHANA?
YEAH...
THAT'S WHAT HE SAID.
BUT WHY?
WELL ...
TAKE CARE OF IT.
DOES HE STILL THINK YOU'RE SACHIHANA SENSEI?
I HAVE NO IDEA.

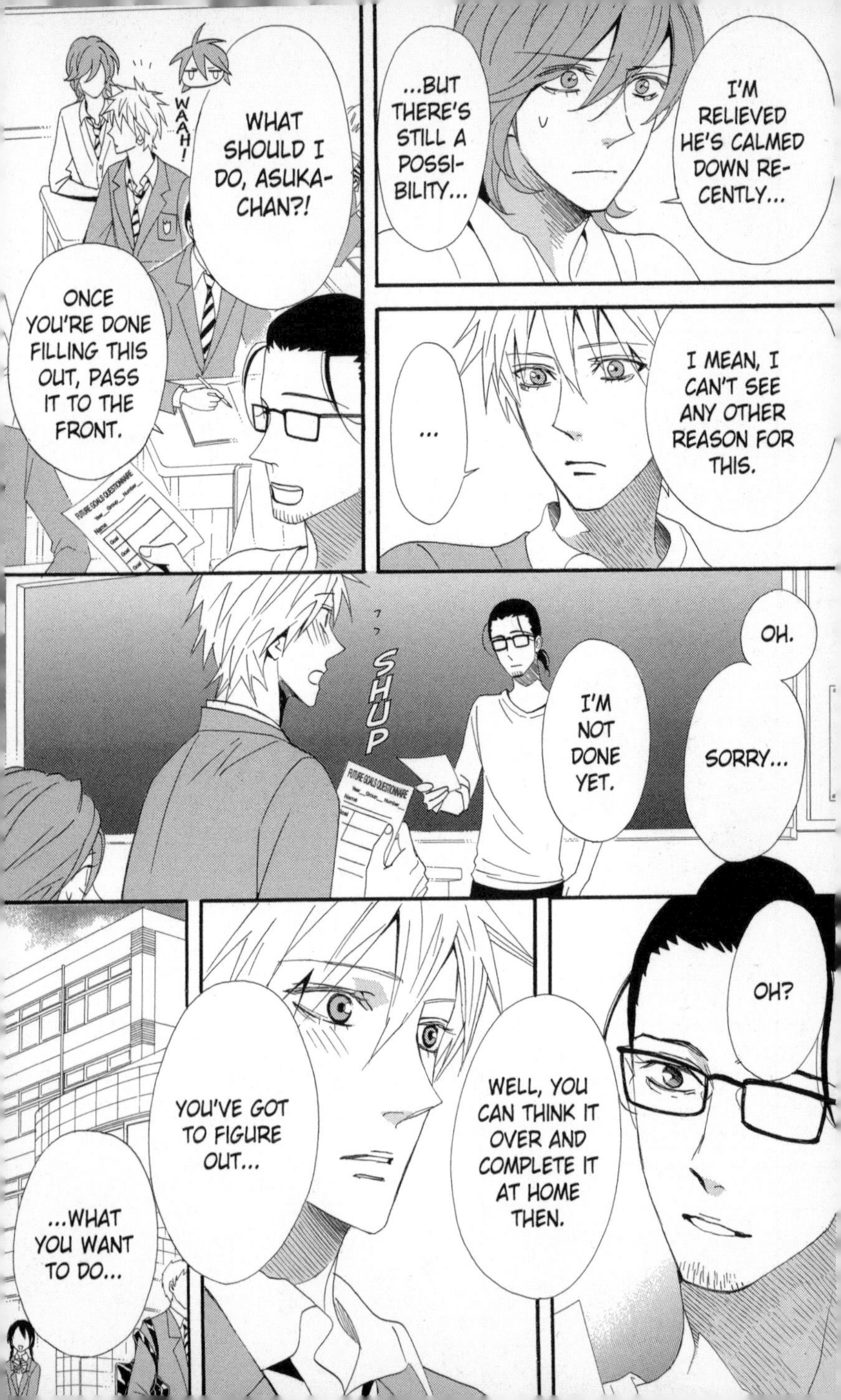
I'M RELIEVED HE'S CALMED DOWN RE-CENTLY...
...BUT THERE'S STILL A POSSI-BILITY...
I MEAN, I CAN'T SEE ANY OTHER REASON FOR THIS.
...
WAAH!
WHAT SHOULD I DO, ASUKA-CHAN?!
ONCE YOU'RE DONE FILLING THIS OUT, PASS IT TO THE FRONT.
FUTURE GOALS QUESTIONNAIRE
OH.
SORRY...
I'M NOT DONE YET.
SHUP
FUTURE GOALS QUESTIONNAIRE
OH?
WELL, YOU CAN THINK IT OVER AND COMPLETE IT AT HOME THEN.
YOU'VE GOT TO FIGURE OUT...
...WHAT YOU WANT TO DO...

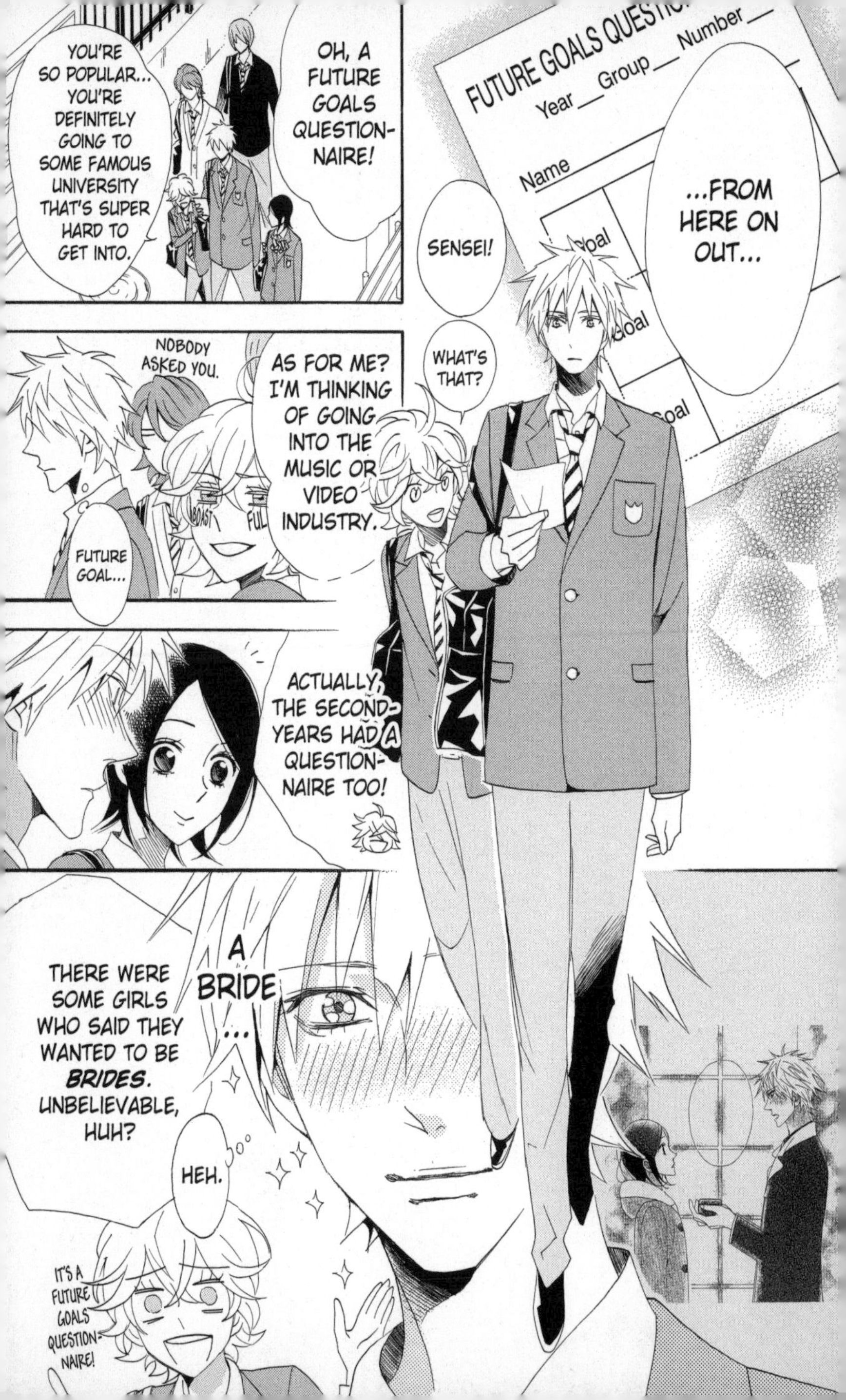

FUTURE GOALS QUESTI
Year ___ Group ___ Number ___
Name
Goal
Goal
Goal
...FROM HERE ON OUT...
SENSEI!
WHAT'S THAT?
OH, A FUTURE GOALS QUESTION-NAIRE!
YOU'RE SO POPULAR... YOU'RE DEFINITELY GOING TO SOME FAMOUS UNIVERSITY THAT'S SUPER HARD TO GET INTO.
AS FOR ME? I'M THINKING OF GOING INTO THE MUSIC OR VIDEO INDUSTRY.
NOBODY ASKED YOU.
BOAST
FUL
FUTURE GOAL...
ACTUALLY, THE SECOND-YEARS HAD A QUESTION-NAIRE TOO!
A BRIDE...
THERE WERE SOME GIRLS WHO SAID THEY WANTED TO BE **BRIDES**. UNBELIEVABLE, HUH?
HEH.
IT'S A FUTURE GOALS QUESTION-NAIRE!

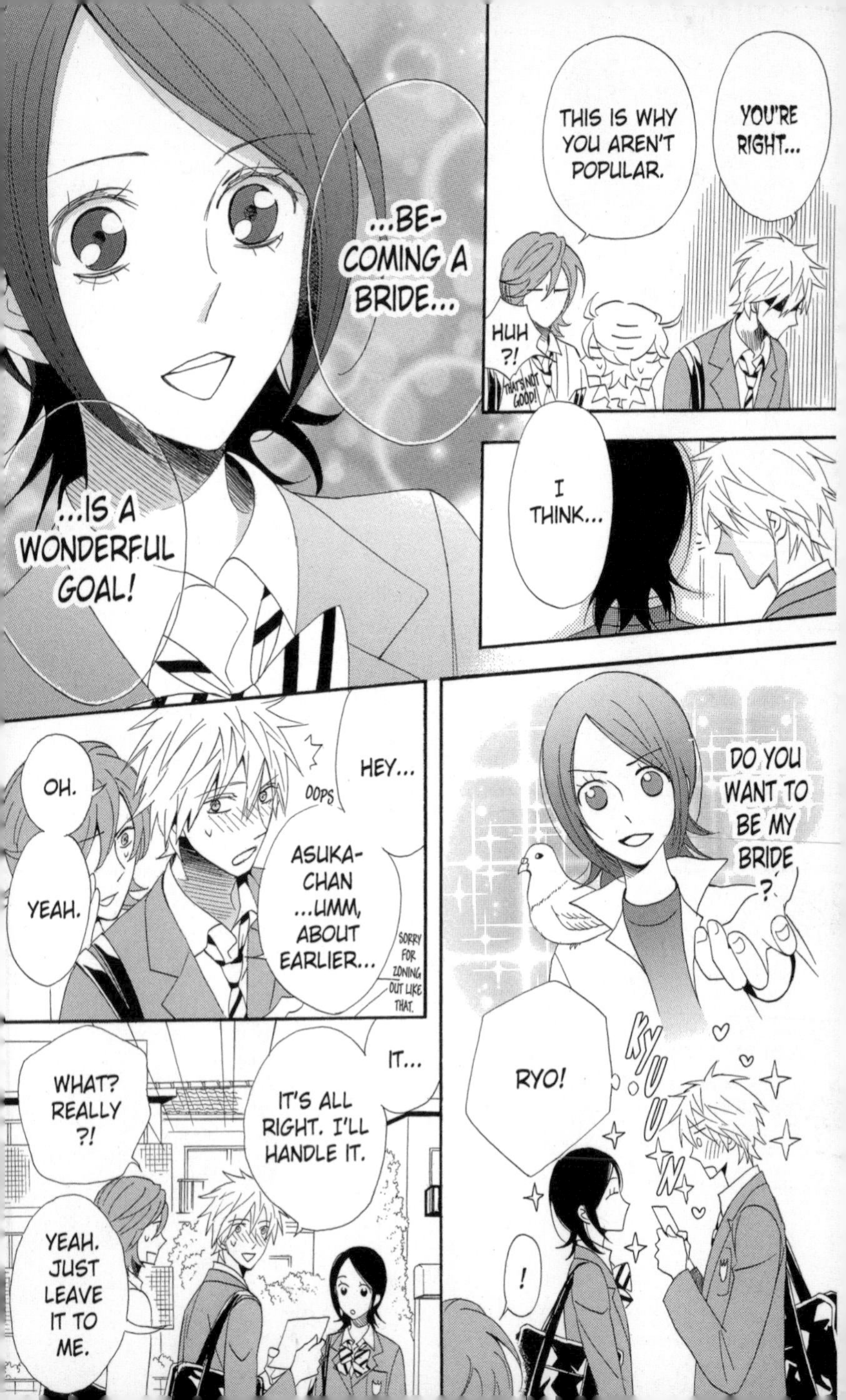
YOU'RE RIGHT...
THIS IS WHY YOU AREN'T POPULAR.
HUH ?!
THAT'S NOT GOOD!
I THINK...
...BE-COMING A BRIDE...
...IS A WONDERFUL GOAL!
DO YOU WANT TO BE MY BRIDE ?
HEY...
OOPS
ASUKA-CHAN ...UMM, ABOUT EARLIER...
SORRY FOR ZONING OUT LIKE THAT.
OH.
YEAH.
KYUUN
RYO!
!
IT...
IT'S ALL RIGHT. I'LL HANDLE IT.
WHAT? REALLY ?!
YEAH. JUST LEAVE IT TO ME.

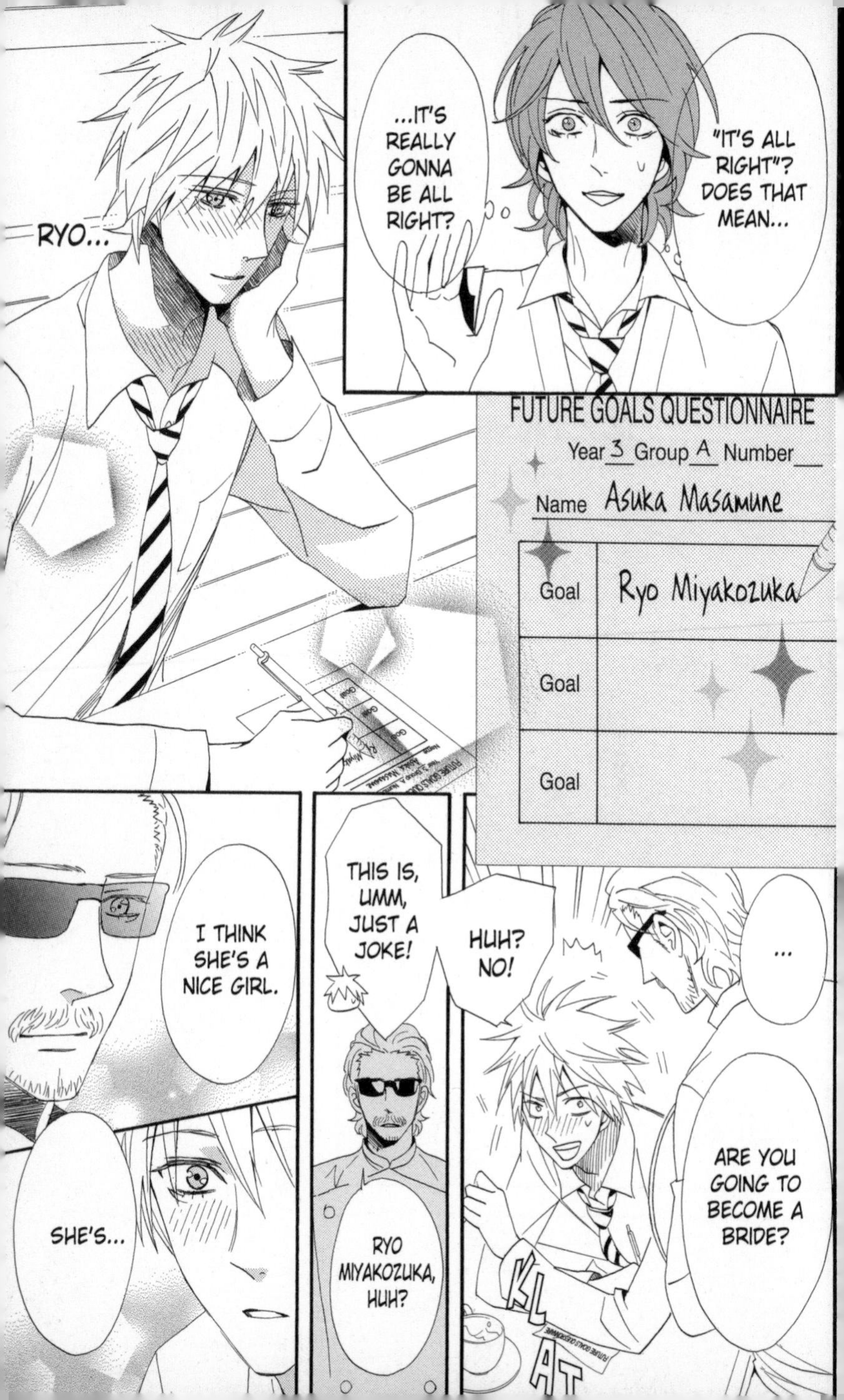

"IT'S ALL RIGHT"? DOES THAT MEAN...
...IT'S REALLY GONNA BE ALL RIGHT?
FUTURE GOALS QUESTIONNAIRE
Year 3 Group A Number
Name Asuka Masamune
Goal Ryo Miyakozuka
Goal
Goal
RYO...
...
ARE YOU GOING TO BECOME A BRIDE?
KLAT
HUH? NO!
THIS IS, UMM, JUST A JOKE!
RYO MIYAKOZUKA, HUH?
I THINK SHE'S A NICE GIRL.
SHE'S...

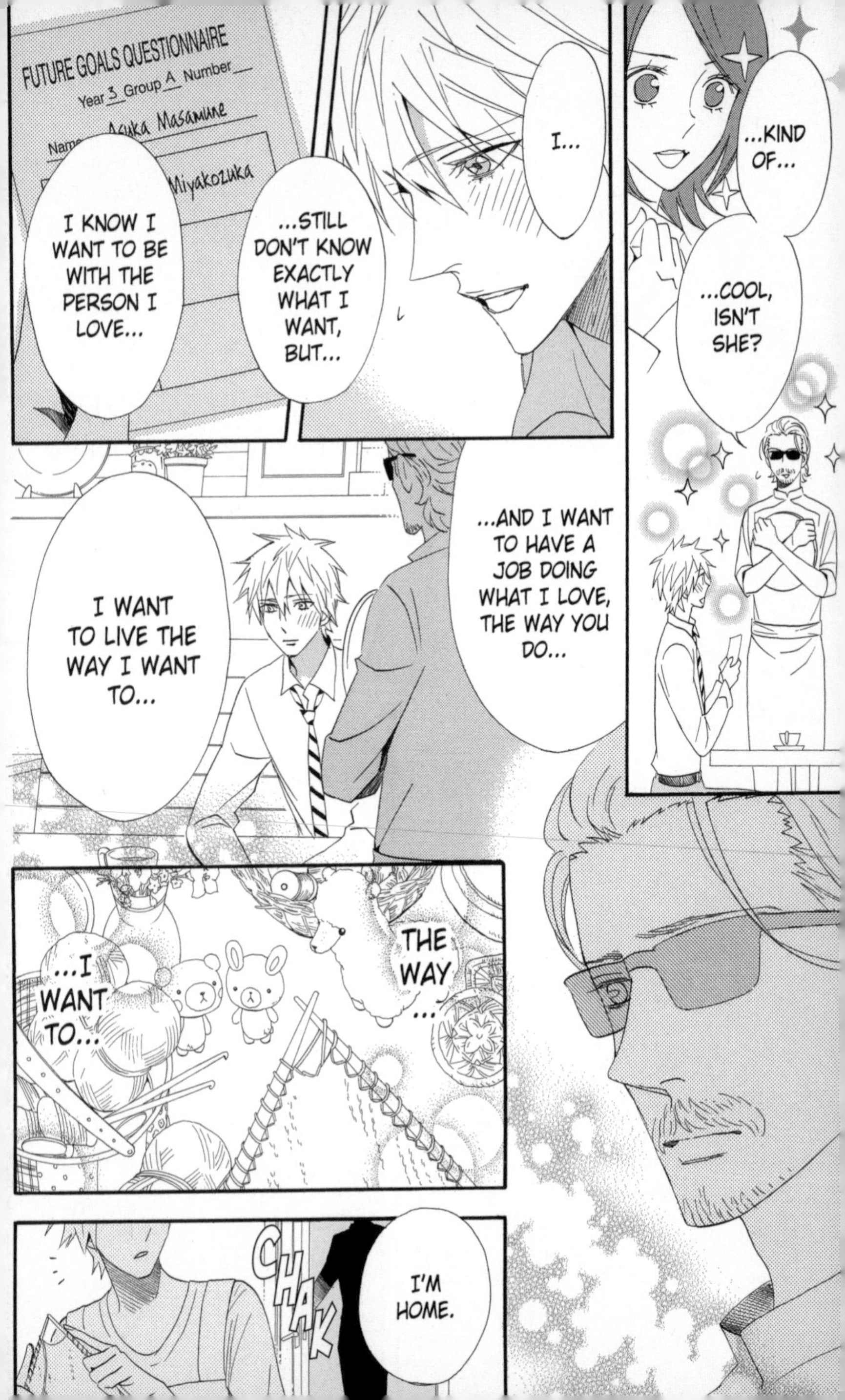
...KIND OF...
...COOL, ISN'T SHE?
I...
...STILL DON'T KNOW EXACTLY WHAT I WANT, BUT...
FUTURE GOALS QUESTIONNAIRE
Year 3 Group A Number
Name Asuka Masamune
Miyakozuka
I KNOW I WANT TO BE WITH THE PERSON I LOVE...
...AND I WANT TO HAVE A JOB DOING WHAT I LOVE, THE WAY YOU DO...
I WANT TO LIVE THE WAY I WANT TO...
THE WAY...
...I WANT TO...
CHAK
I'M HOME.

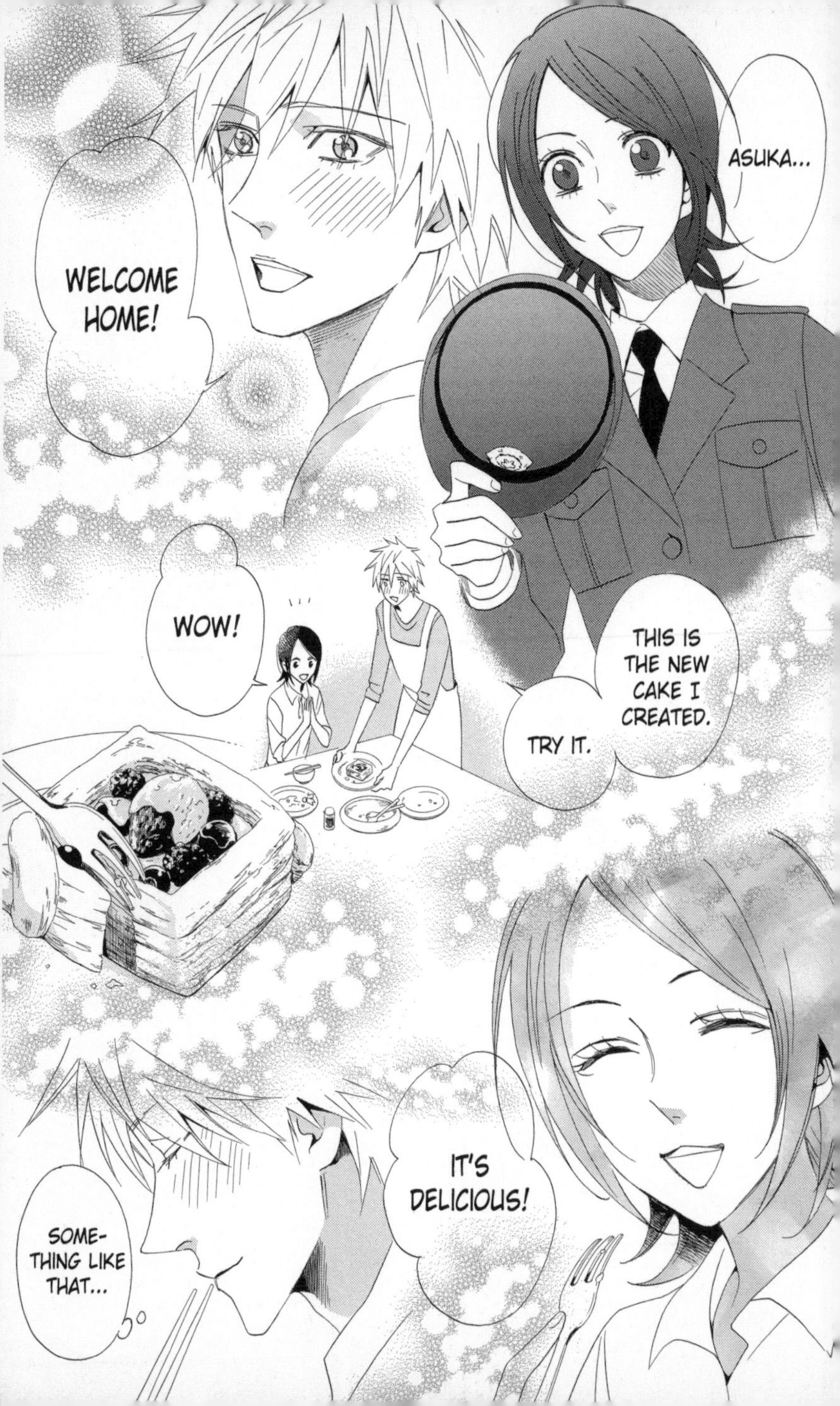
ASUKA...
WELCOME HOME!
THIS IS THE NEW CAKE I CREATED.
TRY IT.
WOW!
IT'S DELICIOUS!
SOME-THING LIKE THAT...

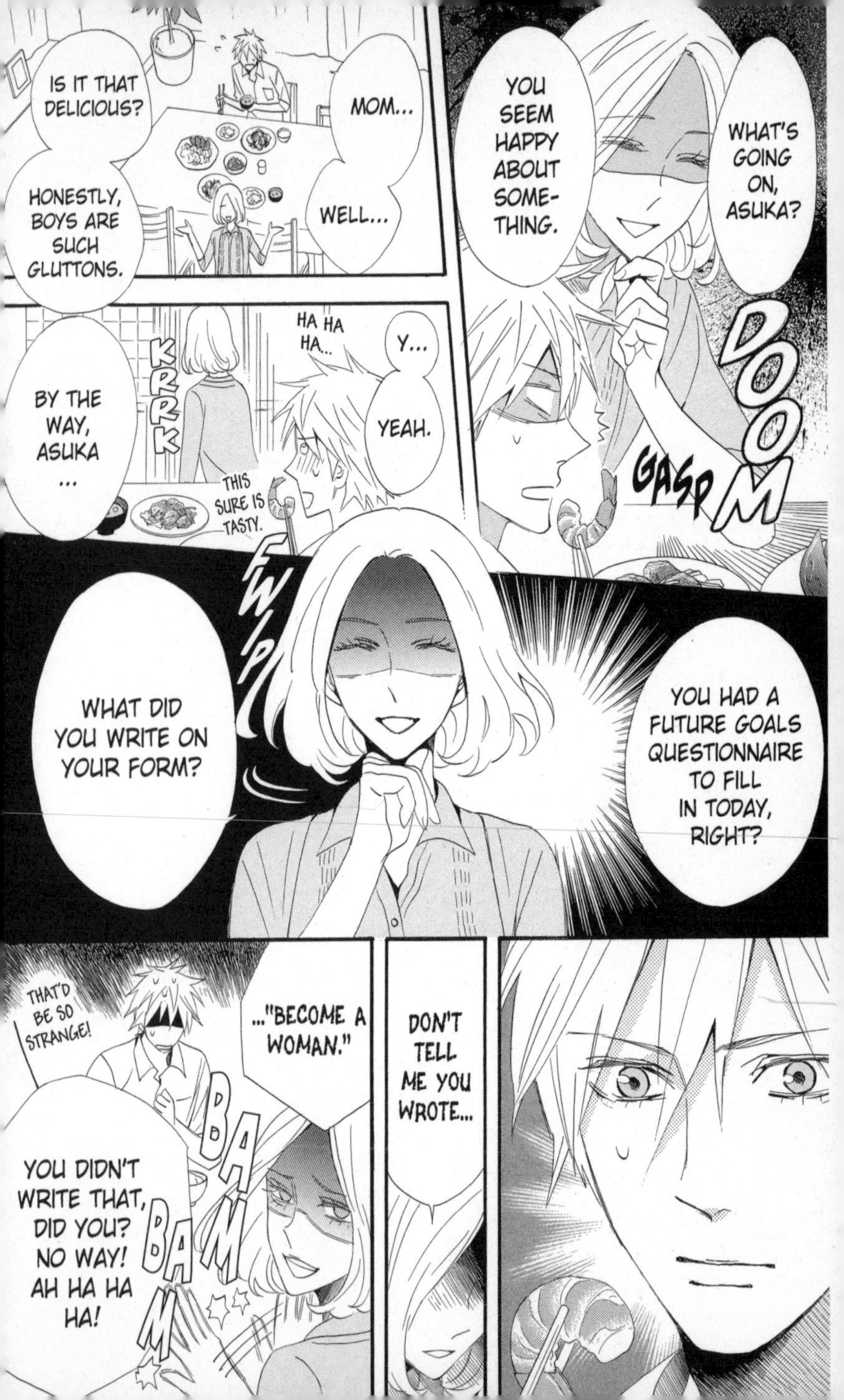
WHAT'S GOING ON, ASUKA?
YOU SEEM HAPPY ABOUT SOME-THING.
DOOOM
GASP
MOM...
WELL...
IS IT THAT DELICIOUS?
HONESTLY, BOYS ARE SUCH GLUTTONS.
Y...
YEAH.
HA HA HA...
KRRK
BY THE WAY, ASUKA...
THIS SURE IS TASTY.
YOU HAD A FUTURE GOALS QUESTIONNAIRE TO FILL IN TODAY, RIGHT?
FWIP
WHAT DID YOU WRITE ON YOUR FORM?
DON'T TELL ME YOU WROTE...
..."BECOME A WOMAN."
THAT'D BE SO STRANGE!
BAM
YOU DIDN'T WRITE THAT, DID YOU? NO WAY! AH HA HA HA!
BAM

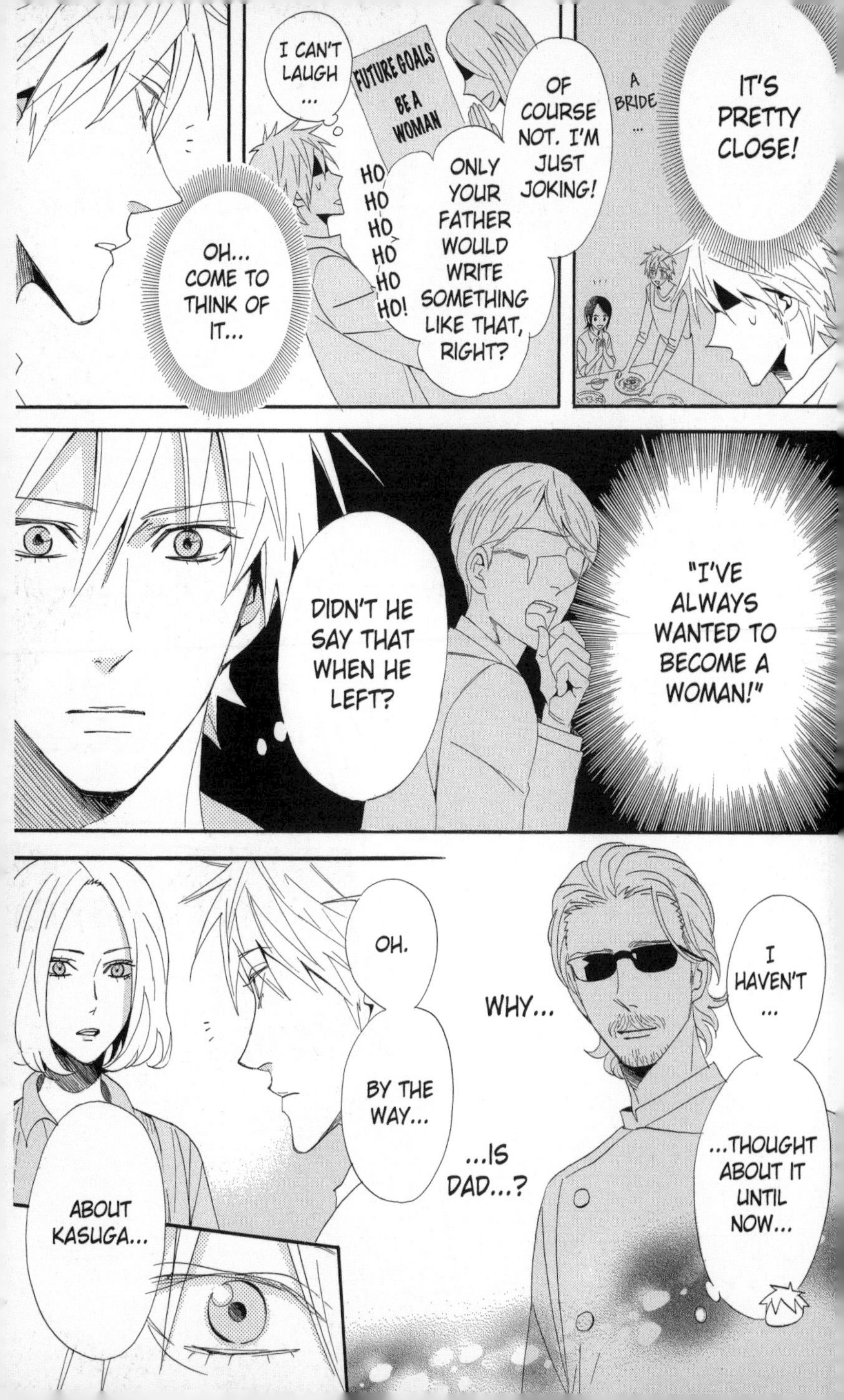
IT'S PRETTY CLOSE!
A BRIDE ...
OF COURSE NOT. I'M JUST JOKING!
ONLY YOUR FATHER WOULD WRITE SOMETHING LIKE THAT, RIGHT?
HO HO HO HO HO HO!
FUTURE GOALS
BE A WOMAN
I CAN'T LAUGH ...
OH... COME TO THINK OF IT...
"I'VE ALWAYS WANTED TO BECOME A WOMAN!"
DIDN'T HE SAY THAT WHEN HE LEFT?
I HAVEN'T ...
...THOUGHT ABOUT IT UNTIL NOW...
WHY...
...IS DAD...?
OH.
BY THE WAY...
ABOUT KASUGA...

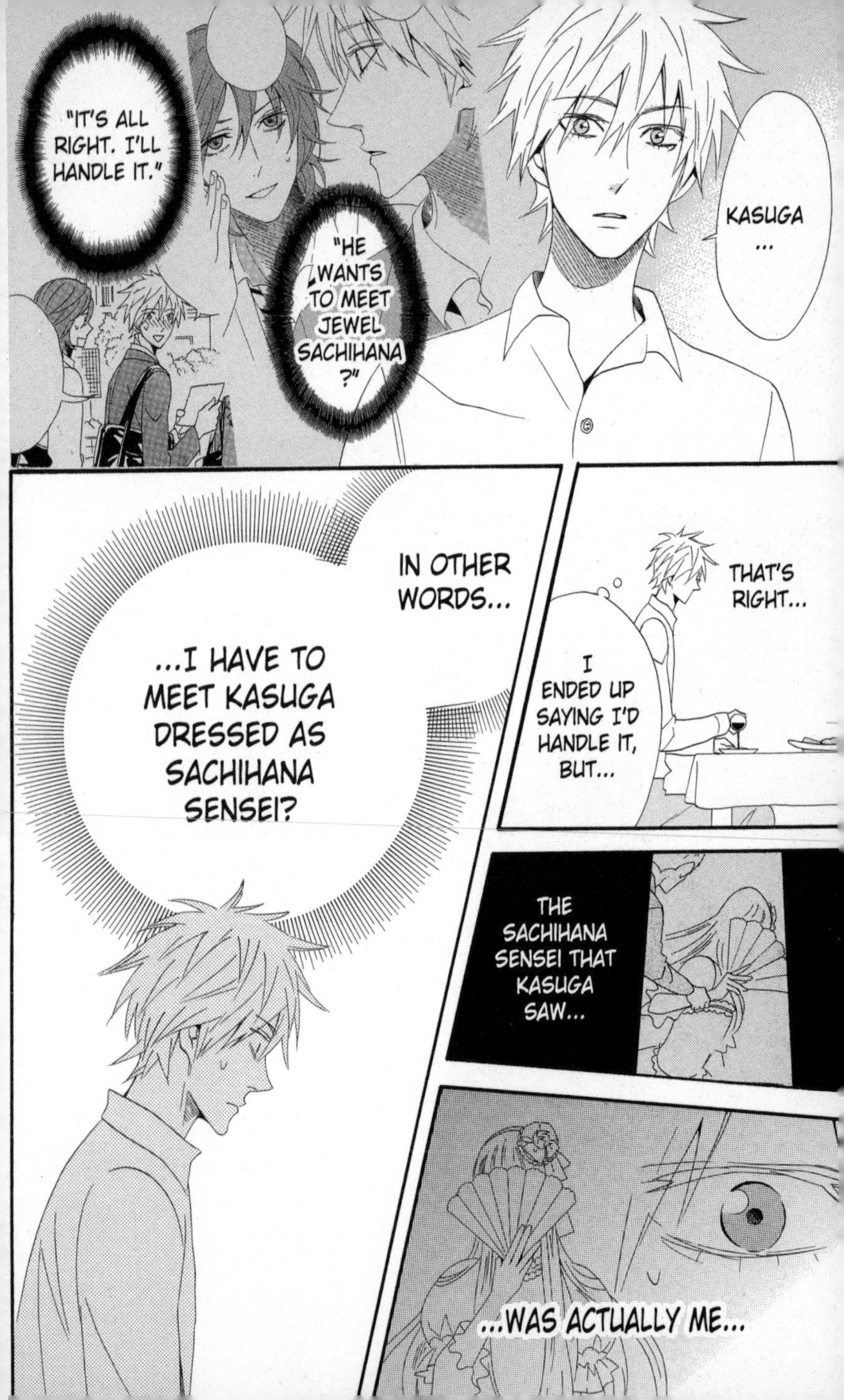
KASUGA ...
"HE WANTS TO MEET JEWEL SACHIHANA?"
"IT'S ALL RIGHT. I'LL HANDLE IT."
THAT'S RIGHT...
I ENDED UP SAYING I'D HANDLE IT, BUT...
THE SACHIHANA SENSEI THAT KASUGA SAW...
...WAS ACTUALLY ME...
IN OTHER WORDS...
...I HAVE TO MEET KASUGA DRESSED AS SACHIHANA SENSEI?

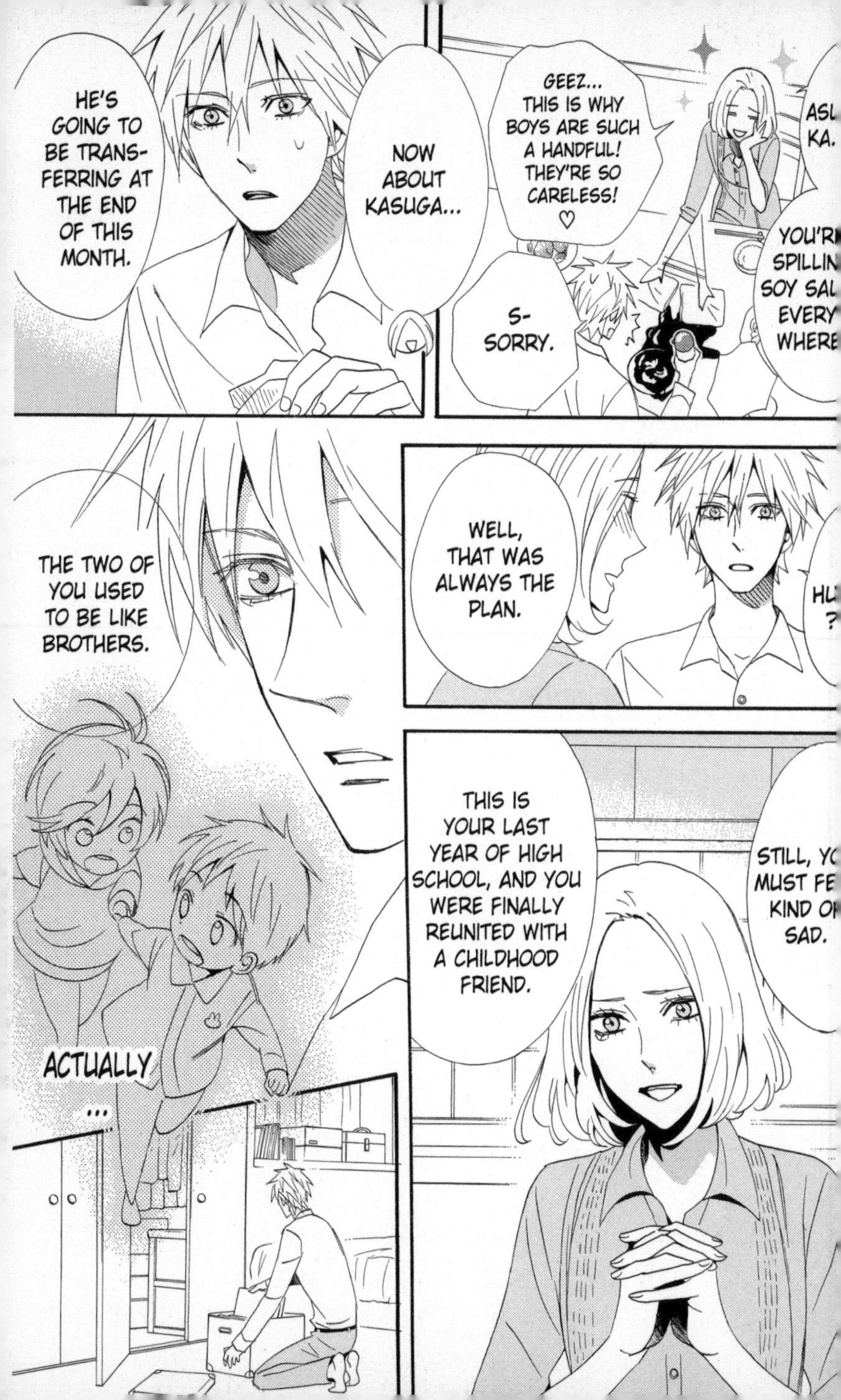
ASU KA.
YOU'R SPILLIN SOY SAU EVERY WHERE
GEEZ... THIS IS WHY BOYS ARE SUCH A HANDFUL! THEY'RE SO CARELESS! ♡
S- SORRY.
NOW ABOUT KASUGA...
HE'S GOING TO BE TRANS- FERRING AT THE END OF THIS MONTH.
HU ?
WELL, THAT WAS ALWAYS THE PLAN.
STILL, YO MUST FE KIND OF SAD.
THIS IS YOUR LAST YEAR OF HIGH SCHOOL, AND YOU WERE FINALLY REUNITED WITH A CHILDHOOD FRIEND.
THE TWO OF YOU USED TO BE LIKE BROTHERS.
ACTUALLY ...

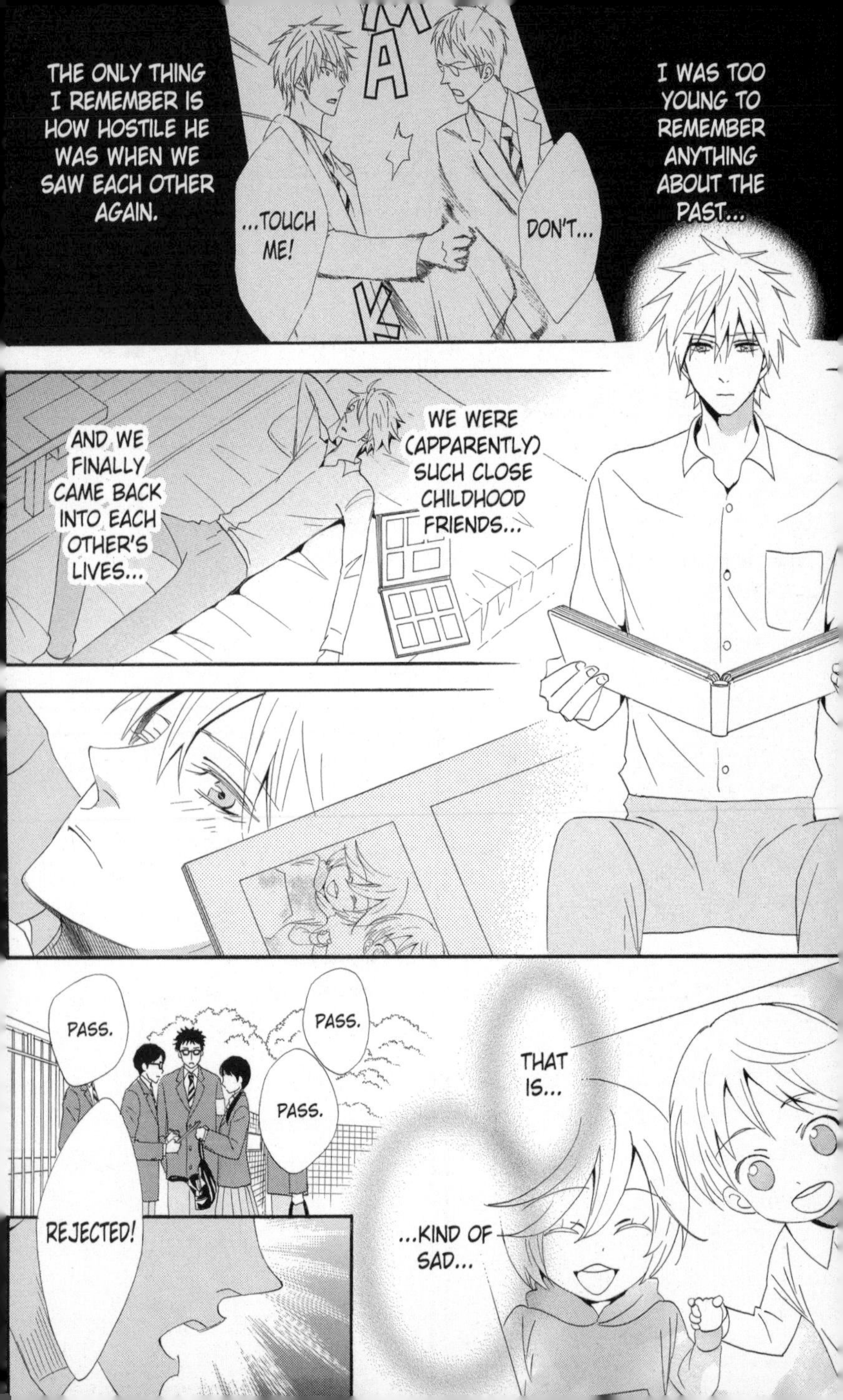
I WAS TOO YOUNG TO REMEMBER ANYTHING ABOUT THE PAST...
DON'T...
...TOUCH ME!
THE ONLY THING I REMEMBER IS HOW HOSTILE HE WAS WHEN WE SAW EACH OTHER AGAIN.
WE WERE (APPARENTLY) SUCH CLOSE CHILDHOOD FRIENDS...
AND WE FINALLY CAME BACK INTO EACH OTHER'S LIVES...
THAT IS...
...KIND OF SAD...
PASS.
PASS.
PASS.
REJECTED!

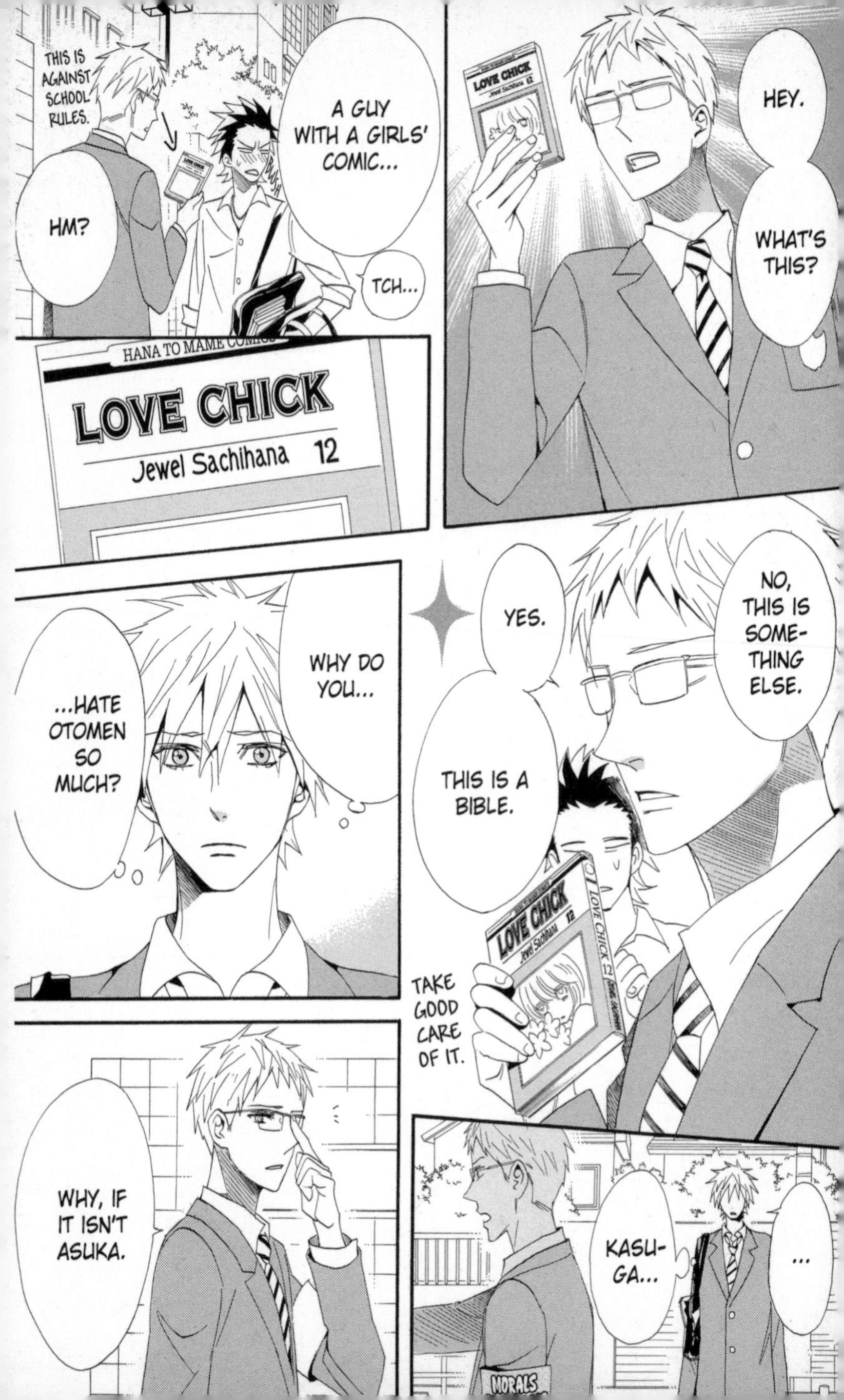
HEY.
WHAT'S THIS?
A GUY WITH A GIRLS' COMIC...
THIS IS AGAINST SCHOOL RULES.
BLUSH
TCH...
HM?
HANA TO MAME COMICS
LOVE CHICK
Jewel Sachihana 12
NO, THIS IS SOME-THING ELSE.
YES.
THIS IS A BIBLE.
TAKE GOOD CARE OF IT.
WHY DO YOU...
...HATE OTOMEN SO MUCH?
...
KASU-GA...
MORALS
WHY, IF IT ISN'T ASUKA.

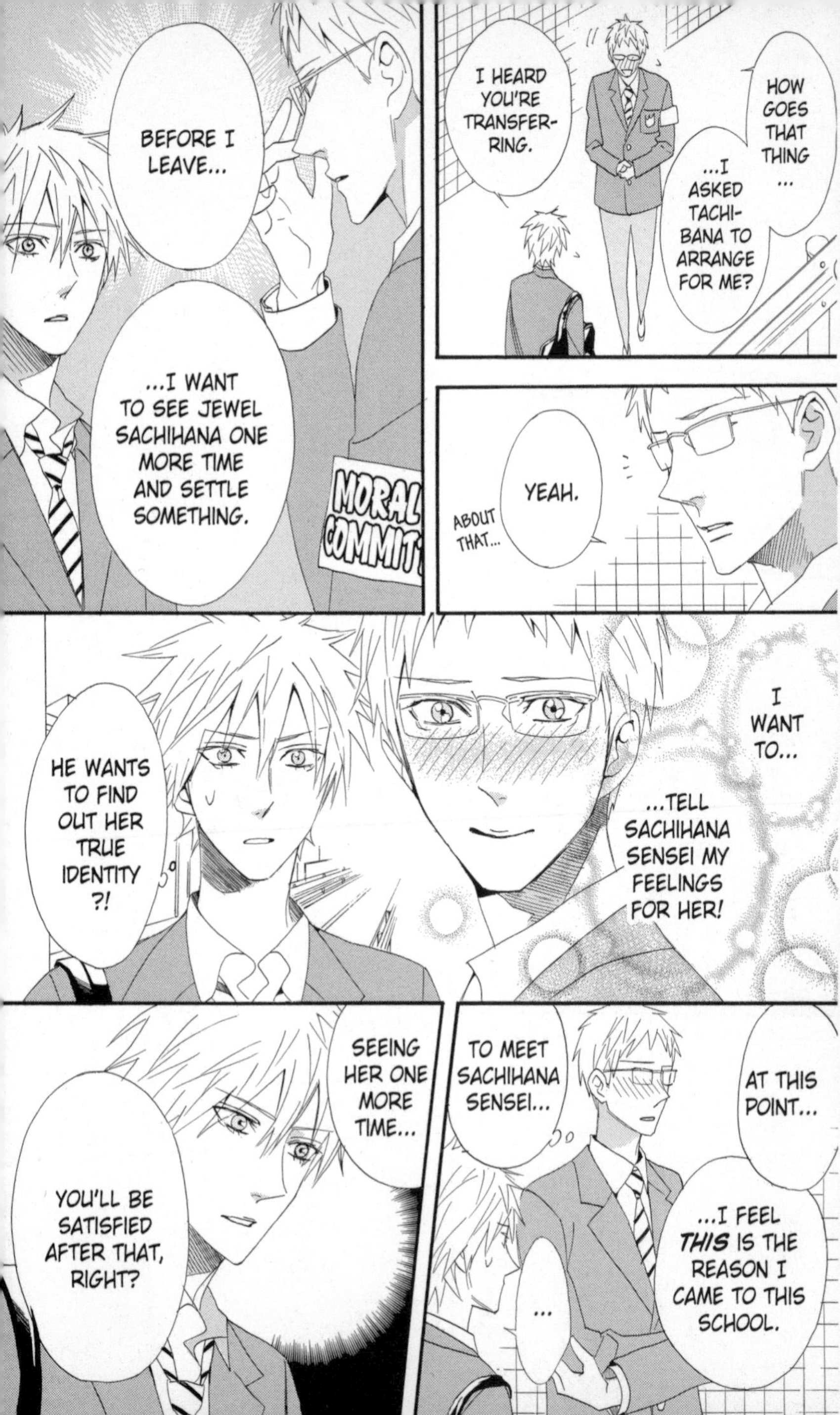
HOW GOES THAT THING...
...I ASKED TACHIBANA TO ARRANGE FOR ME?
I HEARD YOU'RE TRANSFERRING.
YEAH.
ABOUT THAT...
BEFORE I LEAVE...
...I WANT TO SEE JEWEL SACHIHANA ONE MORE TIME AND SETTLE SOMETHING.
MORAL COMMIT
I WANT TO...
...TELL SACHIHANA SENSEI MY FEELINGS FOR HER!
HE WANTS TO FIND OUT HER TRUE IDENTITY?!
AT THIS POINT...
...I FEEL *THIS* IS THE REASON I CAME TO THIS SCHOOL.
TO MEET SACHIHANA SENSEI...
...
SEEING HER ONE MORE TIME...
YOU'LL BE SATISFIED AFTER THAT, RIGHT?

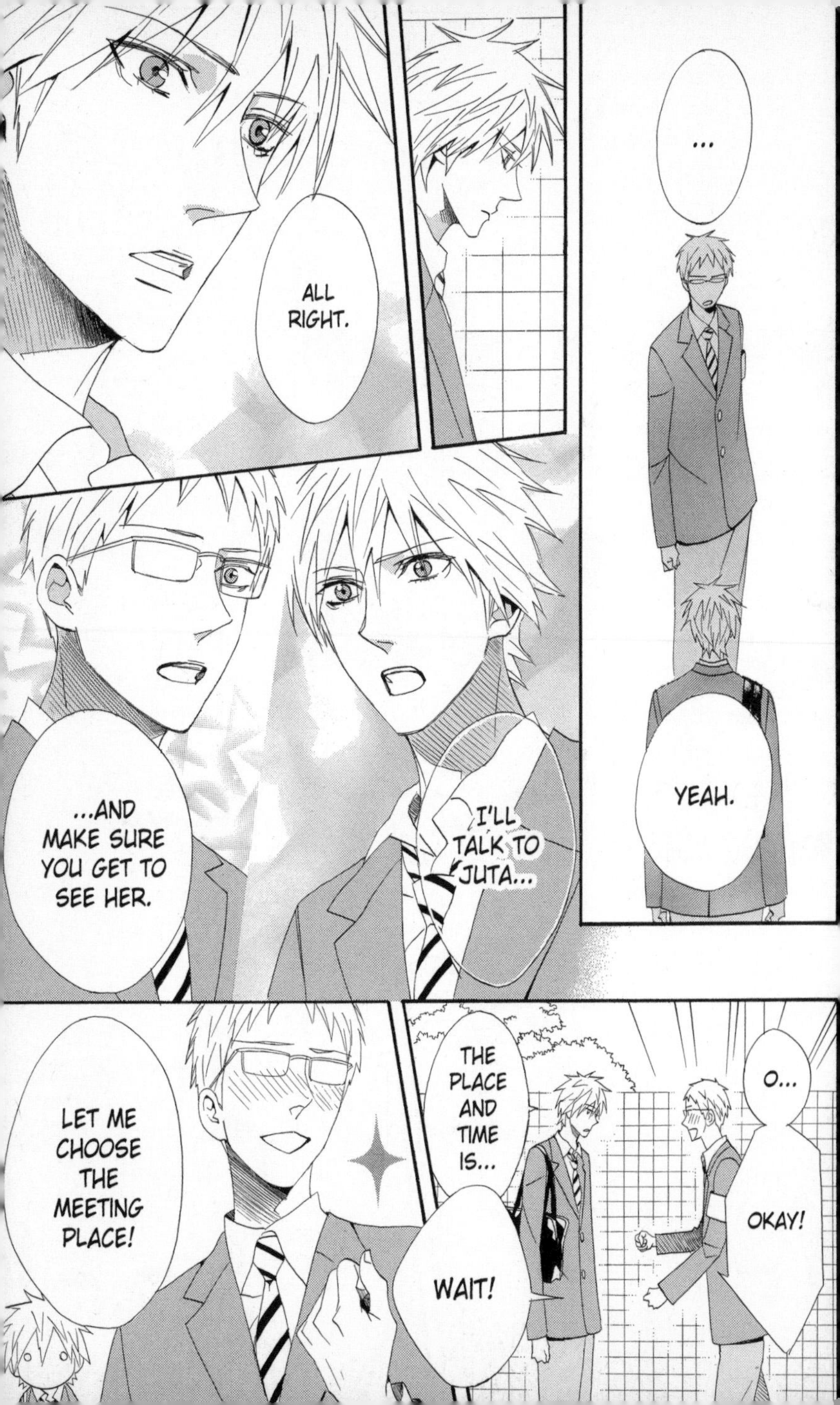
...
YEAH.
ALL RIGHT.
I'LL TALK TO JUTA...
...AND MAKE SURE YOU GET TO SEE HER.
O...
OKAY!
THE PLACE AND TIME IS...
WAIT!
LET ME CHOOSE THE MEETING PLACE!

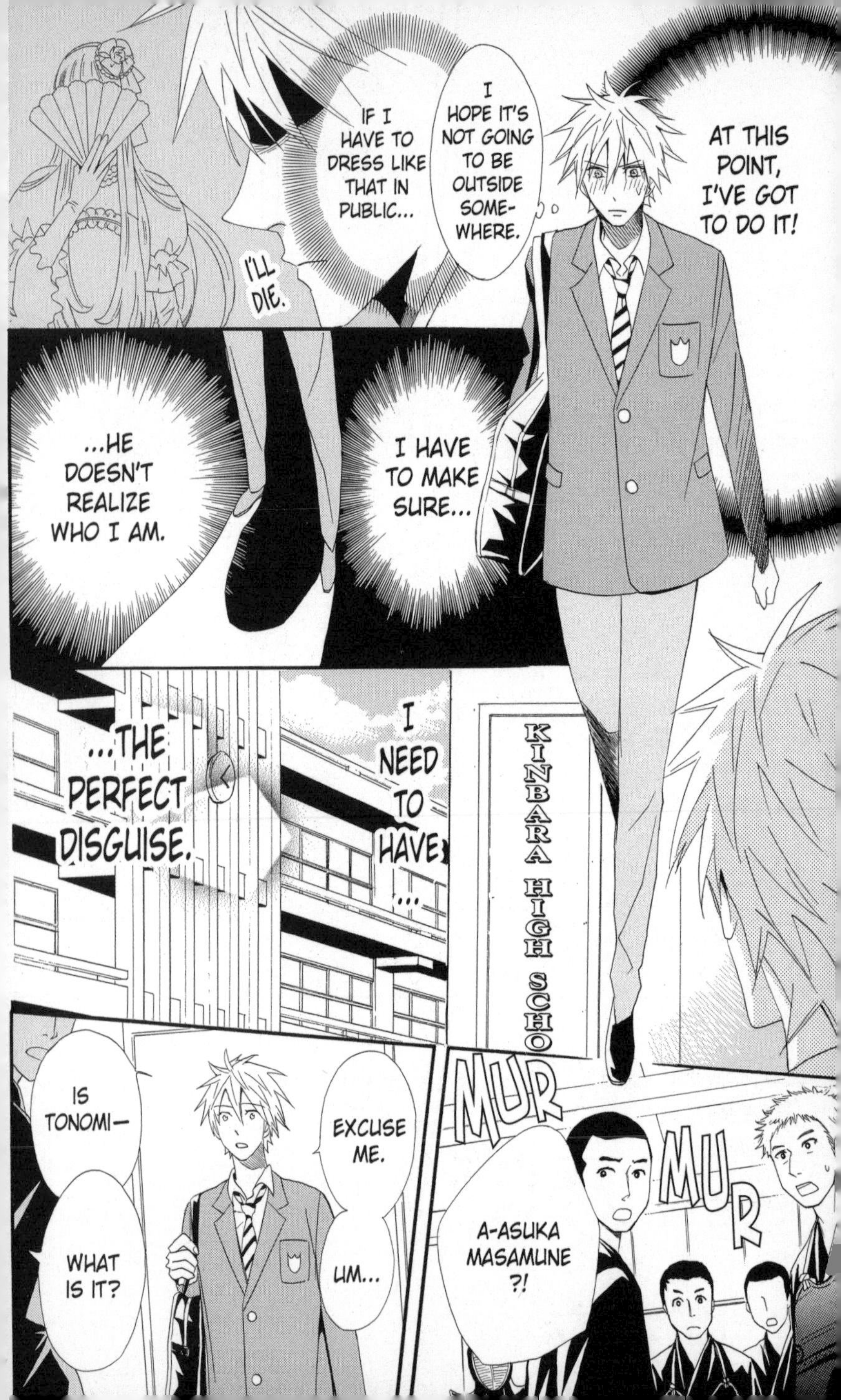
AT THIS POINT, I'VE GOT TO DO IT!
I HOPE IT'S NOT GOING TO BE OUTSIDE SOMEWHERE.
IF I HAVE TO DRESS LIKE THAT IN PUBLIC...
I'LL DIE.
I HAVE TO MAKE SURE...
...HE DOESN'T REALIZE WHO I AM.
KINBARA HIGH SCHO
I NEED TO HAVE...
...THE PERFECT DISGUISE.
MUR
MUR
A-ASUKA MASAMUNE ?!
EXCUSE ME.
UM...
IS TONOMI—
WHAT IS IT?

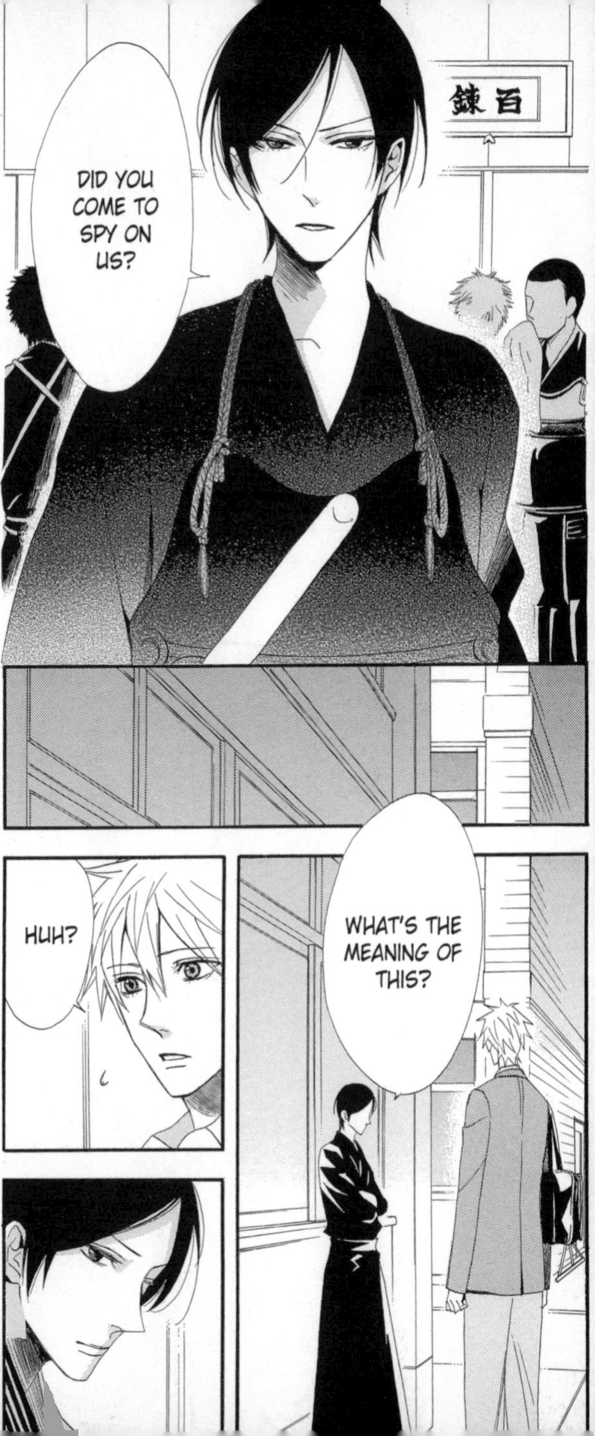
百錬
DID YOU COME TO SPY ON US?
WHAT'S THE MEANING OF THIS?
HUH?

I was actually planning to use Kasuga a lot more.

But because of the way the stories were going, he became rather forgettable.

I'd developed quite a bit of backstory, so I wanted to make use of that.

I think I might make him appear again someday. The next time I do, I'll give him a proper story.

Now it's Tonomine's turn, and his story continues into the next chapter.

I hope the Tonomine fans enjoy it.

Tonomine's father was very popular with my assistants. Ha ha.

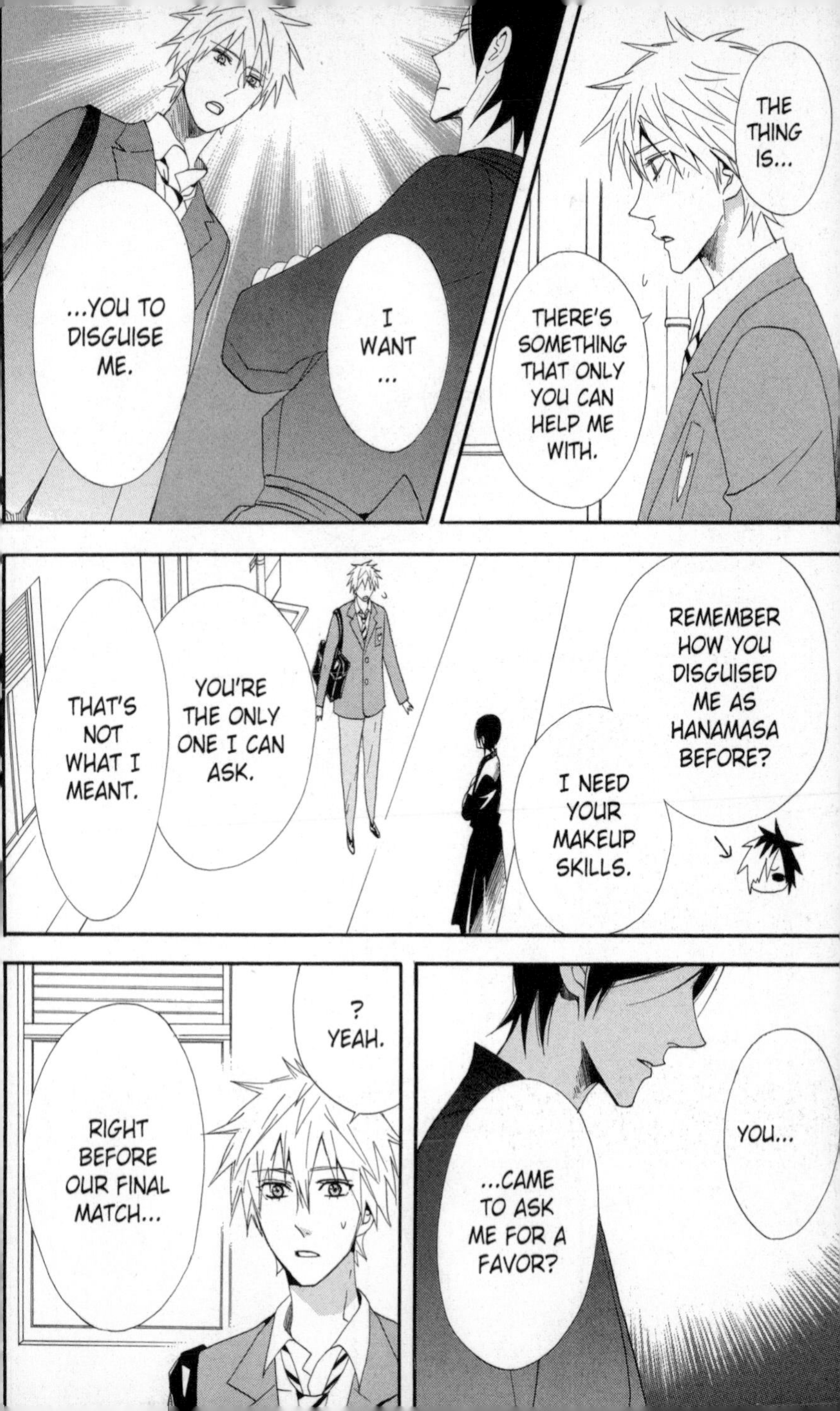
THE THING IS...
THERE'S SOMETHING THAT ONLY YOU CAN HELP ME WITH.
I WANT ...
...YOU TO DISGUISE ME.
REMEMBER HOW YOU DISGUISED ME AS HANAMASA BEFORE?
I NEED YOUR MAKEUP SKILLS.
YOU'RE THE ONLY ONE I CAN ASK.
THAT'S NOT WHAT I MEANT.
YOU...
...CAME TO ASK ME FOR A FAVOR?
? YEAH.
RIGHT BEFORE OUR FINAL MATCH...

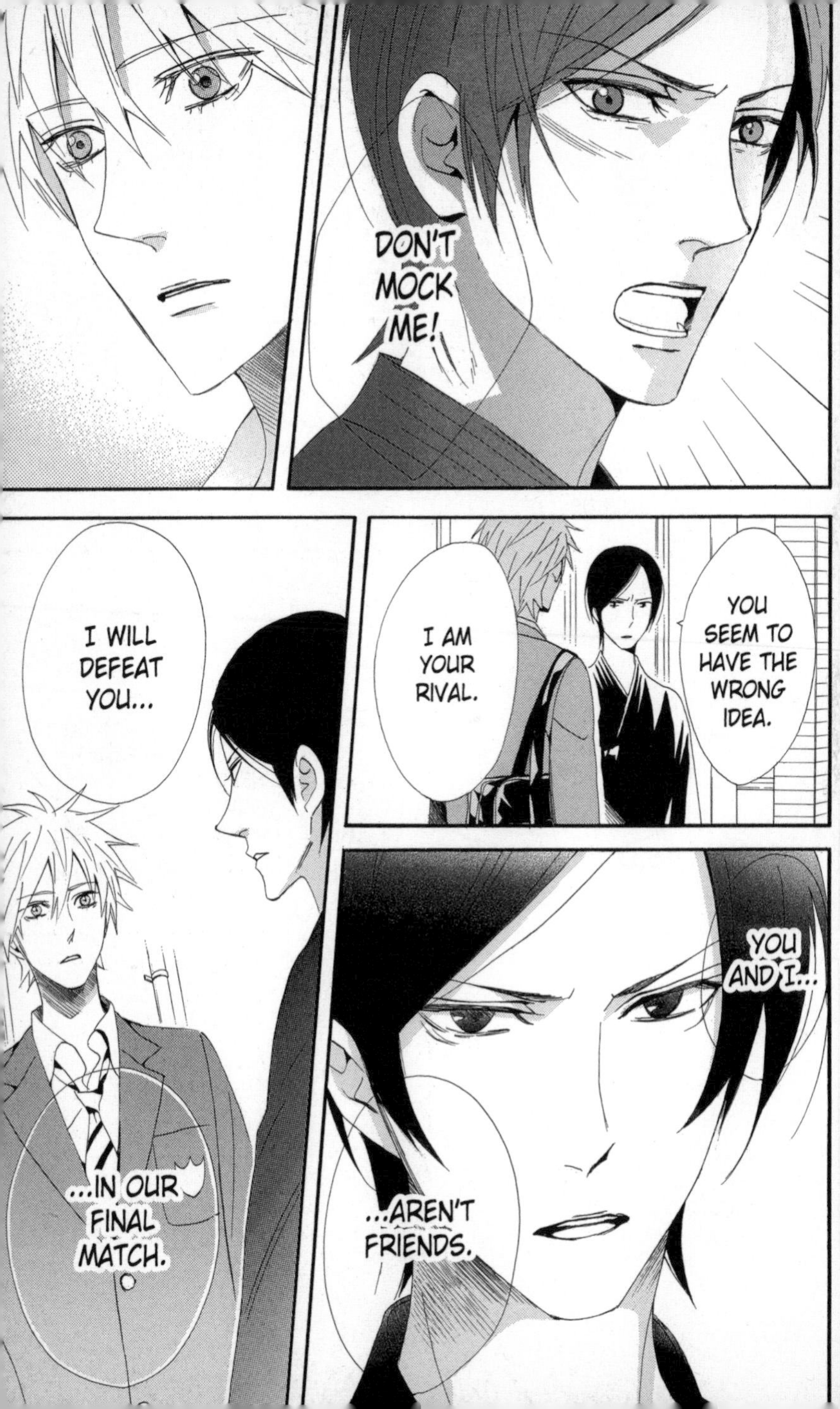
DON'T MOCK ME!
YOU SEEM TO HAVE THE WRONG IDEA.
I AM YOUR RIVAL.
YOU AND I...
...AREN'T FRIENDS.
I WILL DEFEAT YOU...
...IN OUR FINAL MATCH.

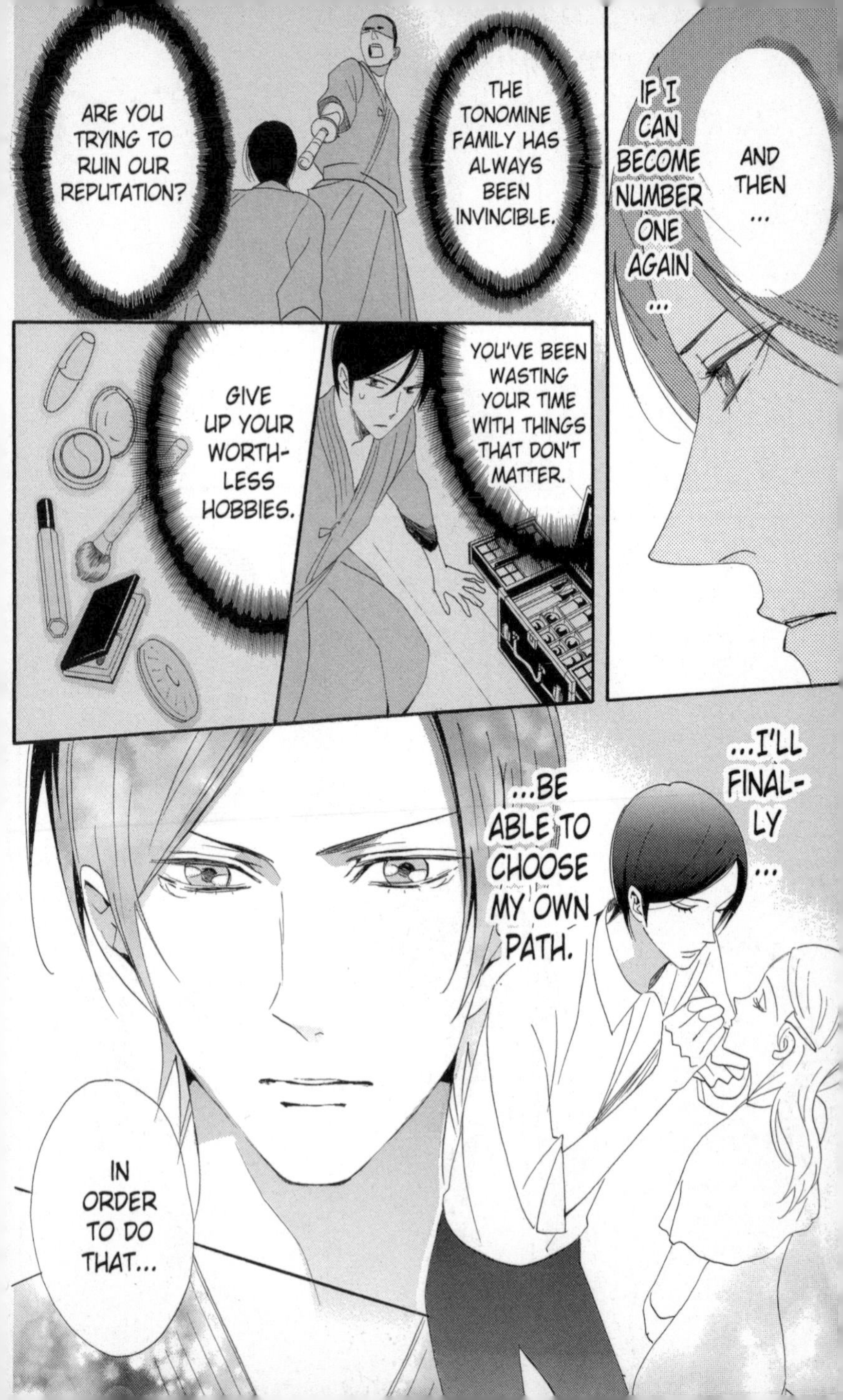
IF I CAN BECOME NUMBER ONE AGAIN...
AND THEN...
THE TONOMINE FAMILY HAS ALWAYS BEEN INVINCIBLE.
ARE YOU TRYING TO RUIN OUR REPUTATION?
YOU'VE BEEN WASTING YOUR TIME WITH THINGS THAT DON'T MATTER.
GIVE UP YOUR WORTH-LESS HOBBIES.
...I'LL FINAL-LY...
...BE ABLE TO CHOOSE MY OWN PATH.
IN ORDER TO DO THAT...

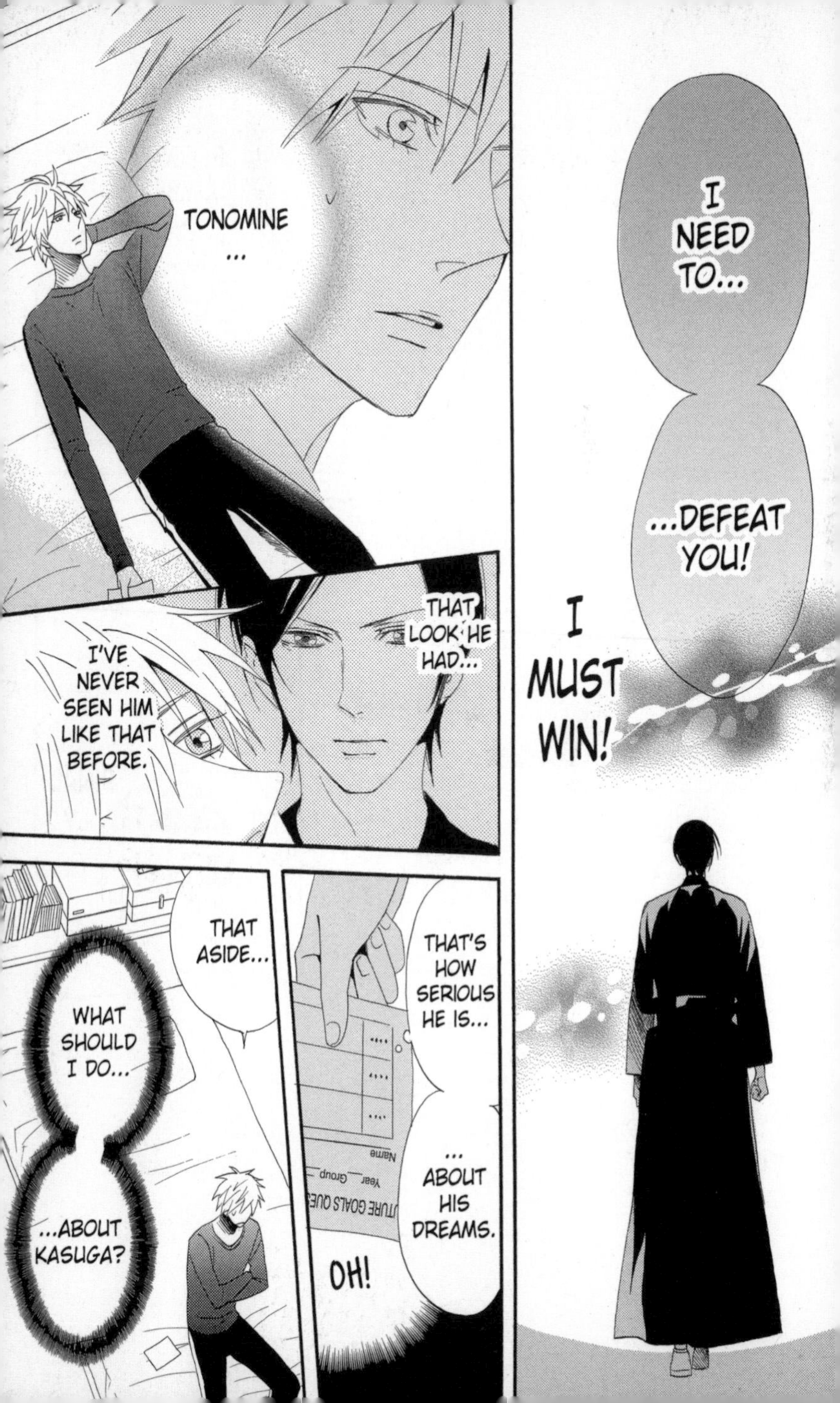
I NEED TO...
...DEFEAT YOU!
I MUST WIN!
TONOMINE ...
THAT LOOK HE HAD...
I'VE NEVER SEEN HIM LIKE THAT BEFORE.
THAT'S HOW SERIOUS HE IS...
... ABOUT HIS DREAMS.
OH!
THAT ASIDE...
WHAT SHOULD I DO...
...ABOUT KASUGA?

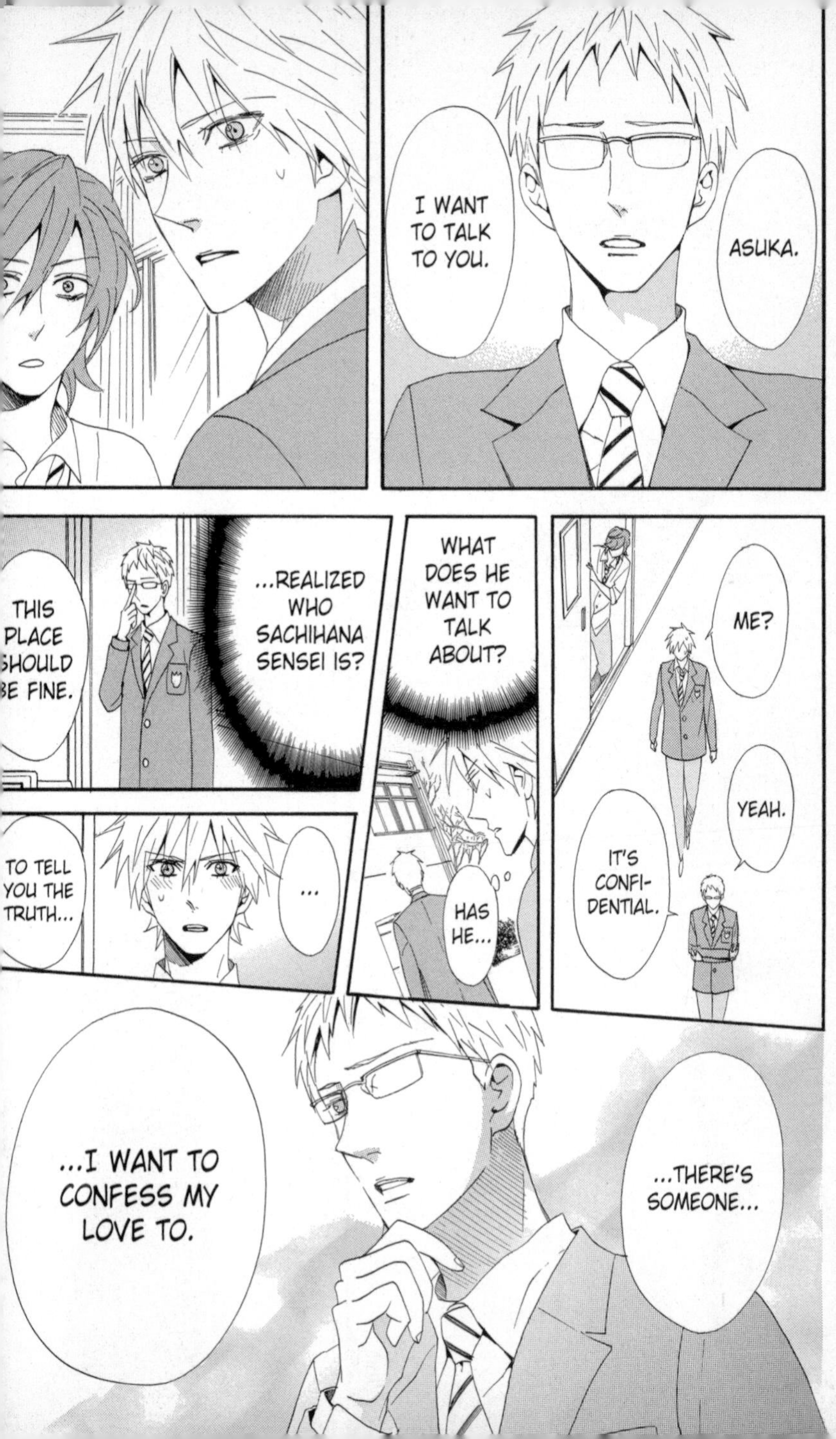
ASUKA.
I WANT TO TALK TO YOU.
ME?
YEAH.
IT'S CONFI-DENTIAL.
WHAT DOES HE WANT TO TALK ABOUT?
HAS HE...
...REALIZED WHO SACHIHANA SENSEI IS?
THIS PLACE SHOULD BE FINE.
...
TO TELL YOU THE TRUTH...
...THERE'S SOMEONE...
...I WANT TO CONFESS MY LOVE TO.

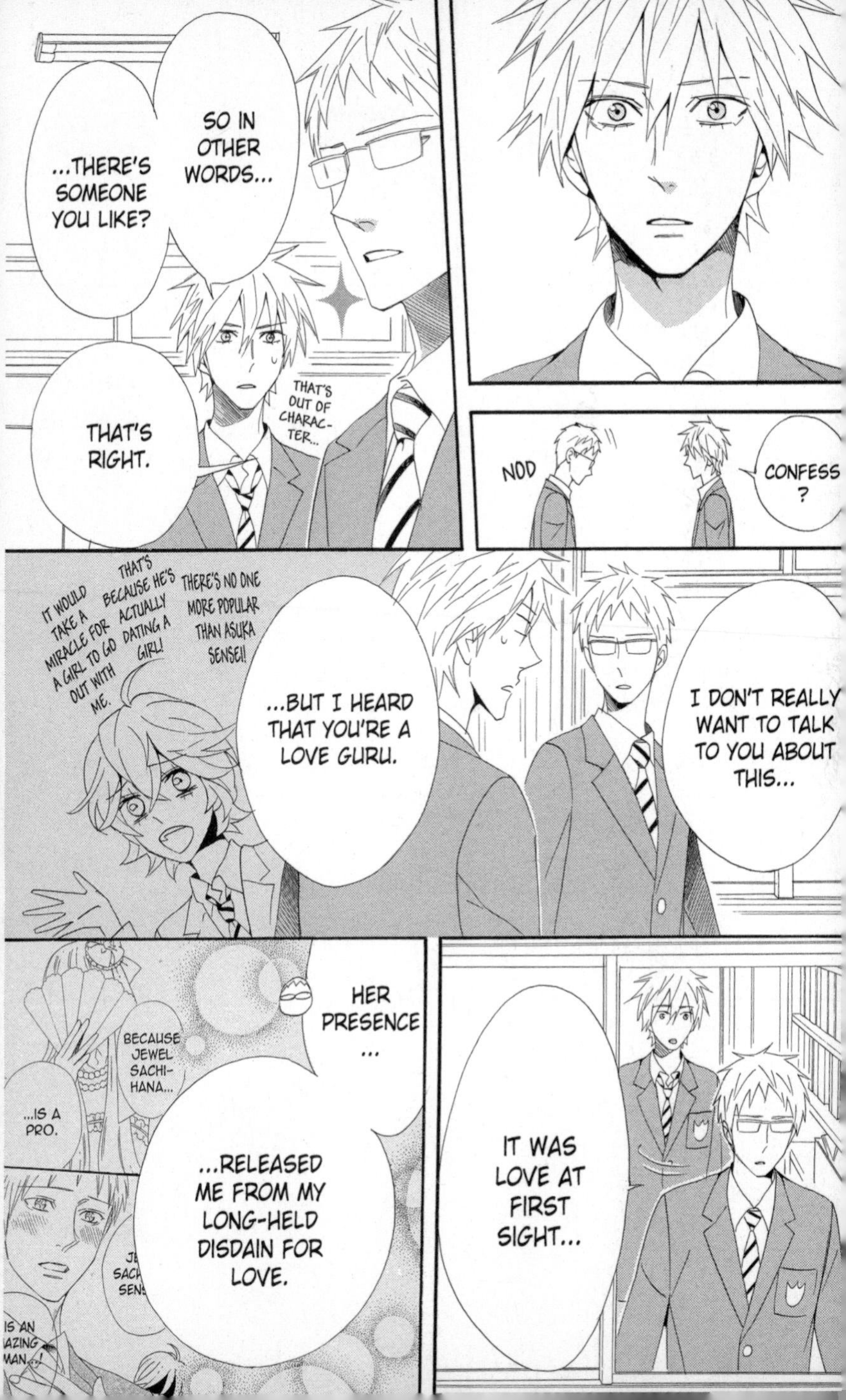
CONFESS?
NOD
SO IN OTHER WORDS...
...THERE'S SOMEONE YOU LIKE?
THAT'S OUT OF CHARACTER...
THAT'S RIGHT.
I DON'T REALLY WANT TO TALK TO YOU ABOUT THIS...
...BUT I HEARD THAT YOU'RE A LOVE GURU.
THERE'S NO ONE MORE POPULAR THAN ASUKA SENSEI!
THAT'S BECAUSE HE'S ACTUALLY DATING A GIRL!
IT WOULD TAKE A MIRACLE FOR A GIRL TO GO OUT WITH ME.
IT WAS LOVE AT FIRST SIGHT...
HER PRESENCE...
...RELEASED ME FROM MY LONG-HELD DISDAIN FOR LOVE.
BECAUSE JEWEL SACHI-HANA...
...IS A PRO.

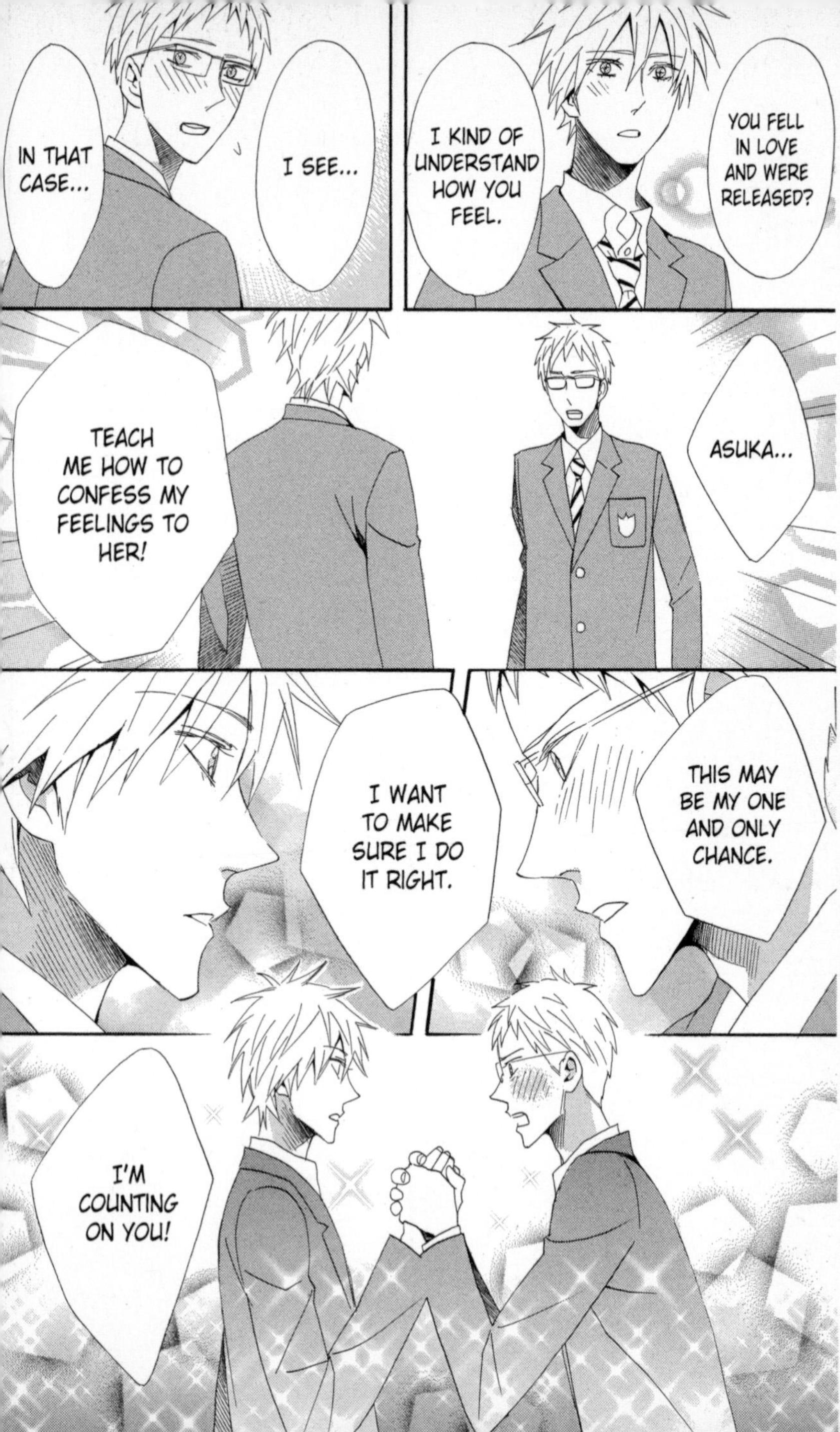
YOU FELL IN LOVE AND WERE RELEASED?
I KIND OF UNDERSTAND HOW YOU FEEL.
I SEE...
IN THAT CASE...
ASUKA...
TEACH ME HOW TO CONFESS MY FEELINGS TO HER!
THIS MAY BE MY ONE AND ONLY CHANCE.
I WANT TO MAKE SURE I DO IT RIGHT.
I'M COUNTING ON YOU!

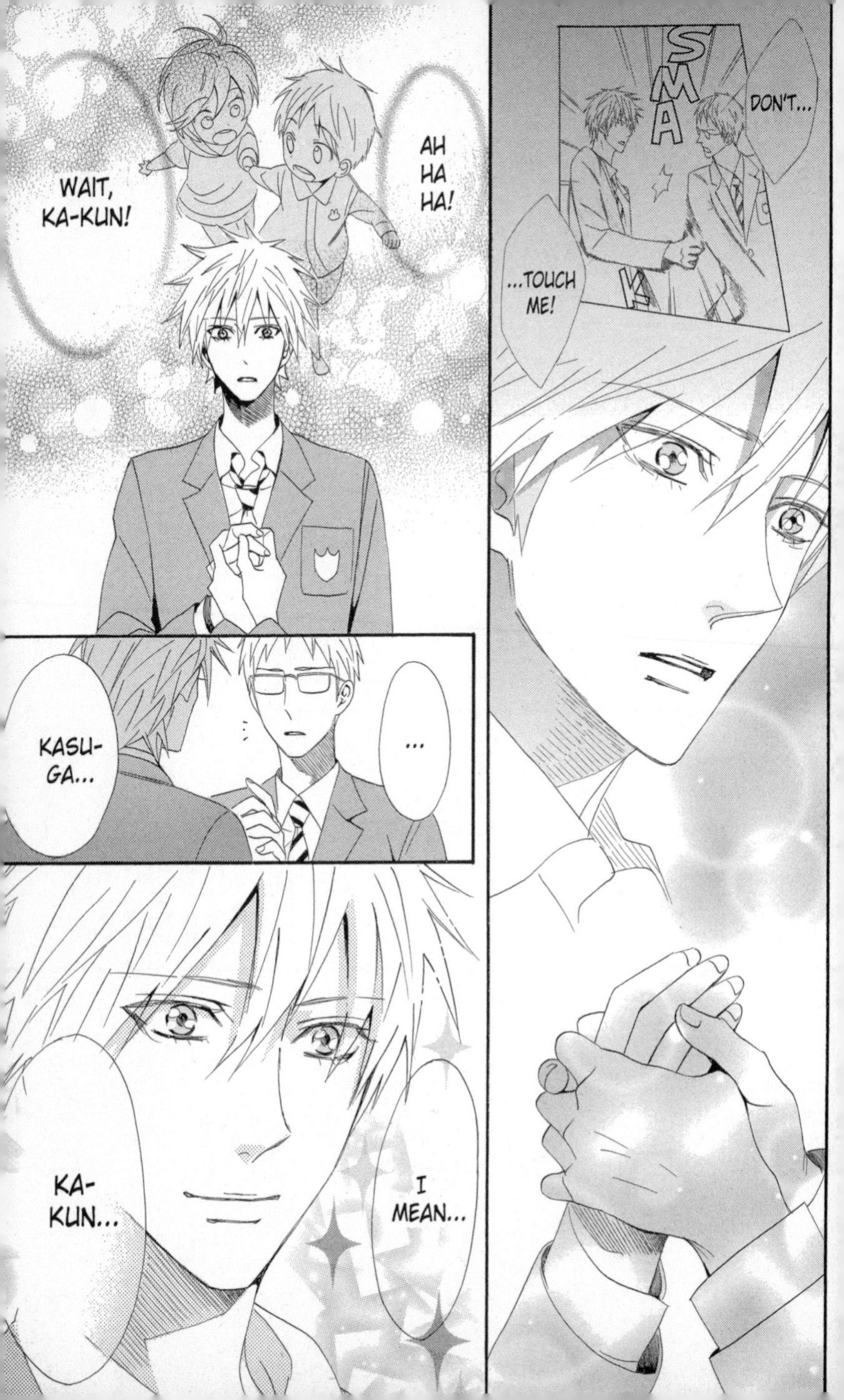
DON'T...
SMA
...TOUCH ME!
AH HA HA!
WAIT, KA-KUN!
...
KASU-GA...
I MEAN...
KA-KUN...

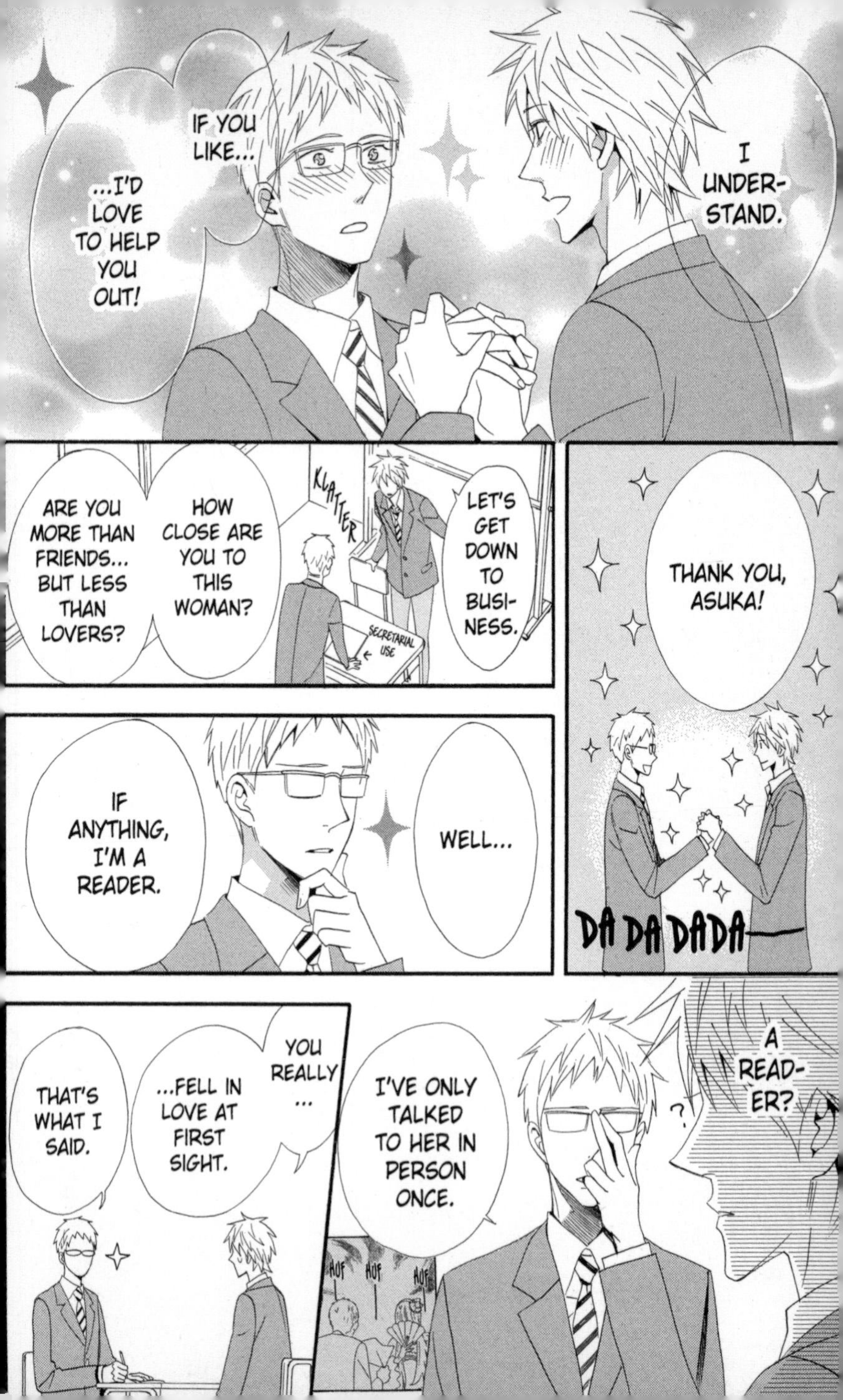
I UNDER-STAND.
IF YOU LIKE...
...I'D LOVE TO HELP YOU OUT!
THANK YOU, ASUKA!
DA DA DADA
LET'S GET DOWN TO BUSI-NESS.
KLATTER
SECRETARIAL USE
HOW CLOSE ARE YOU TO THIS WOMAN?
ARE YOU MORE THAN FRIENDS... BUT LESS THAN LOVERS?
WELL...
IF ANYTHING, I'M A READER.
A READ-ER?
I'VE ONLY TALKED TO HER IN PERSON ONCE.
HUF HUF HUF
YOU REALLY...
...FELL IN LOVE AT FIRST SIGHT.
THAT'S WHAT I SAID.

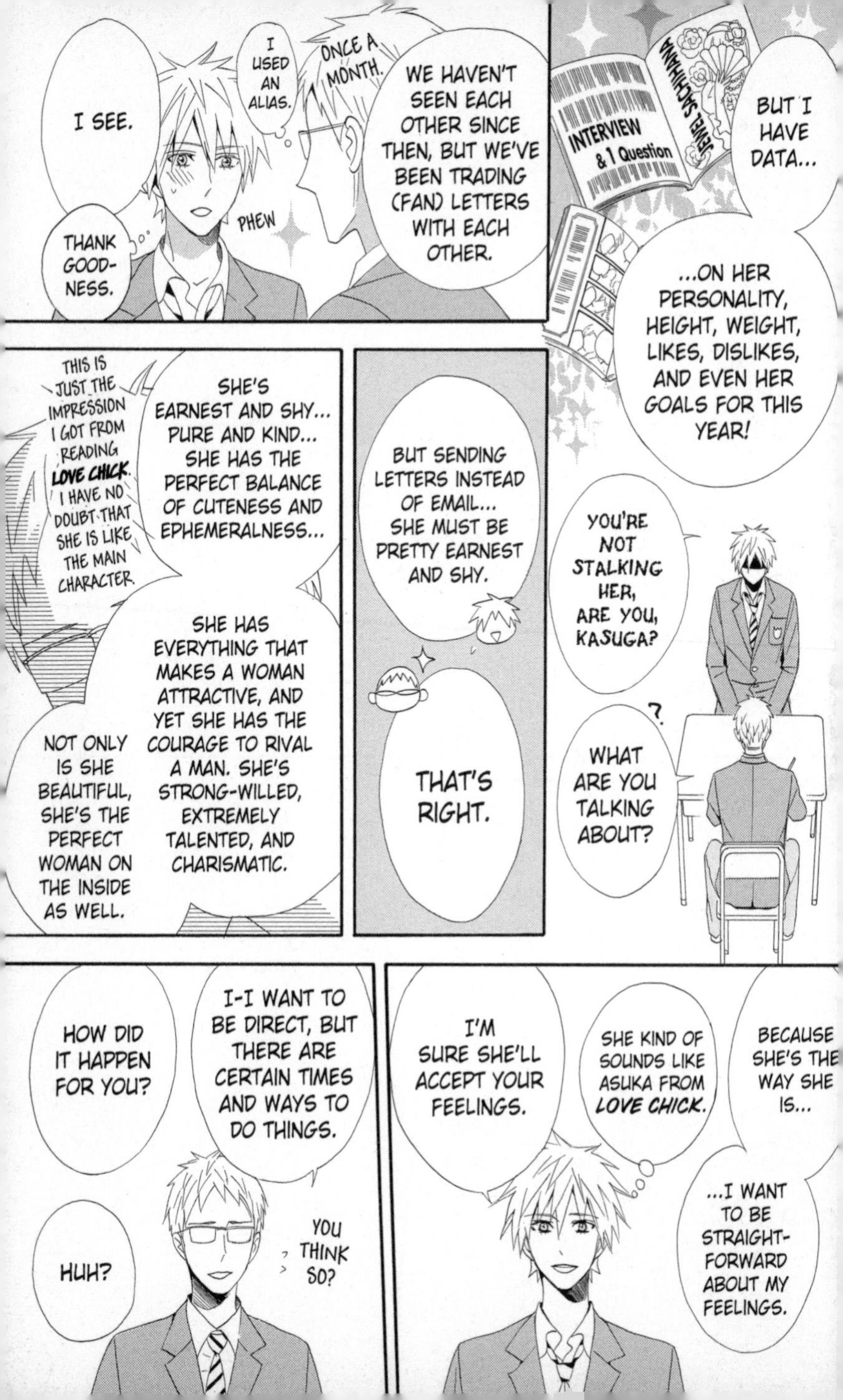
JEWEL SACHIHANA
INTERVIEW & 1 Question
BUT I HAVE DATA...
...ON HER PERSONALITY, HEIGHT, WEIGHT, LIKES, DISLIKES, AND EVEN HER GOALS FOR THIS YEAR!
WE HAVEN'T SEEN EACH OTHER SINCE THEN, BUT WE'VE BEEN TRADING (FAN) LETTERS WITH EACH OTHER.
ONCE A MONTH.
I USED AN ALIAS.
I SEE.
PHEW
THANK GOODNESS.
YOU'RE NOT STALKING HER, ARE YOU, KASUGA?
?
WHAT ARE YOU TALKING ABOUT?
BUT SENDING LETTERS INSTEAD OF EMAIL... SHE MUST BE PRETTY EARNEST AND SHY.
THAT'S RIGHT.
SHE'S EARNEST AND SHY... PURE AND KIND... SHE HAS THE PERFECT BALANCE OF CUTENESS AND EPHEMERALNESS...
THIS IS JUST THE IMPRESSION I GOT FROM READING *LOVE CHICK*. I HAVE NO DOUBT THAT SHE IS LIKE THE MAIN CHARACTER.
SHE HAS EVERYTHING THAT MAKES A WOMAN ATTRACTIVE, AND YET SHE HAS THE COURAGE TO RIVAL A MAN. SHE'S STRONG-WILLED, EXTREMELY TALENTED, AND CHARISMATIC.
NOT ONLY IS SHE BEAUTIFUL, SHE'S THE PERFECT WOMAN ON THE INSIDE AS WELL.
BECAUSE SHE'S THE WAY SHE IS...
...I WANT TO BE STRAIGHTFORWARD ABOUT MY FEELINGS.
SHE KIND OF SOUNDS LIKE ASUKA FROM *LOVE CHICK*.
I'M SURE SHE'LL ACCEPT YOUR FEELINGS.
I-I WANT TO BE DIRECT, BUT THERE ARE CERTAIN TIMES AND WAYS TO DO THINGS.
HOW DID IT HAPPEN FOR YOU?
YOU THINK SO?
HUH?

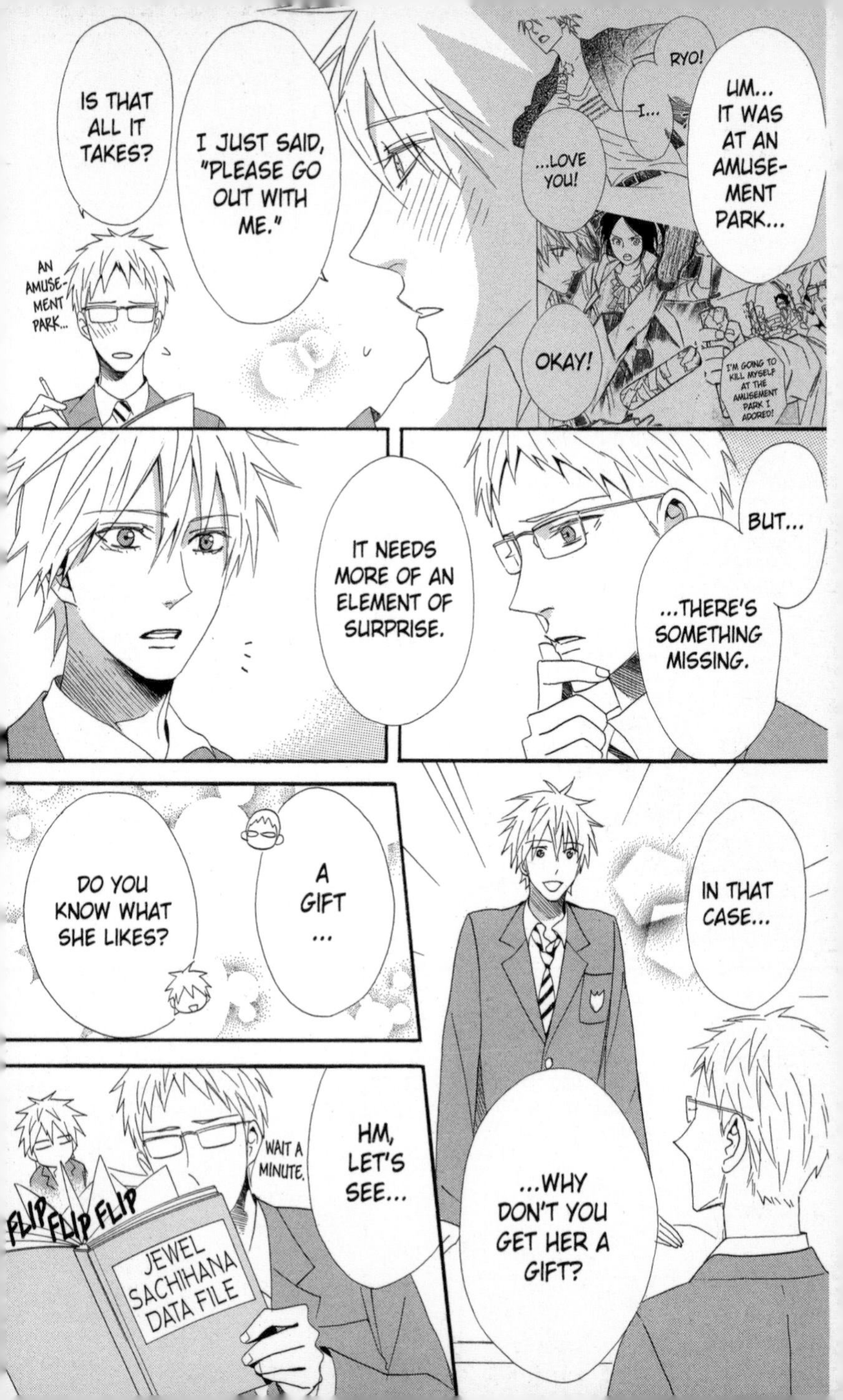
UM... IT WAS AT AN AMUSEMENT PARK...
RYO!
I...
...LOVE YOU!
OKAY!
I'M GOING TO KILL MYSELF AT THE AMUSEMENT PARK I ADORED!
I JUST SAID, "PLEASE GO OUT WITH ME."
IS THAT ALL IT TAKES?
AN AMUSEMENT PARK...
BUT...
...THERE'S SOMETHING MISSING.
IT NEEDS MORE OF AN ELEMENT OF SURPRISE.
IN THAT CASE...
...WHY DON'T YOU GET HER A GIFT?
A GIFT ...
DO YOU KNOW WHAT SHE LIKES?
HM, LET'S SEE...
WAIT A MINUTE.
FLIP FLIP FLIP
JEWEL SACHIHANA DATA FILE

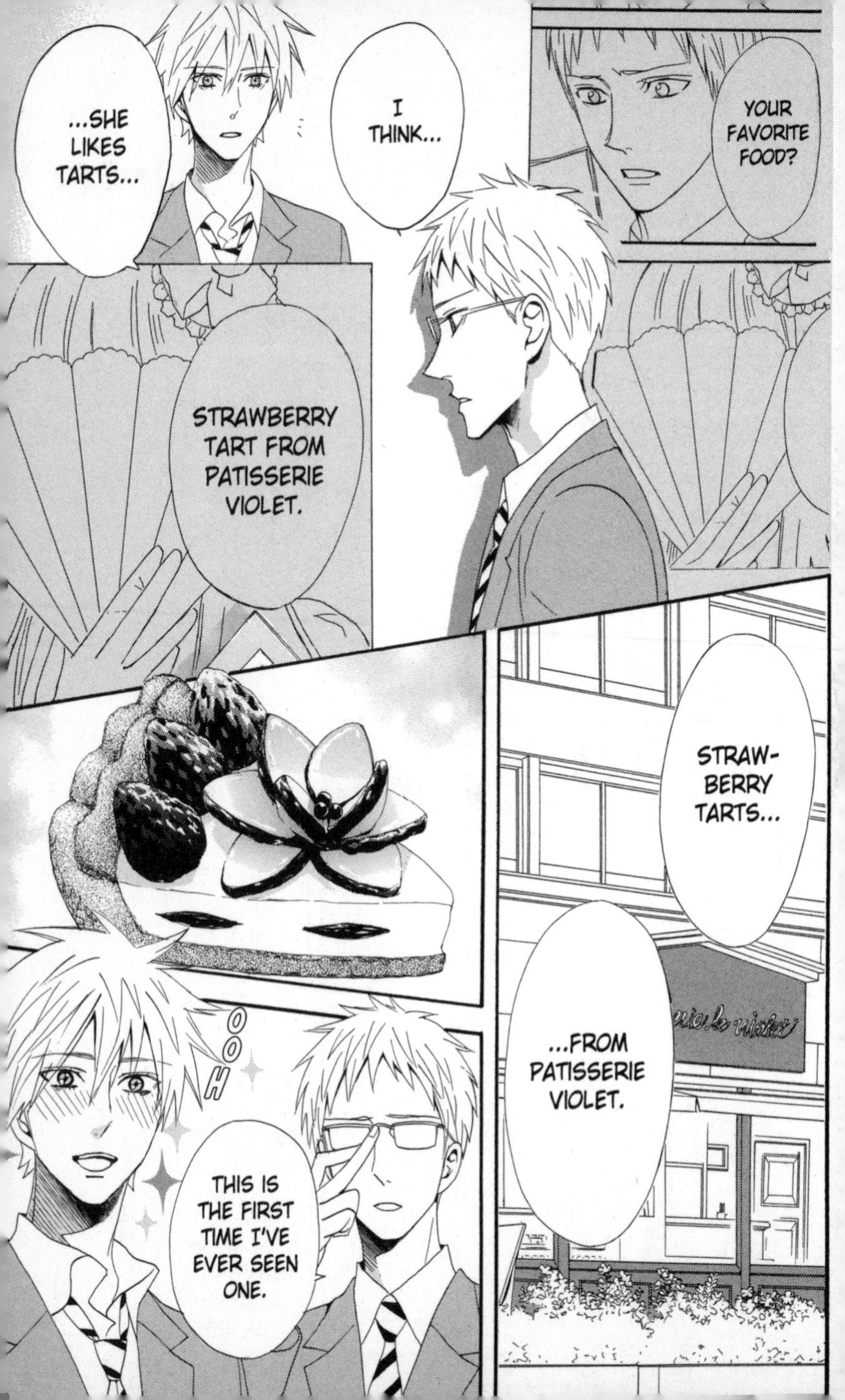
YOUR FAVORITE FOOD?
I THINK...
...SHE LIKES TARTS...
STRAWBERRY TART FROM PATISSERIE VIOLET.
STRAW-BERRY TARTS...
...FROM PATISSERIE VIOLET.
OOH
THIS IS THE FIRST TIME I'VE EVER SEEN ONE.

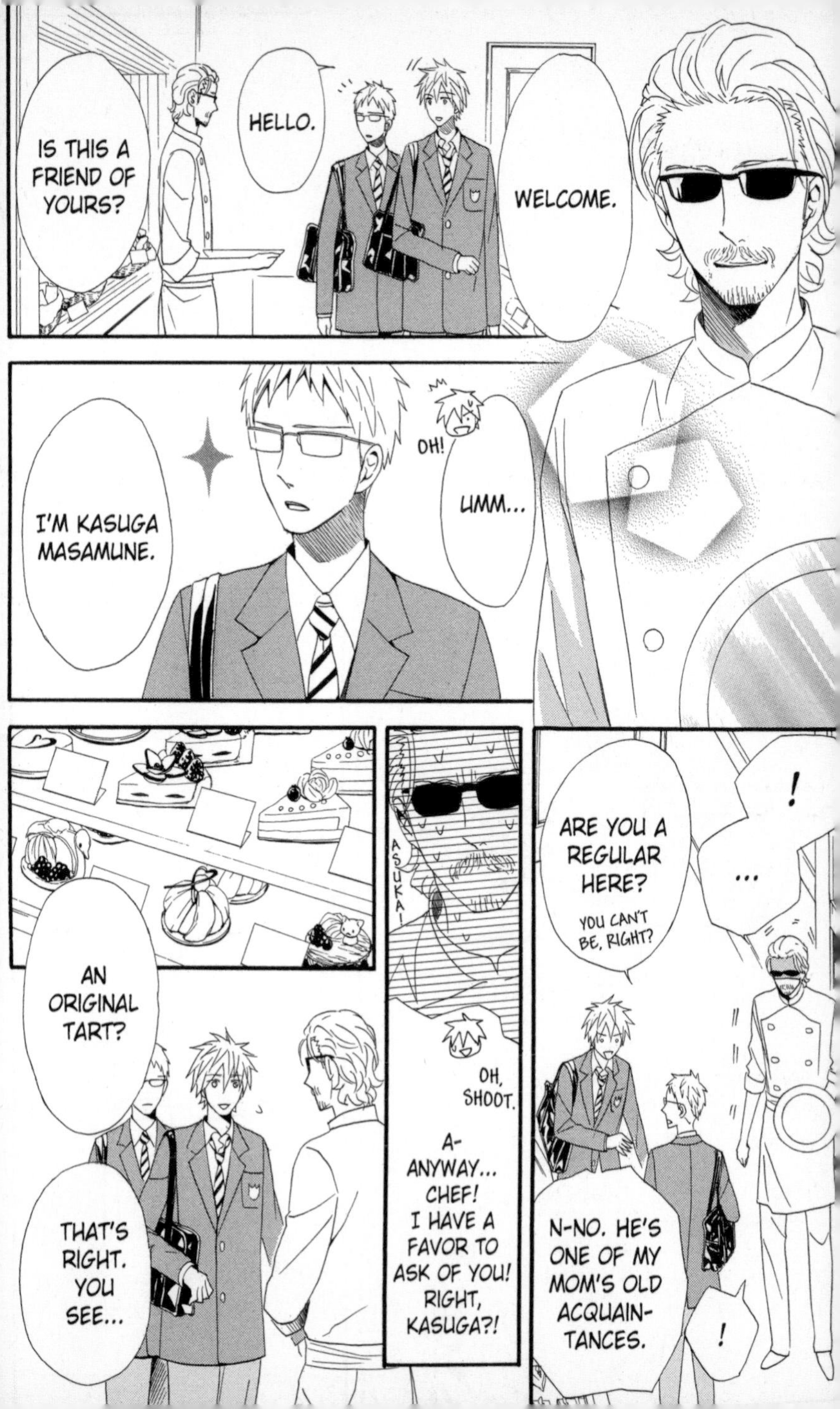
WELCOME.
HELLO.
IS THIS A FRIEND OF YOURS?
OH!
UMM...
I'M KASUGA MASAMUNE.
!
...
ARE YOU A REGULAR HERE?
YOU CAN'T BE, RIGHT?
N-NO. HE'S ONE OF MY MOM'S OLD ACQUAIN-TANCES.
!
ASUKA!
OH, SHOOT.
A- ANYWAY... CHEF! I HAVE A FAVOR TO ASK OF YOU! RIGHT, KASUGA?!
AN ORIGINAL TART?
THAT'S RIGHT. YOU SEE...

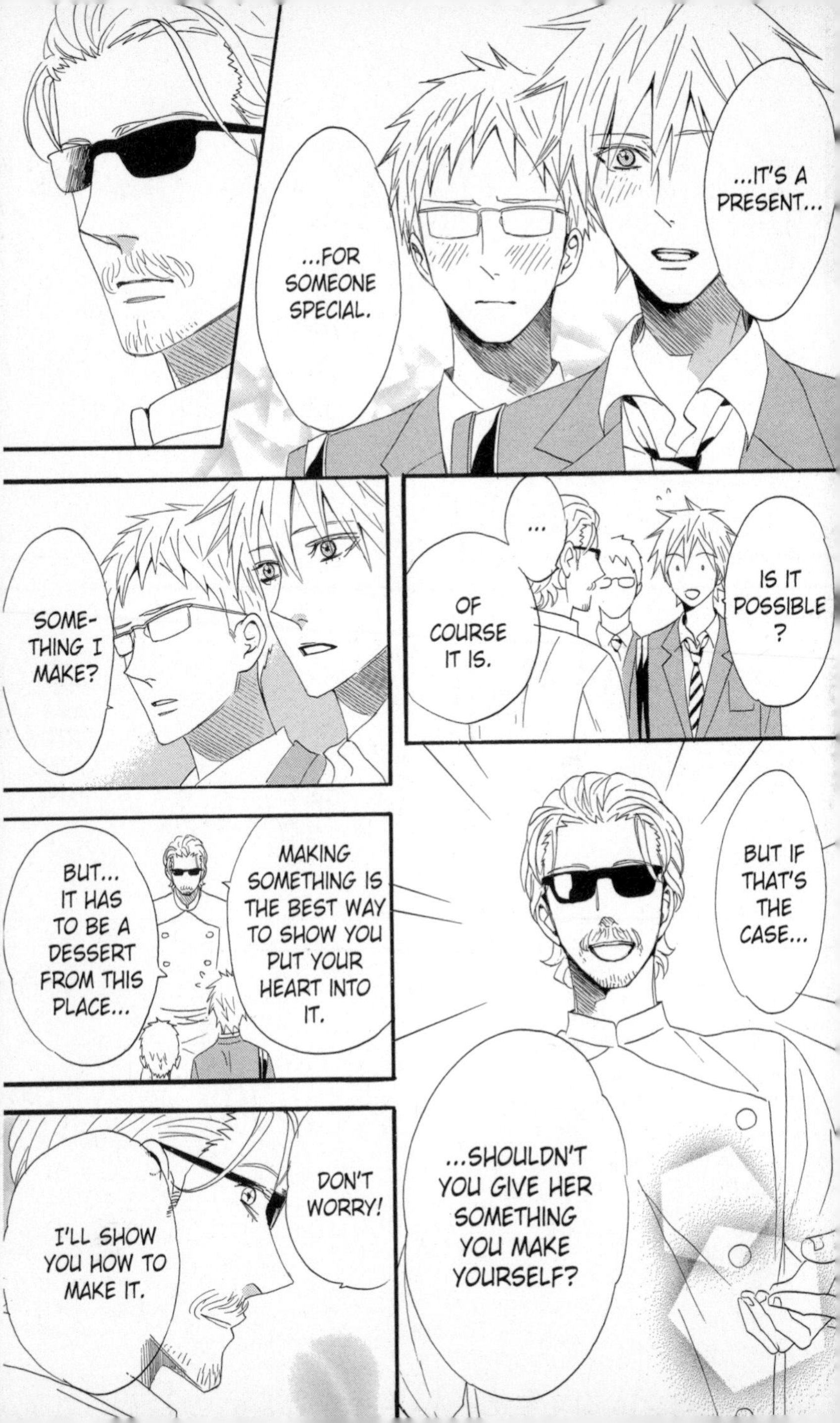
...IT'S A PRESENT...
...FOR SOMEONE SPECIAL.
IS IT POSSIBLE?
...
OF COURSE IT IS.
SOME-THING I MAKE?
BUT IF THAT'S THE CASE...
...SHOULDN'T YOU GIVE HER SOMETHING YOU MAKE YOURSELF?
MAKING SOMETHING IS THE BEST WAY TO SHOW YOU PUT YOUR HEART INTO IT.
BUT... IT HAS TO BE A DESSERT FROM THIS PLACE...
DON'T WORRY!
I'LL SHOW YOU HOW TO MAKE IT.

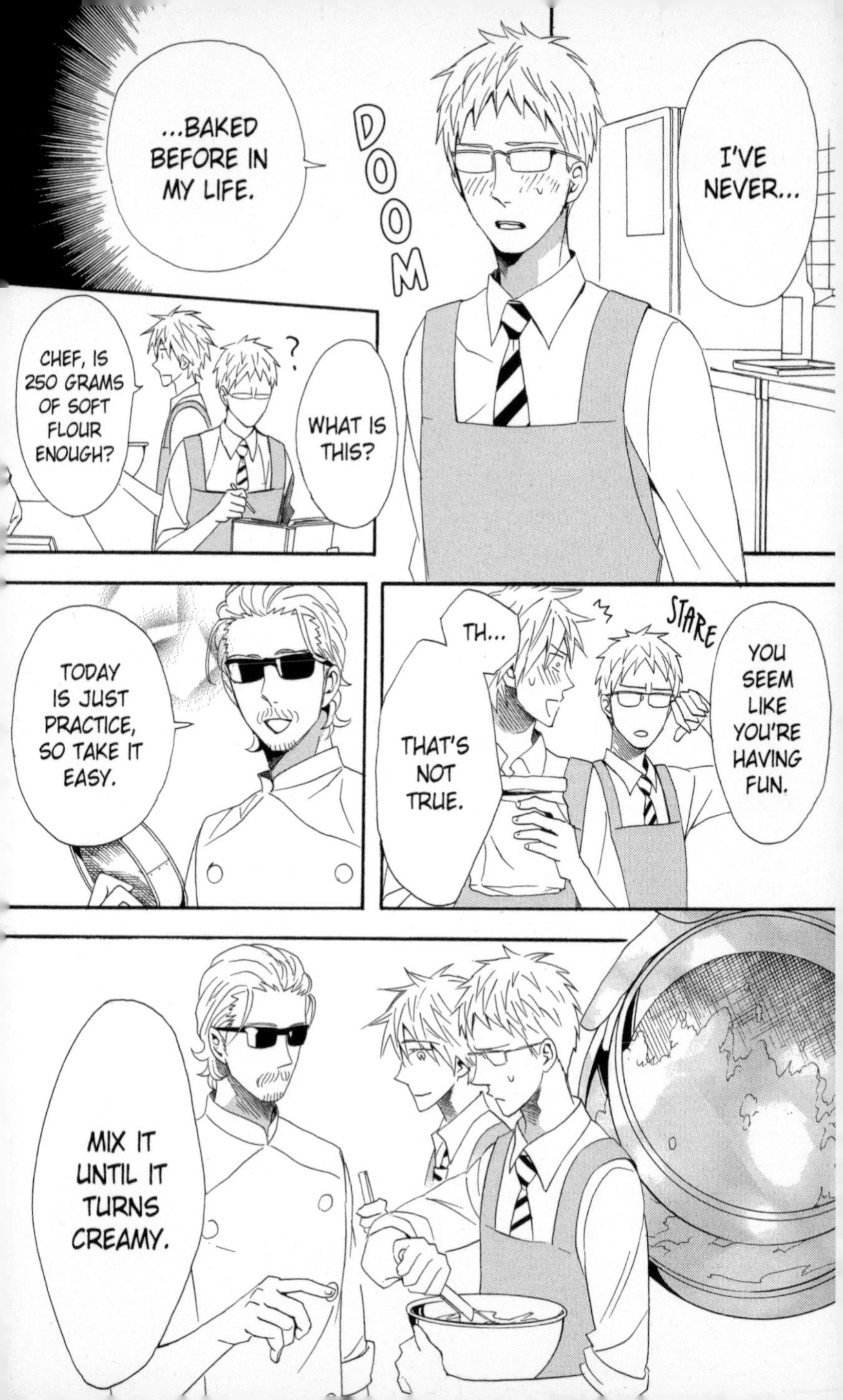
I'VE NEVER...
DOOM
...BAKED BEFORE IN MY LIFE.
?
WHAT IS THIS?
CHEF, IS 250 GRAMS OF SOFT FLOUR ENOUGH?
STARE
YOU SEEM LIKE YOU'RE HAVING FUN.
TH...
THAT'S NOT TRUE.
TODAY IS JUST PRACTICE, SO TAKE IT EASY.
MIX IT UNTIL IT TURNS CREAMY.

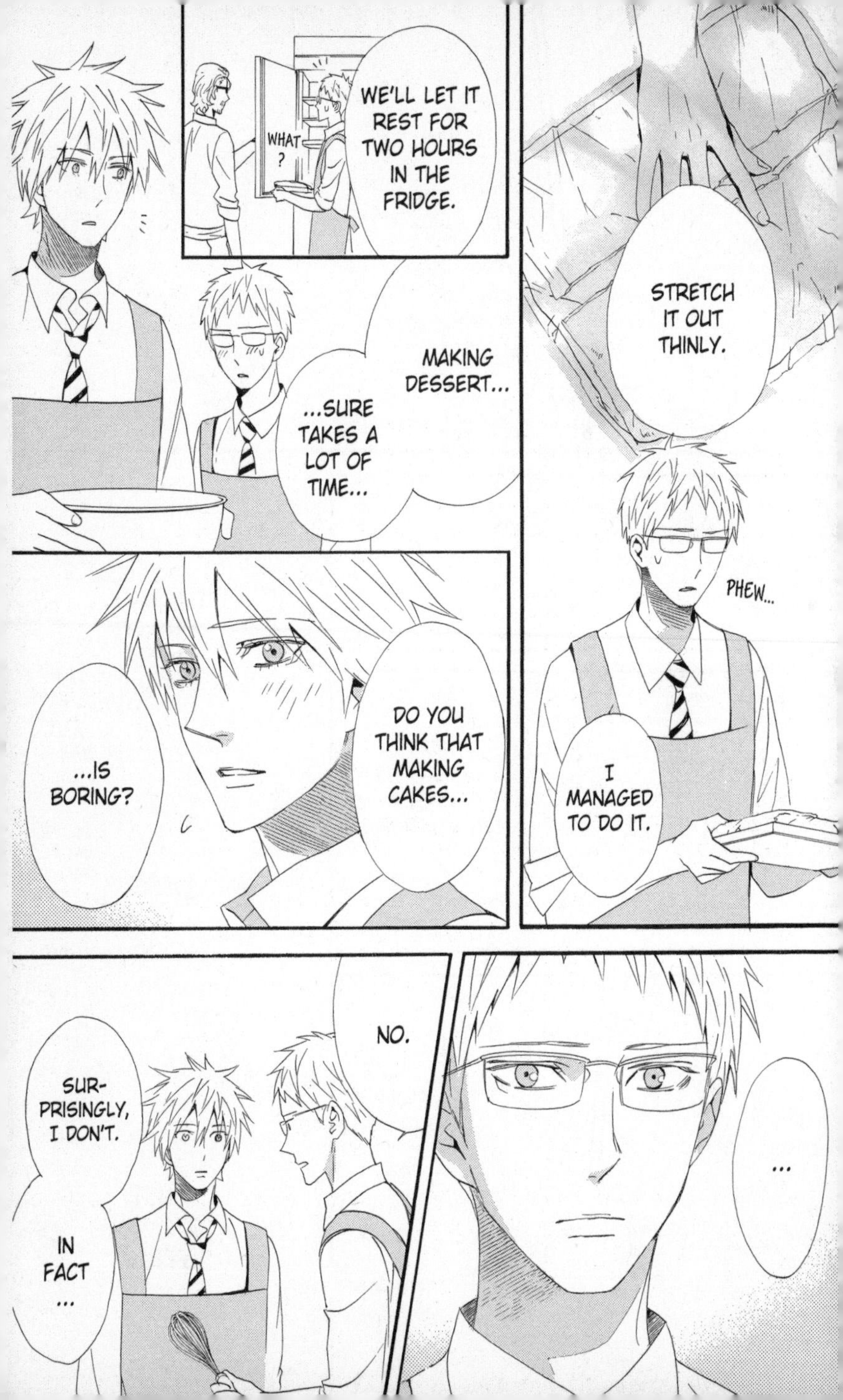
STRETCH IT OUT THINLY.
PHEW...
I MANAGED TO DO IT.
WE'LL LET IT REST FOR TWO HOURS IN THE FRIDGE.
WHAT ?
MAKING DESSERT...
...SURE TAKES A LOT OF TIME...
DO YOU THINK THAT MAKING CAKES...
...IS BORING?
...
NO.
SUR-PRISINGLY, I DON'T.
IN FACT ...

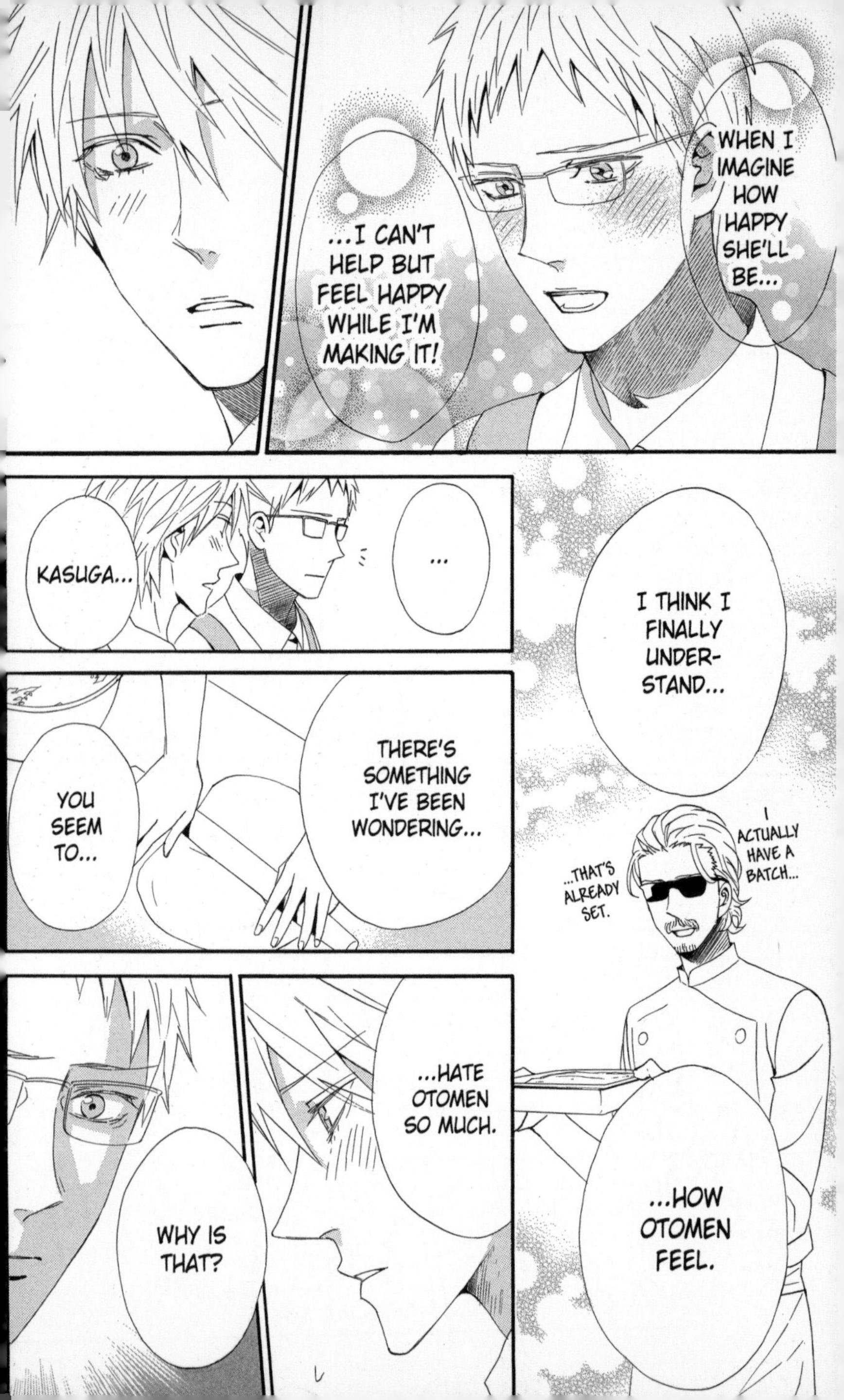
WHEN I IMAGINE HOW HAPPY SHE'LL BE...
...I CAN'T HELP BUT FEEL HAPPY WHILE I'M MAKING IT!
I THINK I FINALLY UNDER-STAND...
I ACTUALLY HAVE A BATCH...
...THAT'S ALREADY SET.
...HOW OTOMEN FEEL.
...
KASUGA...
THERE'S SOMETHING I'VE BEEN WONDERING...
YOU SEEM TO...
...HATE OTOMEN SO MUCH.
WHY IS THAT?

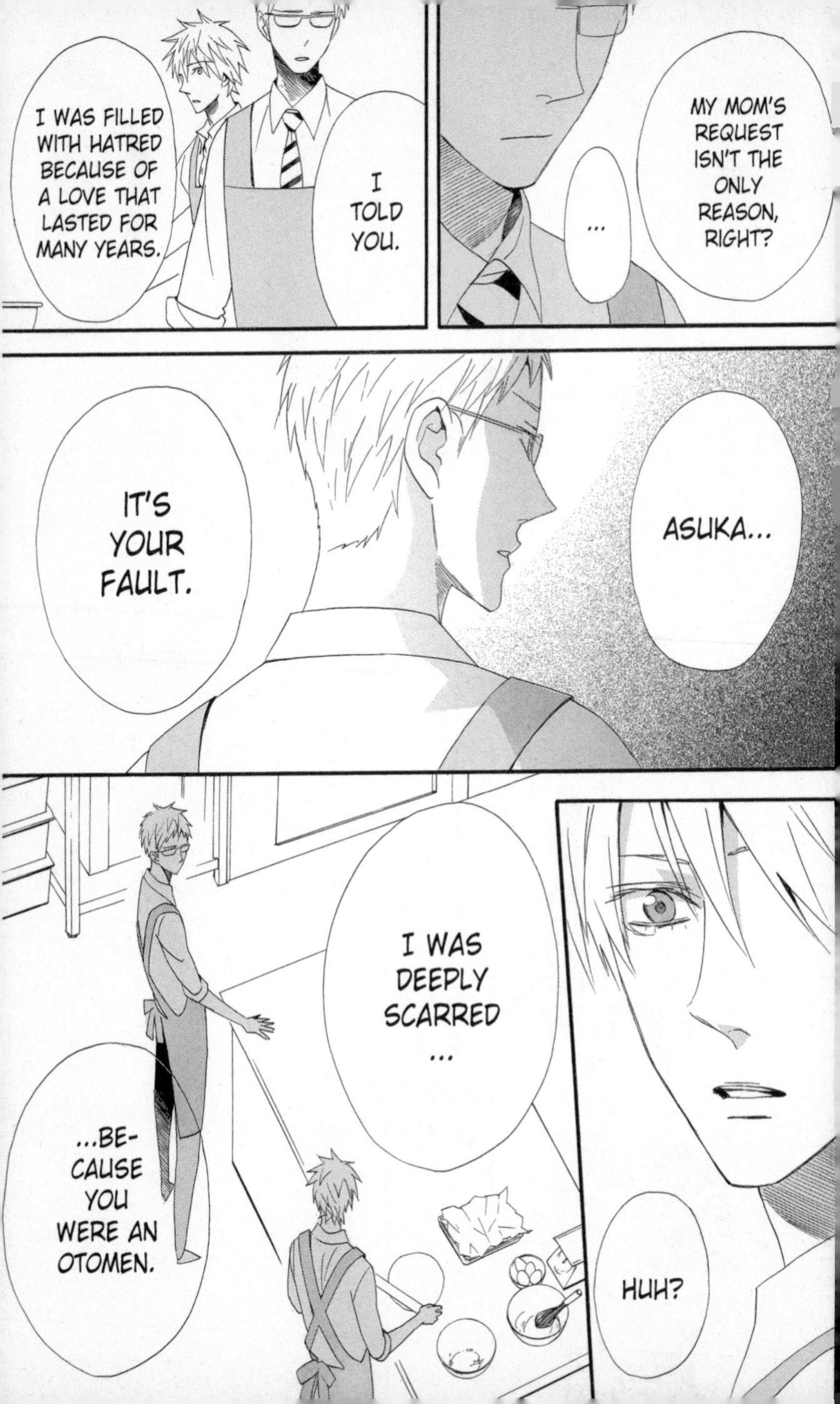
MY MOM'S REQUEST ISN'T THE ONLY REASON, RIGHT?
...
I TOLD YOU.
I WAS FILLED WITH HATRED BECAUSE OF A LOVE THAT LASTED FOR MANY YEARS.
ASUKA...
IT'S YOUR FAULT.
HUH?
I WAS DEEPLY SCARRED...
...BE-CAUSE YOU WERE AN OTOMEN.

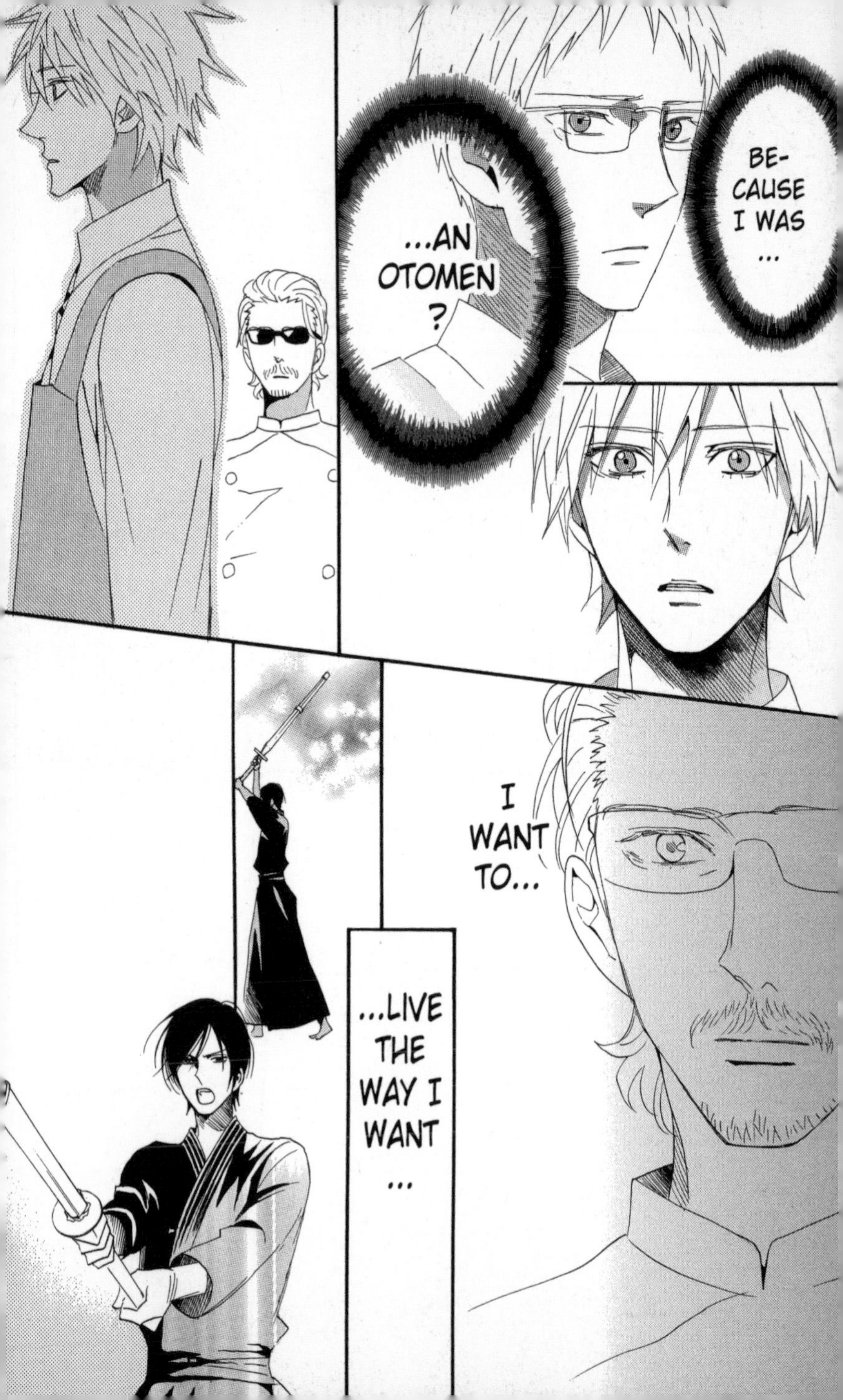

BE-CAUSE I WAS ...
...AN OTOMEN ?
I WANT TO...
...LIVE THE WAY I WANT ...

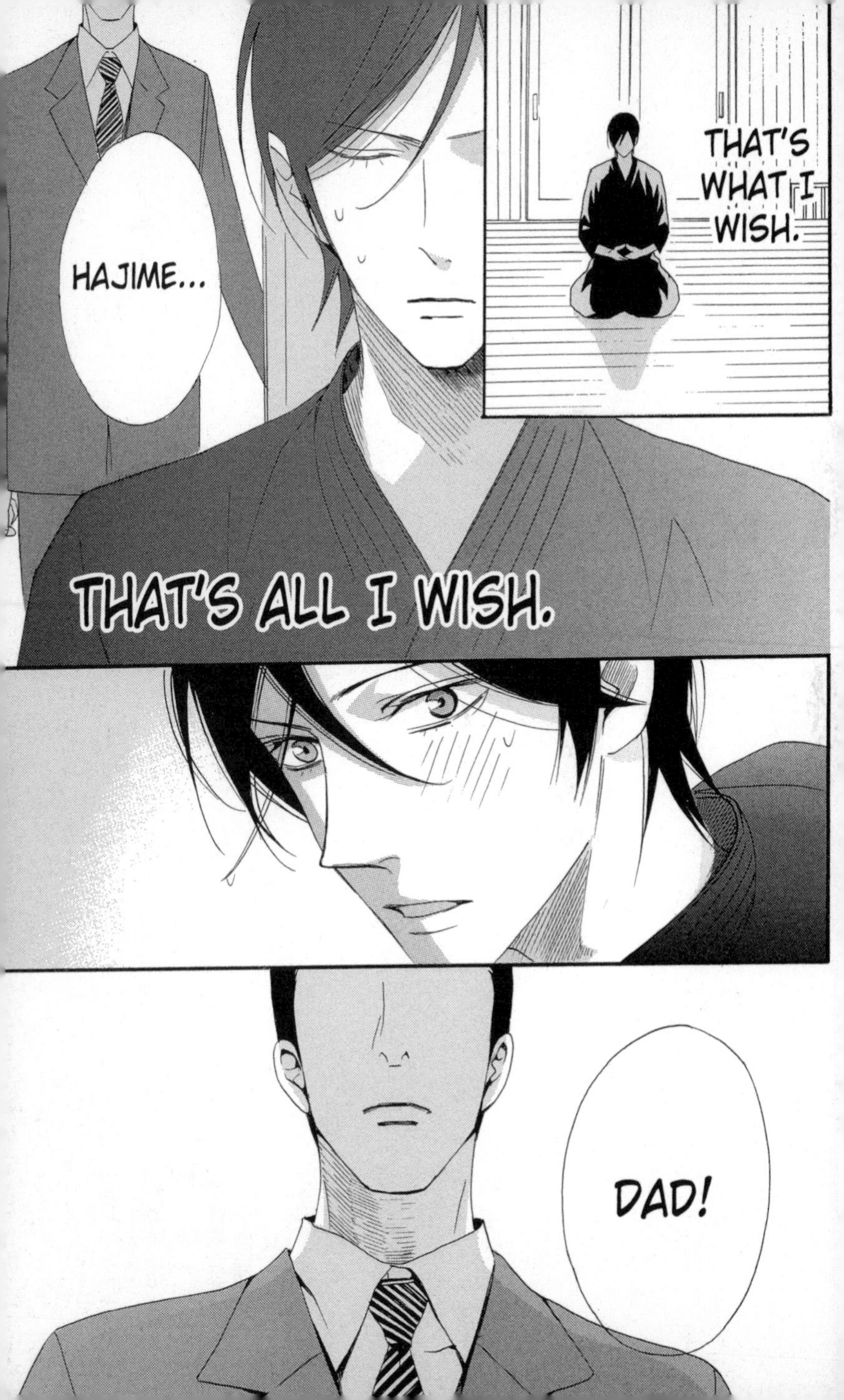
THAT'S WHAT I WISH.
HAJIME...
THAT'S ALL I WISH.
DAD!

OTOMEN

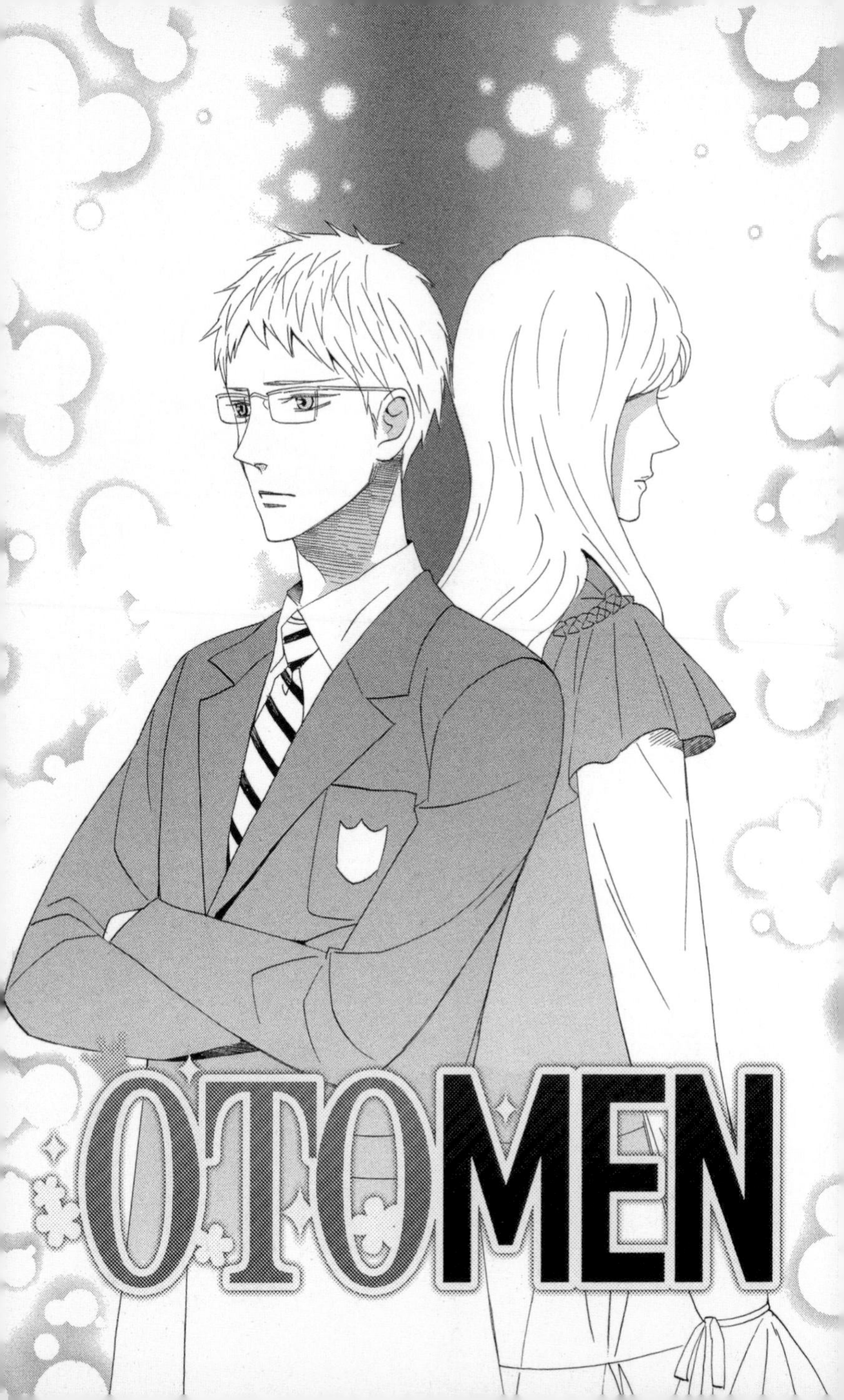
OTOMEN

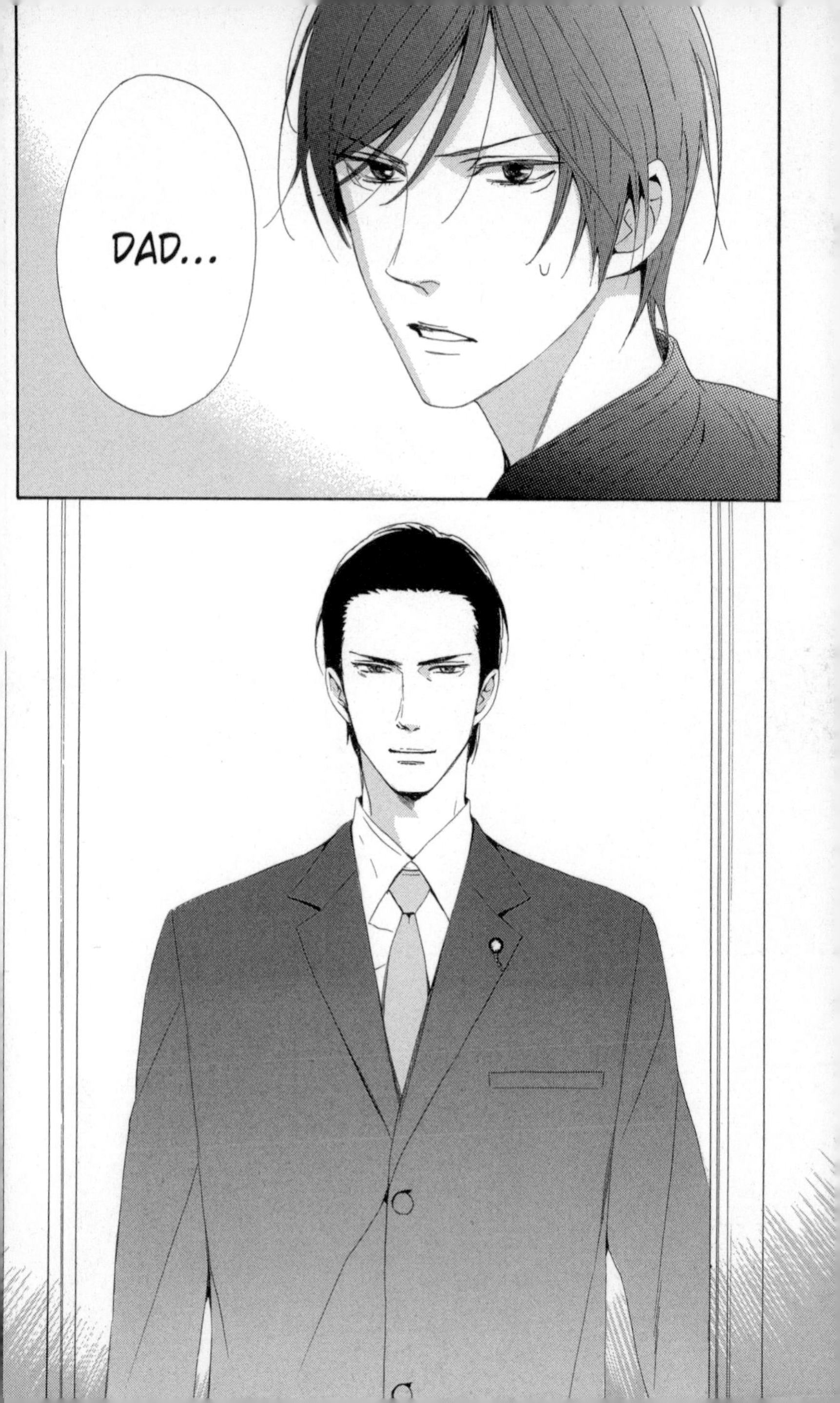
DAD...

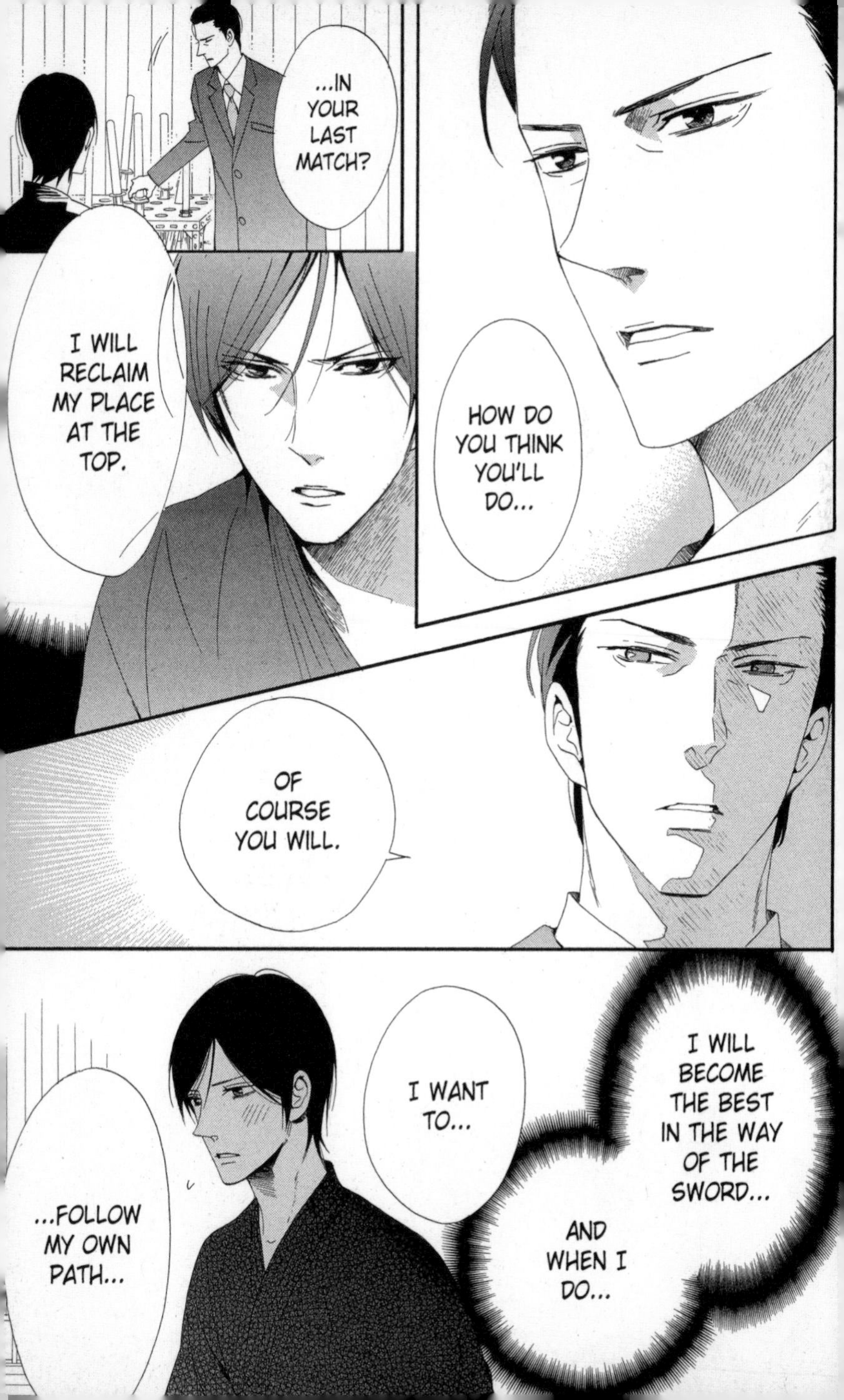
HOW DO YOU THINK YOU'LL DO...
...IN YOUR LAST MATCH?
I WILL RECLAIM MY PLACE AT THE TOP.
OF COURSE YOU WILL.
I WILL BECOME THE BEST IN THE WAY OF THE SWORD...
AND WHEN I DO...
I WANT TO...
...FOLLOW MY OWN PATH...

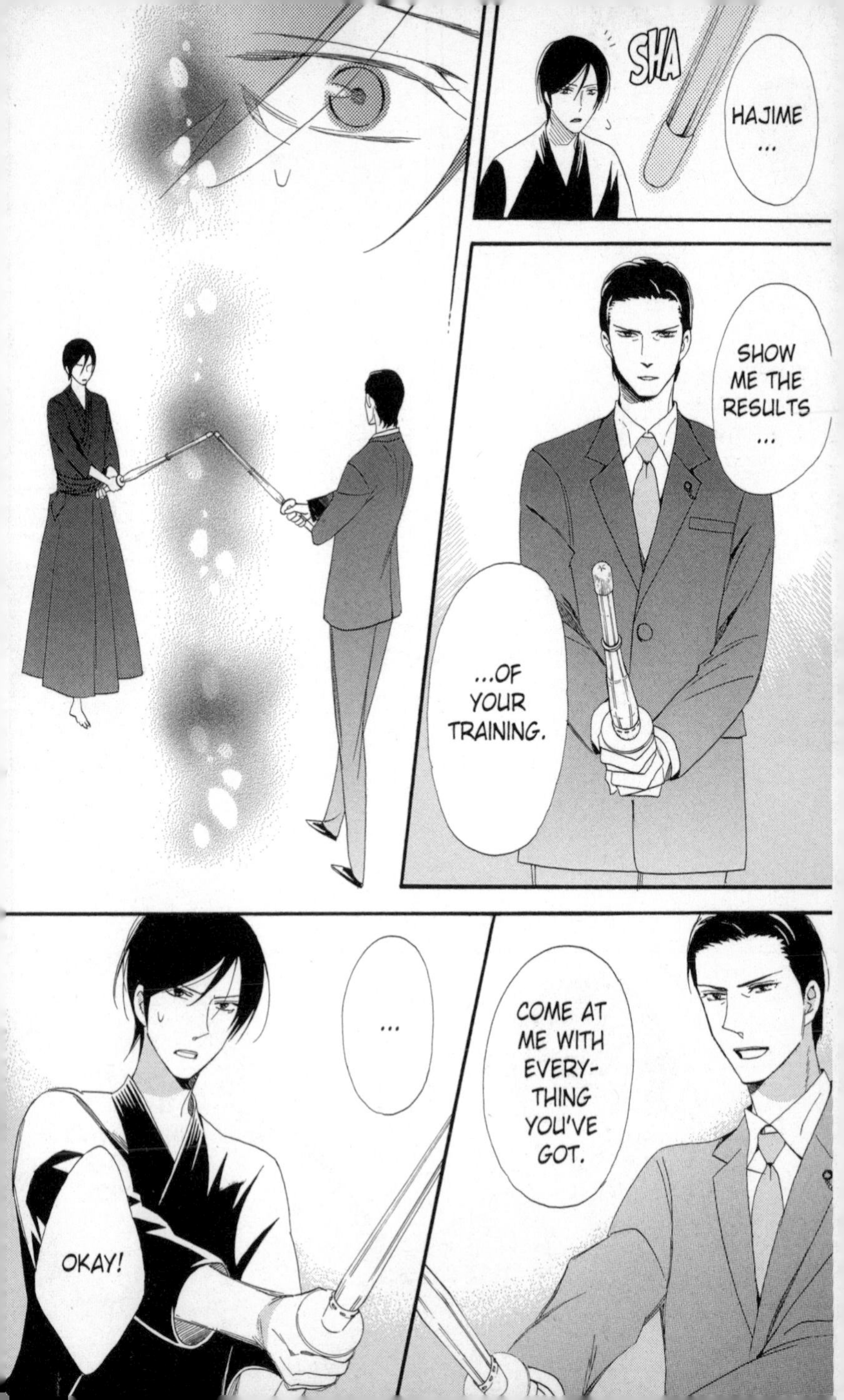
SHA
HAJIME ...
SHOW ME THE RESULTS ...
...OF YOUR TRAINING.
COME AT ME WITH EVERY-THING YOU'VE GOT.
...
OKAY!

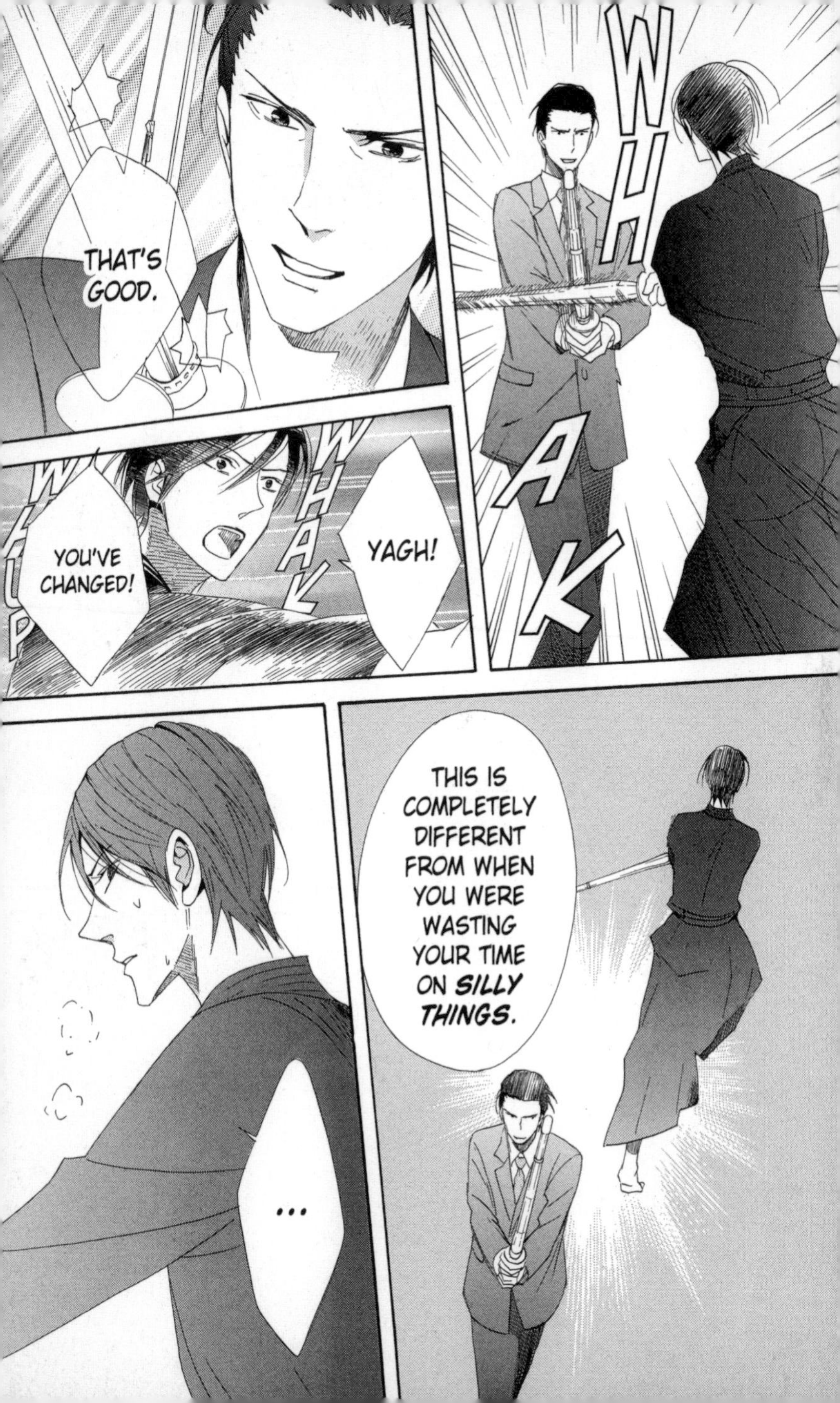
WHAK
THAT'S GOOD.
YAGH!
WHAK
YOU'VE CHANGED!
WHUP
THIS IS COMPLETELY DIFFERENT FROM WHEN YOU WERE WASTING YOUR TIME ON *SILLY THINGS*.
...

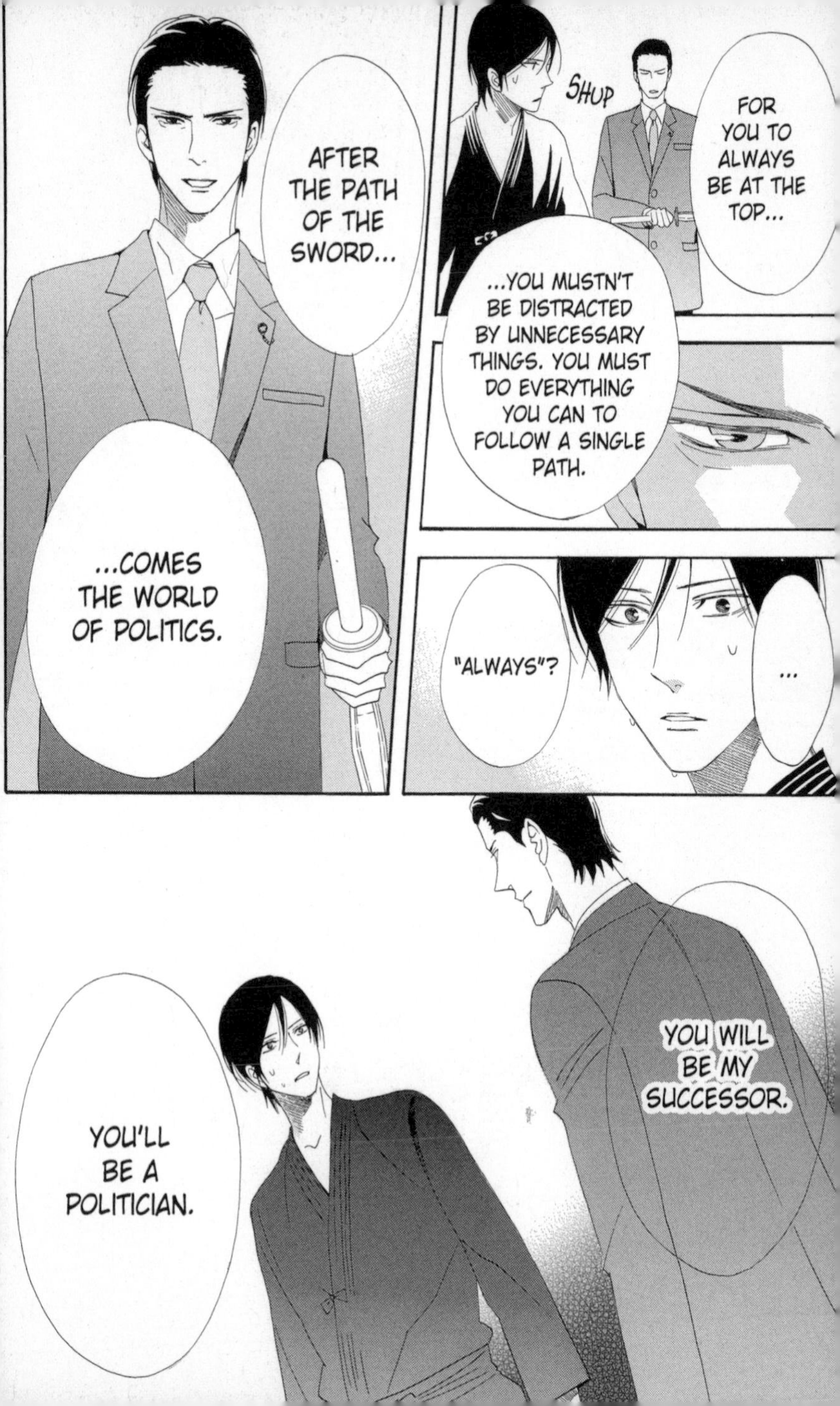
SHUP
FOR YOU TO ALWAYS BE AT THE TOP...
...YOU MUSTN'T BE DISTRACTED BY UNNECESSARY THINGS. YOU MUST DO EVERYTHING YOU CAN TO FOLLOW A SINGLE PATH.
...
"ALWAYS"?
AFTER THE PATH OF THE SWORD...
...COMES THE WORLD OF POLITICS.
YOU WILL BE MY SUCCESSOR.
YOU'LL BE A POLITICIAN.

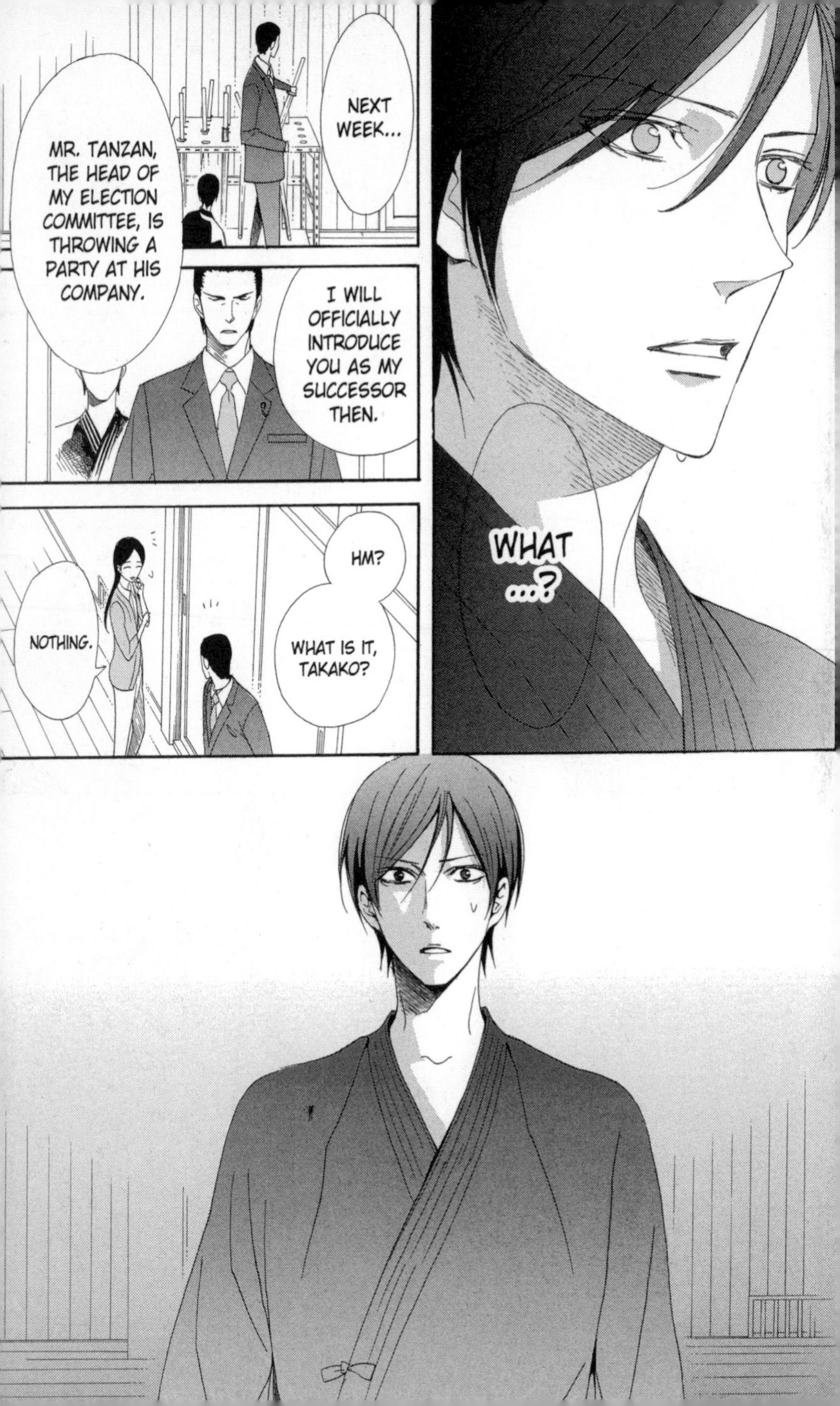
WHAT ...?
NEXT WEEK...
MR. TANZAN, THE HEAD OF MY ELECTION COMMITTEE, IS THROWING A PARTY AT HIS COMPANY.
I WILL OFFICIALLY INTRODUCE YOU AS MY SUCCESSOR THEN.
HM?
WHAT IS IT, TAKAKO?
NOTHING.

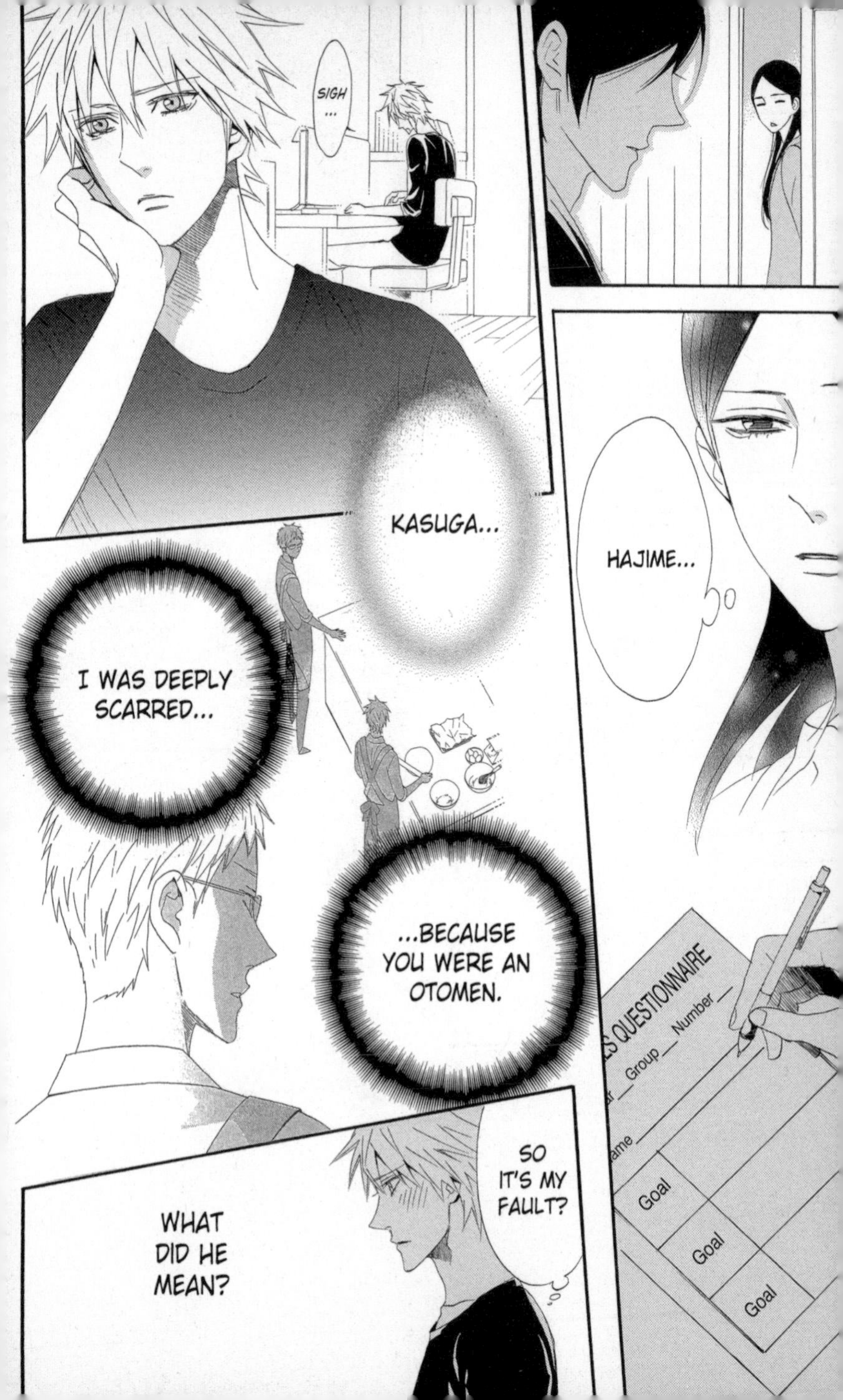
SIGH...
HAJIME...
QUESTIONNAIRE
Group
Number
Goal
Goal
Goal
KASUGA...
I WAS DEEPLY SCARRED...
...BECAUSE YOU WERE AN OTOMEN.
SO IT'S MY FAULT?
WHAT DID HE MEAN?

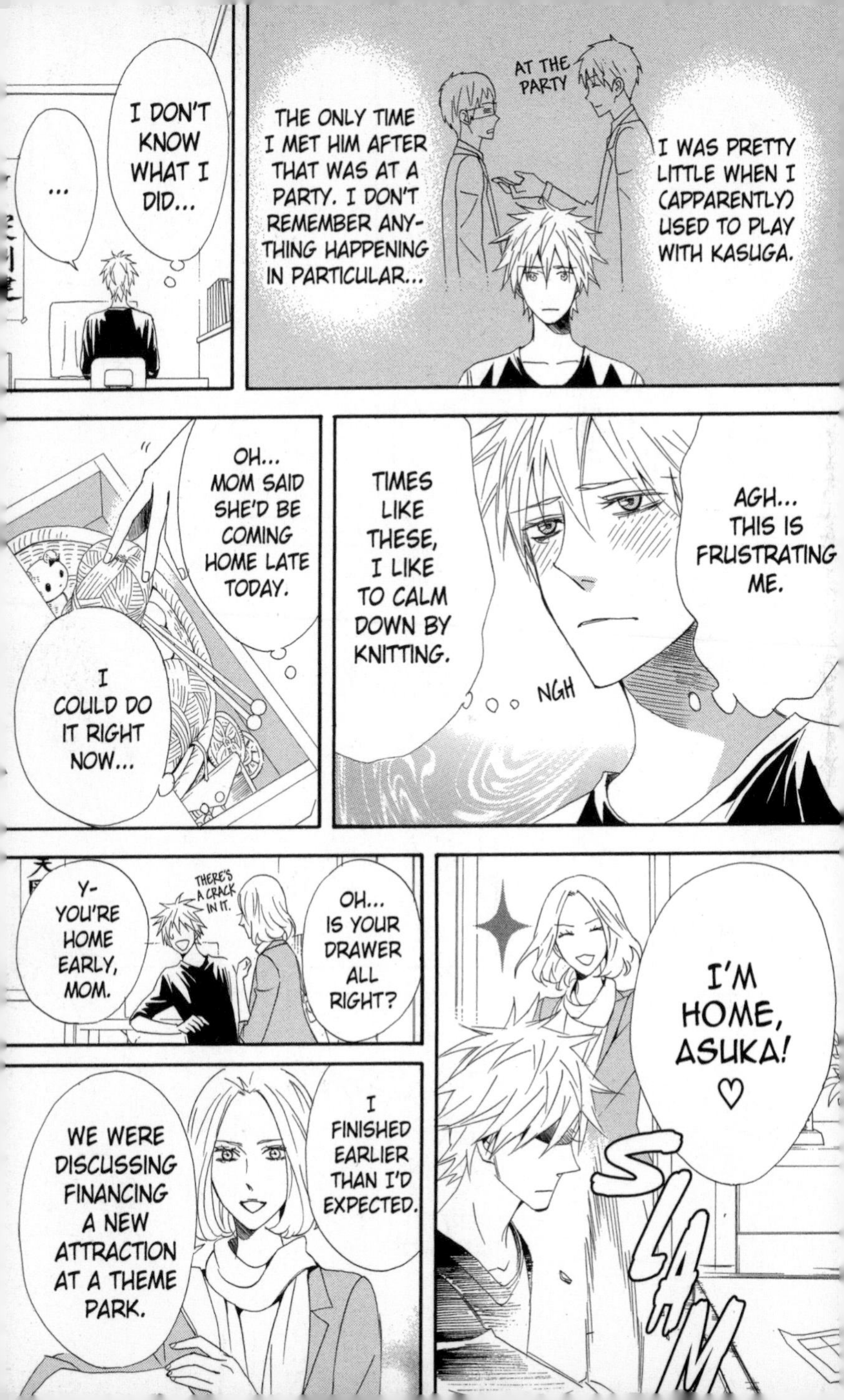
I WAS PRETTY LITTLE WHEN I (APPARENTLY) USED TO PLAY WITH KASUGA.
AT THE PARTY
THE ONLY TIME I MET HIM AFTER THAT WAS AT A PARTY. I DON'T REMEMBER ANY-THING HAPPENING IN PARTICULAR...
I DON'T KNOW WHAT I DID...
...
AGH... THIS IS FRUSTRATING ME.
NGH
TIMES LIKE THESE, I LIKE TO CALM DOWN BY KNITTING.
OH... MOM SAID SHE'D BE COMING HOME LATE TODAY.
I COULD DO IT RIGHT NOW...
I'M HOME, ASUKA! ♡
SLAM
OH... IS YOUR DRAWER ALL RIGHT?
THERE'S A CRACK IN IT.
Y- YOU'RE HOME EARLY, MOM.
I FINISHED EARLIER THAN I'D EXPECTED.
WE WERE DISCUSSING FINANCING A NEW ATTRACTION AT A THEME PARK.

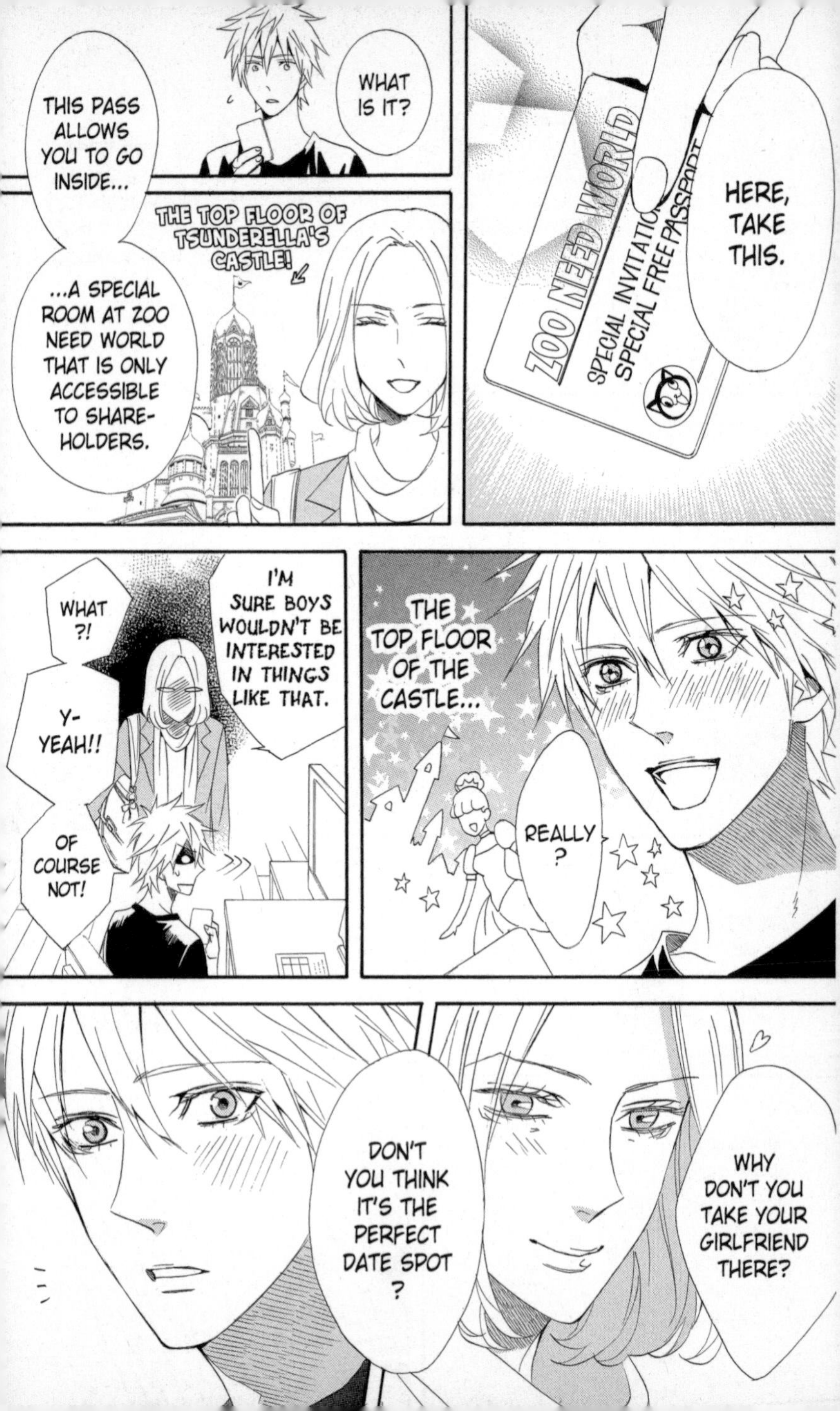
HERE, TAKE THIS.
ZOO NEED WORLD
SPECIAL FREE PASSPORT
WHAT IS IT?
THIS PASS ALLOWS YOU TO GO INSIDE...
THE TOP FLOOR OF TSUNDERELLA'S CASTLE!
...A SPECIAL ROOM AT ZOO NEED WORLD THAT IS ONLY ACCESSIBLE TO SHARE-HOLDERS.
THE TOP FLOOR OF THE CASTLE...
REALLY?
I'M SURE BOYS WOULDN'T BE INTERESTED IN THINGS LIKE THAT.
WHAT?!
Y-YEAH!!
OF COURSE NOT!
WHY DON'T YOU TAKE YOUR GIRLFRIEND THERE?
DON'T YOU THINK IT'S THE PERFECT DATE SPOT?

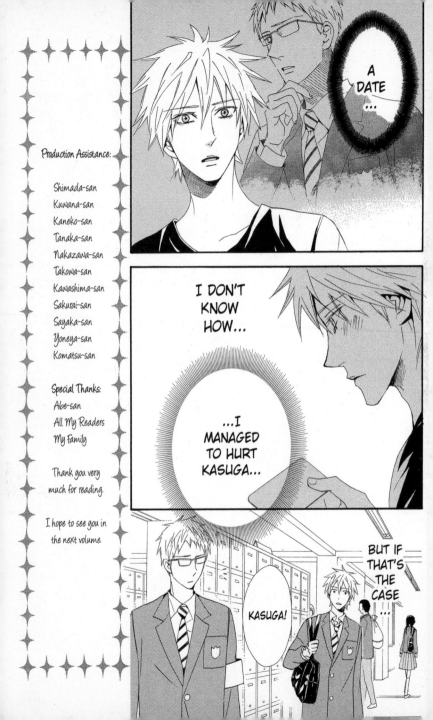

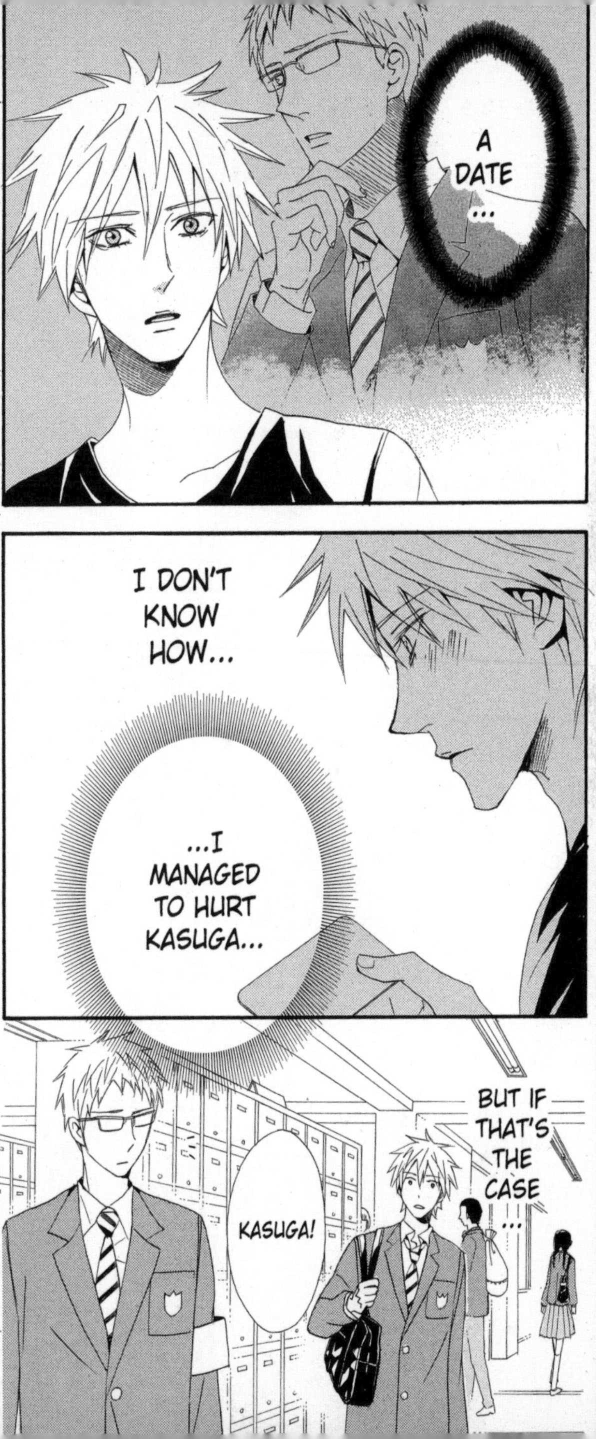
A DATE ...
I DON'T KNOW HOW...
...I MANAGED TO HURT KASUGA...
BUT IF THAT'S THE CASE ...
KASUGA!

Production Assistance:

Shimada-san
Kuwana-san
Kaneko-san
Tanaka-san
Nakazawa-san
Takowa-san
Kawashima-san
Sakurai-san
Sayaka-san
Yoneya-san
Komatsu-san

Special Thanks:
Abe-san
All My Readers
My Family

Thank you very much for reading.

I hope to see you in the next volume.

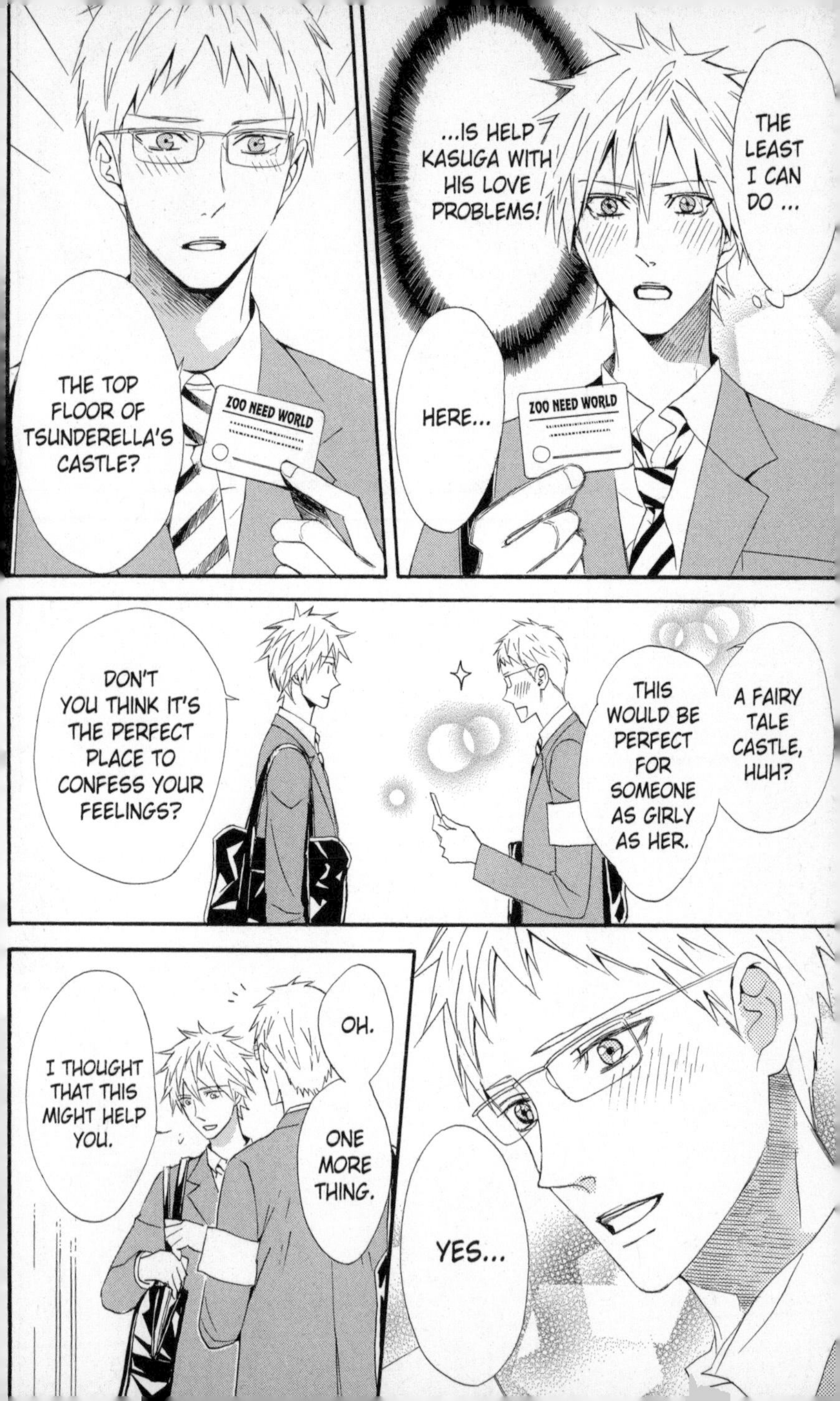
THE LEAST I CAN DO ...
...IS HELP KASUGA WITH HIS LOVE PROBLEMS!
HERE...
ZOO NEED WORLD
THE TOP FLOOR OF TSUNDERELLA'S CASTLE?
ZOO NEED WORLD
A FAIRY TALE CASTLE, HUH?
THIS WOULD BE PERFECT FOR SOMEONE AS GIRLY AS HER.
DON'T YOU THINK IT'S THE PERFECT PLACE TO CONFESS YOUR FEELINGS?
YES...
OH.
ONE MORE THING.
I THOUGHT THAT THIS MIGHT HELP YOU.

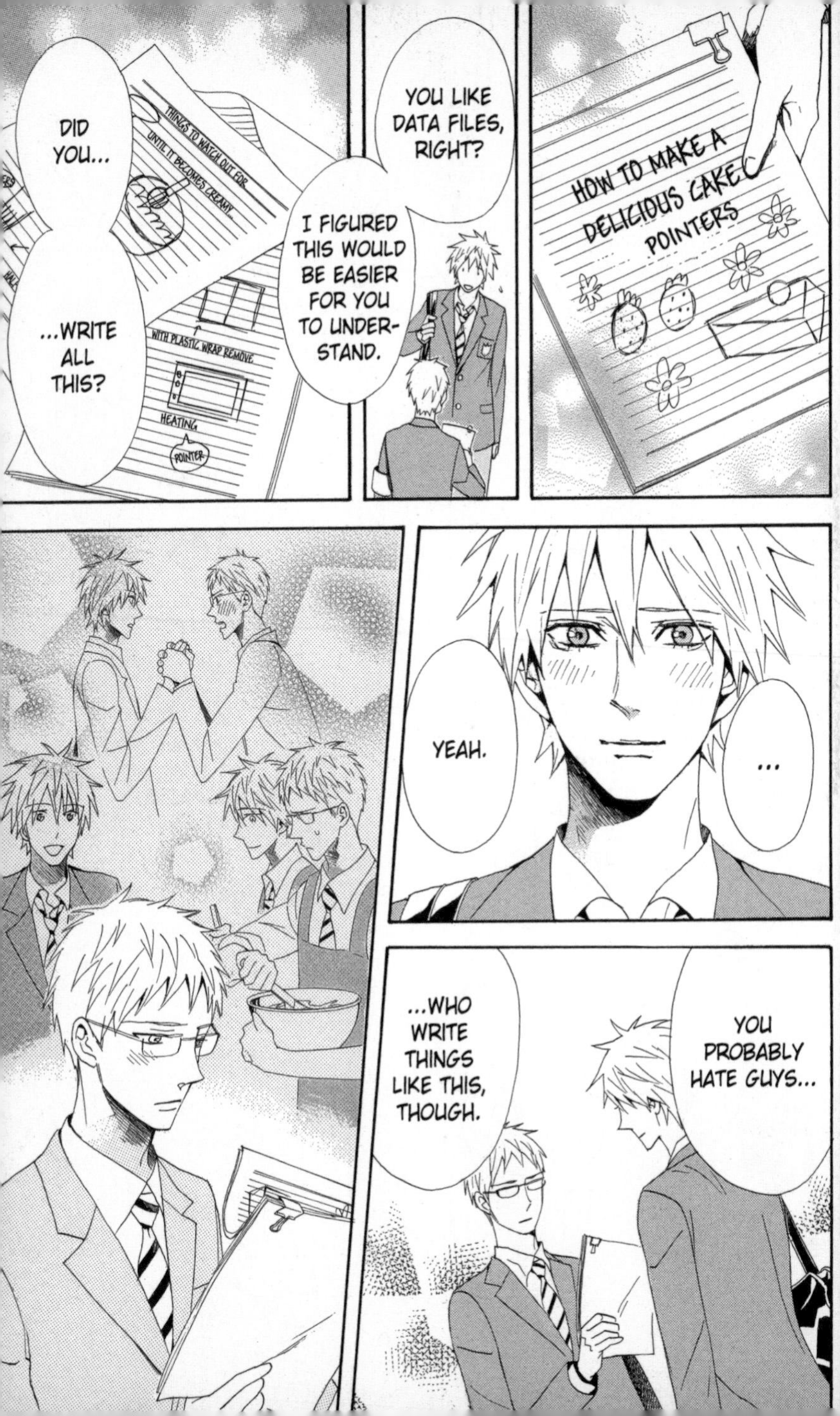
HOW TO MAKE A DELICIOUS CAKE POINTERS
YOU LIKE DATA FILES, RIGHT?
I FIGURED THIS WOULD BE EASIER FOR YOU TO UNDERSTAND.
DID YOU...
...WRITE ALL THIS?
THINGS TO WATCH OUT FOR UNTIL IT BECOMES CREAMY.
WITH PLASTIC WRAP REMOVE
HEATING
POINTER
...
YEAH.
YOU PROBABLY HATE GUYS...
...WHO WRITE THINGS LIKE THIS, THOUGH.
POINTER

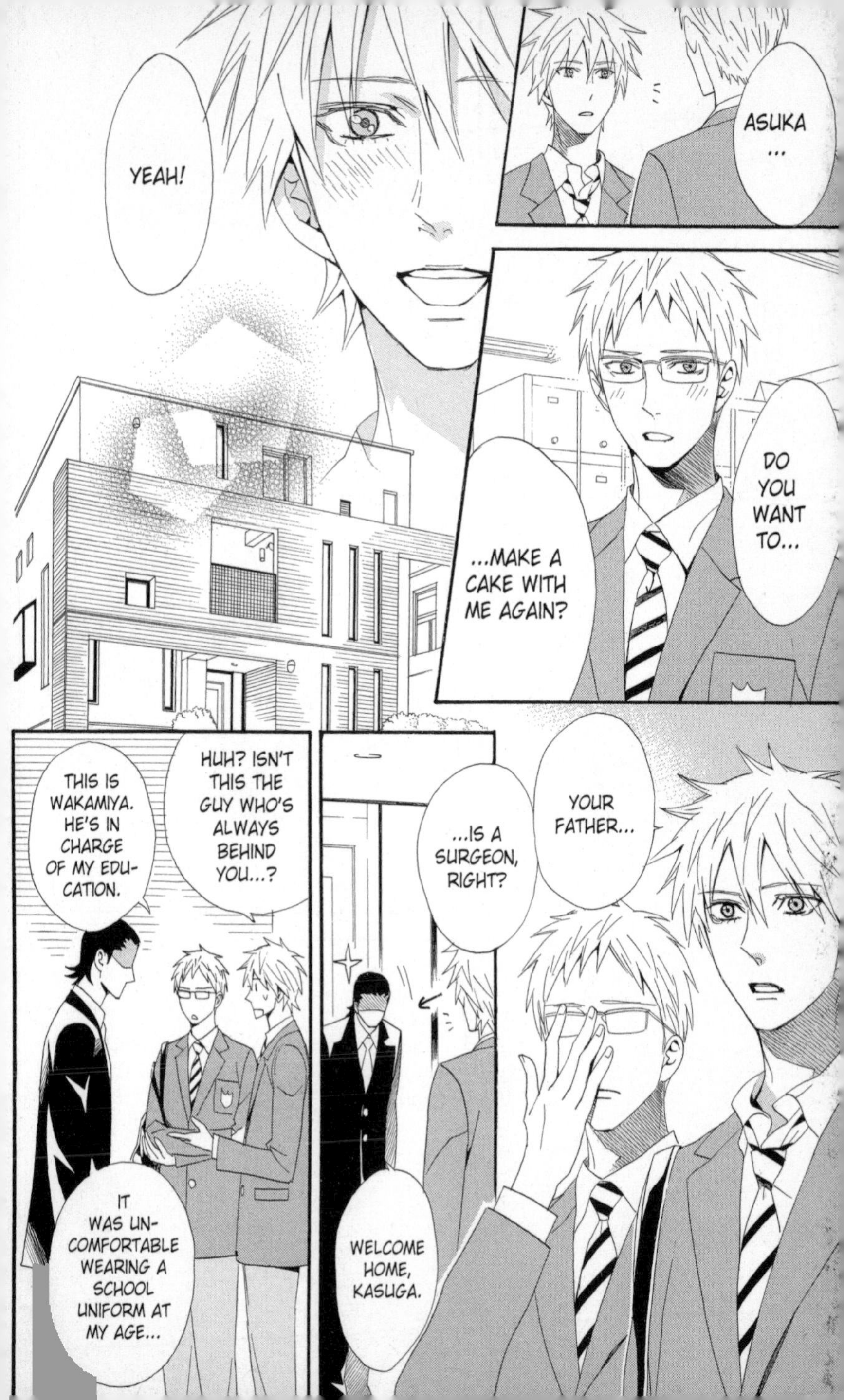
ASUKA...
DO YOU WANT TO...
...MAKE A CAKE WITH ME AGAIN?
YEAH!
YOUR FATHER...
...IS A SURGEON, RIGHT?
WELCOME HOME, KASUGA.
HUH? ISN'T THIS THE GUY WHO'S ALWAYS BEHIND YOU...?
THIS IS WAKAMIYA. HE'S IN CHARGE OF MY EDU-CATION.
IT WAS UN-COMFORTABLE WEARING A SCHOOL UNIFORM AT MY AGE...

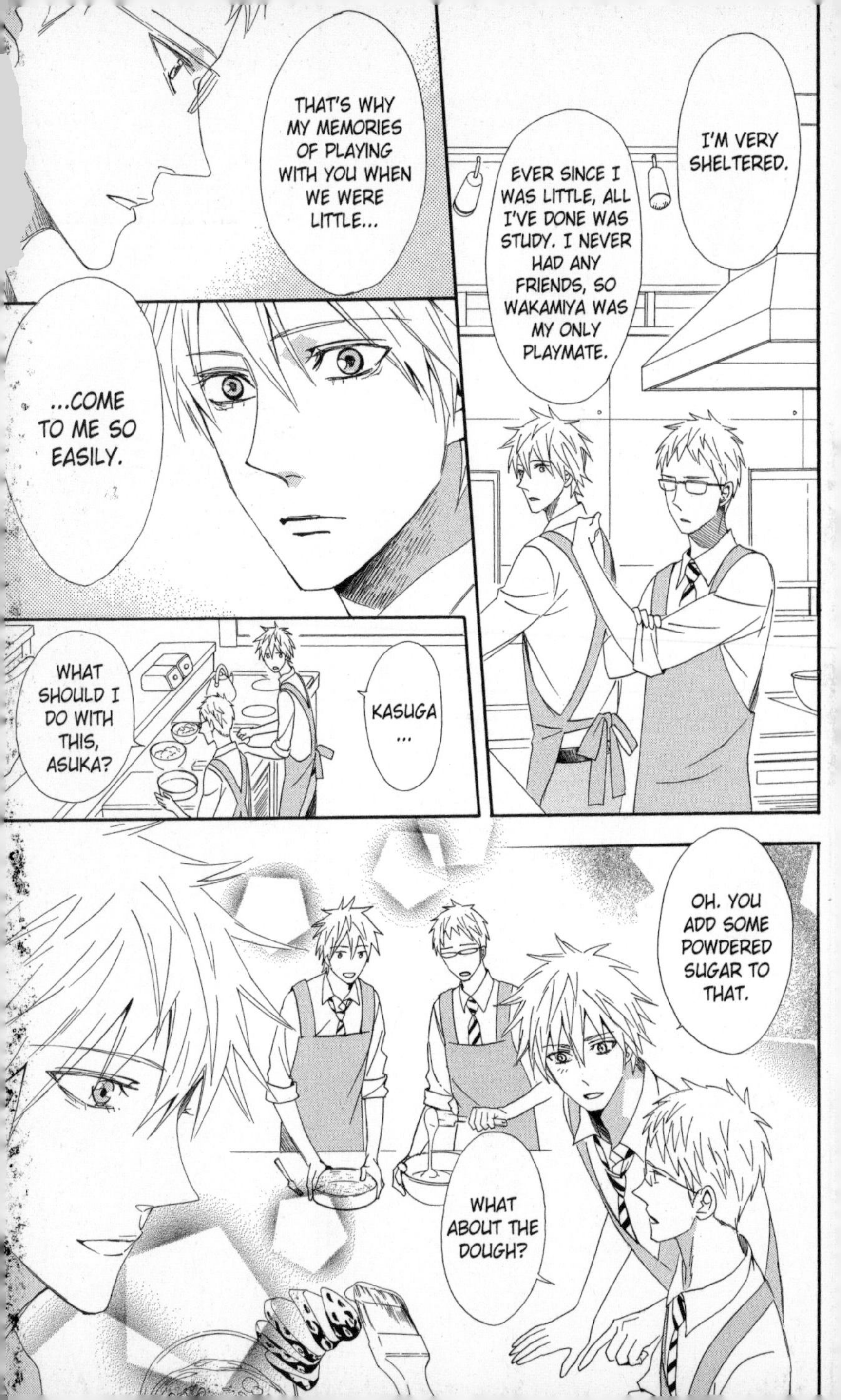
I'M VERY SHELTERED.
EVER SINCE I WAS LITTLE, ALL I'VE DONE WAS STUDY. I NEVER HAD ANY FRIENDS, SO WAKAMIYA WAS MY ONLY PLAYMATE.
THAT'S WHY MY MEMORIES OF PLAYING WITH YOU WHEN WE WERE LITTLE...
...COME TO ME SO EASILY.
KASUGA...
WHAT SHOULD I DO WITH THIS, ASUKA?
OH. YOU ADD SOME POWDERED SUGAR TO THAT.
WHAT ABOUT THE DOUGH?

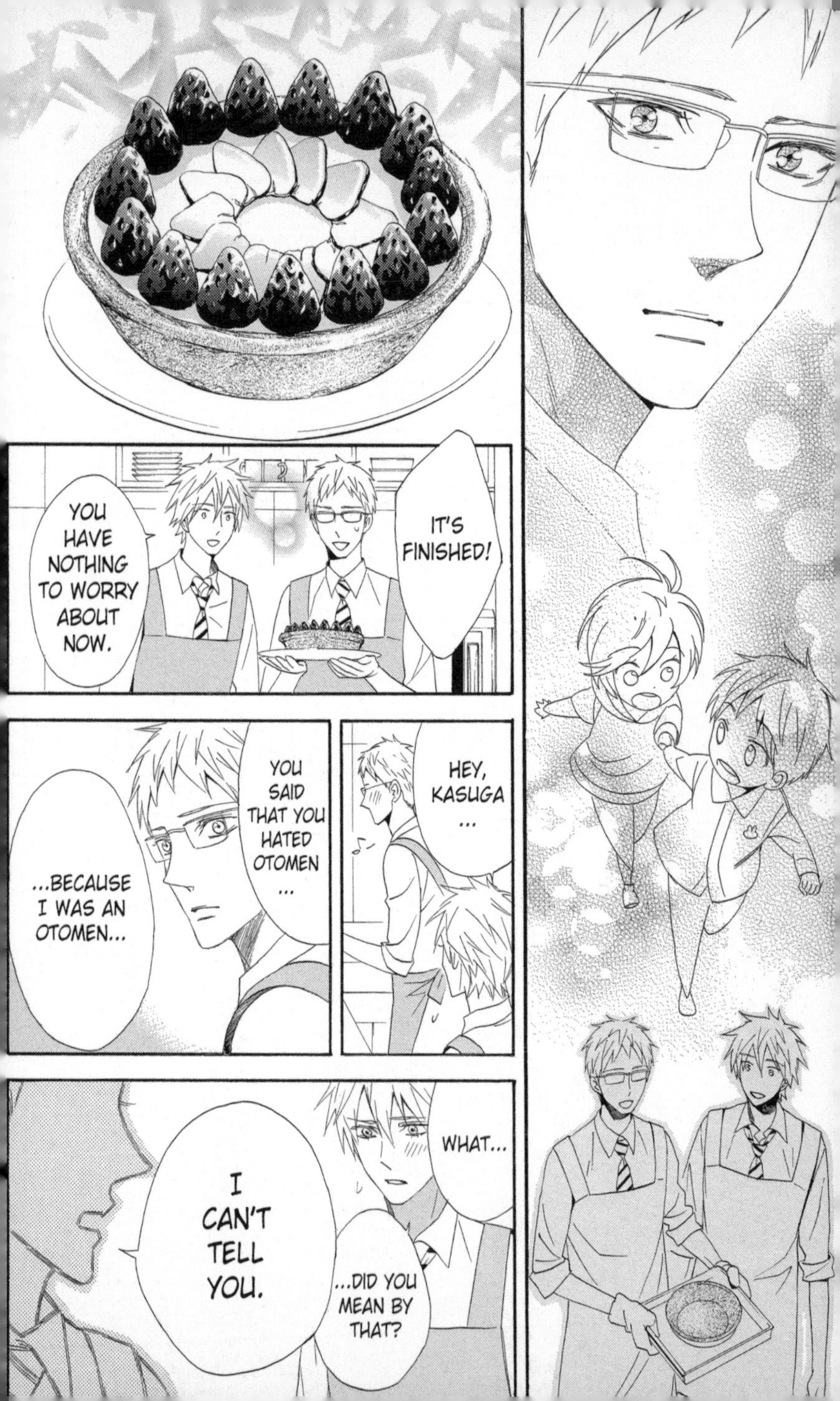
IT'S FINISHED!
YOU HAVE NOTHING TO WORRY ABOUT NOW.
HEY, KASUGA...
YOU SAID THAT YOU HATED OTOMEN...
...BECAUSE I WAS AN OTOMEN...
WHAT...
...DID YOU MEAN BY THAT?
I CAN'T TELL YOU.

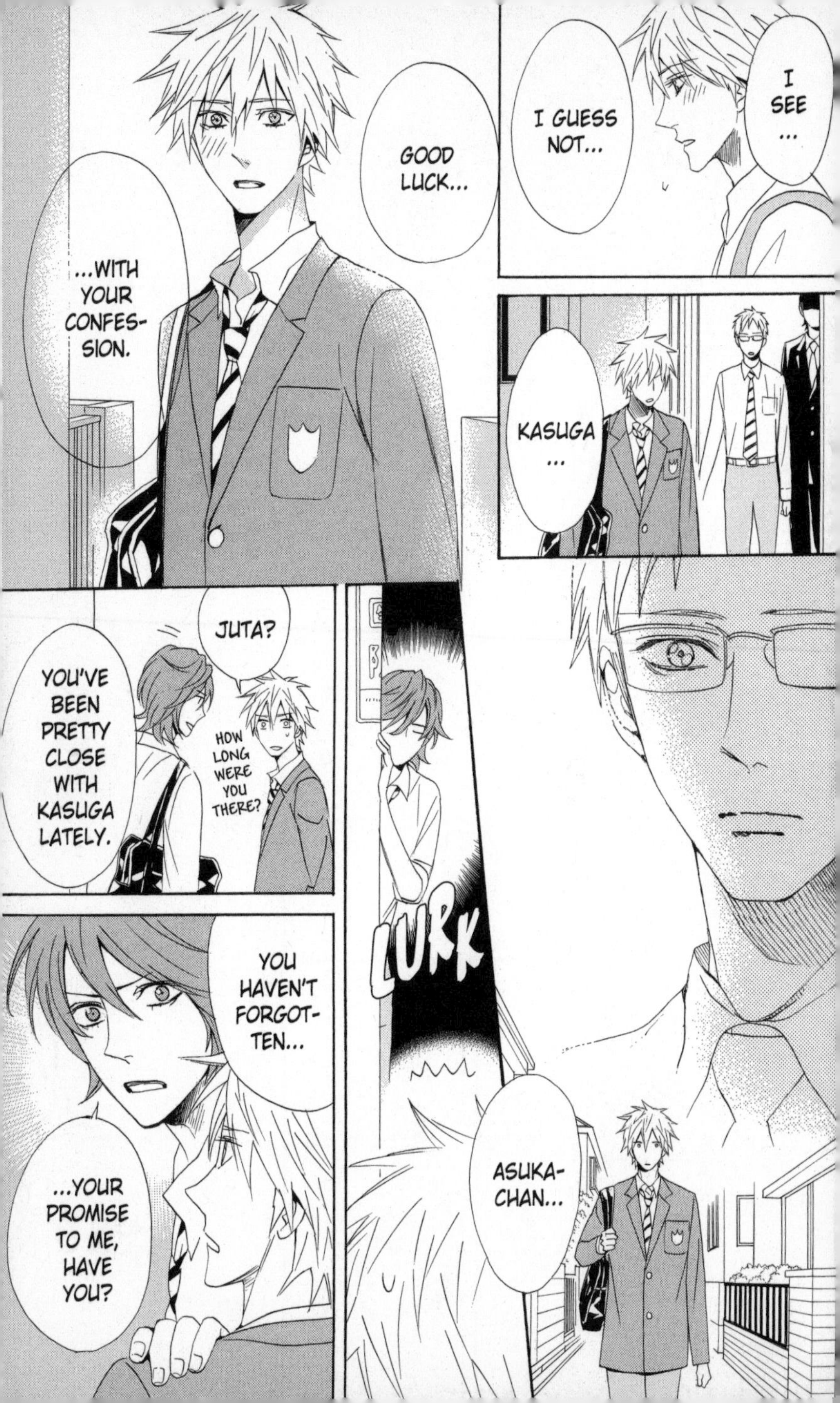
I SEE...
I GUESS NOT...
KASUGA...
GOOD LUCK...
...WITH YOUR CONFESSION.
ASUKA-CHAN...
LURK
JUTA?
HOW LONG WERE YOU THERE?
YOU'VE BEEN PRETTY CLOSE WITH KASUGA LATELY.
YOU HAVEN'T FORGOTTEN...
...YOUR PROMISE TO ME, HAVE YOU?

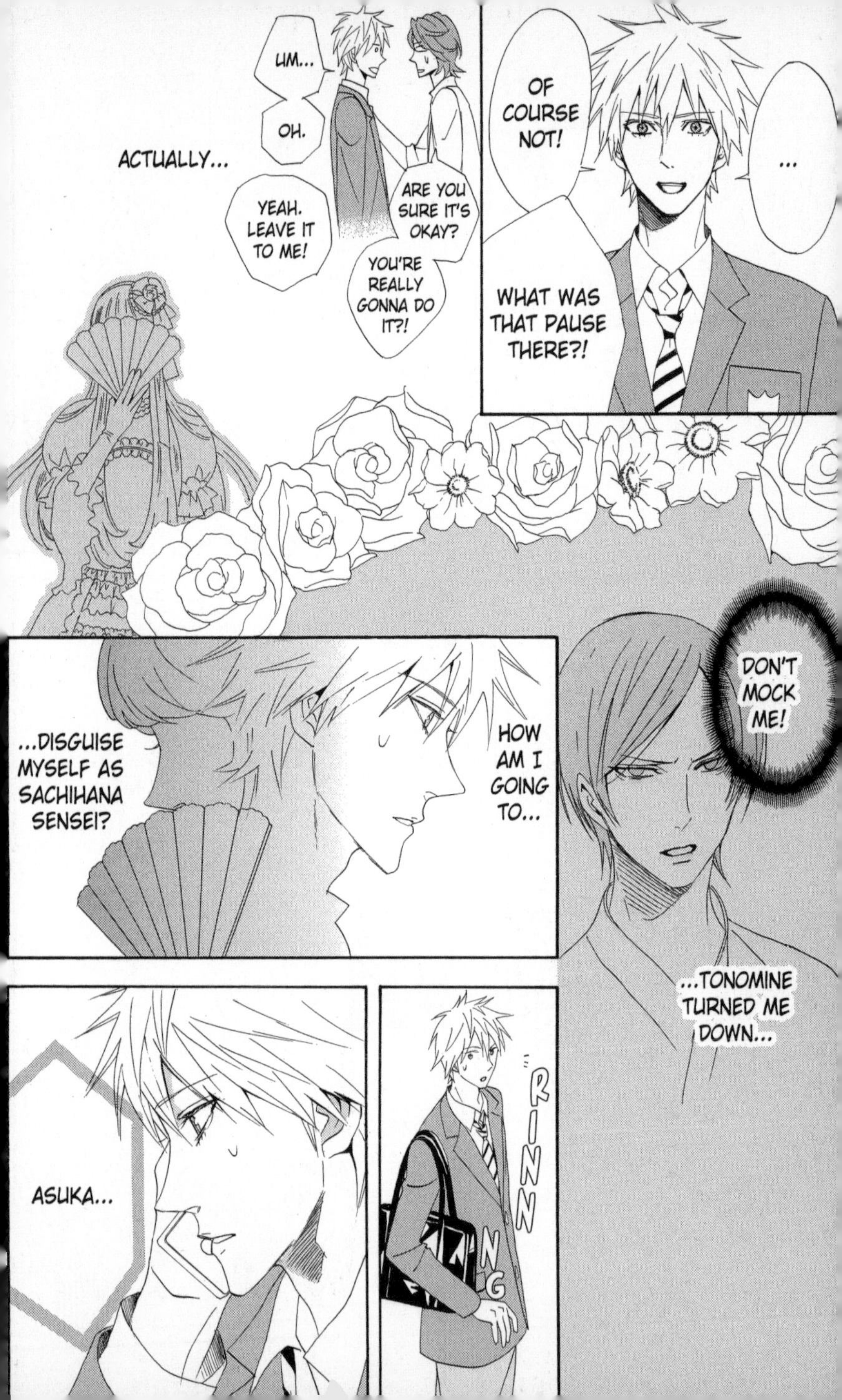

...
OF COURSE NOT!
WHAT WAS THAT PAUSE THERE?!
UM...
OH.
ARE YOU SURE IT'S OKAY?
YOU'RE REALLY GONNA DO IT?!
YEAH. LEAVE IT TO ME!
ACTUALLY...
DON'T MOCK ME!
...TONOMINE TURNED ME DOWN...
HOW AM I GOING TO...
...DISGUISE MYSELF AS SACHIHANA SENSEI?
RINNNG
ASUKA...

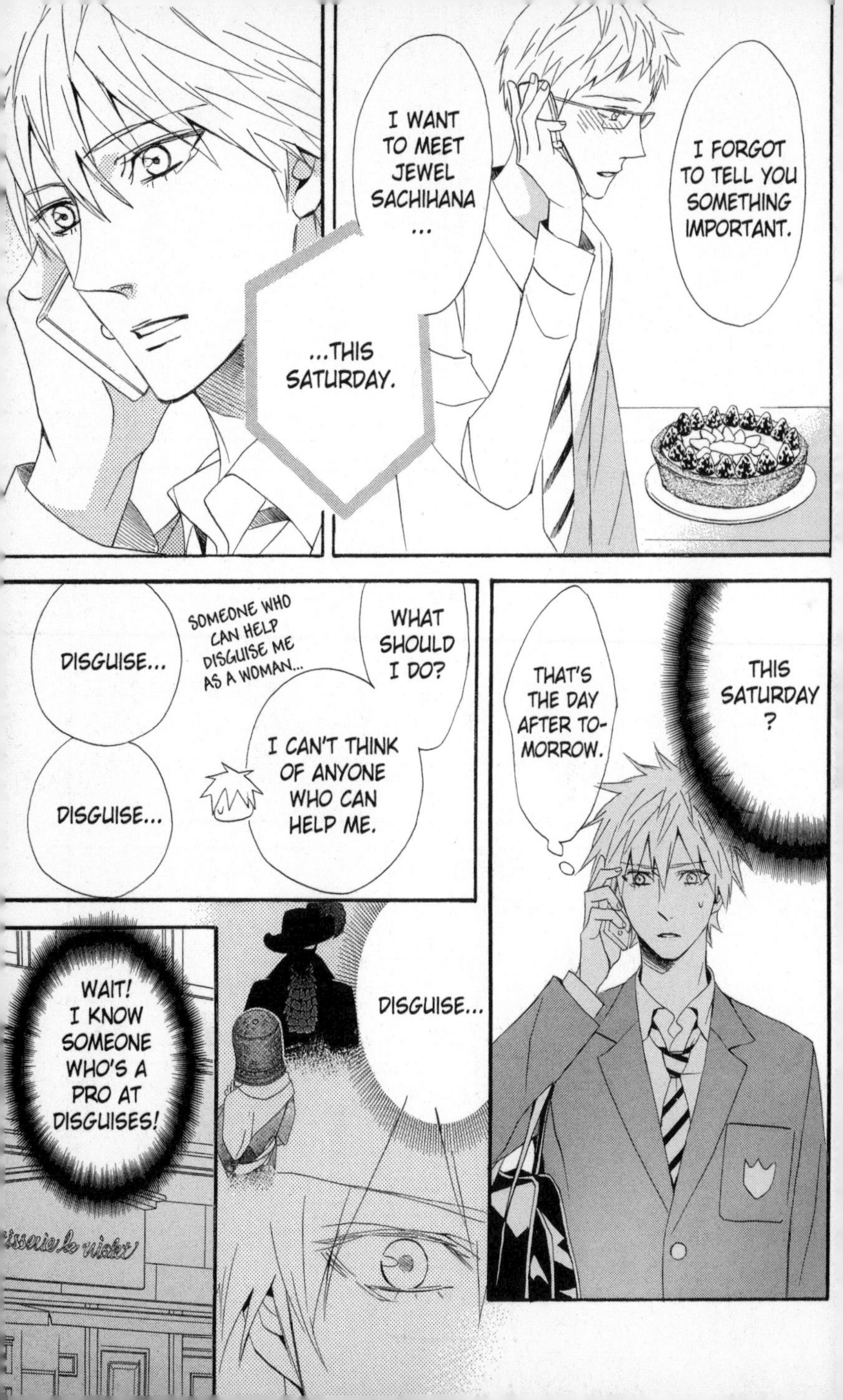
I FORGOT TO TELL YOU SOMETHING IMPORTANT.
I WANT TO MEET JEWEL SACHIHANA ...
...THIS SATURDAY.
THIS SATURDAY ?
THAT'S THE DAY AFTER TO-MORROW.
WHAT SHOULD I DO?
SOMEONE WHO CAN HELP DISGUISE ME AS A WOMAN...
DISGUISE...
I CAN'T THINK OF ANYONE WHO CAN HELP ME.
DISGUISE...
DISGUISE...
WAIT! I KNOW SOMEONE WHO'S A PRO AT DISGUISES!

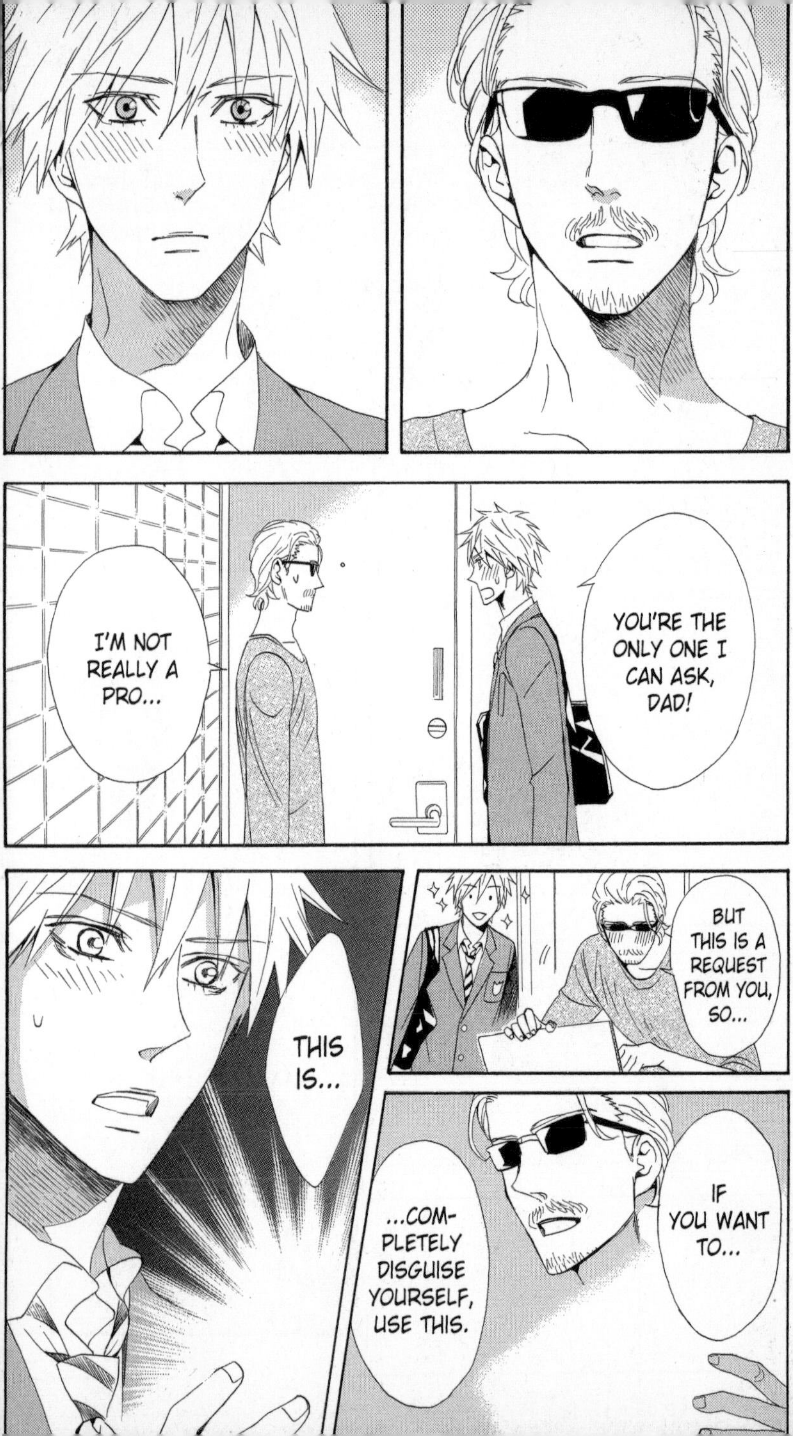
YOU'RE THE ONLY ONE I CAN ASK, DAD!
I'M NOT REALLY A PRO...
BUT THIS IS A REQUEST FROM YOU, SO...
IF YOU WANT TO...
...COM-PLETELY DISGUISE YOURSELF, USE THIS.
THIS IS...

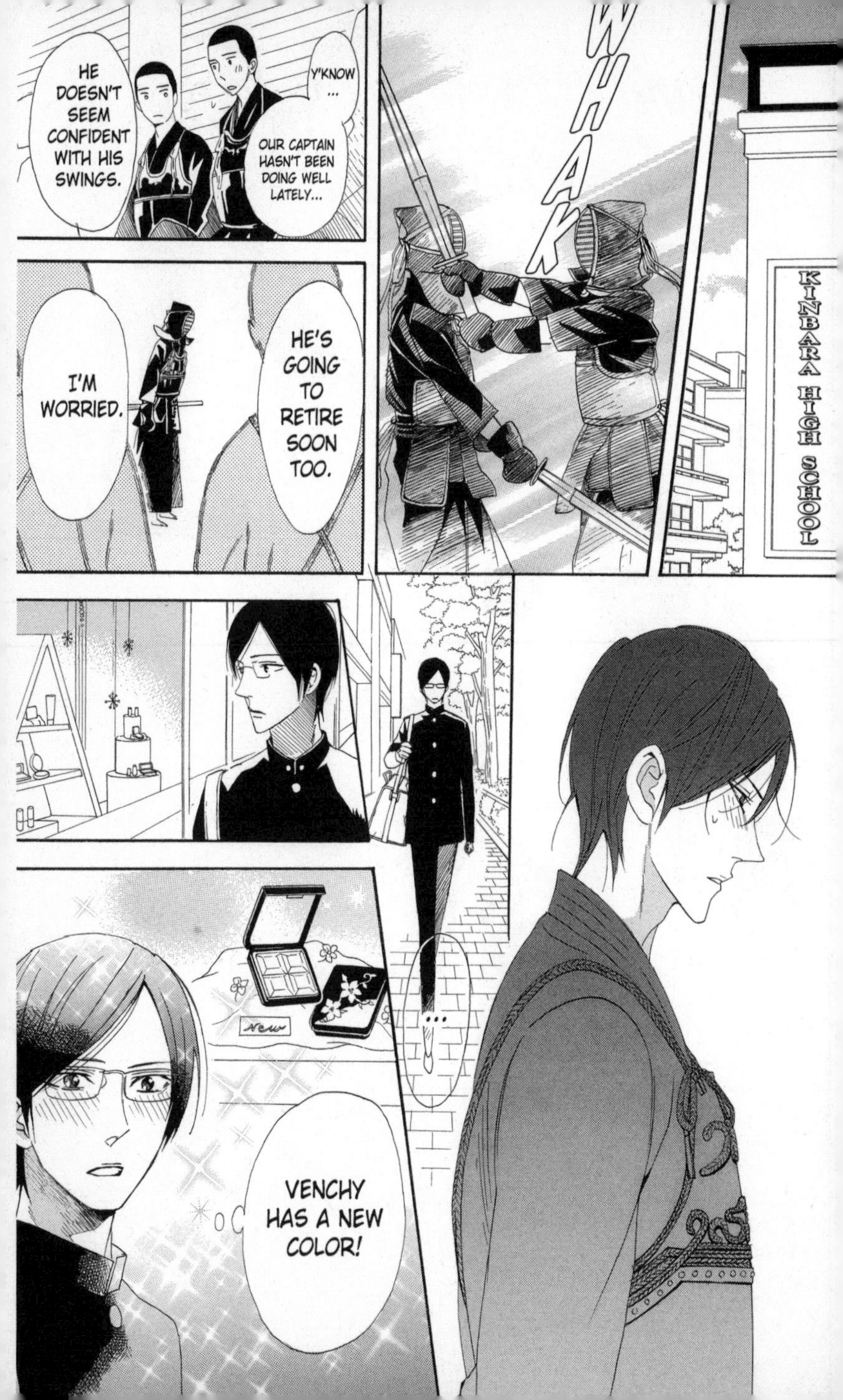
KINBARA HIGH SCHOOL
WHAK
Y'KNOW...
OUR CAPTAIN HASN'T BEEN DOING WELL LATELY...
HE DOESN'T SEEM CONFIDENT WITH HIS SWINGS.
HE'S GOING TO RETIRE SOON TOO.
I'M WORRIED.
...
New
VENCHY HAS A NEW COLOR!

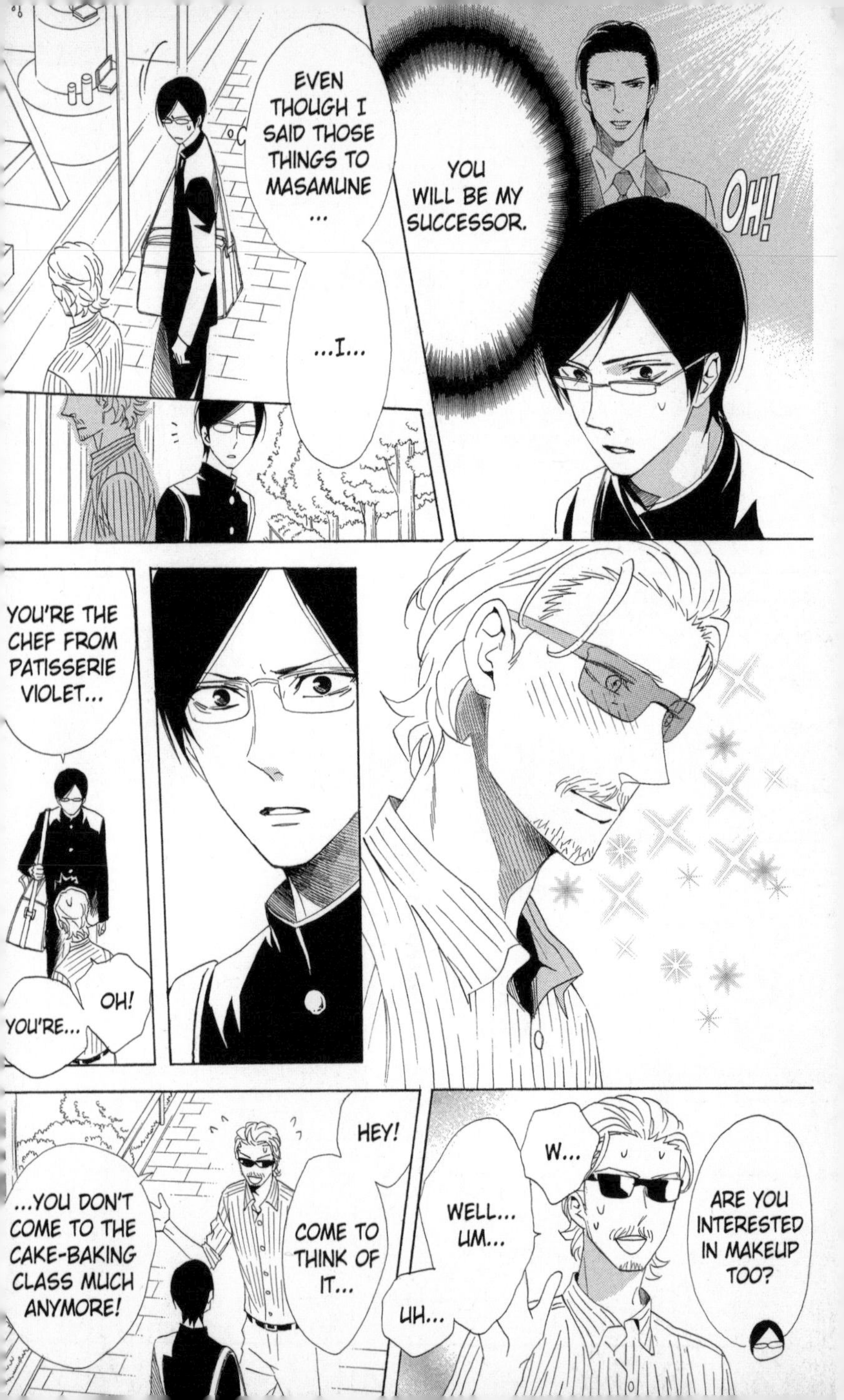
OH!
YOU WILL BE MY SUCCESSOR.
EVEN THOUGH I SAID THOSE THINGS TO MASAMUNE ...
...I...
YOU'RE THE CHEF FROM PATISSERIE VIOLET...
OH!
YOU'RE...
ARE YOU INTERESTED IN MAKEUP TOO?
W...
WELL... UM...
UH...
HEY!
COME TO THINK OF IT...
...YOU DON'T COME TO THE CAKE-BAKING CLASS MUCH ANYMORE!

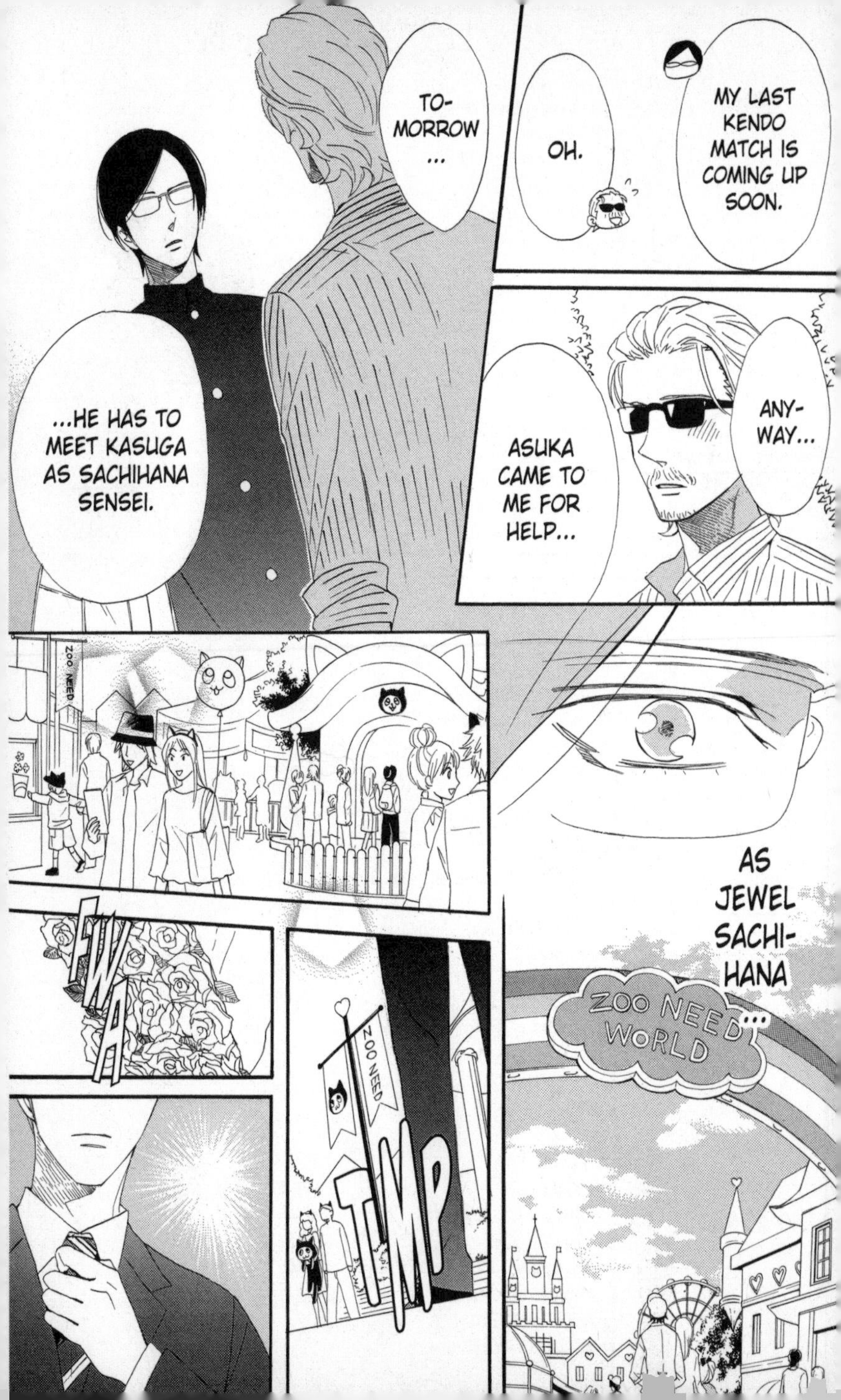
MY LAST KENDO MATCH IS COMING UP SOON.
OH.
ANY-WAY...
ASUKA CAME TO ME FOR HELP...
TO-MORROW...
...HE HAS TO MEET KASUGA AS SACHIHANA SENSEI.
AS JEWEL SACHI-HANA...
ZOO NEED WORLD
ZOO NEED
ZOO NEED
TMP
FWA

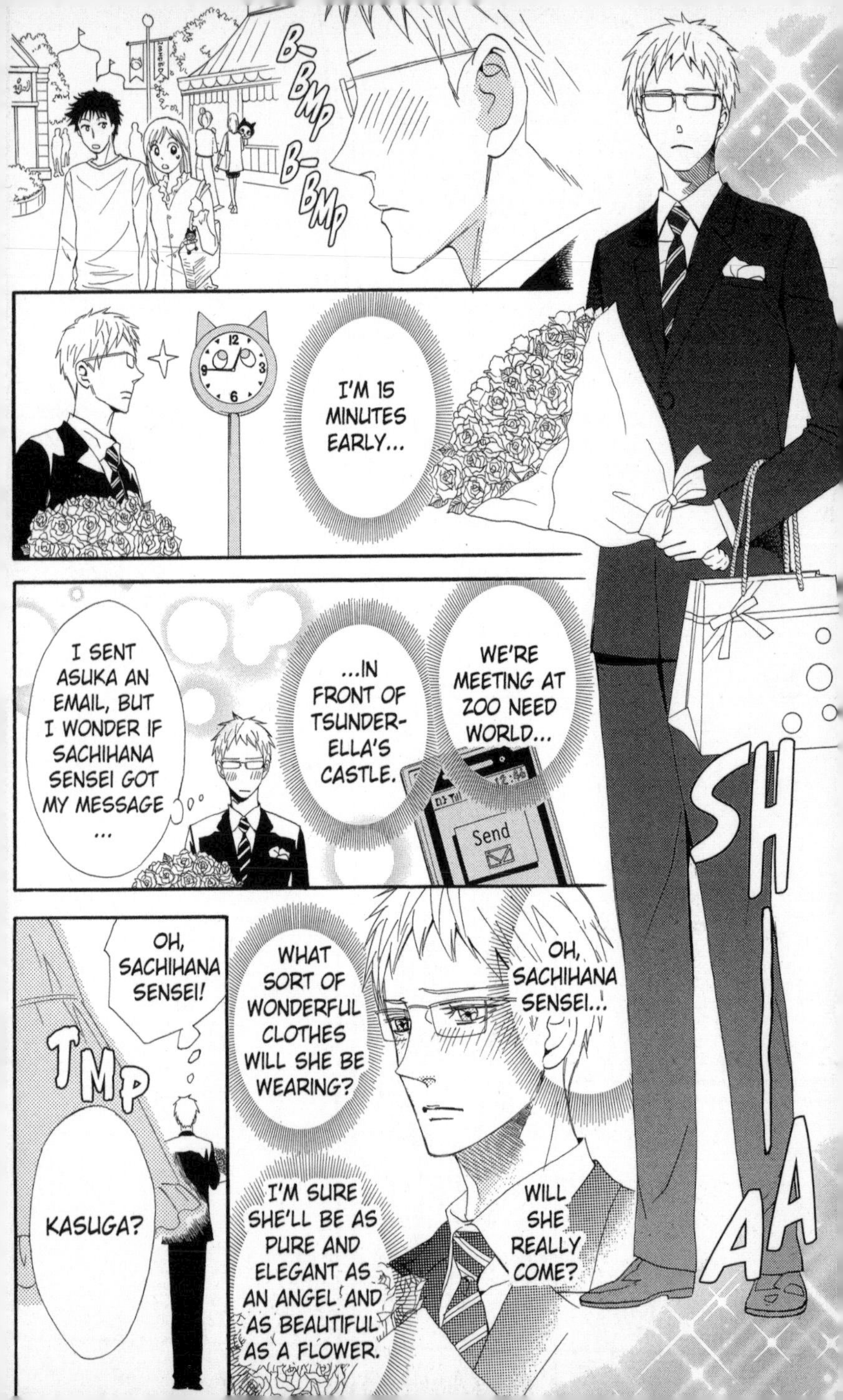
SHIIAA
B-BMP B-BMP
I'M 15 MINUTES EARLY...
WE'RE MEETING AT ZOO NEED WORLD...
...IN FRONT OF TSUNDER-ELLA'S CASTLE.
Send
I SENT ASUKA AN EMAIL, BUT I WONDER IF SACHIHANA SENSEI GOT MY MESSAGE ...
OH, SACHIHANA SENSEI...
WHAT SORT OF WONDERFUL CLOTHES WILL SHE BE WEARING?
WILL SHE REALLY COME?
I'M SURE SHE'LL BE AS PURE AND ELEGANT AS AN ANGEL AND AS BEAUTIFUL AS A FLOWER.
OH, SACHIHANA SENSEI!
TMP
KASUGA?

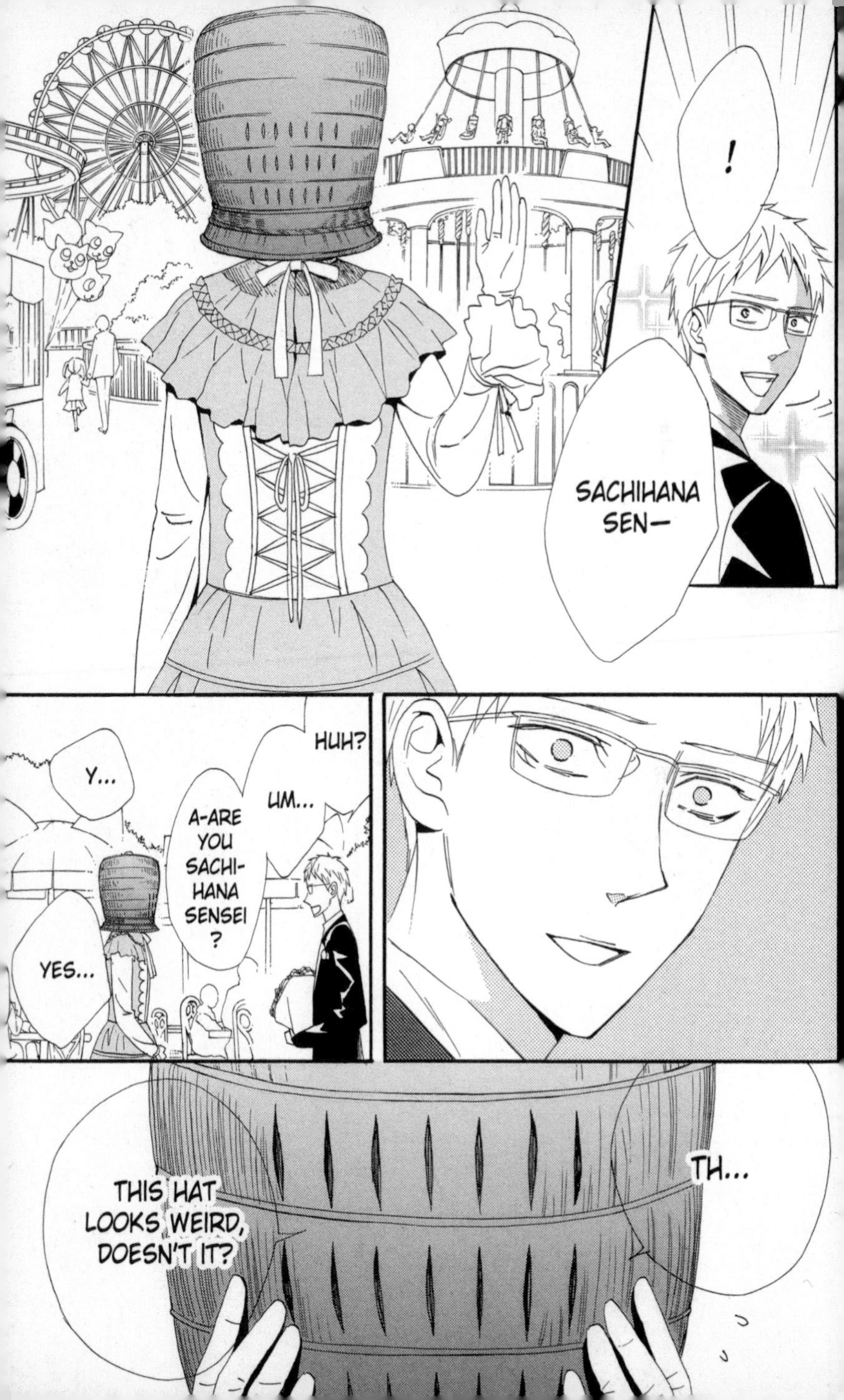
!
SACHIHANA SEN—
HUH?
UM...
A-ARE YOU SACHI-HANA SENSEI?
Y...
YES...
TH...
THIS HAT LOOKS WEIRD, DOESN'T IT?

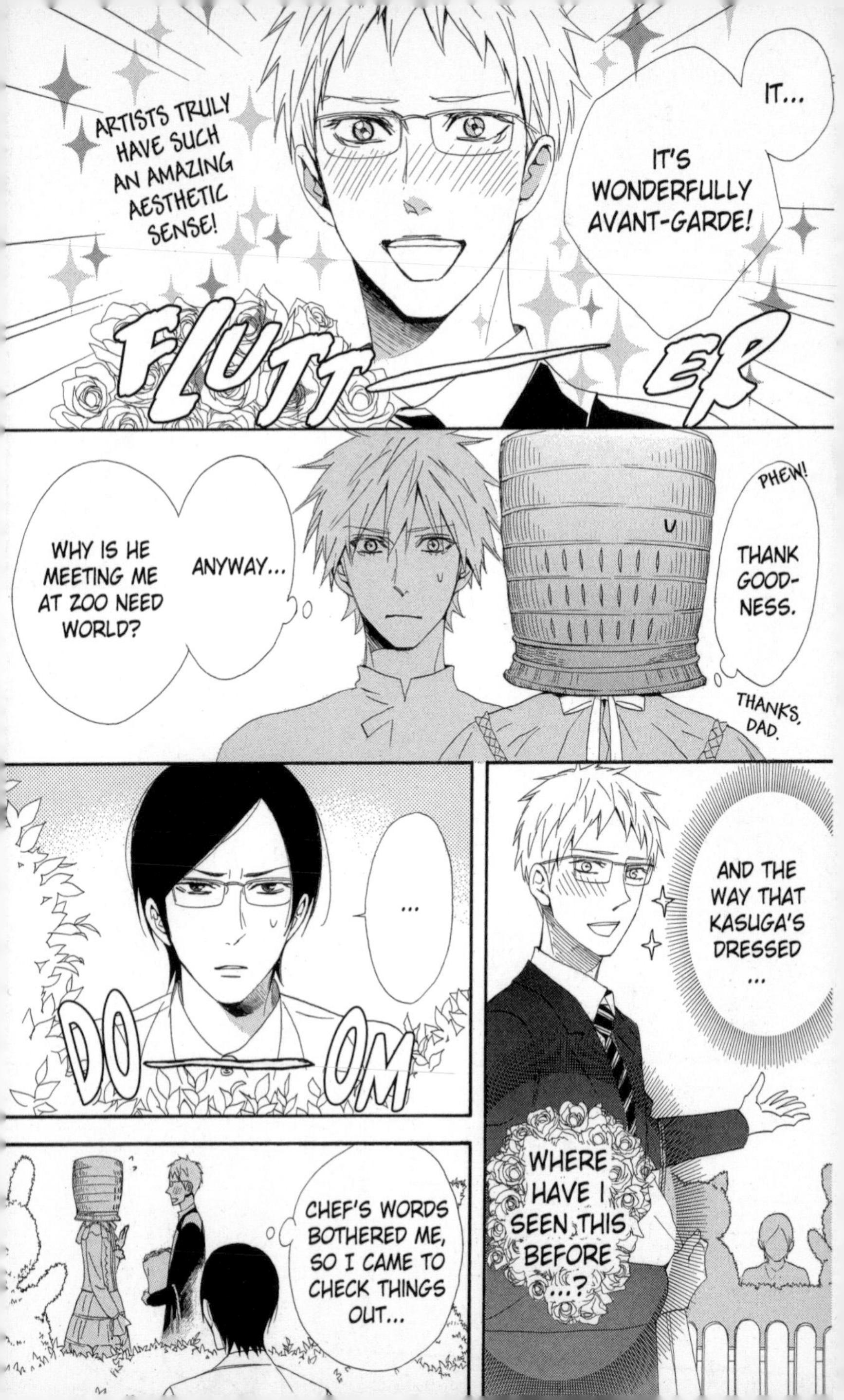
IT...
IT'S WONDERFULLY AVANT-GARDE!
ARTISTS TRULY HAVE SUCH AN AMAZING AESTHETIC SENSE!
FLUTT—ER
PHEW!
THANK GOODNESS.
THANKS, DAD.
ANYWAY...
WHY IS HE MEETING ME AT ZOO NEED WORLD?
AND THE WAY THAT KASUGA'S DRESSED...
WHERE HAVE I SEEN THIS BEFORE...?
...
DO—OM
CHEF'S WORDS BOTHERED ME, SO I CAME TO CHECK THINGS OUT...

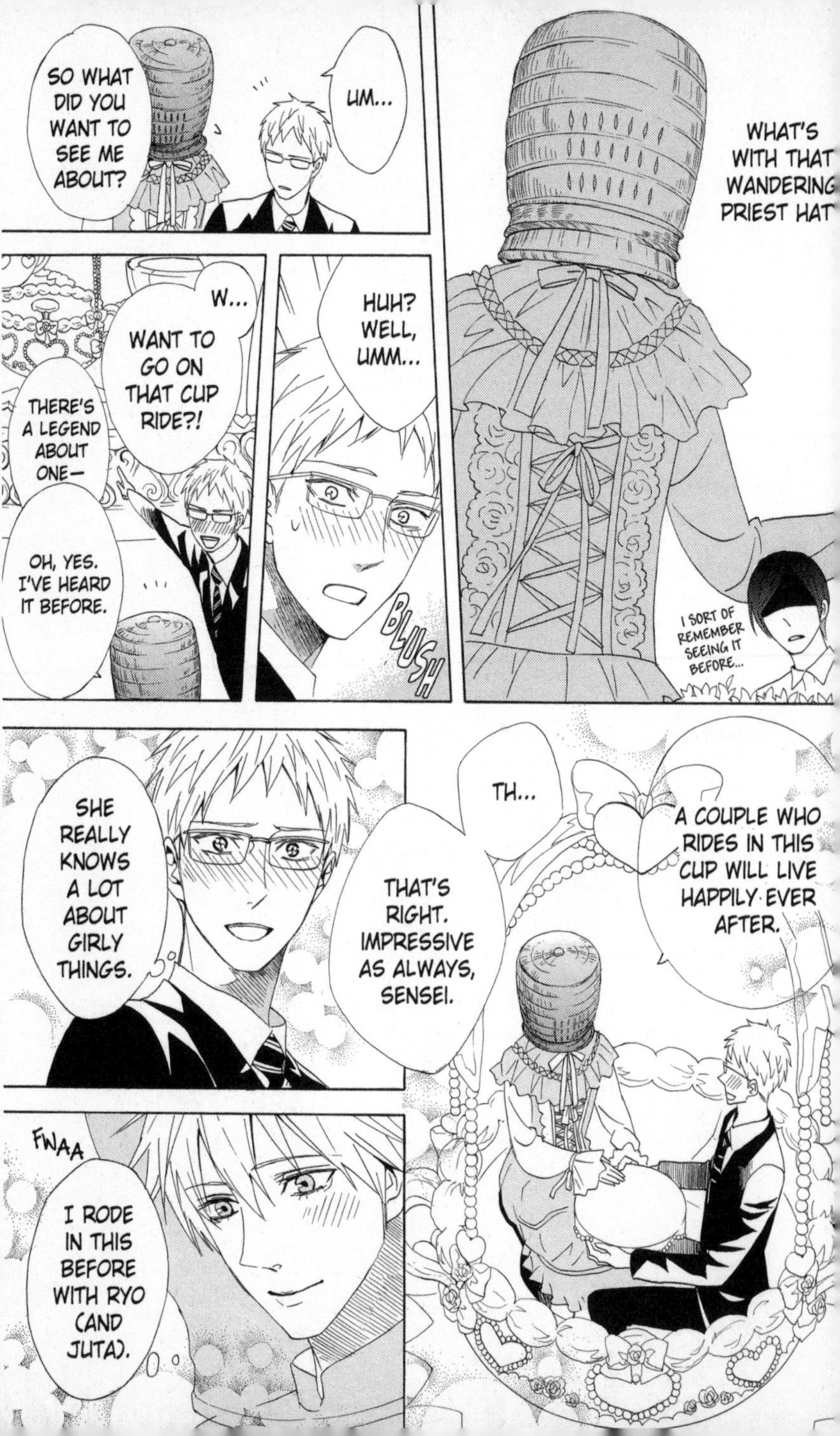
WHAT'S WITH THAT WANDERING PRIEST HAT
I SORT OF REMEMBER SEEING IT BEFORE...
UM...
SO WHAT DID YOU WANT TO SEE ME ABOUT?
HUH? WELL, UMM...
BLUSH
W...
WANT TO GO ON THAT CUP RIDE?!
THERE'S A LEGEND ABOUT ONE—
OH, YES. I'VE HEARD IT BEFORE.
A COUPLE WHO RIDES IN THIS CUP WILL LIVE HAPPILY EVER AFTER.
TH...
THAT'S RIGHT. IMPRESSIVE AS ALWAYS, SENSEI.
SHE REALLY KNOWS A LOT ABOUT GIRLY THINGS.
FWAA
I RODE IN THIS BEFORE WITH RYO (AND JUTA).

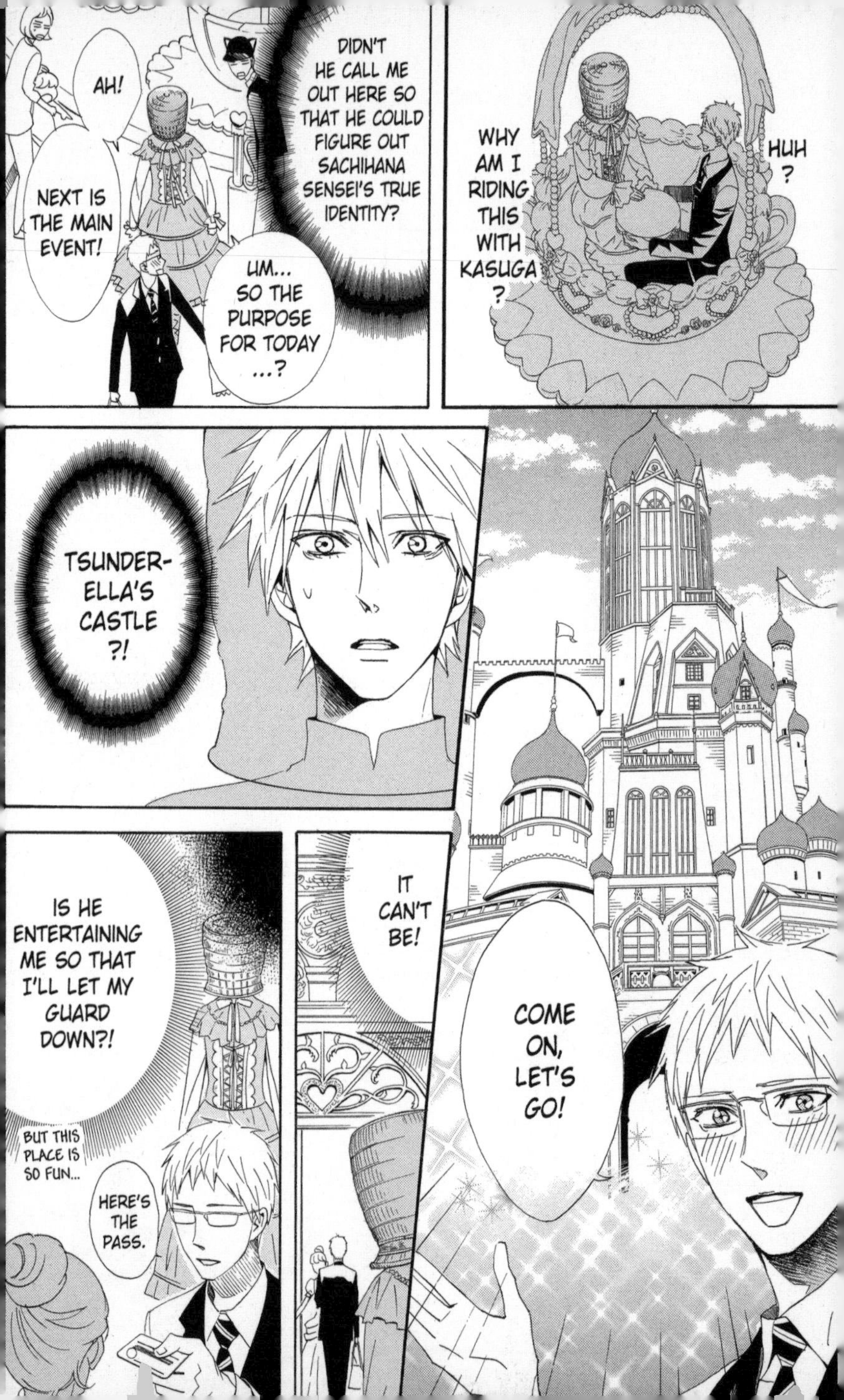
HUH ?
WHY AM I RIDING THIS WITH KASUGA ?
DIDN'T HE CALL ME OUT HERE SO THAT HE COULD FIGURE OUT SACHIHANA SENSEI'S TRUE IDENTITY?
AH!
UM... SO THE PURPOSE FOR TODAY ...?
NEXT IS THE MAIN EVENT!
COME ON, LET'S GO!
TSUNDER-ELLA'S CASTLE ?!
IT CAN'T BE!
IS HE ENTERTAINING ME SO THAT I'LL LET MY GUARD DOWN?!
BUT THIS PLACE IS SO FUN...
HERE'S THE PASS.

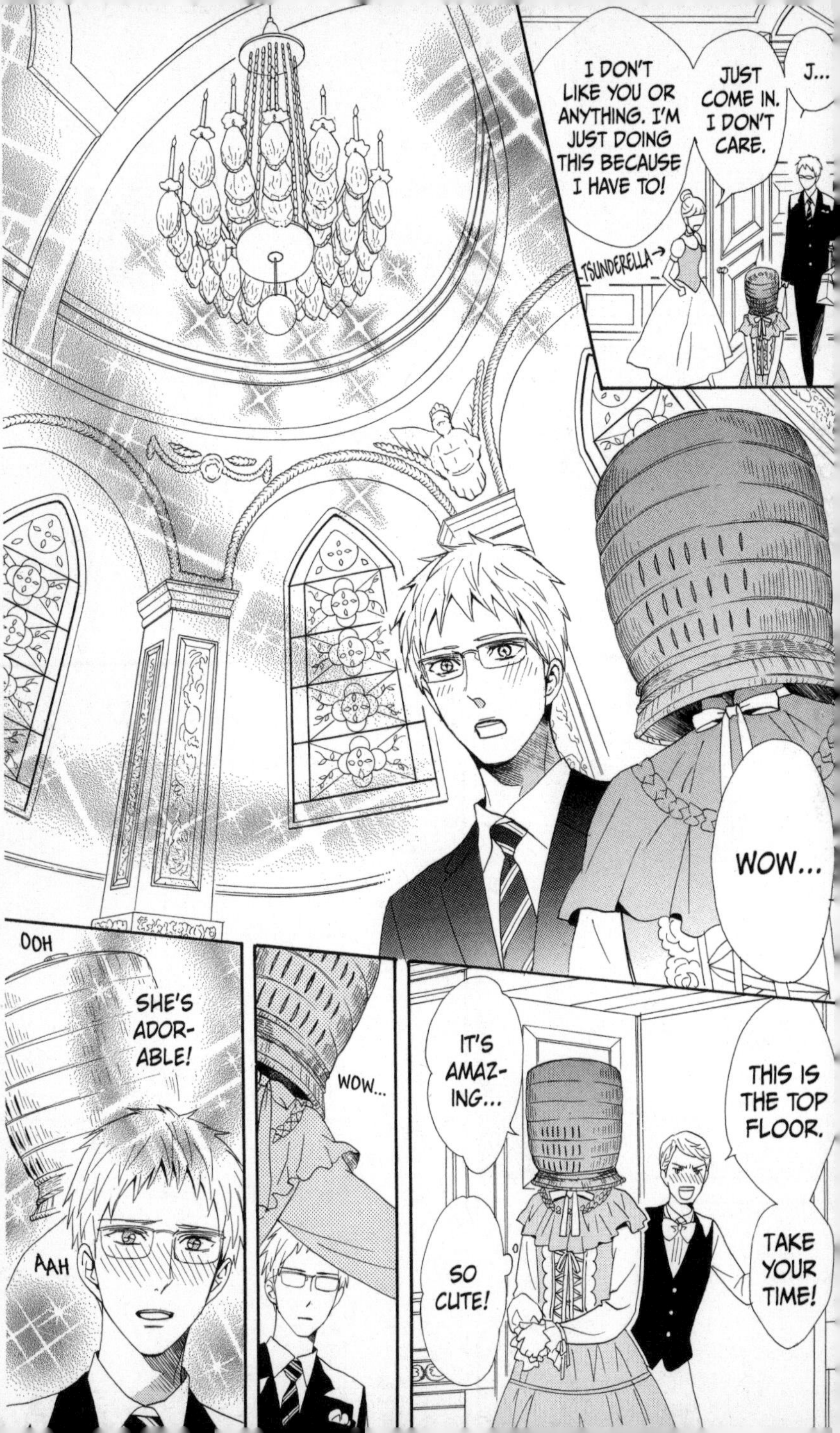
J...
JUST COME IN. I DON'T CARE.
I DON'T LIKE YOU OR ANYTHING. I'M JUST DOING THIS BECAUSE I HAVE TO!
TSUNDERELLA→
WOW...
THIS IS THE TOP FLOOR.
IT'S AMAZ-ING...
TAKE YOUR TIME!
SO CUTE!
WOW...
OOH
SHE'S ADOR-ABLE!
AAH

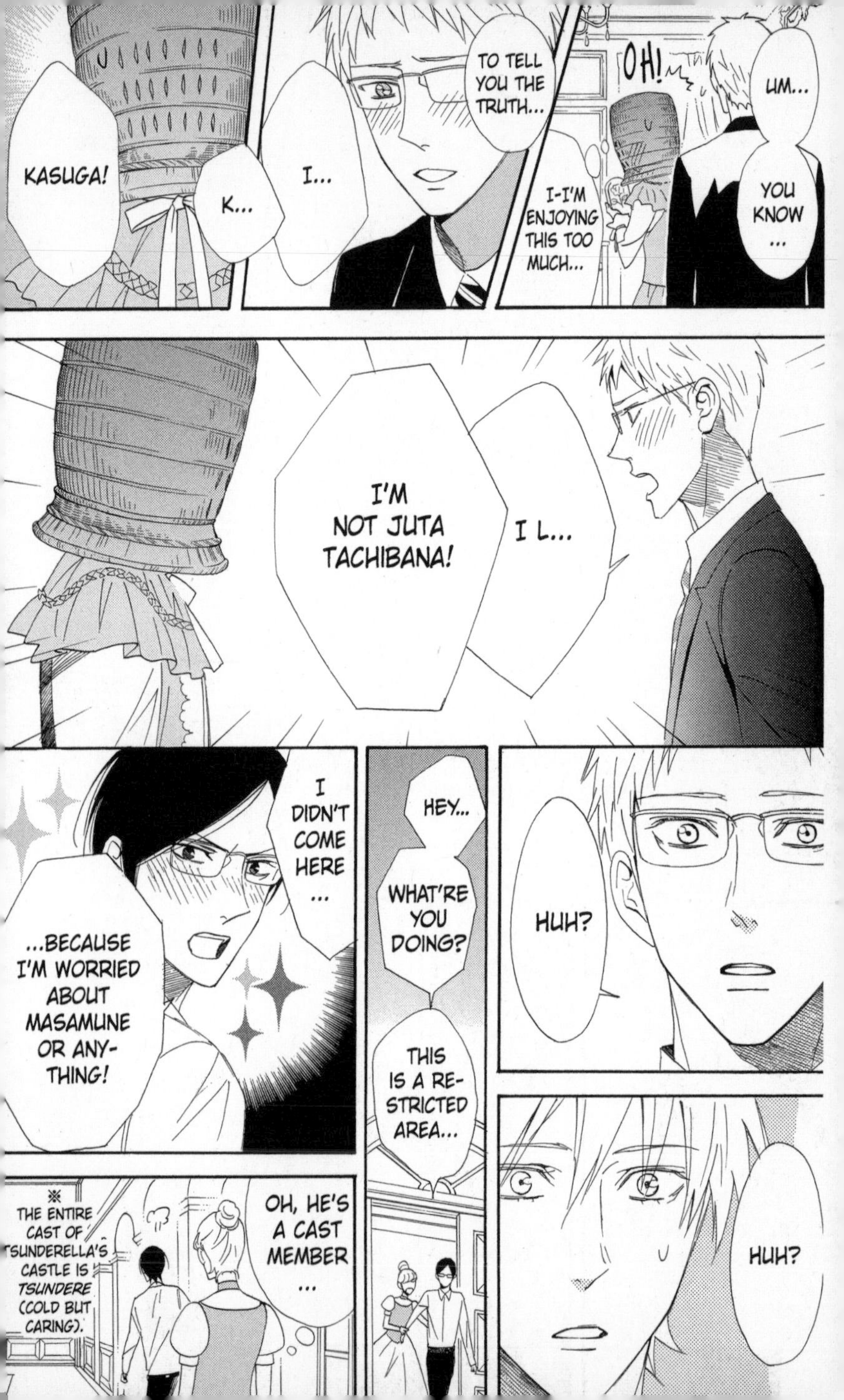
UM...
YOU KNOW ...
OH!
I-I'M ENJOYING THIS TOO MUCH...
TO TELL YOU THE TRUTH...
I...
K...
KASUGA!
I L...
I'M NOT JUTA TACHIBANA!
HUH?
HUH?
HEY...
WHAT'RE YOU DOING?
THIS IS A RE-STRICTED AREA...
I DIDN'T COME HERE ...
...BECAUSE I'M WORRIED ABOUT MASAMUNE OR ANY-THING!
OH, HE'S A CAST MEMBER ...
※ THE ENTIRE CAST OF TSUNDERELLA'S CASTLE IS TSUNDERE (COLD BUT CARING).

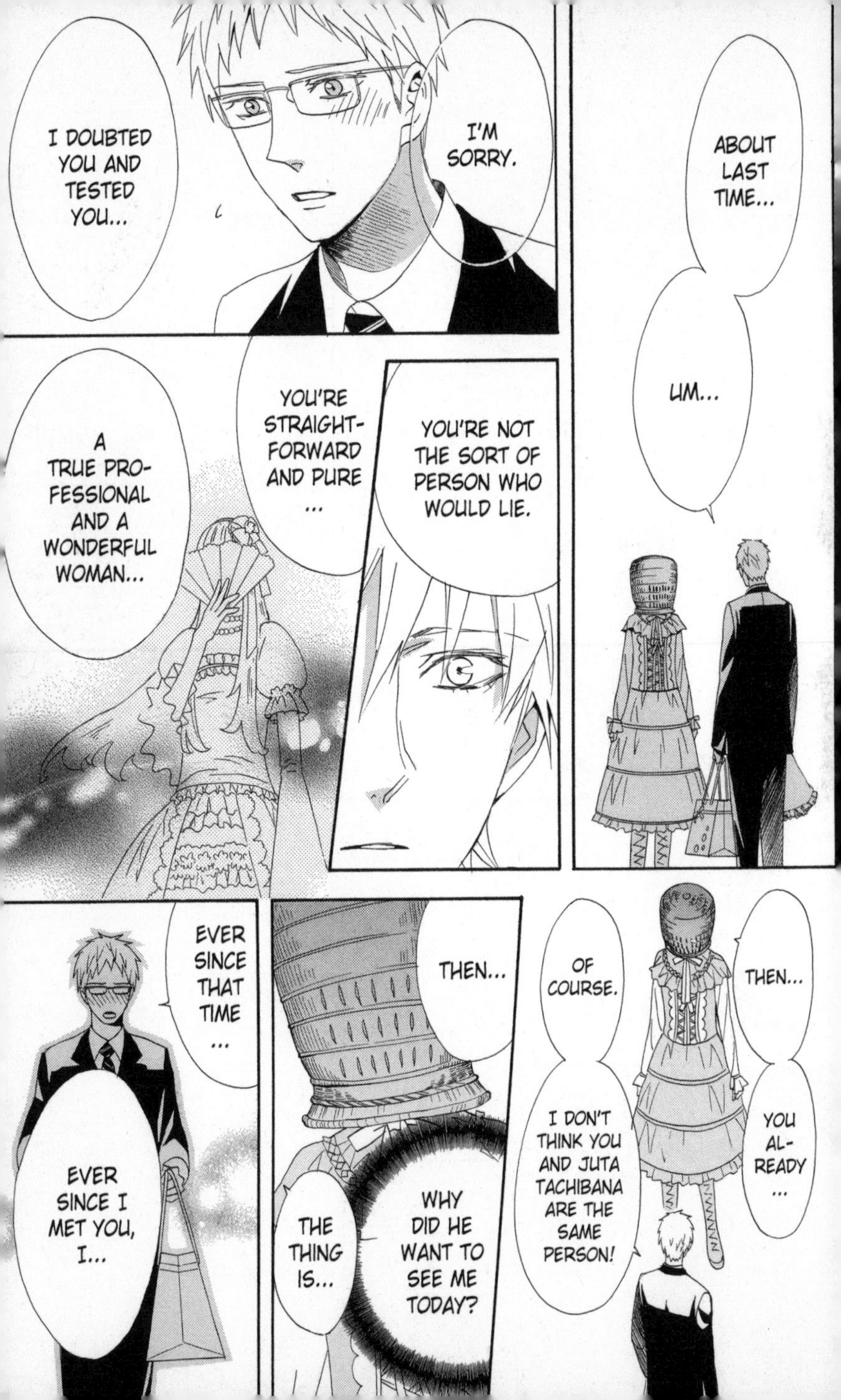
ABOUT LAST TIME...
UM...
I'M SORRY.
I DOUBTED YOU AND TESTED YOU...
YOU'RE NOT THE SORT OF PERSON WHO WOULD LIE.
YOU'RE STRAIGHT-FORWARD AND PURE ...
A TRUE PRO-FESSIONAL AND A WONDERFUL WOMAN...
THEN...
YOU AL-READY ...
OF COURSE.
I DON'T THINK YOU AND JUTA TACHIBANA ARE THE SAME PERSON!
THEN...
WHY DID HE WANT TO SEE ME TODAY?
THE THING IS...
EVER SINCE THAT TIME ...
EVER SINCE I MET YOU, I...

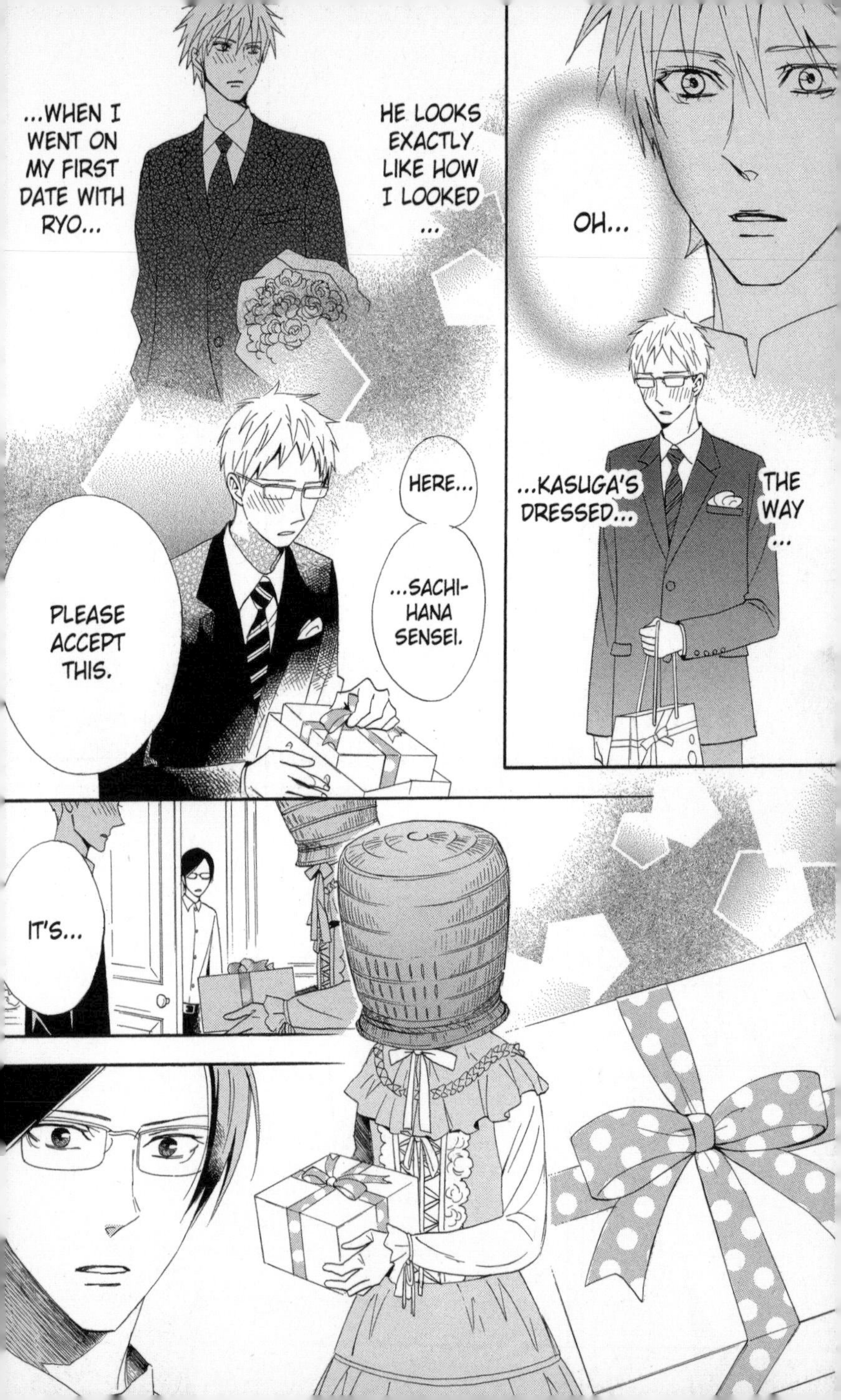
OH...
THE WAY...
...KASUGA'S DRESSED...
HE LOOKS EXACTLY LIKE HOW I LOOKED...
...WHEN I WENT ON MY FIRST DATE WITH RYO...
HERE...
...SACHI-HANA SENSEI.
PLEASE ACCEPT THIS.
IT'S...

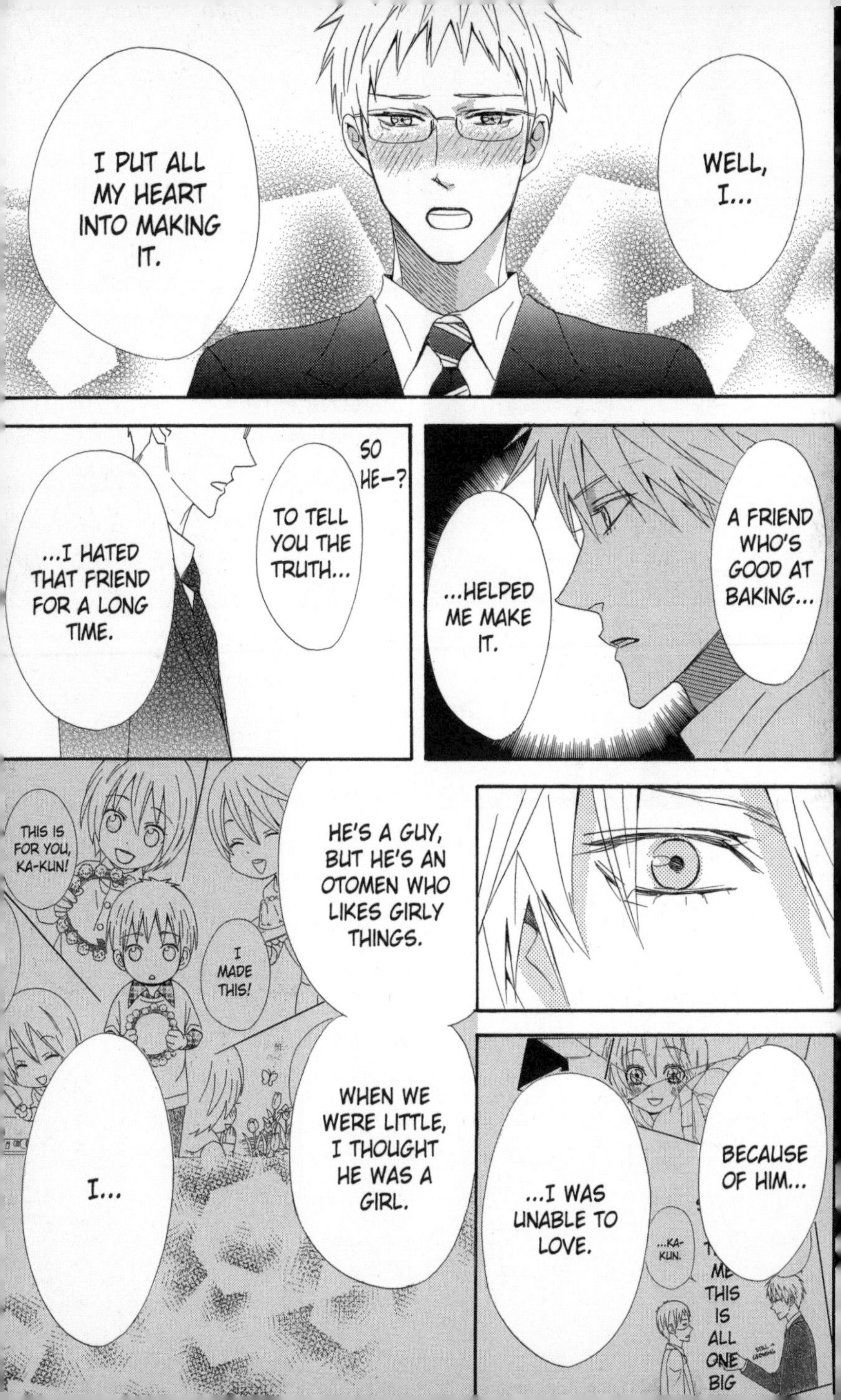
WELL, I...
I PUT ALL MY HEART INTO MAKING IT.
A FRIEND WHO'S GOOD AT BAKING...
...HELPED ME MAKE IT.
SO HE—?
TO TELL YOU THE TRUTH...
...I HATED THAT FRIEND FOR A LONG TIME.
BECAUSE OF HIM...
...I WAS UNABLE TO LOVE.
...KA-KUN.
THIS IS ALL ONE BIG
HE'S A GUY, BUT HE'S AN OTOMEN WHO LIKES GIRLY THINGS.
WHEN WE WERE LITTLE, I THOUGHT HE WAS A GIRL.
THIS IS FOR YOU, KA-KUN!
I MADE THIS!
I...

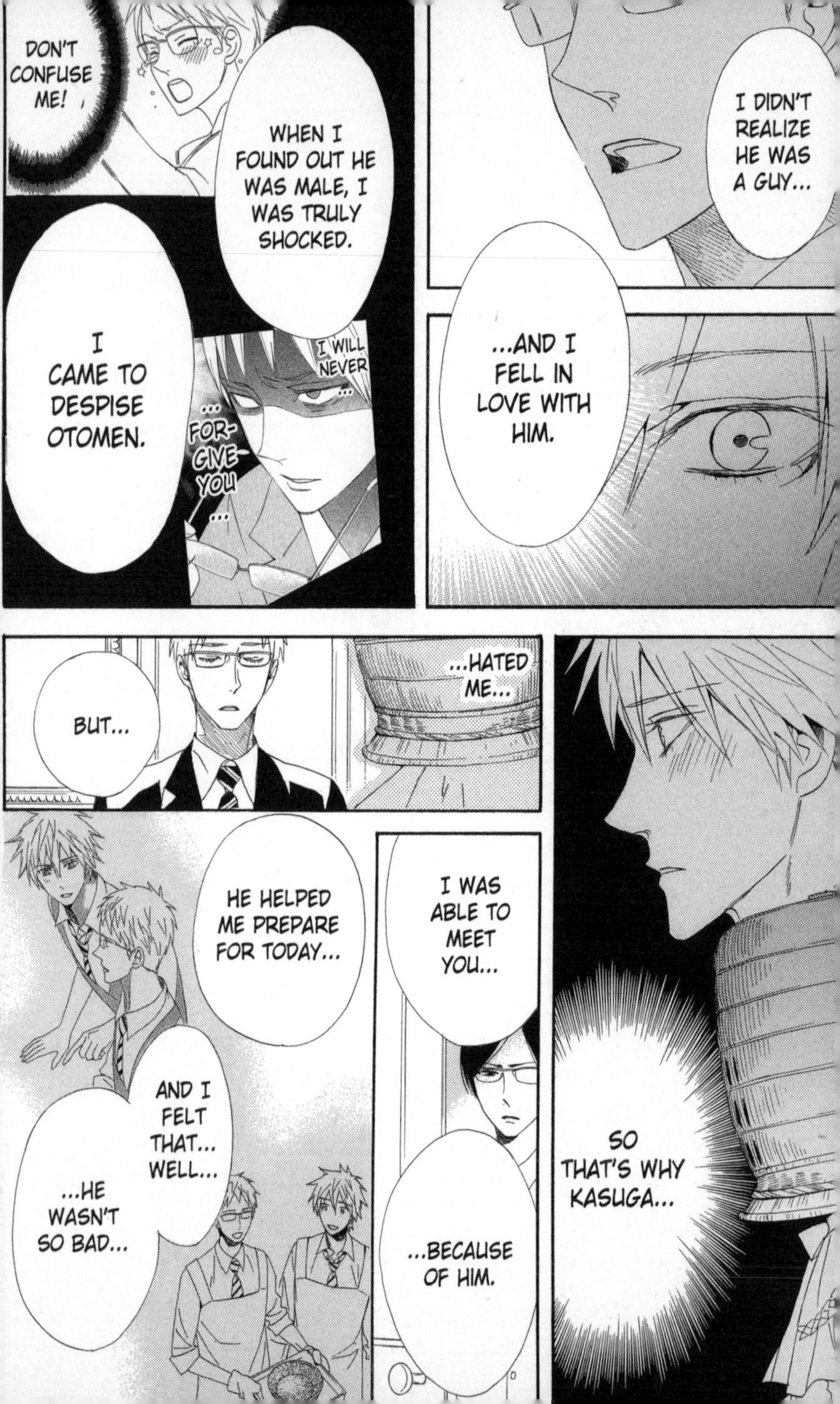
I DIDN'T REALIZE HE WAS A GUY...
...AND I FELL IN LOVE WITH HIM.
WHEN I FOUND OUT HE WAS MALE, I WAS TRULY SHOCKED.
DON'T CONFUSE ME!
I WILL NEVER...
...FOR-GIVE YOU...
I CAME TO DESPISE OTOMEN.
SO THAT'S WHY KASUGA...
...HATED ME...
BUT...
I WAS ABLE TO MEET YOU...
...BECAUSE OF HIM.
HE HELPED ME PREPARE FOR TODAY...
AND I FELT THAT... WELL...
...HE WASN'T SO BAD...

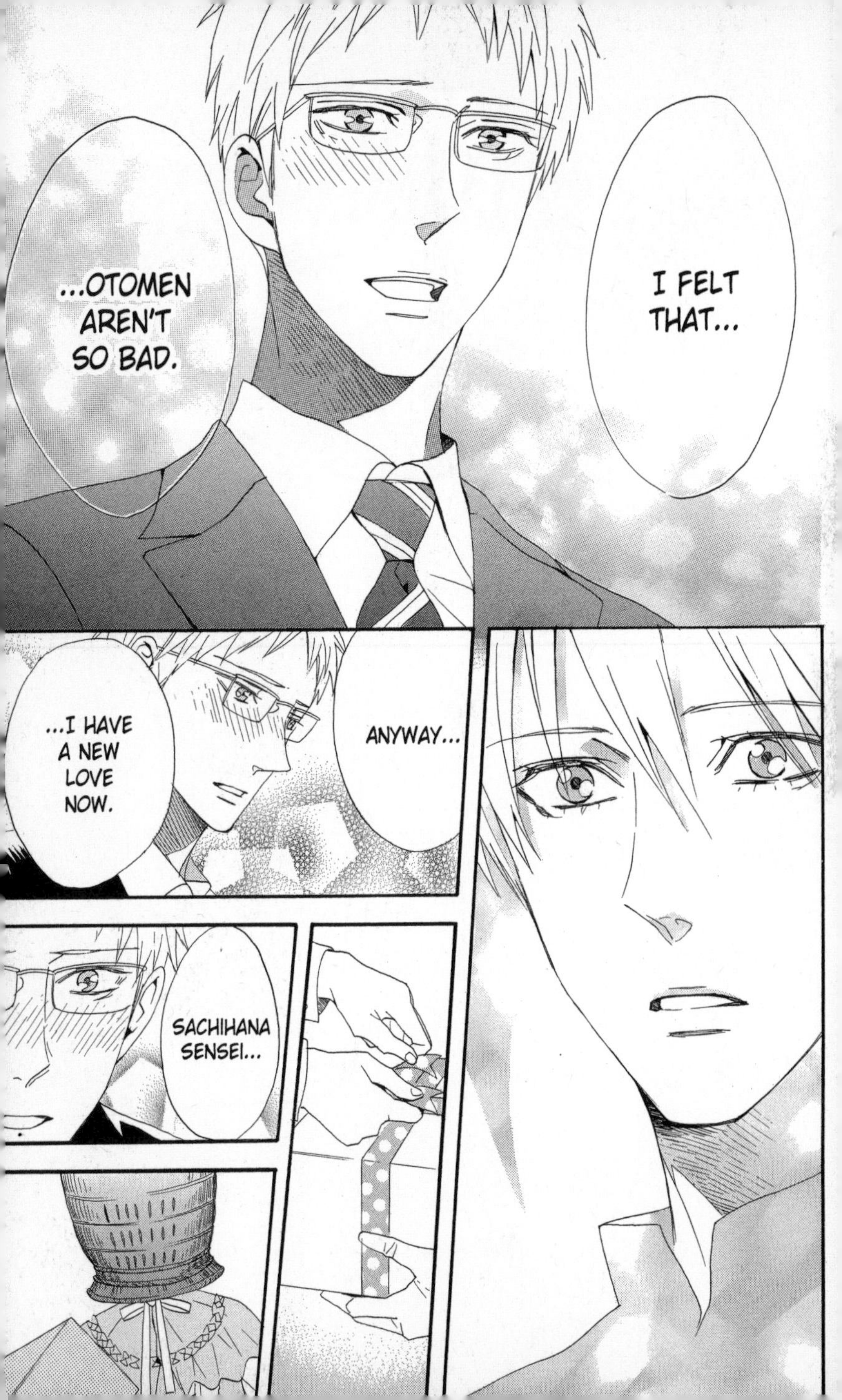
I FELT THAT...
...OTOMEN AREN'T SO BAD.
ANYWAY...
...I HAVE A NEW LOVE NOW.
SACHIHANA SENSEI...

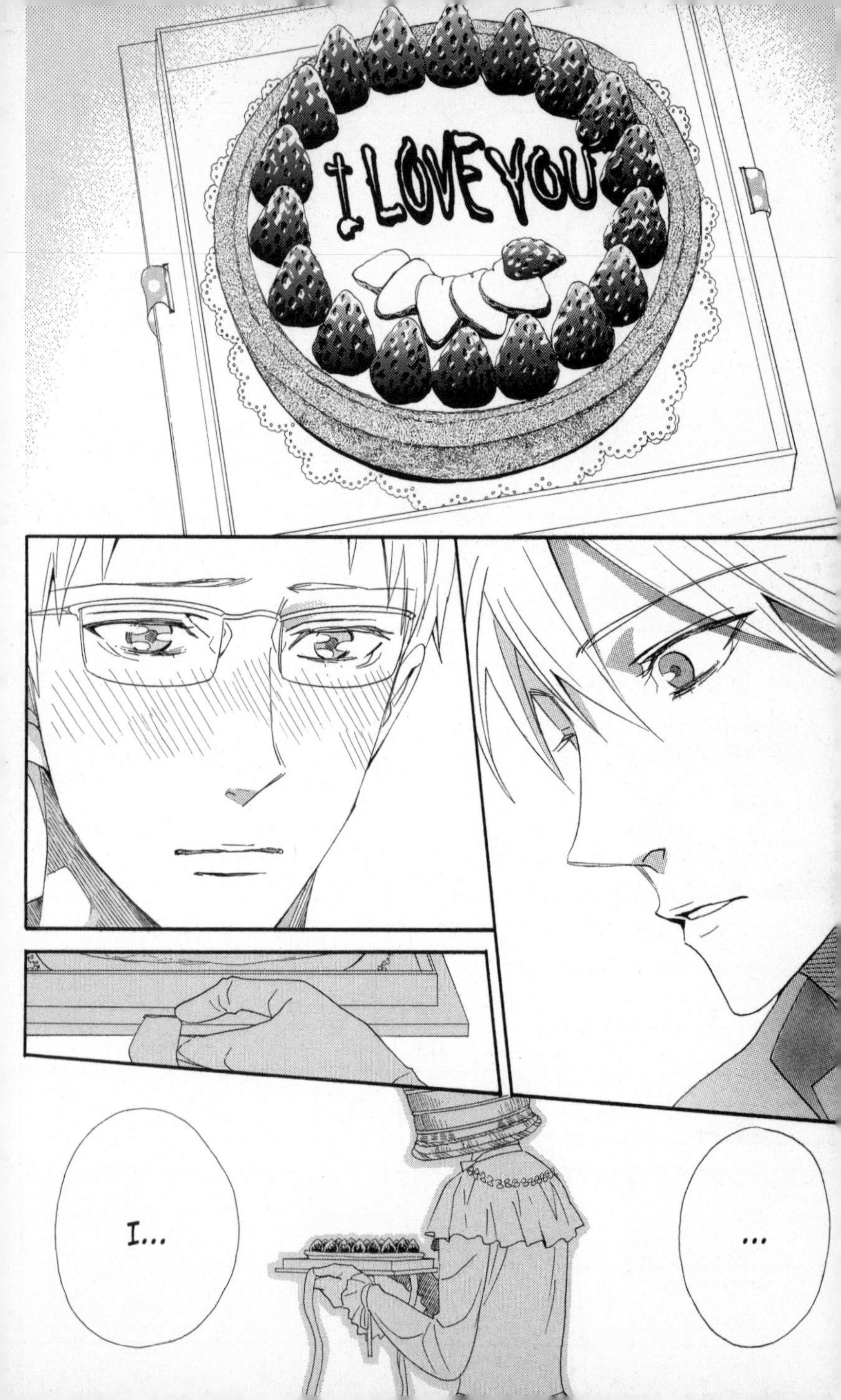
I LOVE YOU
...
I...

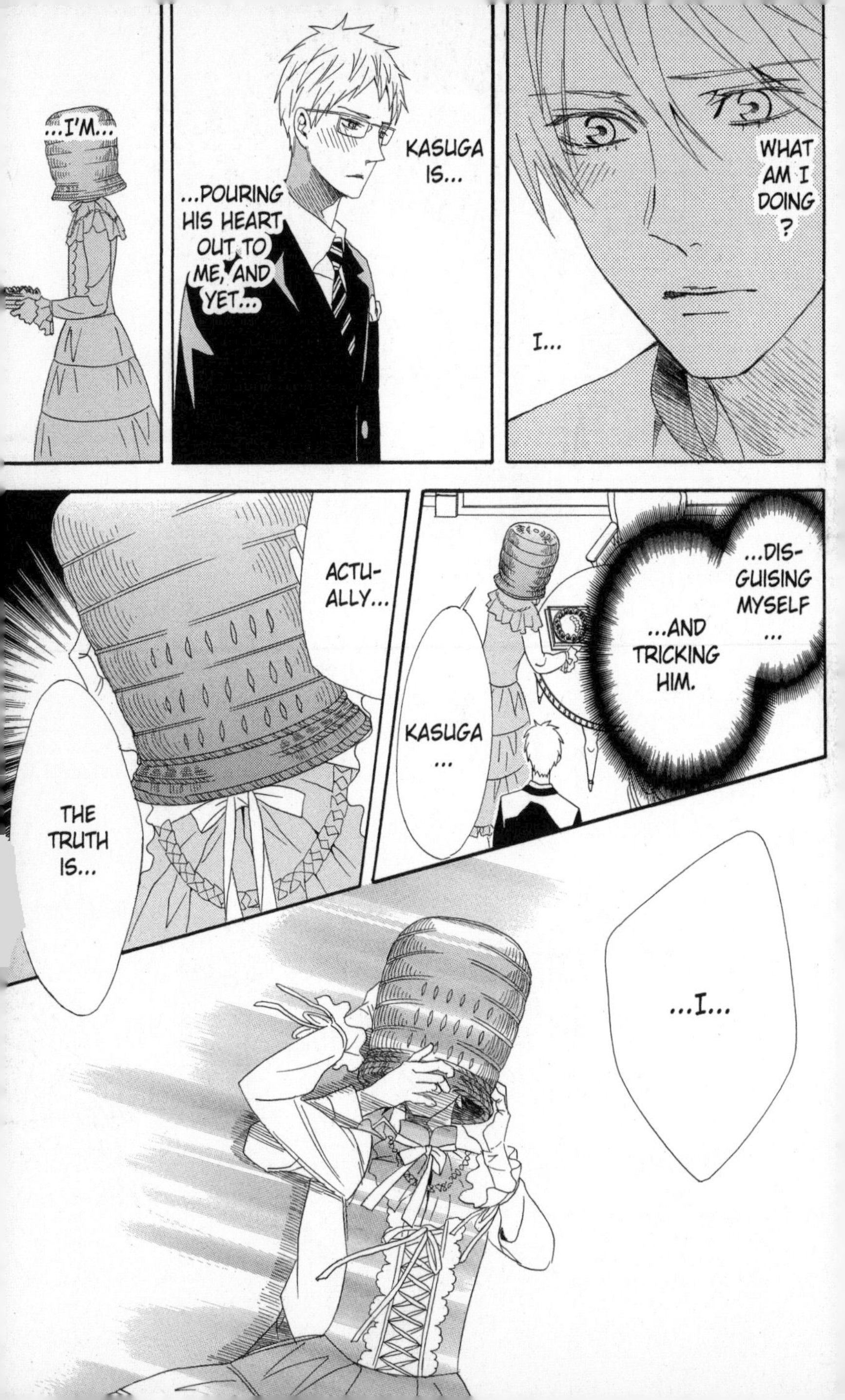
WHAT AM I DOING?
I...
KASUGA IS...
...POURING HIS HEART OUT TO ME, AND YET...
...I'M...
...DIS-GUISING MYSELF...
...AND TRICKING HIM.
KASUGA...
ACTU-ALLY...
THE TRUTH IS...
...I...

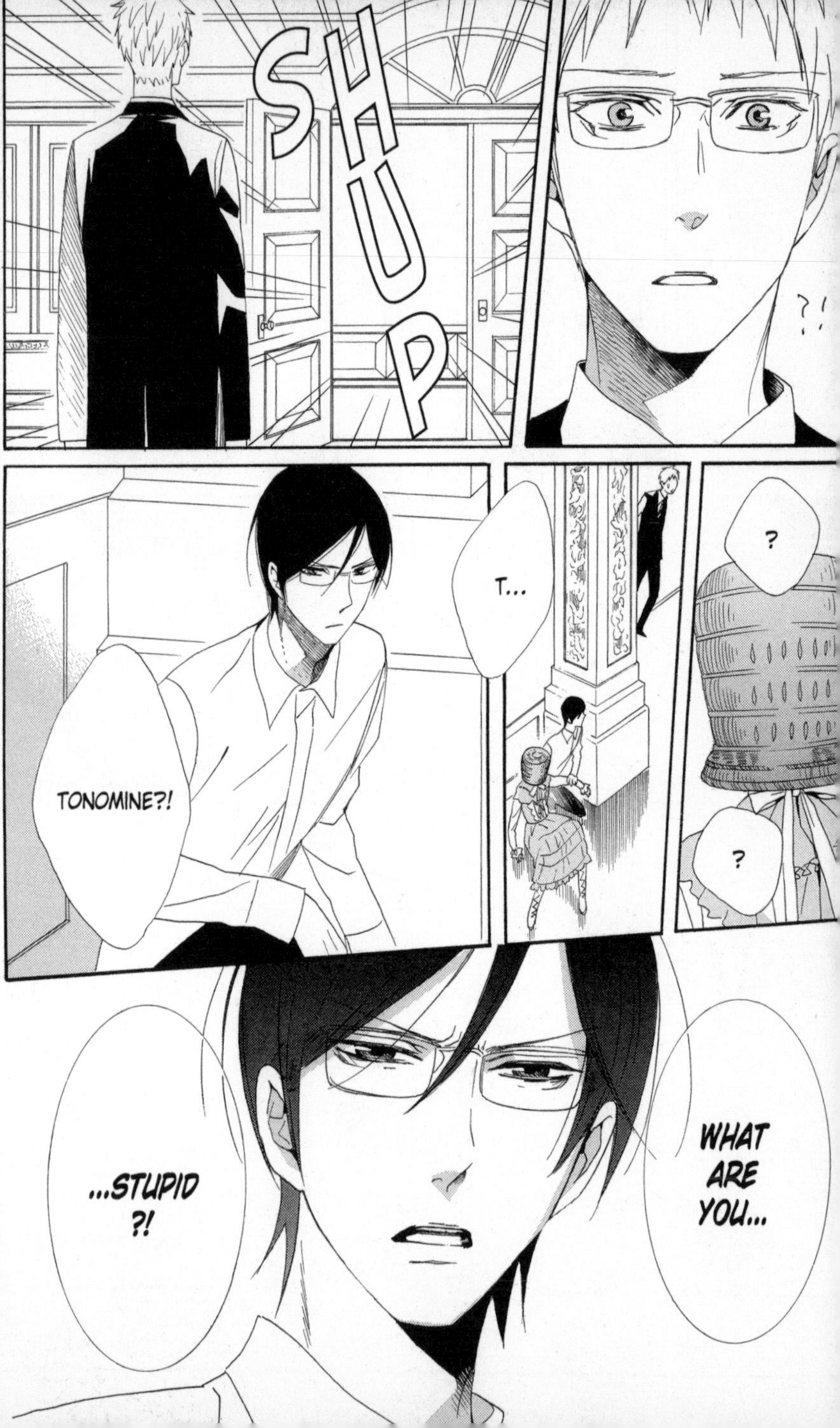
?!
SHUP
?
?
T...
TONOMINE?!
WHAT ARE YOU...
...STUPID ?!

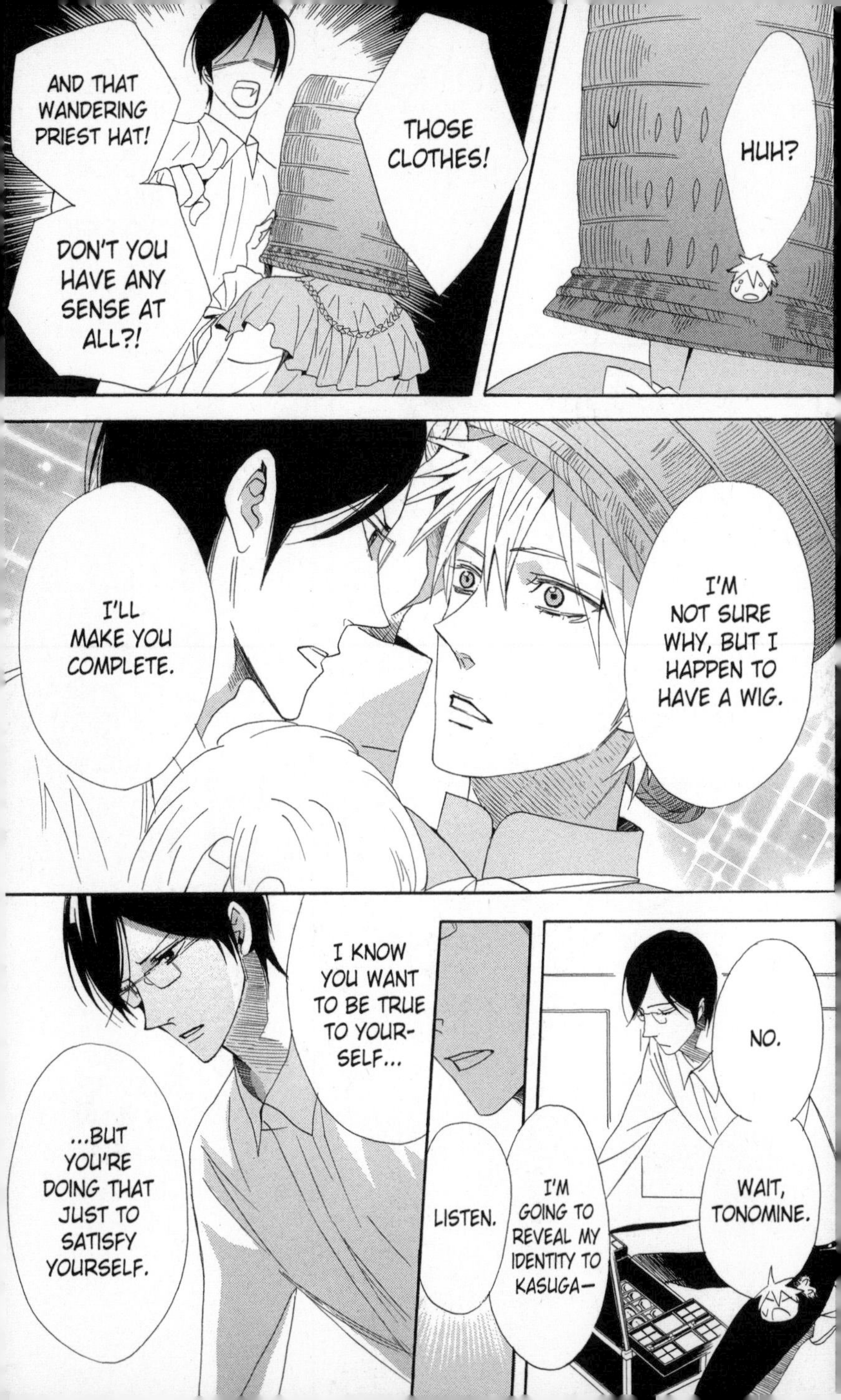

HUH?
THOSE CLOTHES!
AND THAT WANDERING PRIEST HAT!
DON'T YOU HAVE ANY SENSE AT ALL?!
I'M NOT SURE WHY, BUT I HAPPEN TO HAVE A WIG.
I'LL MAKE YOU COMPLETE.
NO.
WAIT, TONOMINE.
I'M GOING TO REVEAL MY IDENTITY TO KASUGA—
LISTEN.
I KNOW YOU WANT TO BE TRUE TO YOURSELF...
...BUT YOU'RE DOING THAT JUST TO SATISFY YOURSELF.

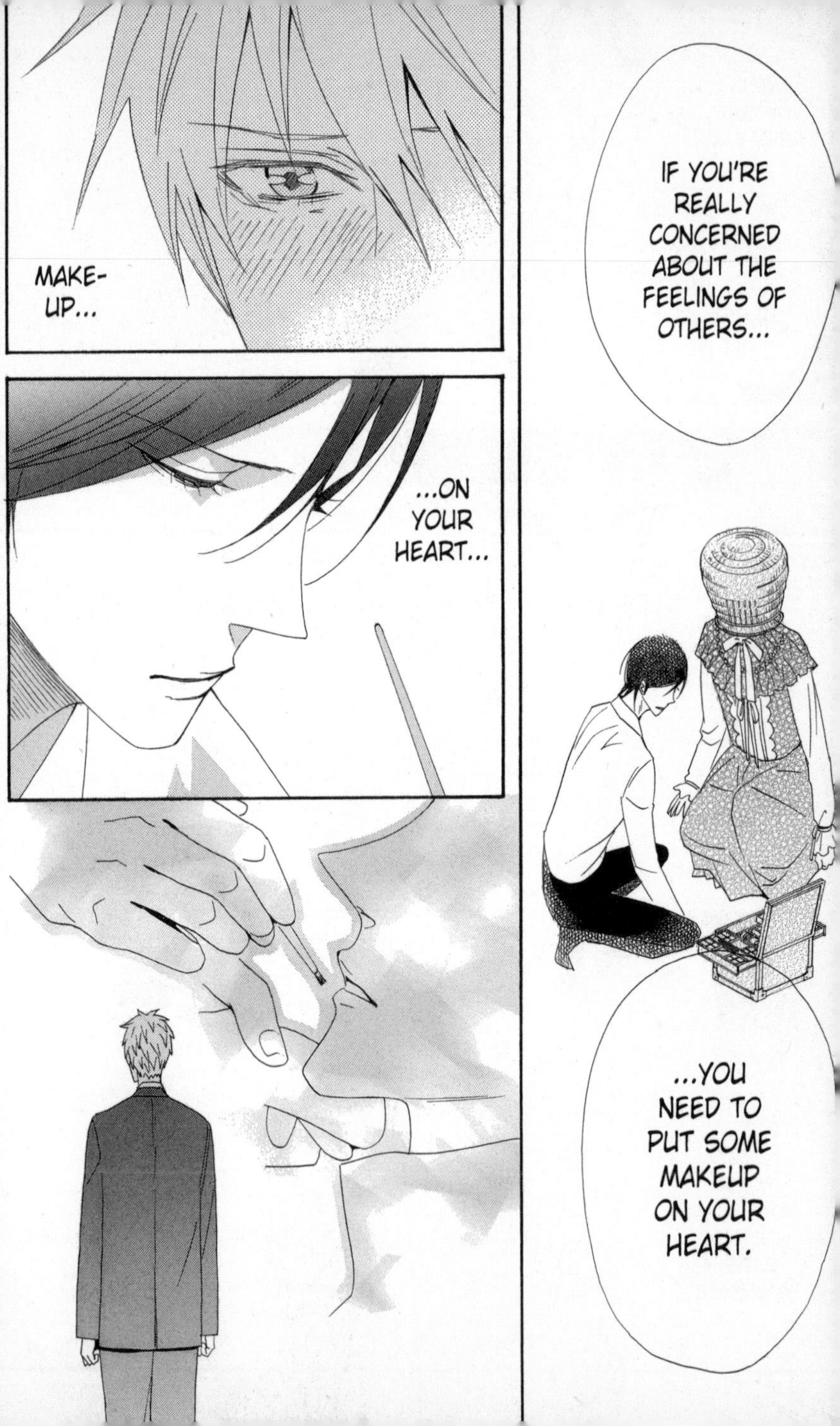
IF YOU'RE REALLY CONCERNED ABOUT THE FEELINGS OF OTHERS...
...YOU NEED TO PUT SOME MAKEUP ON YOUR HEART.
MAKE-UP...
...ON YOUR HEART...

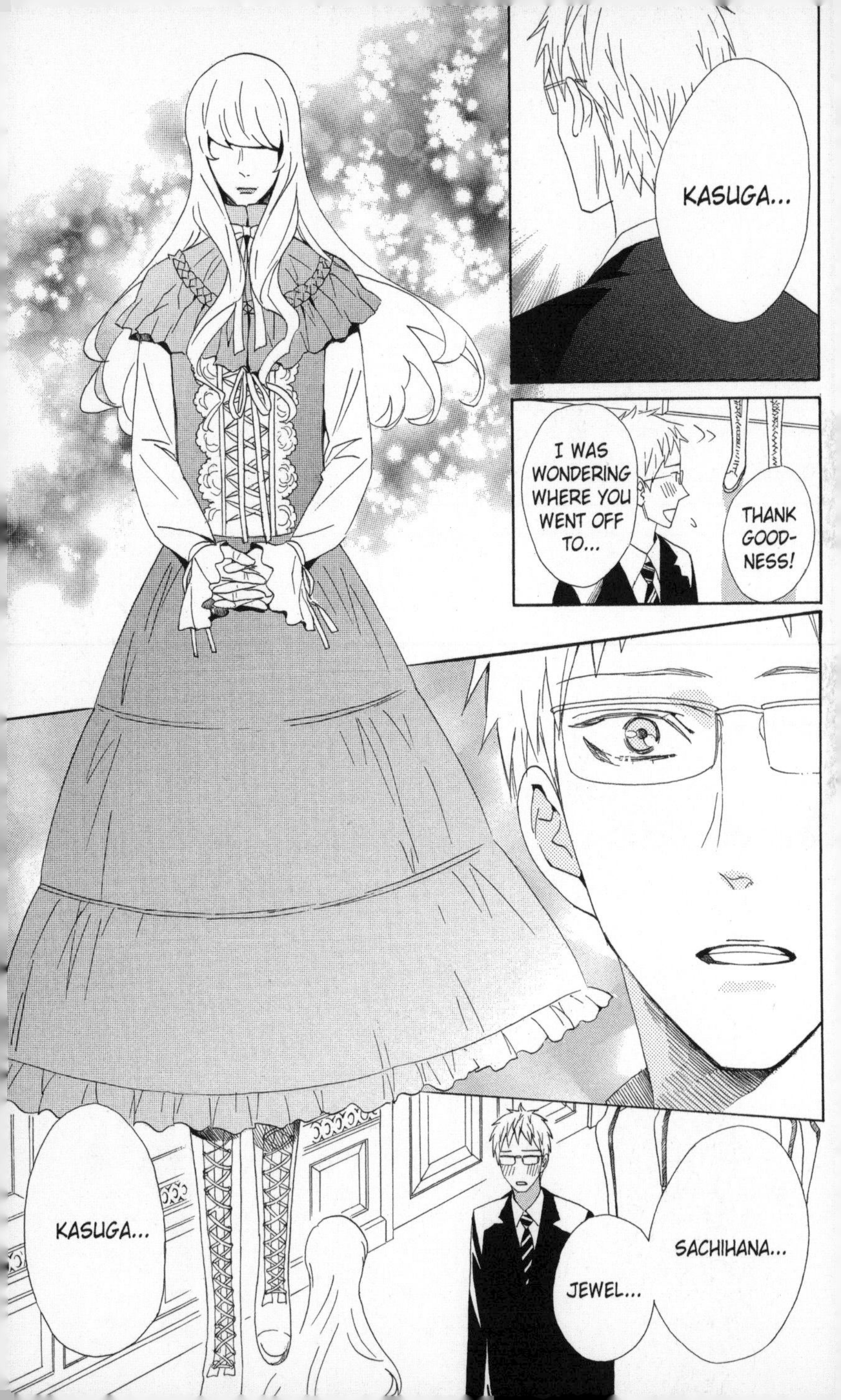
KASUGA...
THANK GOODNESS!
I WAS WONDERING WHERE YOU WENT OFF TO...
SACHIHANA...
JEWEL...
KASUGA...

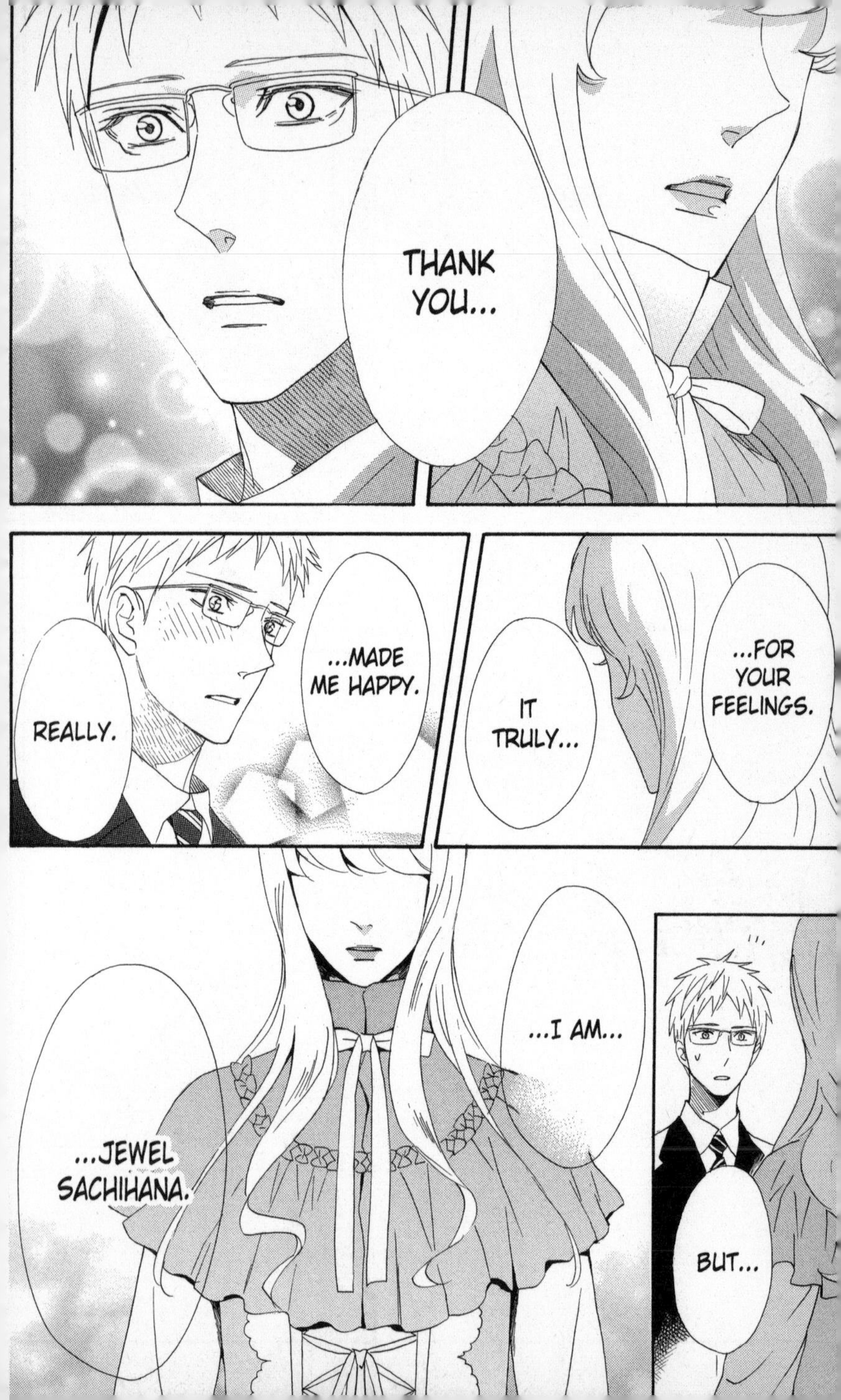
THANK YOU...
...FOR YOUR FEELINGS.
IT TRULY...
...MADE ME HAPPY.
REALLY.
BUT...
...I AM...
...JEWEL SACHIHANA.

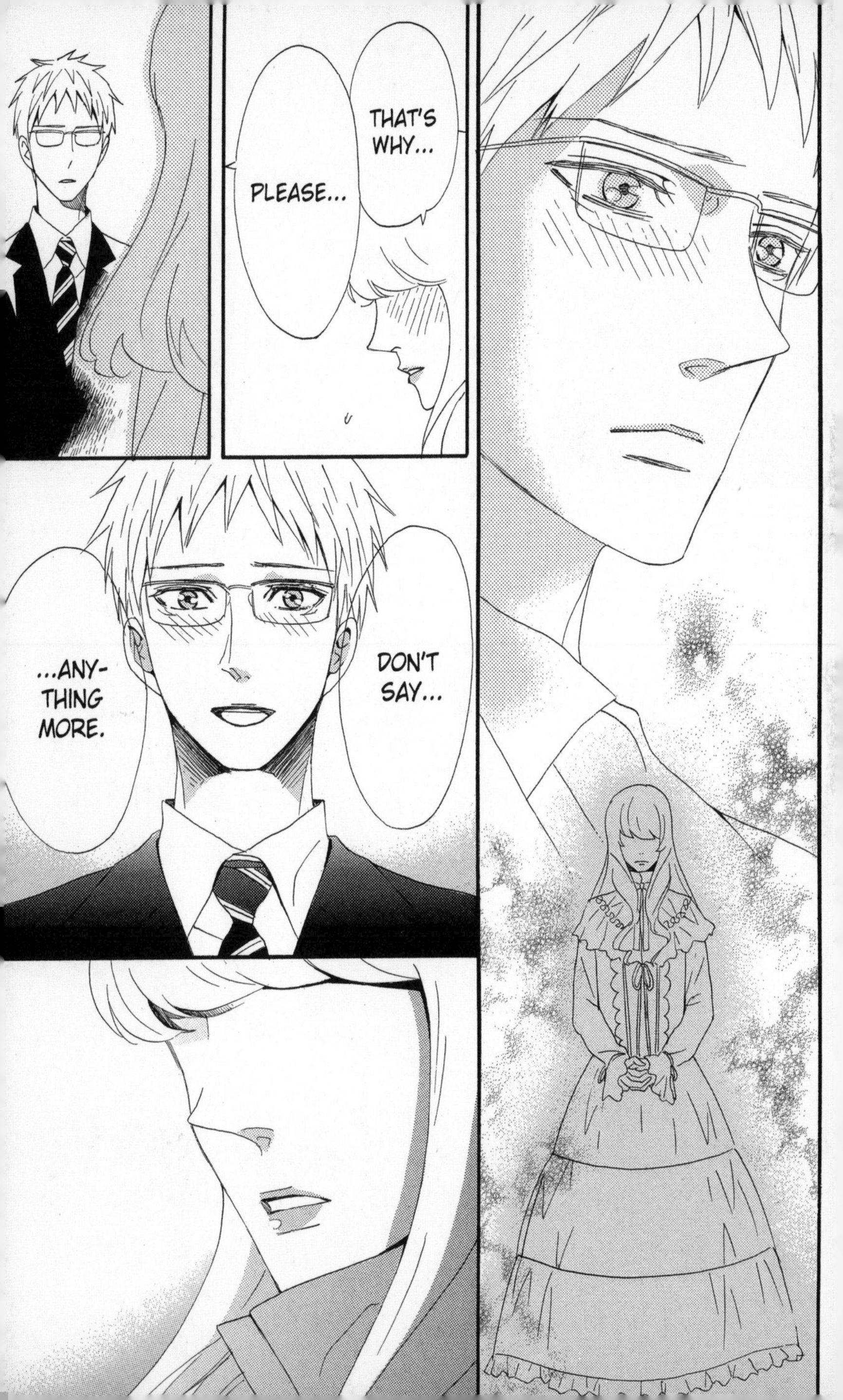
THAT'S WHY...
PLEASE...
DON'T SAY...
...ANYTHING MORE.

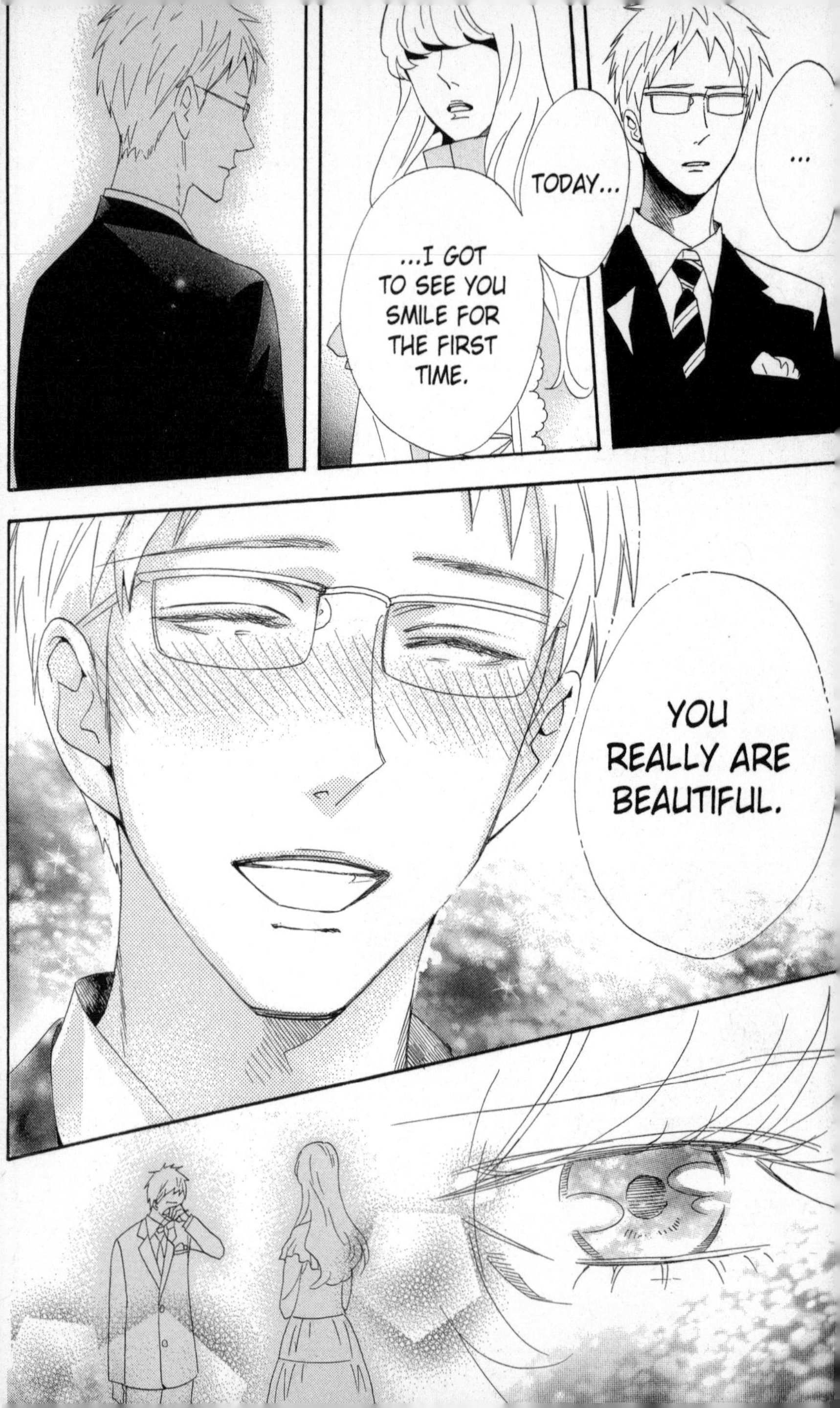
...
TODAY...
...I GOT TO SEE YOU SMILE FOR THE FIRST TIME.
YOU REALLY ARE BEAUTIFUL.

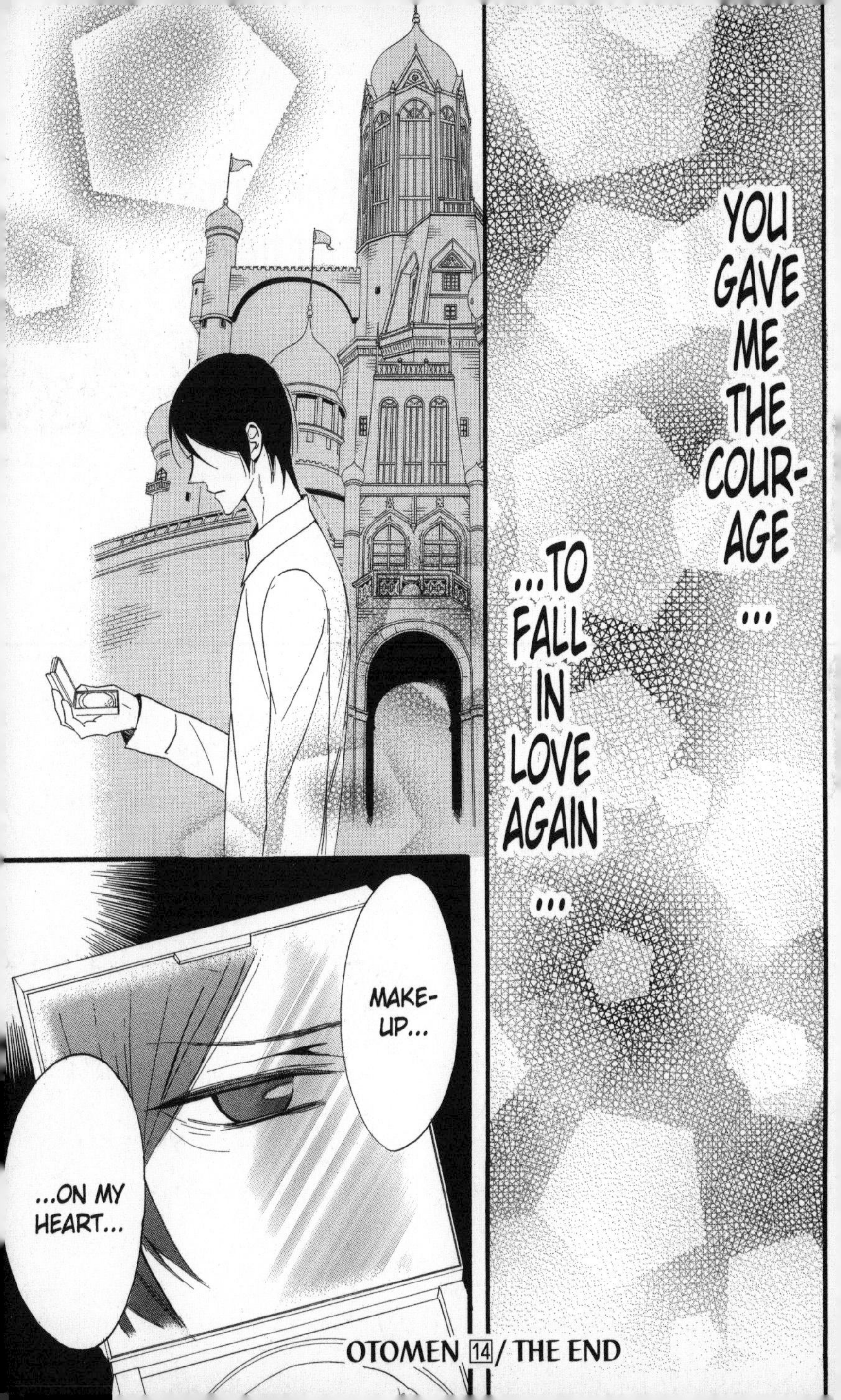
YOU GAVE ME THE COUR-AGE...
...TO FALL IN LOVE AGAIN...
MAKE-UP...
...ON MY HEART...

OTOMEN 14 / THE END

Confused by some of the terms, but too MANLY to ask for help?

Here are some **cultural notes** to assist you!

HONORIFICS

Chan – an informal honorific used to address children and females. *Chan* can also be used toward animals, lovers, intimate friends and people whom one has known since childhood.

Kun – an informal honorific used primarily toward males; it can be used by people of more senior status addressing those junior to them or by anyone addressing male children.

San – the most common honorific title. It is used to address people outside one's immediate family and close circle of friends.

Sensei – honorific title used to address teachers as well as professionals such as doctors, lawyers and artists.

Aya Kanno was born in Tokyo, Japan.
She is the creator of *Soul Rescue* and *Blank Slate*
(originally published as *Akusaga* in Japan's
BetsuHana magazine). Her latest work, *Otomen*,
is currently being serialized in *BetsuHana*.

OTOMEN
Vol. 14
Shojo Beat Edition

Story and Art by | **AYA KANNO**

Translation & Adaptation | **JN Productions**
Touch-up Art & Lettering | **Mark McMurray**
Design | **Fawn Lau**
Editor | **Amy Yu**

Otomen by Aya Kanno © Aya Kanno 2012
All rights reserved. First published in Japan in 2012 by HAKUSENSHA, Inc., Tokyo.
English language translation rights arranged with HAKUSENSHA, Inc., Tokyo.

The rights of the author(s) of the work(s) in this publication to be so identified
have been asserted in accordance with the Copyright, Designs and Patents Act 1988.
A CIP catalogue record for this book is available from the British Library.

The stories, characters and incidents mentioned in this publication are entirely fictional.

Printed in the U.S.A.

Published by VIZ Media, LLC
P.O. Box 77010
San Francisco, CA 94107

10 9 8 7 6 5 4 3 2 1
First printing, January 2013

www.viz.com

www.shojobeat.com